DEVELOPMENTALLY APPROPRIATE CURRICULUM IN ACTION

MARJORIE J. KOSTELNIK
University of Nebraska, Lincoln

MICHELLE RUPIPER
University of Nebraska, Lincoln

ANNE K. SODERMAN
Michigan State University

ALICE PHIPPS WHIREN
Michigan State University

PEARSON

Boston Columbus Indianapolis New York San Francisco Upper Saddle River
Amsterdam Cape Town Dubai London Madrid Milan Munich Paris Montréal Toronto
Delhi Mexico City São Paulo Sydney Hong Kong Seoul Singapore Taipei Tokyo

Vice President and Editorial Director: Jeffery W. Johnston
Senior Acquisitions Editor: Julie Peters
Editorial Assistant: Andrea Hall
Vice President, Director of Marketing: Margaret Waples
Senior Marketing Manager: Krista Clark
Senior Managing Editor: Pamela D. Bennett
Project Manager: Kerry Rubadue
Senior Operations Supervisor: Matthew Ottenweller
Senior Art Director: Diane Lorenzo
Text Designer: Candace Rowley

Cover Designer: Laura Gardner
Cover Art: (left to right) Lukas, Camden, Gianna; images provided by Artsonia.com
Media Project Manager: Noelle Chun
Full-Service Project Management: Amy Gehl, S4Carlisle Publishing Services
Composition: S4Carlisle Publishing Services
Printer/Binder: RR Donnelley
Cover Printer: Lehigh Phoenix Color/Hagerstown
Text Font: Adobe Garamond Pro Regular 11/13

Photo credits are listed on page xiv, which constitutes a continuation of this copyright page.

Every effort has been made to provide accurate and current Internet information in this book. However, the Internet and information posted on it are constantly changing, so it is inevitable that some of the Internet addresses listed in this textbook will change.

Library of Congress Cataloging-in-Publication Data
Kostelnik, Marjorie J., author.
  Developmentally appropriate curriculum in action / Marjorie J. Kostelnik, University of Nebraska, Lincoln, Anne K. Soderman, Michigan State University, Alice Phipps Whiren, Michigan State University, Michelle Rupiper, University of Nebraska, Lincoln.
    pages cm
  Includes index.
  ISBN-13: 978-0-13-705807-5
  ISBN-10: 0-13-705807-1
1. Early childhood education—United States. 2. Early childhood education—Curricula—United States. 3. Child development—United States. I. Soderman, Anne Keil, author. II. Whiren, Alice Phipps, author. III. Rupiper, Michelle, author. IV. Title.
  LB1139.25.K68 2014
  372.21—dc23
                                                                        2012045036

10 9 8 7 6 5 4 3 2 1

PEARSON

ISBN 10:   0-13-705807-1
ISBN 13: 978-0-13-705807-5

About the Authors

MARJORIE J. KOSTELNIK began her career as a Head Start teacher and is now serving as dean of the College of Education and Human Sciences at the University of Nebraska, Lincoln. Over the years she has also been an early childhood program director, teacher educator, researcher, T.E.A.C.H. advocate, and school district consultant. A former vice president of NAEYC, Marjorie currently serves on the Dimensions Foundation Board (focused on early childhood nature education), and the Malaika Foundation Board (focused on global education).

MICHELLE RUPIPER is an associate professor of practice and the director of the Ruth Staples Child Development Laboratory at the University of Nebraska-Lincoln, where she has taught since 1994. She has served as a classroom teacher for infants through school-aged children as well as directed community-based programs during her career. She is active in the National Association for the Education of Young Children (NAEYC), having served on the Affiliate Council of NAEYC and as president of Midwest AEYC and Nebraska AEYC. She is currently on the board of the National Coalition for Campus Children's Centers (NCCCC).

ANNE K. SODERMAN had 14 years of classroom experience before joining the faculty of Michigan State University, where she is now professor emeritus. She continues to consult with international schools in Beijing, China, writing and conducting research about dual-language immersion. She is currently an adjunct professor in early childhood education at the University of South Florida. Soderman is also co-author of *Guiding Children's Social Development and Learning*, 7th ed. (2012), *Creating Literacy-Rich Preschools and Kindergartens* (2008), and *Scaffolding Emergent Literacy* (2005).

ALICE PHIPPS WHIREN is a professor emeritus of the Department of Family and Child Ecology, Michigan State University. She taught curriculum in early childhood and child development to undergraduate and graduate students and was supervisor of the Child Development Laboratories. Early in her career, she taught young children in an inner-city public school in Michigan. She also served as a Head Start assistant director and has provided a variety of training sessions for preprimary teachers nationally and internationally. Currently, Dr. Whiren continues to write and consult with early childhood programs.

As you can see, as authors, we have had many years of experience interacting directly with young children and their families and with educators in national and international preprimary and primary settings. We have worked in urban, suburban, and rural programs; large, medium, and small classes; public, private, not-for-profit, and profit-seeking organizations; half- and full-day programs; preschool classes; and the elementary grades. Currently, all of us are actively engaged in educating young children and the professionals who work with them. We are eager to have you join us in this wonderful profession as teachers who touch the future by working with young children!

Preface

"I touch the future—I teach!"

Christa McAuliffe

Welcome to the field of early childhood education! Chances are, you are thinking about becoming a teacher of children ages 3 through 6 because you want to make a positive difference in young children's lives. Nowhere will that difference be more keenly felt than in an early childhood classroom. Whether you work in a preschool, child-care setting, Head Start classroom, or kindergarten, you will be someone who introduces children to the world of formal learning early in their lives. What you say and do will either enhance or detract from children's sense of themselves as learners. That is an awesome responsibility.

Our goal in writing *Developmentally Appropriate Curriculum in Action* is to provide you with the professional knowledge and skills you will need to be an effective early childhood teacher. For example, you will learn such things as:

- How to plan learning activities for the children in your classroom
- What you might do when children have difficulty getting along
- Ways to communicate with families about what their children are learning
- Sample strategies for supporting children who are dual-language learners

The material in this text has been thoroughly researched, making use of the latest theories and findings about how young children learn and about how great teachers teach. As a result, it is filled with the latest information about effective practices in early education. This means you will learn *what* to do with young children as well as *how* to translate your knowledge into effective actions. We expect this combination of knowledge and skills to enhance your work with children and your enjoyment of the profession you have chosen.

Distinctive Features of This Text

Developmentally Appropriate Curriculum in Action incorporates several unique features to increase your understanding and skill development.

- This **comprehensive book addresses all aspects of classroom life**, including children and adults, the physical and social environments, and teaching and learning from a "whole-child" perspective. It also covers all portions of the classroom day from preplanning through implementing a daily routine to post-session reflections.
- **Developmentally appropriate practice** (DAP) is woven throughout the book. Every chapter addresses principles of age appropriateness, individual appropriateness, and sociocultural appropriateness. All of the DAP material incorporates the latest version of *Developmentally Appropriate Practice in Early Childhood* (NAEYC, 2009).
- We **combine** a **play-based approach** with **intentional teaching strategies** in every chapter.
- **National standards and NAEYC guidelines** are referenced in every chapter.
- Many chapters open with an example of an **artifact a teacher or child might create** to represent work in the classroom. These items help readers recognize the wide array of artifacts that teachers may use throughout the year to assess children's learning.
- Each chapter includes a **glossary of terms**. This helps readers identify professional vocabulary.

- Each chapter includes a *Try It Yourself* feature. These are exercises embedded within the chapter to encourage you to pause and reflect on what you are learning and to apply a concept immediately, based on your personal experience.
- *Newsletter/Web-Ready* features are incorporated into all chapters. These items give you actual words you might use to explain chapter-related content to family members via a newsletter, bulletin board, blog, web site, or social media outlet.
- Examples of **children with special needs and diverse families** are integrated within each chapter.
- All chapters end with a feature entitled *Applying What You've Learned.* These are specific exercises and assignments that enable readers to translate the reading into practical applications in early childhood settings.
- The curriculum focuses on **developmental domains (aesthetics, affective, cognitive, language, social, and physical)**. Each domain incorporates cutting-edge **subject matter content** and skills.
- This text addresses individual curricular domains (in separate chapters) as well as curriculum integration in multiple chapters and in Chapter 16, which focuses on projects and themes.
- All of the curriculum chapters (9 through15) include the following:

   Sample content: Examples of terms and facts associated with the domain and relevant subject matter.

   Sample materials and resources: You will get clear ideas about specific materials, common objects, and children's books that can be used to teach within each domain.

   Sample teaching strategies: Focus on methods—specific guidelines for teaching in all portions of the program including individual, small-group, and whole-group teaching methods.

   Sample activities: Written as short-form lesson plans, these provide concrete examples of activities for younger and older preschoolers and kindergartners. There is one example for each of six types of lessons: exploratory play, guided discovery, problem solving, discussions, demonstrations, and direct instruction.

   Tech Tips: Explicit examples of how teachers can use technology to support early learning in every curricular domain.

This is very much a "how-to" book that emphasizes teaching methods and strategies. We believe it provides the foundations you need to begin a productive career in early childhood education.

Special Note to Instructors

Over the years, many instructors have asked us to write a book for entry-level practitioners that has a strong emphasis on the *how* of teaching and a briefer emphasis on the *why. Developmentally Appropriate Curriculum in Action* represents our response to those requests. Although we have used the same curricular domains and curricular goals as in *Developmentally Appropriate Curriculum* (Pearson), our original text on early childhood curriculum, nothing else has been duplicated. This volume does not repeat any of the same stories, examples, or sample activities of the original text, which emphasized theory and research. In addition, *Developmentally Appropriate Practices in Action* is firmly focused on young children ages 3 to 6, rather than 3 to 8 years, as in our other texts. Finally, this book has only half the number of pages. We made these modifications to the present text to give instructors the opportunity to choose the book that best fits their needs and the needs of their students. We hope you enjoy the results.

Chapter Sequence

Developmentally Appropriate Curriculum in Action is divided into two parts. **Part 1,** *Teaching in Early Childhood Programs,* consists of an introduction to developmentally appropriate practice and the fundamental things teachers must know to create effective programs for children. Within a series of eight chapters, readers become familiar with the principles of DAP as well as basic teaching strategies that are useful in all domains and in all parts of the early childhood day. Child guidance strategies and how to assess children's learning are addressed in detail. Next comes lesson planning, with attention to lessons for younger and older children as well as strategies for adapting lessons to children of varying abilities and interests. Attention to the physical learning environment indoors and outdoors as well as strategies for teaching children in small groups or in whole group scenarios are also covered within the eight chapters that make up Part 1. These chapters are viewed as fundamental building blocks of effective teaching. **Part 2,** *The Curriculum,* consists of Chapters 9 through 16. These chapters address six developmental domains (aesthetic, affective, cognitive, language, social, and physical). Because there is such keen interest in cognition as it relates to mathematics and science at the preprimary level, we have divided cognition into two chapters to allow adequate coverage of these important curricular areas. The curricular domains are presented in alphabetical order to underscore the idea that no one domain is more important than any of the others. The curriculum chapters are written in such a way that instructors may introduce them in any order that makes sense to them and their students. Chapter 16, *Putting It All Together: Organizing Children's Learning Over Time,* is the last chapter in this volume. It introduces the notion of daily planning, planning for multiple days, and making use of themes and projects to extend children's learning over time. The book closes with an appendix that presents a series of six long-form lessons plans that provide an example of each of six activity types—exploratory play, guided discovery, problem-solving, discussions, demonstrations, and direct instruction. These plans give readers tangible models to emulate in their own work.

Supplementary Materials for Instructors

All of our instructor supplements are posted online at www.pearsonhighered.com. Click on "Educators," then click on "Download Instructor Resources." You may register there, and download and print ancillaries.

Online Instructor's Manual

The Instructor's Manual supports lesson planning and the concepts and terms students learn in this course.

PowerPoint® Slides

Slides are provided for each chapter to support learning in any class format.

Online Test Bank

The Test Bank consists of multiple-choice, true-false, and essay questions for each chapter.

Acknowledgments

We are indebted to the teachers in the child development laboratories at Michigan State University for their early work on curriculum, for providing continuous and easy access to their classrooms for observation, and for inspiring many of the ideas represented in this book. Teachers in the Ruth Staples Child Development Laboratory School and the 3E International School in Beijing, China, also contributed significantly to our work.

We thank the following reviewers for their comments and suggestions: Jeanne W. Barker, Tallahassee Community College; Cindy Calhoun, Southern Union State Community College; Berta Harris, San Diego City College; Bonny Headley, University of Alaska Anchorage; Kathryn Hollar, Catawba Valley Community College; Dawn L. Kolakoski, Hudson Valley Community College; Tara Mathien, William Rainey Harper College; Nicole D. Reiber, Coastal Carolina Community College; and Gwen Walter, Forsyth Technical Community College.

Julie Peters, our editor at Pearson, was a tremendous support, as were all members of the production team. During the preparation of this manuscript, we discussed our ideas with and received feedback from a number of University of Nebraska students and faculty members, as well as Head Start, Chapter 1, child-care, preschool, and elementary school teachers and administrators. We heard the concerns of many parents of young children and listened to the children themselves as they responded to diverse program practices in their classrooms. We are especially grateful for all these contributions in shaping our vision of appropriate practices and in motivating us to share this vision with others.

Marjorie J. Kostelnik

Michelle Rupiper

Anne K. Soderman

Alice Phipps Whiren

Brief Contents

Contents

Part 2 The Curriculum

9 The Aesthetic Domain: Celebrating the Artist Within 156

10 The Affective Domain: Developing a Sense of Self 178

11 The Cognitive Domain: Nurturing Young Scientists 204

12 The Cognitive Domain: Fostering Mathematical Thinking 222

Photo Credits

Credits and acknowledgments for materials borrowed from other sources and reproduced, with permission, in this textbook appear on the appropriate page within the text.

Photo Credits: © Mykola Velychko/Fotolia, p. 2; © Gennadiy Poznyakov/Fotolia, p. 4; © Jaren Wicklund/Fotolia, p. 6; © Thomas Perkins/Fotolia, p. 12; © Igor Negovelov/Fotolia, p. 14; © HP_Photo/Fotolia, p. 15; Shirley Shi, p. 18, 66, 68, 222, 226, 229, 231, 235, 240, 250 (top), 256; © nyul/Fotolia, p. 21; Purestock/Getty Images, p. 22; © kristall/Fotolia, p. 30; Annie Fuller/Pearson, p. 31, 53, 129, 130, 193 (btm), 193 (top left), 193 (top right), 265 (top), 285, 286, 317; © Yuri Arcurs/Fotolia, p. 32; Amy Loveday-Hu, p. 33, 34, 69, 75, 233; Felicia Martinez/PhotoEdit, p. 40; © JenKedCo/Fotolia, p. 42; © Anatoliy Samara/Fotolia, p. 45, 60; © Iurii Sokolov/Fotolia, p. 48; © Monkey Business/Fotolia, p. 49, 51, 142, 143, 180, 287; © mangostock/Fotolia, p. 54; © denys_kuvaiev/Fotolia, p. 55; © iofoto/Fotolia, p. 61; Jupiterimages/Getty Images - Brand X Pictures/Thinkstock, p. 63; Michelle Rupiper, p. 73 (bottom), 73 (top left), 73 (top right), 128, 204 (left), 204 (right), 209 (left), 209 (right) 284, 330; © Andrey Kiselev/Fotolia, p. 79; © WavebreakmediaMicro/Fotolia, p. 80; © micromonkey/Fotolia, p. 88; © Dan Race/Fotolia, p. 89; © Philipe Minisini/Fotolia, p. 91; Thinkstock/Comstock/Getty Images, p. 93, 311; © dmitryelagin/Fotolia, p. 101; Lynne Carpenter/Shutterstock, p. 102; © Eléonore H/Fotolia, p. 104; © Kablonk Micro/Fotolia, p. 105, 280; © matka_Wariatka/Fotolia, p. 107, 216, 301; © Andy Dean/Fotolia, p. 108; © Ints Vikmanis/Fotolia, p. 110; © Paulus Nugroho R/Fotolia, p. 112; © Cheryl Casey/Fotolia, p. 124; Tony Freeman/PhotoEdit, p. 125 (top); Laurie Linscott, p. 125 (bottom), 127 (top), 131 (top), 262 (top); Imagesource RF/Glow Images, p. 126; Bounce/Cultura/Getty Images, p. 127 (bottom); © Sergiy Bykhunenko/Shutterstock, p. 131 (bottom); © alexandre zveiger/Fotolia, p. 147; © asem arab/Fotolia, p. 149; © Pavel Losevsky/Fotolia, p. 150, 211, 263; © arztsamui/Fotolia, p. 151; © Kenishirotie/Fotolia, p. 158; © lunamarina/Fotolia, p. 160; © Isaiah Love/Fotolia, p. 162; © ampyang/Fotolia, p. 163; © Artem Furman/Fotolia, p. 171; David Kostelnik, p. 178, 184 (left), 184 (mid), 184 (right), 188 (btm left), 188 (btm right), 188 (top left); © terraformer/Fotolia, p. 183; © michaeljung/Fotolia, p. 186; Artsonia, p. 195 (left), 195 (right); Created by Anne Soderman, p. 198; © Chepko Danil/Fotolia, p. 207; © photophonie/Fotolia, p. 213; © mitgirl/Fotolia, p. 224; © James Peragine/Shutterstock, p. 228; Patrick White/Merrill, p. 242; © waldru/Fotolia, p. 250 (bottom); © Mirma/Fotolia, p. 261; © Mat Hayward/Fotolia, p. 262 (bottom); Regina Yip, p. 265 (bottom); © .shock/Fotolia, p. 267; © cantor pannatto/Fotolia, p. 268; © Benjamin Gelman/Fotolia, p. 274; © Nikolay Levitskiy/Fotolia, p. 290; Bob Ebbesen/Alamy, p. 291; © darko64/Fotolia, p. 293; © Nikolaj Kondratenko/Fotolia, p. 295 (bottom); © Konstantin L/Fotolia, p. 295 (bottom); © wojtek/Fotolia, p. 295 (mid); © Inge Knol/Fotolia, p. 295 (mid); © Firma V/Fotolia, p. 295 (top); © Stephanie Frey/Fotolia, p. 297 (btm left); © Prod. Nume´rik/Fotolia, p. 297 (btm right); © Jasmin Merdan/Fotolia, p. 297 (top); Krista Greco/Merrill, p. 314; © Vladislav Gajic/Fotolia, p. 315 (bottom); © robhainer/Fotolia, p. 315 (top); © sinuswelle/Fotolia, p. 320; © Brebca/Fotolia, p. 325.

DEVELOPMENTALLY APPROPRIATE CURRICULUM IN ACTION

1 Ready, Set, Go! Teaching in Developmentally Appropriate Programs

Tanya examined her sunflower closely. She said it had yellow petals, brown "fuzz" inside, and green leaves. The words she used to describe parts of the flower were *pretty*, *big*, *soft*, *scratchy*, and *hard*. Then she put the biggest flower on her head and said it would make a good hat. We all laughed at that!

Tanya learned several lessons this day—she learned about petals and stems and leaves. She learned to be a better observer, she expanded her vocabulary, and she learned that her teacher valued her playfulness.

Tanya is fortunate. She is in a high-quality early childhood program. According to James Hymes, a pioneer in early education, "a high quality early childhood program, no matter what its name, is proud of the youngness of its children. It is geared to honest, real-life children, the noisy, messy, active, dirty, imaginative kind" (1994, p. 23).

Appreciating the unique qualities of young children is a hallmark of the very best early childhood education programs worldwide. Think about what a program would look like if it were tailored to match the traits of young children described by James Hymes. For instance, if children are noisy, messy, active, and imaginative, what kinds of activities should occupy their time? What kinds of materials should teachers provide? What kind of schedule should they follow from the start of their day to the end? How should adults behave toward children and what should be the content of the lessons they plan? Questions like these have been asked and studied for years. Based on much research and conversation among practitioners, early childhood professionals have come to agree that certain principles and practices characterize programs that respect and celebrate what makes young children special and different from their older peers. These principles and strategies are known as *developmentally appropriate practices*, or DAP.

Today it is nearly impossible to discuss early childhood education without knowing about DAP. Every aspect of children's learning in the early childhood classrooms in which you will teach will be influenced by your understanding of DAP. Thus, learning more about DAP is the first step you will take in becoming an effective teacher of young children.

LEARNING OUTCOMES

After you read this chapter, you will be able to:

- Describe the principles that define developmentally appropriate practices and how these principles influence curriculum.
- Identify your role in supporting a developmentally appropriate approach to teaching young children.
- Recognize developmentally appropriate practices in action.

A Sample Developmentally Appropriate Classroom

Early childhood classrooms characterized by DAP have a certain look and feel. Most important is that these classrooms are action-oriented places where children are on the move, exploring one material and then another, talking with peers and adults, and seldom sitting still. In developmentally appropriate classrooms children gain knowledge and skills through hands-on experiences with people and objects. They construct, create, explore, experiment, invent, find out, build, and compose throughout the day. Teachers are moving and learning too. They hold conversations with children, guide activities, question children, challenge children's thinking, observe, draw conclusions,

TECH TIP

Virtual Museum

Use the Internet to familiarize yourself with famous works of art. Google Rivera's *Girl with Sunflowers* and Van Gogh's *Sunflowers* to view the sunflower paintings mentioned.

and plan for and monitor children's learning. To further understand DAP, consider the learning going on in this early childhood setting.

In the art area Sara, Raj, and Emma are examining two posters: Rivera's *Girl with Sunflowers* and Van Gogh's *Sunflowers*. The children are discussing what they like best about each painting. Leon is seated nearby at a table with a vase of real sunflowers, painting a still life with watercolors. Not far away, Tanya and Simone are also looking at sunflowers of different sizes spread out on a table. They tell a teacher words that describe the look, feel, and smell of the sunflowers. (See the Teacher's Observation Record in the chapter opening.) In the block area, four boys are discussing how to create a tower that doesn't fall over. They use trial and error as they balance blocks atop one another, adjusting their approach with each attempt. Jason and Mara are each rocking baby dolls in the dramatic play area. As they rock, Jason sings quietly to his doll. Another child approaches Mara and announces, "The doctor is ready to see you." The "doctor" holds a stethoscope to the doll and then writes *babe nedz medsn* (baby needs medicine) on a piece of paper and hands it to Mara.

Developmentally appropriate classrooms are action-oriented places where children are engaged in a variety of activities.

Other children in the classroom are looking at books, building puzzles, and talking with one another. Some work individually, some in pairs or small groups. A buzz of happy voices fills the air. The adults in the classroom are active as well. They move among groups of children, asking questions, helping them solve problems, and listening to children's ideas and theories. The teachers make note of what children are doing and how they are doing it. They participate with the children in their activities to understand the children's thinking and to support children's learning. Although it may look as though the children are *only playing*, the teachers have planned the environment and activities with specific goals and objectives in mind. They document children's progress toward these goals by observing children in action. Adult observations help them to see what children are trying to figure out and to consider ways in which children's active learning can be facilitated.

From this description of an active classroom, you can see that teachers in developmentally appropriate classrooms take seriously something the Chinese philosopher Confucius observed more than 2,500 years ago:

> I hear, and I forget.
> I see, and I remember.
> I do, and I understand.

To find out how DAP has become such an important influence today, let us begin by looking at the history of developmentally appropriate practice.

Some Background on Developmentally Appropriate Practices

Following is some discussion about how DAP came about and how it will affect you as an early childhood professional. In the mid-1980s, early childhood educators became worried that many early education programs were not as high quality as they needed to be. Some were too rigid in their approach to teaching, requiring preschoolers to sit still for long periods of time or asking children to fill out many worksheets. Other programs were lacking in appropriate stimulation, with too few materials and not enough interesting things for children to do. In light of this dilemma, in 1986 the National Association for the Education of Young Children (NAEYC) published a position statement on developmentally appropriate practice to provide more specific guidance to professionals in early care and education (Bredekamp, 1987). From the beginning, DAP was seen as evolving in order to reflect the best thinking of the field (Copple & Bredekamp, 2006). In 1997, the statement was revised to reflect new research, experiences of early education professionals, and changing perspectives in the field (Bredekamp & Copple, 1997). The most recent version of the position statement was published in 2009 and addresses three challenges present in early childhood education today:

1. Reducing learning gaps among certain groups of children and increasing the achievement of all children
2. Creating improved, better connected education for preschool and elementary children
3. Recognizing teacher knowledge and decision making as vital to educational effectiveness (Copple & Bredekamp, 2009)

position statement A statement examining a specific issue pertinent to an organization and a declaration of the organization's stance on the issue.

What Does It Mean to Be Developmentally Appropriate?

Understanding how young children develop and learn informs our practice and acts as a guide to planning activities and experiences for the children in our care. When working with young children, it is easy to see that a one-size-fits-all approach does not work well. You must meet children where they are, both as individual learners and as a group. Developmentally appropriate practice means utilizing your knowledge and skills about how children learn and adapting your teaching strategies to fit the age, ability, interests, and experience of individual children. Teachers using DAP consider three fundamental questions when planning and carrying out activities:

1. Is it age appropriate?
2. Is it individually appropriate?
3. Is it socially and culturally appropriate?

Let's look at each of these questions in more detail.

DAP IS AGE APPROPRIATE

To address age appropriateness, first think about what children are like within a general age range. Next, develop activities, routines, and expectations that accommodate and complement these characteristics. Early childhood teachers recognize that expectations appropriate for 4-year-olds are not appropriate for 18-month-old children. Think about how two children of different ages might use the same material. Rae, who is 2 years old, fills a bucket with small wooden blocks, dumps the blocks out, and fills the bucket once again. Malik, age 4, uses the same blocks to build a skyscraper, complete with windows and doors. You would not expect Rae and Malik to use the blocks in the same way because they are not the same age. Different materials, environments, and activities are needed to challenge and support children in these different age groups. Knowing the typical expectations of an age group is helpful in predicting the interests and abilities you are likely to observe. However, knowing a child's age is not sufficient by itself to provide developmentally appropriate experiences. You also need to continually observe the specific children in your classroom to identify their particular abilities, interests, and needs.

DAP IS INDIVIDUALLY APPROPRIATE

Children come to preschool with different developmental strengths. All children within a given age group are not alike; each child has individual strong points, dispositions, interests, needs, and abilities. What is appropriate for one 4-year-old might not be appropriate for another. For example, Melody and LaTisha are each age 4 and were born in the same month. LaTisha has participated in dance lessons and gymnastics for the past year; she spends a lot of time outdoors with her family and enjoys riding a two-wheeler. Melody spends much of her free time exploring books and being read to by her grandmother. She can already identify many written words by sight and enjoys copying down print she sees in the environment. These two girls have had different experiences and demonstrate different abilities and interests. Expectations that may be appropriate for Melody in physical development may be surprisingly easy for LaTisha. On the other hand, LaTisha may not demonstrate Melody's strength in language development. Teachers must take into account the individual knowledge, experience, and skills of each child to determine if a practice is developmentally appropriate.

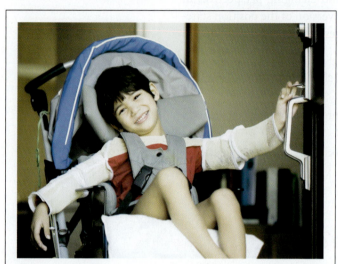

What might you need to consider to plan appropriate experiences for this child?

DAP IS SOCIALLY AND CULTURALLY APPROPRIATE

Children and families live in the context of their communities and cultures and need meaningful, supportive early childhood programs. From early on, children learn rules about values, attitudes, and what is considered appropriate behavior. These rules may be directly taught to children or may be absorbed as children watch people important in their lives. For example, Sue Yeon has learned to look down and smile politely when an adult corrects her. Kendra has learned to look an adult in the eye and keep an expressionless face under the same conditions. Culture also influences how you interpret behaviors exhibited by children. Based on Western practice, you might think Sue Yeon finds it amusing that she is being corrected and is not taking what you are saying seriously, or that Kendra is not remorseful for her behavior. Don't assume that just because children share an ethnic or cultural group that they also share a common cultural experience. There may be differences within an ethnic group based on the region from which they emigrated and also between families from the same region, especially determined by when they emigrated.

Practices appropriate in one culture might not be considered appropriate in another. Think about Brook, who is Navajo. She stands back and watches as other children in the class gleefully experiment with new materials the teacher has just introduced. The teacher tries to engage Brook by offering her some of the items, but Brook just shakes her head 'no' and continues to observe. After several minutes, the teacher comments to her assistant, "I don't know what to do; Brook never wants to try new things!" The teacher doesn't understand that traditional Navajo culture expects children to observe carefully before trying something new and that Brook's behavior is in keeping with her culture. A more culturally appropriate adult response would be to keep the materials available for more than one day and to allow Brook to gradually become involved in using them as she feels more comfortable.

General Practices Associated with Developmentally Appropriate Practice

Teachers using DAP choose goals that are challenging yet achievable for children. Of course what is challenging and achievable will vary depending on the individual child. Children also need multiple opportunities to practice skills related to these goals.

DAP provides a framework for thinking about, planning, and implementing high-quality programs for young children. It informs our decision making and gives us a basis for continually scrutinizing our professional practices. In 2009, NAEYC published the third edition of the book *Developmentally Appropriate Practice in Early Childhood Programs: Serving Children from Birth through Age 8* (Copple & Bredekamp, 2009). This publication contains examples of appropriate practices (effective practices supported by research) and contrasting practices (less effective or even harmful strategies) for infants and toddlers, 3- to 5-year-olds, 5- to 6-year-olds, and for 6- through 8-year-olds. (See Table 1.1 for an example.)

As you can tell from Table 1.1, inappropriate practices sometimes reflect errors of omission (missing an opportunity to assist or support children as they problem solve) as well as errors of commission (teachers focus only on teaching children to count). Appropriate practices are often defined between these extremes (to promote reasoning and problem solving, teachers engage children in thinking about solutions to everyday situations). Although many examples of appropriate or less appropriate practices could be described, the spirit of DAP can be captured in 12 overarching principles (Kostelnik & Grady, 2009; Miller, 2009).

1. Adults develop warm, caring relationships with children.
2. Adults acknowledge children's positive behaviors, reason with children, and treat their misbehaviors as learning opportunities to help children learn to manage their emotions and behaviors.
3. Programs focus on the "whole child," addressing all domains of child development: the children's aesthetic, emotional, cognitive, language, social, and physical needs.
4. Programs address the learning needs of *all* children, including children who have special needs and those who do not speak English as their home language.

TABLE 1.1 • Examples of Appropriate Practices and Inappropriate Practices Related to Mathematics with Children Ages 3 to 5		
AGE GROUP	**APPROPRIATE PRACTICES**	**CONTRASTING/INAPPROPRIATE PRACTICES**
3- to 5-year-olds	To promote reasoning and problem solving, teachers engage children in thinking about solutions to everyday situations (e.g., balancing a block structure, dividing crackers fairly) and in interesting, pre-planned mathematics activities. They talk about the problem, draw children into the process of investigating and solving it, and ask how children came up with their solutions.	Teachers focus heavily on children getting the right answer to a problem. Instead of teachers giving children time and guidance to assist their reasoning and problem solving, teachers tell children the answers or solve problems for them. Teachers stand back and leave children to solve problems on their own without adult assistance or support, therefore missing important opportunities to scaffold children's mathematical thinking and reasoning.

5. Indoor and outdoor environments are safe and stimulating; routines are well suited to the needs of young children.

6. Children have numerous opportunities to learn by doing through hands-on activities that are relevant and meaningful to them.

7. Children are active decision makers in their own learning. They have many opportunities to initiate activities and to make choices about what and how they will learn.

8. Children have many opportunities to play throughout the day.

9. Teachers are intentional in their teaching. They have specific goals in mind for children's learning and use relevant instructional strategies to address those goals.

10. Activities address more than one discipline, such as reading and science, and more than one developmental domain at a time.

11. Assessment takes place continuously throughout the day and addresses all developmental domains. Adults gather information about what children know and can do through observations and annotation by collecting work samples and by inviting children to document their own learning.

12. Early childhood practitioners establish positive, two-way relationships with children's families.

RESEARCH SUPPORTS THE USE OF DEVELOPMENTALLY APPROPRIATE PRACTICE

What began as common sense for many people is becoming a confirmed reality. Documentation is mounting that using developmentally appropriate principles in early childhood programs leads to positive outcomes for children. When compared to programs that ignore such principles, developmentally appropriate curricula are more likely to produce long-term gains in children's cognitive development, social and emotional skills, and life-coping capabilities (Montie, Claxton, & Lockhart, 2007; Payton et al., 2008; UNICEF, 2008). Although more remains to be learned, we have a growing body of research that supports the idea that DAP has long-lasting benefits for children, as summarized in Figure 1.1.

FIGURE 1.1 Research findings associated with DAP

Several research studies have examined the performance of children in DAP-oriented classrooms and the performance of children in classrooms not characterized by DAP. Following are sample findings related to children's social and cognitive learning.

Social outcomes

Children whose teachers use DAP tend to exhibit:

Better social problem-solving skills

More cooperation

More favorable attitudes toward school and teachers

More positive attitudes about themselves as learners

Fewer negative social behaviors

Fewer stress-related behaviors

Cognitive outcomes

Children whose teachers use DAP tend to exhibit better:

Creative-thinking skills

Memory skills

Mathematical problem-solving skills

Grasp of mathematical concepts

Ability to generalize numeracy skills from one situation to another

Reading comprehension

Listening skills

Letter-word identification

Source: Based on Barnett, 2008; Dunn, Beach, & Kontos, 1994; Hart, Burts, Durland, Charlesworth, DeWolf, & Fleege, 1998; Jambunathan, Burts, & Pierce, 1999; Mantzicopoulos, Neuharth-Pritchett, & Morelock, 1994; Payton et al., 2008; Sherman & Mueller, 1996; UNICEF, 2008; Wiltz & Klein, 2001.

Addressing the Needs of Diverse Learners

The population of the United States is becoming more and more diverse. Most early childhood programs today already serve children from varied cultural and linguistic backgrounds as well as children with a range of abilities. To be successful, you will need to embrace this diversity in order to help all the children in your group to reach their full potential. You will need to utilize materials, activities, and teaching strategies that reflect the diversity of the children and families in your program. DAP provides a framework for you to individualize curriculum to meet the needs of each child. Your knowledge of child development combined with your knowledge of individual children will enable you to provide these developmentally appropriate educational experiences. Figure 1.2 includes ideas you can use to support linguistically and culturally diverse learners in your classroom.

The nature of DAP encourages the placement of children with and without disabilities in the same classrooms (Filler & Xu, 2006). Inclusive programs, those serving children with disabilities alongside their nondisabled peers, benefit all young children. At the heart of DAP is meeting children where they are and supporting them to meet achievable yet challenging goals. Effective teachers support children who have special learning and developmental needs to participate fully in classroom activities and routines. However, it is not enough simply to place children with disabilities in

inclusive programs Programs emphasizing the acceptance and full participation of all students regardless of the student's ability. Children are included in all program activities as members who belong, with the supports and services they need to participate.

FIGURE 1.2 Supporting linguistically and culturally diverse learners in your classroom

Support the child's home language

- Know words the child uses for basic needs and wants (*What words does the child use to indicate having to go to the bathroom?*).
- Learn key phrases (*Good morning*) in the child's home language.
- Post simple phrases (*Tell me what you're building*) in children's home languages in interest areas so that

you can communicate in the child's home language. Include pronunciations if needed.

- Label classroom areas and items in all the languages spoken by children in your class.
- Provide books, games, and other materials written in other languages.
- Sing simple songs in children's home languages. Learn and sing familiar songs (*Twinkle, Twinkle, Little Star*) in different languages.

English Version	Spanish Version	French Version
Twinkle, Twinkle Little Star	**Estrellita, Donde Estas**	**Petite Etoile**
Twinkle, twinkle little star,	Estrellita, donde estas?	Petite étoile, où es-tu?
How I wonder what you are,	Me pregunto qué seras.	Je me demande ce que tu peux être.
Up above the world so high,	En el cielo y en el mar,	Dans le ciel et dans la mer,
Like a diamond in the sky,	Un diamante de verdad.	Un véritable diamant.
Twinkle, twinkle little star,	Estrellita, donde estas?	Petite étoile, où es-tu?
How I wonder what you are!	Me pregunto qué seras.	Je me demande ce que tu peux être.

- Include authentic items from each child's culture in all interest areas.
- Provide puzzles, pictures, and books that represent various cultures and languages.
- Display art from around the world.
- Play authentic music from different cultures.
- Ask parents or family members to create audio-taped versions of books by telling the story in

their home language. Add these versions to your listening area.

- Include photographs or posters of international buildings or icons in the block area.
- Add empty food containers, restaurant menus, magazines, and newspapers written in children's home languages to the dramatic play area.
- Serve foods from various cultures at meals and snacks.

an inclusive classroom without making appropriate accommodations. Many special education experts believe that DAP is not sufficient on its own to meet the needs of young children with disabilities (Gargiulo & Kilgo, 2005). Specialized services for children with identified disabilities are also needed. These are most effective when built on a developmentally appropriate foundation that recognizes that children with disabilities are children first and foremost. The DAP guidelines and those developed by the Division for Early Childhood (DEC) and the Council for Exceptional Children (CEC) have many similarities. They both stress:

- individualization of instruction
- appropriate and meaningful assessment
- integration of assessment and curriculum
- focus on child-initiated activities
- emphasis on child's active engagement
- importance of social interaction
- social and cultural appropriateness (Fox, Hanline, Vail, & Galant, 1994)

In order for children to benefit from inclusion, we must ensure the full participation of *all* children. Full participation often means that materials, routines, or activities must be adapted in some way to accommodate the needs of a child with a disability. The physical setup of the room should also be considered. Are pathways wide enough to accommodate a child in a wheelchair? Are materials that are meant for children placed where they are accessible to all children? It may be overwhelming at first to think of accommodating a child with special needs in your classroom. However, early childhood teachers make accommodations all the time. Adding a step stool so that children can reach the water fountain, providing paint smocks to keep clothes clean, and encouraging shoes with Velcro are all examples of accommodations for young children. Of course, the accommodations you make for any individual child will depend on the needs of that specific child. For children who have verified disabilities, early childhood teachers will work with a team of specialists to determine appropriate goals and strategies to meet that child's specific needs, which will be outlined in the child's individualized education plan (IEP).

individualized education plan (IEP) A program that determines what services children with special needs will receive, how services will be provided, and the outcomes a child might reasonably be expected to accomplish in a year. Every IEP includes these elements: a description of the child's strengths, needs, goals; short-term objectives; special education services and program modifications; and the frequency, duration, and location of the services to be provided.

Federal law mandates that all children with a documented special need that adversely affects educational performance receive special education services early in life. For children age 3 and older, the local school system develops and coordinates an IEP. Every IEP includes the same elements: a description of the child's strengths; needs; goals; short-term objectives; special education services; program modifications; and the frequency, duration, and location of the services to be provided. These services must take place in the least restrictive environment possible. For young children, that often includes an early childhood classroom. What services children receive, how services are provided, and the outcomes a child might reasonably be expected to accomplish in a year are described within an IEP. In each case, these elements are *individualized* to address the educational needs of a specific child. Figure 1.3 provides additional information about an IEP.

Teachers must be knowledgeable about the needs of the children they teach in order to utilize the strategies most effective in supporting children's learning. Families will likely be the best source of information about the specific needs, strengths, and interests of individual children. Listening attentively, demonstrating interest, and asking open-ended questions of family members can further your understanding of children's competence. This is one reason that developing positive, two-way relationships with families is essential for effective teachers.

At this point you may be wondering if developmentally appropriate practices work for all children or if it meets the needs of some children but not others. Studies conducted a decade ago seem to indicate that these practices are widely applicable. Researchers at the time noted that DAP "has the potential to provide strong foundational experiences

FIGURE 1.3 Carmen's individualized education plan

Carmen is a 3-year-old girl with an engaging smile and big brown eyes; she has also been identified as having a speech delay. Carmen likes to play with dolls, draw at the art table, and listen to books. She spends much of her time in solitary play but appears to enjoy playing near other children in her preschool class. If a teacher draws her attention to a peer, she will join in, but she needs the teacher's help to continue the interaction. Currently, she uses very few words but is learning to use picture cards and gestures to aid her communication. Sometimes Carmen becomes frustrated and will scream in protest when others do not understand what she wants or needs. Carmen is enrolled in a full-day program that includes children who are developing typically as well as children who have special needs.

Carmen's IEP was created in a group meeting that included her mom, dad, and grandmother (who lives with Carmen, her parents, and younger brother Luis). Her early childhood special education (ECSE) teacher, her pre-K teacher, an occupational therapist, and a speech pathologist also attended. The adults first reviewed Carmen's assessment data, noting when her last formal assessment was given and the results. Her family offered examples of what she likes to do at home. The teachers brought written notes as well as checklists of behaviors they had observed Carmen display at preschool. The pre-K teacher also had work samples of Carmen's art, a list of words she has used at preschool, and digital photographs of her playing at school to share with the group.

Together the team created specific social, behavior, and communication goals and objectives for Carmen to address during the year. They agreed that the plan would be reviewed and revised annually. Following are three examples of *individually appropriate goals* identified for Carmen.

IEP goals

- Carmen will imitate a pretend play sequence of 4 to 6 steps with peer and adult models to facilitate and maintain the play activity.

- Carmen will use appropriate social greetings with familiar adults and children (hi, bye), using names when appropriate.

- Carmen will request a desired item or activity by giving a picture to an adult or peer.

Supporting practices

The pre-K teacher agreed to incorporate the following *individually appropriate practices* in his classroom to facilitate Carmen's progress toward her IEP goals. Carmen's family will also use some of these techniques at home.

Create communication opportunities

- Teach Carmen to get a peer's attention by tapping the peer on the shoulder and then saying the peer's name. She could then give the peer a picture card to request an item or activity. (The teacher will also work to teach the other children how to respond appropriately to Carmen.)

- Provide Carmen multiple opportunities throughout each day to greet different people including peers, teachers, and other adults in the building (e.g., lunch personnel, custodian, principal).

- Encourage peers to ask questions and make comments to Carmen.
  - "Luke, ask Carmen where she would like to play next."
  - "Sasha, tell Carmen what you are building."

Facilitate social opportunities

- If Carmen is playing alone, bring a peer to her play area or ask a peer to invite Carmen to play along.

- When transitioning in the classroom or going outside, have a peer hold Carmen's hand.

- Utilize Carmen's preferred play materials (e.g., dolls) as a way to encourage interaction with her peers. Draw Carmen's attention to peer's actions. For example, "Carmen, Justin is brushing his doll's hair. Do what Justin is doing."

for males and females from different racial and socioeconomic backgrounds" (Hart et al., 1997, p. 8). Later studies have supported these findings. Over the past 10 years, the favorable results reported in Figure 1.1 have been found to be true for boys and for girls, for children from higher- and lower-income families, for children of color as well as white children in the United States, and for children in many countries around the world (e.g., Australia, England, France, Greece, Poland, Indonesia, and Thailand) (Bennett, 2008; National Institute of Child Health and Human Development [NICHHD], 2005). Such results indicate that DAP is a promising approach for working with various populations of children. However, more research specifically designed to answer questions of diversity are necessary before we can say with certainty that DAP meets the needs of *all* the children and families that early childhood educators serve.

Research indicates that developmentally appropriate practices are effective with children of various backgrounds.

DEVELOPMENTALLY APPROPRIATE PRACTICE AND CURRICULUM

DAP affects every component of the curriculum. Your understanding of DAP will affect your choices as teachers, including:

- How we structure the physical learning environment
- How we organize the schedule of the day and daily routines
- How we interact with children and families
- What goals we choose for children

The key ideas addressed in DAP center on what children know and can do, and adults working with children make intentional decisions about curriculum with these characteristics in mind. Developmentally appropriate curriculum is created while considering specific children's strengths, needs, interests, and abilities. Table 1.2 provides key principles associated with appropriate curriculum and examples of what these principles look like in operation.

DEVELOPMENTALLY APPROPRIATE PRACTICE INVOLVES JUDGMENT

Teachers make hundreds of large and small decisions in their classrooms every day. Such decision making lies at the center of effective teaching. Teachers must rely on their knowledge and understanding of young children to determine what is appropriate for the children they teach. Good teachers are intentional in everything they do (Epstein, 2007). They think carefully about the decisions they make and are able to articulate the rationale for their decisions. They make informed decisions based on what they know about children in general as well as what they know about the specific children in their care.

TABLE 1.2 • Five Principles Associated with Appropriate Curriculum

PRINCIPLE	EXAMPLE
Curricula address the whole child, providing for all areas of development.	Tracy makes sure that her daily lesson plans include math, science, language, art, music, social, affective, and physical experiences.
Curricula include content that is meaningful to children.	After observing children watching insects while outdoors, Tracy adds several insect-related books to the reading area and provides collection jars and magnifying glasses for the children to use in their observations.
Curricula are culturally relevant and value children's home cultures and languages while also supporting all children to participate in the shared culture of the school.	Tracy invites the families of her class to share experiences from their homes with the children. Meijing's parents make dumplings with the class, Josh's grandmother brings quilts for the children to examine, and Ezra's mother teaches the children a Yiddish song.
Curricula have clearly stated outcomes for children. Effective teachers also plan teaching strategies appropriate for helping children make progress towards these outcomes.	Tracy carefully chooses materials for the writing center in her classroom to encourage children to put their thoughts on paper. Throughout the week she gathers writing samples for the children to determine their current writing abilities.
Curricula are developed by teachers who believe in themselves and their abilities to influence children's learning.	Tracy reflects on her day and smiles as she thinks of Jenna's pride at writing her name on her painting. Tracy recalls the numerous writing opportunities she has planned throughout the year and is pleased with the progress Jenna has made.

Source: Based on Jalongo and Isenberg (2008).

Thinking about what you have just read regarding DAP, consider whether or not the following scenarios are examples of developmentally appropriate practice.

- Jenny Wolensky has read the book *It Looked Like Spilt Milk* to her group of 4-year-olds and now is engaging in an art activity where children have made fold-over paintings with white paint on blue paper. She asks each child to describe what his or her painting looks like and records the responses on the bottom of the painting.
- Marcus Wentworth has planned a trip for his morning preschool class to the petting zoo, which features goats, pigs, and sheep.
- Mrs. McNamara has a workbench in her classroom for 3-year-olds, complete with an authentic hand saw that the young preschoolers can use to saw wood.

Your first impression might be that creating paintings based on a book the children enjoyed and planning a trip to the petting zoo are clear examples of DAP. You may have concerns about the safety of a hand saw being used by 3-year-olds and think a sharp saw is not a developmentally appropriate choice of materials. However, closer scrutiny may prompt you to reassess your original judgments.

You may revise your assessment of the painting activity after viewing the following interaction between Leo and his teacher, Jenny. When Leo tells Jenny his painting looks like a truck, she responds, "Look, Leo, it looks like a bunny. See the long ears here?" and points to the painting. Leo replies, "No, a truck." Jenny again points to the painting and says, "Leo, your painting looks like a bunny. It has long ears just like a bunny." Leo simply replies, "Truck." Jenny writes at the bottom of his painting "*It looks like a bunny*," and tells Leo to put the painting in his cubby. Leo takes the painting and sulks off toward his cubby. Although the painting activity was appropriate for young children, the interaction between Leo and his teacher created an inappropriate experience for Leo. It is not enough to simply choose activities that are appropriate; teachers must implement the activity in an appropriate manner as well.

A trip to the petting zoo would be appropriate for many preschool classes, but further examination of the children in Marcus' class reveals that two of the children are Muslim, and petting a pig would not be appropriate for them. Another child in the class is tactile defensive and becomes very agitated and distraught when asked to touch unfamiliar things, and a third child has autism and would likely react negatively to this change in the schedule. Considering the individual and cultural needs of the children in this class, you may decide that the trip is not appropriate.

Further examination of Mrs. McNamara's class shows us that the children are very interested in building and woodworking. They have been well instructed in the correct use of all the tools, including the saw, and take using the saw very seriously. Mrs. McNamara makes sure the work bench area is well supervised and that the tools are not accessible to the children at other times. Based on these observations, you may determine that the materials are developmentally appropriate.

As the previous examples show, the answer to whether or not a specific practice is developmentally appropriate is "It depends." It depends on the experiences, abilities, and cultures of the individual children with whom you are working. Scenarios such as these illustrate that determining what does or does not constitute DAP requires more than simply memorizing a set of dos and don'ts or looking at children's activities in isolation. It involves considering every practice within the context in which it is occurring and making a judgment about what is happening to a particular child in a particular place at a particular time. The best judgments are those you make consciously.

To determine whether specific teaching practices are developmentally appropriate, many early childhood educators ask three questions:

1. Does this practice support what I know about child development and learning?
2. Does this practice take into account children's individual strengths and needs?
3. Does this practice demonstrate respect for children's social and cultural lives?

What questions might you ask this parent to help you design experiences that are individually and culturally appropriate for her child?

Teachers may use these questions to answer immediate concerns or to think about more long-term DAP issues. These questions might be considered by an individual teacher or by an entire program staff. You might use these questions to consider the appropriateness of a specific activity or program policy. In every circumstance, the answer to each question should be "yes." Answering no to any question is a strong indication that the practice is not appropriate and should be reconsidered, adapted, or discarded. Your knowledge of child development and learning, your understanding of curriculum, your awareness of family and community relationships, your knowledge of assessment, and your interpretation of your professional role will also influence what you do (Copple & Bredekamp, 2009). All of these factors, combined with an understanding of DAP, should guide early childhood decision making.

THE ROLE OF THE TEACHER IN DAP PROGRAMS

In developmentally appropriate programs, the teacher has a critical role. The guidelines developed by NAEYC (Copple & Bredekamp, 2009) for DAP describe five interrelated functions of excellent early childhood teachers:

1. creating a caring community of learners
2. teaching to enhance development and learning
3. planning curriculum to achieve important goals
4. establishing reciprocal relationships with families
5. assessing children's development and learning

Successful teachers are intentional in each aspect of their jobs. That is, they leave little to chance. They think carefully about the children, their goals in the program, and how they will address those goals every day. They realize that each feature of DAP is related to the rest, and none can be shortchanged without seriously undermining the others.

CREATING A CARING COMMUNITY OF LEARNERS

Good teachers realize that children learn best in an environment where they feel valued and safe. Teachers make a genuine effort to get to know each child and family well and develop a warm and positive relationship with each individual. Everyone is included and treated with respect as a part of the classroom community. This community of learners provides the positive relationships through which children learn best.

TEACHING TO ENHANCE DEVELOPMENT AND LEARNING

Effective early childhood teachers need specialized knowledge about how children learn and develop as well as effective strategies to teach children. Teachers make intentional decisions about which materials to use, how to design the environment, and what learning experiences are most appropriate for the group and each individual child within it. Successful teachers utilize a broad array of teaching formats such as small groups, whole group, and learning centers for different learning purposes. They also use a wide variety of teaching strategies to best address the goals and situation at hand. In later chapters you will learn more about these topics.

PLANNING CURRICULUM

Teachers of young children must plan curriculum to assist children in meeting important goals. The curriculum includes the knowledge and skills you plan to have

classroom community A sense of common purpose and values that is shared by the teachers and children within a classroom, which leads to a sense of belonging by classroom members.

the children acquire as well as the experiences through which the children's learning will take place. Good curriculum should address all the domains associated with childhood development and learning (aesthetic, cognitive, physical, social, emotional, and language). Activities should be flexible in order to be adapted to the needs of individuals and be worthy of children's time. Much of this text is devoted to creating meaningful and effective curriculum for young children.

ASSESSING CHILDREN'S DEVELOPMENT AND LEARNING

Another role of the teacher is linking assessment and curriculum to guide planning and decision making. Intentional teachers use assessment to monitor children's progress and base subsequent curriculum planning on assessment results. Teachers ensure that any assessment used is appropriate for the child's age and developmental status and is individually and culturally appropriate. Most often in a preschool classroom, useful assessment data is gathered by close observation of children, talking with them, and examining their work. We address assessment further in Chapter 4.

Communicating with Families About Developmentally Appropriate Practice
ESTABLISHING RECIPROCAL RELATIONSHIPS WITH FAMILIES

Excellent teachers recognize that family members are the most important people in a child's life. Parents and other family members have knowledge and understanding of the child that the teacher does not. This information helps the teacher to better understand the child as an individual, and therefore better meet the child's needs. Reciprocal relationships with families can be enhanced by ongoing, two-way communication with families where information is regularly exchanged. Welcoming families and consistently treating them with respect and as a valued partner in their child's education communicates to families their importance as a member of the classroom community. Figure 1.4 includes information you can share with families regarding developmentally appropriate practice.

Certain activities may be developmentally appropriate for some children but not for others.

TRY IT YOURSELF

Prepare to interview a family member of a young child. Develop a set of questions to ask during the interview. What information do families have that will assist you in developing appropriate activities and experiences for this child? What questions will help you determine which activities will be *individually appropriate* for this child? What questions will help you determine which activities would be *socially and culturally appropriate* for this child? Compare your ideas with some of the questions listed here.

1. What are your child's favorite activities?

2. How does your child respond to new people or new situations?

3. What family rituals, routines, or holidays do you follow?

4. What hobbies or interests might you be willing to share with our program?

NEWSLETTER/WEB READY COMMUNICATION

FIGURE 1.4 • Our Classroom Is Developmentally Appropriate

Early childhood classrooms are abuzz with excitement and activity. Children are busy building with blocks, creating masterpieces in the art area, and moving to music during group time. It may look as though the children are *only playing*, but there is learning going on within the commotion! As children play, they are able to test their theories about how things work, develop social skills that enable them to cooperate with each other, and solve problems they encounter with materials. Research and experiences tell us that in order for us to foster children's learning, we must be *developmentally appropriate*. This means teachers must have a thorough understanding of how children grow and develop and what to expect at what age. At the same time, teachers must also meet the needs of each individual child in their classes. Developmentally appropriate practice means teaching that takes into account children's ages, experiences, abilities, interests, and cultures while helping them reach challenging and achievable goals. For example, some children have had little experience being a part of a group and may need help taking turns or sharing materials. Other children have already developed these skills. Good teachers strive to be developmentally appropriate in their interactions with children and families, and are eager to learn about each family's culture and circumstances.

FIGURE 1.5 Ways to advocate for appropriate practices

- Connect with other early childhood professionals in your community—begin small and work toward change in your local environment

- Develop relationships with education and political leaders such as school board and city council members—you may be able to provide insight on issues from an early childhood perspective

- Read about current early childhood policy issues—sign up for e-mail alerts, newsletters, and other ways to get information

- Join professional organizations—organizations provide the opportunity to work with others to make change on a larger scale

Source: Based on Brown (2008).

DEVELOPMENTALLY APPROPRIATE PRACTICE IS STILL EVOLVING

The guidelines for DAP were developed as a living document that would continue to evolve in order to reflect the current educational context (Copple & Bredekamp, 2009). The guidelines are subject to change as thinking and recommended practices in the field change over time. This means that you will need to continue developing as a professional, thinking carefully about changing perspectives in the field and how they affect your work. Early childhood teachers should also advocate for policies based on what research has demonstrated is effective in supporting children's learning and development. Figure 1.5 suggests several ways that early childhood teachers can advocate for appropriate practices.

As you have learned in this chapter, early childhood professionals approach their work with the understanding that young children's learning differs significantly from that of older children and adults. The application of DAP makes the nature and well-being of children the central focus of professional practice. Now take what you have learned and apply it within the professional activities that follow.

1 Applying What You've Learned

1. Describe the principles that define developmentally appropriate practice and how these principles influence curriculum.

2. Identify your role in supporting a developmentally appropriate approach to teaching young children.

Review several websites or activity books that contain activities for preschool children. Choose two to three activities and analyze each activity by answering the following questions:

- How does this activity match with what I know about child development and learning?

- How does this activity take into account children's individual strengths and needs?

- How does this activity demonstrate respect for children's social and cultural lives?

- How might this activity need to be adapted or modified to make it more developmentally appropriate?

■ 3. Recognize developmentally appropriate practices in action.

- Observe two classrooms that have adopted a developmentally appropriate philosophy.

Describe ways the adults use the principle of *age appropriateness* in terms of materials, activities, and routines in each classroom. Identify the similarities and the differences between the two rooms and write a summary of your findings.

- Observe an inclusive early childhood classroom. Describe ways in which the materials, routines, and activities have been modified to be *individually appropriate* for a child with special needs.

References

Barnett, W. S. (2008). *Preschool education and its lasting effects: Research and policy implications.* Boulder and Tempe: Education and the Public Interest Center & Education Policy Research Unit. Retrieved March 30, 2008 from http://epicpolicy.org/publication/preschool-education.

Bennett, J. (2008). Early Childhood Services in the OECD Countries: Review of the literature and current policy in the early childhood field. *Innocenti Working Paper* No.2008-01. Florence, Italy: UNICEF Innocenti Research Centre.

Bredekamp, S. [Ed.] (1987). Developmentally appropriate practice in early childhood programs serving children from birth through age 8. Washington, D.C.: NAEYC.

Bredekamp, S., & Copple, C. [Eds.] (1997). Developmentally appropriate practice in early childhood programs. Rev. ed. Washington, D.C.: NAEYC.

Brown, C. P. (2008). Advocating for policies to improve practice. *Young Children, 63*(4), 70–77.

Copple, C., & Bredekamp. S. (2006). Basics of developmentally appropriate practice: An introduction for teachers of children 3 to 6. Washington, D.C.: NAEYC.

Copple, C., & Bredekamp, S. (2009). *Developmentally appropriate practice in early childhood programs serving children from birth through age 8.* Washington, D.C.: National Association for the Education of Young Children.

Dunn, L., Beach, S. A., & Kontos, S. (1994). Quality for the literacy environment in day care and children's development. *Journal of Research in Childhood Education, 9,* 24–34.

Epstein, A. S. (2007). *The intentional teacher: Choosing the best strategies for young children's learning.* Washington, D.C.: National Association for the Education of Young Children.

Filler, J., & Xu, Y. (2006). Including children with disabilities in early childhood education programs: Individualizing developmentally appropriate practices. *Childhood Education, 83*(2), 92–99.

Fox, L., Hanline, M., Vail, C., & Galant, K. (1994). Developmentally appropriate practices: Applications for young children with disabilities. *Journal of Early Intervention, 18*(3), 243–257.

Gargiulo, R., & Kilgo, J. (2005). *Young children with special needs* (2nd. ed.). Clifton Park, NY: Thompson/Delmar Learning.

Hart, C. H., Burts, D. C., & Charlesworth, R. (1997). Integrated developmentally appropriate curriculum: From theory to research to practice. In C. H. Hart, D. C. Burts, & R. Charlesworth (Eds.), *Integrated curriculum and developmentally appropriate practice: Birth to age eight* (pp. 1–27). Albany: State University of New York Press.

Hart, C. H., Burts, D. C., Durland, M. A., Charlesworth, R., DeWolf, M., & Fleege, P. O. (1998). Stress behaviors and activity type participation of preschoolers in more or less developmentally appropriate classrooms: SES and sex differences. *Journal of Research in Childhood Education, 12*(2), 176–196.

Hymes, J. (1994). *The child under six.* Englewood Cliffs, NJ: Prentice Hall.

Jalongo, M. R., & Isenberg, J. P. (2008). Exploring your role: An introduction to early childhood education. Upper Saddle River, NJ: Pearson.

Jambunathan, S., Burts, D. C., & Pierce, S. H. (1999). Developmentally appropriate practices as predictors of self-competence among preschoolers. *Journal of Research in Childhood Education, 13*(2), 167–174.

Kostelnik, M. J., & Grady, M. L. (2009). *Getting it right from the start: The principal's guide to early childhood education.* Thousand Oaks, CA: Corwin Press.

Mantzicopoulos, P. Y., Neuharth-Pritchett, S., & Morelock, J. B. (1994, April). *Academic competence, social skills, and behavior among disadvantaged children in developmentally appropriate and inappropriate classrooms.* Paper presented at the annual meeting of the American Educational Research Association, New Orleans, LA.

Miller, E. (2009). *Positive child guidance* (6th ed.). Clifton Park, NY: Delmar Learning.

Montie, J. E., Claxton, J., & Lockhart, S. D. (2007). A multinational study supports child-initiated learning. *Young Children, 62*(6), 22–26.

National Institute of Child Health and Human Development, Early Childcare Research Network (Ed.). (2005). *Childcare and child development: Results from the NICHD study of early childcare and youth development.* New York: Guildford Press.

Payton, J., Weissberg, R. P., Durlak, J. A., Dymnicki, A. B., Taylor, R. D., Schellinger, K. B., & Pachan, M. (2008). *The positive impact of social and emotional learning for kindergarten to eighth-grade students: Findings from three scientific reviews.* Chicago, IL: Collaborative for Academic, Social, and Emotional Learning.

Sherman, C. W., & Mueller, D. P. (1996, June). Developmentally appropriate practice and student achievement in inner-city elementary schools. Paper presented at Head Start's Third National Research Conference, Washington, D.C.

UNICEF. (2008). UNICEF Innocenti Report Card 8, The Childcare Transition: A league table of early childhood education and care in economically advanced countries. United Nations, Florence, Italy.

Wiltz, N. W., & Klein, E. L. (2001). What do you do in child care? Children's perceptions of high and low quality classrooms. *Early Childhood Research Quarterly, 16*(2), 209–236.

2 What You Need to Know to Help Children Grow: Preparing to Teach

Kate had always wanted to be an early childhood teacher—and she was determined to be a good one. As she sat through her course work to earn her degree, she found her instructors emphasizing three areas of knowledge. First, she learned that it was important to gain a good understanding of how children develop and learn, and she felt she had worked hard on that. Second, she found that she needed a good grasp of content knowledge in a variety of areas, such as language and literacy, social learning, mathematics, and science, as well as an understanding of relevant learning outcomes. Her administrator identified what the program expected children to learn during the preschool, kindergarten, and primary years. Finally, she discovered that she needed to develop a broad repertoire of effective teaching strategies. Her readings, volunteer experience, and student teaching had helped with that. Today was her first day on the job—her chance to put it all together.

This chapter explores these essential facets of early education (see Figure 2.1) and how to combine them to create a holistic approach to teaching and learning in the early years.

Early Childhood Educators Need to Know About Child Development and Learning

Three-year-old Megan and her 6-year-old sister Anna are enjoying playing with paper dolls, though it's clear they are playing in entirely different ways. Megan talks out loud about what her doll is thinking and pretends she is "going inside and outside" again and again, changing the doll's clothing each time. Anna is intent on creating new clothes for both dolls, skillfully measuring and cutting them out. She carefully arranges her created doll clothes in distinct piles, sorting them at first as "tops" and "bottoms" and then categorizing them further into sweaters, jackets, tee shirts, skirts, and pants. When Megan mistakenly puts a "bottom" into the tee-shirt pile, an exasperated Anna says, "Megan, look. No bottoms here. I told you that!"

An early myth about early childhood education was that anyone with a "good heart" could teach young children—that it was mostly intuitive and dependent on having lots of activities to keep children busy. Evidence shows that this is not true. Effective delivery of high-quality programs demands that early childhood teachers know when children are expected to benefit from certain experiences and how children are likely to differ from one another (Copple & Bredekamp, 2009; Stronge, 2002). Equally important is knowledge of strategies to logically move children along in their learning. Teachers who are unskilled in understanding the unique characteristics of the children they serve are most likely to "drop out of the field" (Horowitz, Darling-Hammond, & Bransford, 2005), have management problems with children, and find teaching on a day-to-day basis difficult and unrewarding.

LEARNING OUTCOMES

After you read this chapter, you will be able to:

- Connect principles of child development and learning to your teaching practices.
- Describe the cycle of learning or how children gain new knowledge and skills.
- Describe content knowledge and the role that content standards play in early learning programs.
- Identify instructional strategies connected with developmentally appropriate practices.
- Explain how to adapt your teaching to meet the needs of diverse learners.
- Communicate with families about how and what you are teaching.

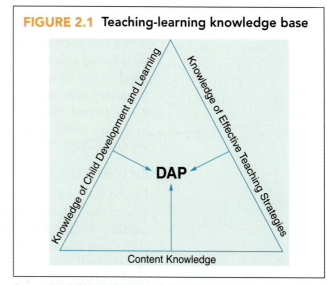

FIGURE 2.1 Teaching-learning knowledge base

Source: Kostelnik, M. J., Soderman, A. K., & Whiren, A. P. *Developmentally appropriate curriculum: Best practices in early childhood education,* 5th ed., © 2011. Reprinted and electronically reproduced by permission of Pearson Education, Inc., Upper Saddle River, NJ.

PRINCIPLES OF CHILD DEVELOPMENT AND LEARNING

Understanding child development and learning will influence how you interact with children, the kinds of environments you create for them, and the kinds of learning outcomes you will expect of children of different ages and abilities. Following are nine principles consistently cited by early educators throughout the world. As you make them a natural part of your practice, they will allow you to make informed decisions about your thinking, planning, and teaching as an early childhood educator.

CHILDREN DEVELOP HOLISTICALLY

When you think about the children you will teach, remember that the six developmental domains—aesthetic, affective, cognitive, language, physical, and social—are continuously interrelated. One developmental domain never functions without the others. Look back at Megan and Anna's paper doll play and consider how the play was influenced by each facet of the children's development: Their activity included aesthetic development (creating the dolls and clothes), affective development (experiencing satisfaction with their work), cognitive development (sorting, measuring), social development (exchanging ideas), language (creating verbal scenarios), and fine motor development (cutting, coloring). Although one domain may sometimes be more dominant than others in a given task, children always function holistically.

CHILD DEVELOPMENT FOLLOWS AN ORDERLY SEQUENCE

Researchers have been able to identify step-wise processes in which children's understandings, knowledge, and skills build on each other (Berk, 2009). Benchmarks in the six developmental domains emerge in a predictable order and are dependent on children's maturation and opportunities to learn. For example, the various categories for the different types of doll clothes were clear to 6-year-old Anna, but her younger sister did not yet fully understand and needed further coaching, prompting, experience, and time in order to reach the same clarity. It's important to remember, however, that developmental processes are not rigid; they vary with individual children's motivation, special needs, and exposure to certain experiences. A child's current development and your knowledge of how development proceeds will provide reliable clues about what comes next.

CHILDREN DEVELOP AT VARYING RATES

If you were to observe a classroom of 15 three-year-olds as they approach certain developmental milestones, you would find considerable variation in their development based on maturation and experience (Trawick-Smith, 2009). For example, Megan has had plenty of access to construction materials and the modeling of an older sister who enjoys playing with her (at least most of the time!). Some of the children may never have had a chance or the motivation to hold scissors, sort materials, or even play with another child.

CHILDREN LEARN BEST WHEN THEY FEEL SAFE AND SECURE

During their doll play, Anna may have been irritated with Megan, but she communicated that irritation without being abusive, preserving the girls' ability to play well together. Warm, loving relationships form the context for optimal learning. Thus, one of the most important things that you will do as a teacher is to develop a warm relationship with each child in the classroom so that children can relax, knowing that you genuinely like and value them. When children come to know that you are interested in what they are saying, that you will be patient with them as they are learning, that routines are predictable, and that they can rely on you to set reasonable limits, they feel safe. Such environments are perceived by children as a good place to spend time, and they look forward to each day of school.

CHILDREN ARE ACTIVE LEARNERS

Learning is most apt to take place when children are engaged in plenty of hands-on experiences where they have freedom to investigate, move, and act on their environments as they learn, using all their senses. In our opening scenario, both Megan and Anna have different ideas about what they want to "act on" in their play with the paper dolls and most likely would have lost interest quickly in the activity if it were being overly supervised by a teacher or parent. Although the girls had different goals and were not directly interacting with one another, their play was mobilized by Anna's active desire to produce the materials and Megan's equally active enjoyment in using them.

CHILDREN LEARN THROUGH PHYSICAL EXPERIENCE, SOCIAL INTERACTION, AND REFLECTION

Young children have a powerful need to make sense of everything they encounter. Their efforts to do so begin at birth and continue as they directly manipulate, listen to, smell, taste, and act on objects. These are the primary ways they gain knowledge about the properties of things, how they work, and how they are similar or different. To the extent that children have opportunities to explore, they develop increasingly complex thinking, which they use to interpret and draw conclusions about the world.

Continuing with our example of Megan and Anna, there is no doubt that Megan's ability to sort and categorize is enhanced as she pays attention to Anna's insistence on "only tops in one pile; only bottoms in another." At first, Megan is thrown out of balance by this, thinking, "Why does it matter?" However, after reflecting further about Anna's reasoning and then replacing the doll clothing in the relevant categories, her thinking becomes more complex.

Children are unable to learn everything totally on their own. Their interactions with others will yield the names of objects, customs, historical facts, the rules for interacting socially, and certain skills such as learning to read and write. As children talk, work, and play with others, they generate hypotheses, ask questions, and formulate answers (Copple & Bredekamp, 2009). As they do so, they reflect internally on their experiences, recognize discrepancies in their reasoning and that of others, continually shaping, expanding, and reorganizing their thinking.

What can these two boys learn from one another while playing together here?

CHILDREN ARE MOTIVATED TO LEARN THROUGH A CONTINUOUS PROCESS OF CHALLENGE AND MASTERY OF CONCEPTS AND SKILLS

We saw an example of this process of challenge and **mastery** when Anna challenged Megan to get things "in the right pile" during their paper doll play. With prompting and practice, Megan's *mastery* of Anna's rule became internalized or automatic, no longer needing a reminder. Young children have so many things to learn, and the excitement of doing so is what prompts them to continue pursuing concepts and skills just slightly beyond their current levels of proficiency. However, if children lack stimulation and support to master new tasks or become highly stressed because a task

mastery Demonstrated control of a skill or concept.

How does this fish bowl serve as a learning resource in this classroom?

is too demanding, they eventually give up. You will play a major role in structuring the learning environment so that children remain motivated and engaged rather than frustrated.

CHILDREN'S LEARNING PROFILES VARY

Everyone has preferred ways of learning. Think about what your learning preferences are. Now think about Anna and Megan. Anna preferred to create materials while Megan preferred to use them in an imaginative way. These differences probably had more to do with their individual learning styles than they did with other factors. As you get to know the children you are teaching, you will find that each child is a unique combination of eight *frames of mind* or *multiple intelligences* (Gardner, 1993). These intelligences (see Table 2.1) are predictive of the way children like to spend their time, where they seem to excel, and where they may need additional support to learn.

CHILDREN LEARN THROUGH PLAY

Play is a powerful teaching and learning medium—at all stages of life, but particularly in early childhood. It is voluntary activity, pursued without ulterior purpose and generally with enjoyment or expectation of enjoyment (English, & English, 1958). Play is how children prefer to gather and process information, learn new skills, and practice old ones (Kostelnik, Gregory, Soderman, & Whiren, 2011).

Table 2.2 summarizes these nine principles of child development and learning.

Early childhood educators feel strongly that young children must be given time to play so that they can come to understand the use of objects and symbols, explore

TABLE 2.1 • Eight Intelligences That Contribute to Children's Learning Styles

INTELLIGENCE	CHILD LEARNS BEST BY
Linguistic *The Word Player*	Reading, writing, and talking
Logical-mathematical *The Questioner*	Exploring patterns and relationships, working with numbers, doing experiments
Spatial *The Visualizer*	Drawing, building, designing, creating things, using the mind's eye
Musical *The Music Lover*	Listening to and making music, using rhythm and melody
Bodily-kinesthetic *The Mover*	Touching, moving, processing knowledge through bodily sensations
Intrapersonal *The Individual*	Working alone; pursuing own interests; being aware of inner moods, intentions, motivations, temperaments, and self-desires
Interpersonal *The Socializer*	Sharing, comparing, relating to others, cooperating
Naturalistic *The Nature Lover*	Observing nature, interacting with plants and animals, perceiving relationships among natural things

Source: Kostelnik, M. J., Soderman, A. K., & Whiren, A. P. *Developmentally appropriate curriculum: Best practices in early childhood education,* 5th ed., © 2011. Reprinted and electronically reproduced by permission of Pearson Education, Inc., Upper Saddle River, NJ.

■■ **TRY IT YOURSELF**

Consider each of Gardner's eight intelligences. In which of these would you rate yourself highest? In which would you rate yourself lowest? Think back to when you were in high school. How did your talents and interests affect your performance in certain subjects or other activities? How might your talents and interests contribute to your skill as a teacher?

TABLE 2.2 • Connecting Knowledge of Development and Learning to Teaching Practices	
PRINCIPLES OF CHILD DEVELOPMENT AND LEARNING	**CORRESPONDING DEVELOPMENTALLY APPROPRIATE TEACHING PRACTICES**
Children develop holistically	Teachers plan daily activities and routines to address all aspects of children's development—aesthetic, emotional, intellectual, language, physical, and social.
Child development follows an orderly sequence	Teachers use their knowledge of developmental sequences to gauge whether children are developing as expected, to determine reasonable expectations for children, and to figure out what steps are next in the learning process.
Children develop at varying rates	Children need opportunities to pursue activities at their own pace. Teachers plan flexible activities to address the wide range of development represented in their group, including opportunities for more or less advanced learners. They provide experiences according to children's changing needs, interests, and abilities.
Children learn best when they feel safe and secure	Teachers develop nurturing relationships with children, as well as predictable daily routines, activities, and transitions that respect children's attention span and need for movement. Adults use positive discipline to enhance children's self-esteem, self-control, and problem-solving abilities. Teachers address aggression and bullying calmly, firmly, and proactively. The early childhood environment complies with the safety requirements of the appropriate licensing or accrediting agency. Children have access to images, objects, and activities in the early childhood program that reflect their home experiences, and there is effective two-way communication between teachers and families.
Children are active learners	Teachers plan many hands-on experiences. Children investigate, move, and act on their environments as they learn, using all their senses.
Children learn through a combination of physical experience, social experience, and reflection	Teachers use a variety of strategies to engage learners. They pose questions, offer information, and challenge children's thinking. They encourage children to handle objects every day and to reflect on their ideas.
Children learn through mastery and challenge	Teachers simplify, maintain, or extend activities in response to children's functioning and comprehension. Teachers help children figure out alternative approaches when the task is beyond their current capabilities. Children learn from interacting with others as they engage in activities within or slightly beyond their ability to carry out independently.
Children's learning profiles vary	Teachers present the same information and skills in more than one modality (seeing, hearing, touching) and through different types of activities across all domains. Children choose from an array of multi-sensory activities every day.
Children learn through play	Teachers prepare the environment, provide the materials, observe, and interact playfully with the children. Play is integrated throughout the day within all aspects of the program.

Source: Kostelnik, M. J., Soderman, A. K., & Whiren, A. P. *Developmentally appropriate curriculum: Best practices in early childhood education,* 5th ed., © 2011. Reprinted and electronically reproduced by permission of Pearson Education, Inc., Upper Saddle River, NJ.

TABLE 2.3 • Mildred Parten's Classification of Stages of Play	
PLAY CLASSIFICATION	**CHILD'S ACTIONS**
Unoccupied Activity	The child is not actually "playing" but watches anything that happens to catch his interest. He may become intrigued with his own body, move around, remain in one location, or follow a teacher.
Onlooker Behavior	This stage is termed "behavior" instead of play because this child is content in watching other children.
Solitary Independent Play	Children prefer to play by themselves and are not comfortable interacting with other children. They may play apart from other children with chosen toys, yet within listening/speaking distance, and demonstrate little interest in making contact.
Parallel Play	Children occupy space near others, but seldom share toys or materials. They may talk, but each has his or her own conversation and there is no attempt to communicate with each other. As an example, one child may talk about going to the circus while another interrupts about going to a fast food restaurant.
Associate Play	Children lend, borrow, and take toys from others. However, it's still "every child for himself." At this stage, the children are beginning to engage in close personal contact; however, they still consider their own viewpoint as most important. Children are not yet ready to participate in teams or group work, but there should be opportunities for group work so they can gradually learn how to communicate their needs.
Cooperative Play	This stage is the highest form of children playing together. They share, take turns, and allow some children to serve as leaders for the group. For example, one child may be the police officer, another a nurse, while another is the mother in cooperative play. Three-year-olds play best with approximately three other children; 5-year-olds can play successfully with approximately five children.

social relationships, work out their differences with others, extend skills in all learning domains, express their emotions appropriately, and release the tensions they experience (Wenner, 2009). Think about all the meaningful learning that was taking place as Megan and Anna enjoyed what they were doing with their paper dolls.

When observing a number of children at play in any single classroom, you'll see that children's participation styles can be very different. Mildred Parten's early study is now a classic classification system used for describing children's developing play behaviors (see Table 2.3) (Parten, 1932).

When watching children at play, you'll also find that their play takes different forms, including movement play, object play, language play, pretend play, construction play, and games. Figure 2.2 describes these forms of play.

TECH TIP

Whenever possible, introduce concepts and skills to young children by using real objects and concrete materials before substituting with technology. Technology should never be a replacement when the real thing is available.

The Cycle of Learning: Gaining New Knowledge and Skills

Ms. Bendick wants to expand the children's understanding of numbers. She realizes that her 3- and 4-year-olds are all in a very different place in their knowledge. When asked how old he is, Max holds up three fingers correctly. Kevin can write numerals from 1 to 5, even though many are backwards, and Michaela can easily count to 25 but cannot count out seven paper cups. Ms. Bendick begins by providing sets of different materials in small baskets and counting the objects one at a time with the children, moving the objects from the basket to a plate as she counts. Today, she introduces a new finger play where she has them pretending to pick apples from a tree, jumping up to get them—1, 2, 3, 4, 5—and then throwing them down into an imaginary basket—5, 4, 3, 2, 1.

FIGURE 2.2 Forms of play

Movement play

The first playthings children have at their disposal are their own bodies. Physical movement is fun! Children delight in racing down a hill, imitating the actions of the "chicken dance," or twirling until dizzy. All of these activities involve playing with motion itself. Children enjoy both exercise play (such as running, climbing, or hopping) and practice play (a child persists in walking a balance beam over and over until slips off of the beam happen less frequently). In each case, children gain pleasure and confidence from mastering physical challenges and using their bodies in invigorating ways. Children who are proficient at movement play—tossing balls into the parachute, chasing on the playground, or racing to the top of the climber—tend to be admired by peers, making them desirable playmates.

Object play

Children of all ages play with just about anything, starting with everyday materials such as sticks, pots and pans, boxes, or blankets. Obviously, children also play with toys, sports equipment, games and electronic media. No matter the object, children spend time investigating and manipulating to find out what the object can do (this object opens and closes, pulls apart, is heavy, or beeps when you push this button). They also discover what they can do to and with objects to achieve certain outcomes (I can pound, build, or make sounds with this object). Eventually, children transform objects into something else in the context of their play. Thus, two "jet pilots" may transform a block to serve as a cell phone, a can of food, or a battery for their plane. These kinds of manipulations and transformations provide a basis for the development of abstract thinking, creativity, and problem solving.

Language play

Playing with language begins in toddlerhood and continues into grade school. It involves experimenting with and coming to understand words, syllables, sounds, and grammatical structures through playful means. Children who play with language have a vehicle for manipulating and controlling it (Isenberg, J. P., & Jalongo, M. R. 2012). They find humor in imitating or making up sounds and in changing the volume and speed of their words (such as chanting, "red rover, red rover, red rover" more and more quickly until the words tumble over themselves). They enjoy repeating rhymes and making up rhymes of their own ("I'm a whale. This is my tail."). Although substituting letter sounds and transposing letters leads to hilarity among the preschool set (Anna Banana, Tony Baloney, etc.), it also serves as a key skill in later reading and writing.

Pretend play

Pretending to be someone else, making believe an object is something other than it is, and carrying out imaginary activities are fun things to do. Any child can pretend at any time alone or with someone else. This play begins around 15 months of age with simple actions such as pretending to sleep or putting the dolly to bed (Smith & Pellegrini, 2008). Sociodramatic play, common from around 3 years of age, involves pretending with others. It requires role-playing ("I'm the mom."), assigning meaning to objects ("This brush is our magic wand."), and developing story lines ("Let's play dinosaurs."). Due to its interactive nature, sociodramatic play gives children plenty of chances to engage in turn taking and sharing, negotiating and compromising ("Okay, we can have two moms."), and problem solving ("Let's ask Sara to be the aunt."). As children navigate these situations with greater success, their social competence increases.

Construction play

Construction play happens when a child envisions something mentally (a house, a car, or a town) and then makes it out of tangible materials such as blocks, sand, or art supplies. This kind of play first becomes evident at about 3 years of age when children name the things they make ("Teacher, see my house."). From then on, children's constructions become more elaborate, both in terms of what they represent and in the skills children use to produce them. You see this in the constructions by older preschoolers and kindergartners, who may create entire towns out of boxes or make elaborate props for their pretend play.

Games

Games enjoyed by preschoolers and kindergarten-aged children range from the Farmer in the Dell, to Simon Says, to Candy Land, to Hide and Seek, to Pocket Frogs. They might or might not include props. Some games require physical movement (Hot Potato, Hokey Pokey, Red Light/Green Light); others are table games or ones children play sitting down. Some are played in small groups (Memory), but some can be played only with many children (parachute activities). What games like these have in common are other players, simple rules, and a high degree of social interaction. Children are not automatic experts in the protocol of games— waiting one's turn is challenging, following rules is a trial and error business, and moving through a structured game such as Candy Land from beginning to end does not happen all at once. Children need many chances to perfect the skills necessary to play increasingly long and complicated games.

As this last principle makes clear, careful attention must be paid to constructing a learning environment that fosters the young child's preference for acquiring knowledge and skills through play.

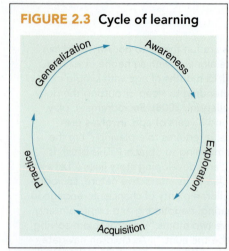

FIGURE 2.3 **Cycle of learning**

Source: Kostelnik, M. J., Soderman, A. K., & Whiren, A. P. *Developmentally appropriate curriculum: Best practices in early childhood education,* 5th ed., © 2011. Reprinted and electronically reproduced by permission of Pearson Education, Inc., Upper Saddle River, NJ.

cycle of learning The 5-phase process (i.e., awareness, exploration, acquisition, practice, and generalization) of learning something new whereby gaining new knowledge and skills.

Learning something completely new requires moving from initial awareness to actually gaining new knowledge and skills that we can then apply on our own. This happens in what is called the cycle of learning and consists of five phases, each supporting and leading to the next phase: awareness, exploration, acquisition, practice, and generalization (Epstein, 2007; Robertson, 2007) (see Figure 2.3). Let's look at each of these separately.

- *Awareness.* Young children are constantly confronted with new events, objects, and people. That does not mean that everything catches their attention equally, but adults can mediate awareness through the environments and experiences they create for children. For example, Ms. Bendick knows how important it is to have her children begin to understand one-to-one correspondence, an important early mathematics concept. She frequently plans for engaging activities and materials to draw their attention to mathematical ideas.

- *Exploration.* Once Ms. Bendick has gained the children's attention, she knows they need plenty of opportunities and time to explore the things that have captured their interest. This is a critical period of discovery as children spontaneously manipulate materials, "play around," and engage in informal interactions with classmates and adults. They have a chance to talk about their experiences, ask questions, relate what they are doing to prior learning, propose explanations and construct new understandings (the marble can't get down the chute, which is smaller in the middle than on top), and develop personal meanings that lead them to want to know or do more.

In the exploration phase, it is important that teachers act as facilitators. For example, 3-year-old Ezra was exploring different ways to balance a push-cart. He kept tipping it up on its side, standing it on the front two wheels. The teacher reminded him to keep all the wheels on the floor and helped him put it back down. As she left, he picked it up again, tipped it on its side, removed his hands to see that it was stable, and then placed it back on the floor. The teacher, recognizing that he was exploring how to balance the cart differently, returned and acknowledged his efforts to do so. "You know that the cart usually rolls on the floor, Ezra, but you've figured out that it can also sit up on only two wheels as well and want to try that out. You're being very careful not to let it fall on anyone."

- *Acquisition.* By signaling that they want to do something else with the materials or activity, children are letting you know that they are no longer satisfied with just exploring and want to refine their understanding or make new connections ("Ms. Bendick, let's pretend that we pick one apple for every kid who's here today! Instead of 5, we can pick 17, 'cause there are 17 kids, right?"). This is when teachers tune in carefully to what children want to learn, offering support as needed and instruction as appropriate.

- *Practice.* Once new knowledge and skills have been acquired, children enjoy practicing what they have learned. For example, when Ms. Bendick suggested substituting a new finger play to replace the familiar apple-picking activity at the beginning of large group, she was met with resistance from a number of children who weren't yet ready to give it up. When Ezra understood that the push-cart could stand on end, he delighted in going through the entire process, again and again. The expression on his face each time it balanced without holding on to it registered both pride and satisfaction that he had discovered something new and exciting. You will need to offer plenty of time for this important phase as well as find ways to vary the practice conditions to sustain children's interest.

- *Generalization.* Eventually, sufficient practice results in a child's ability to apply the newly learned skills in a variety of ways and in new circumstances. In the process of doing so, new discoveries are made that prompt reentry into the cycle of learning at the awareness phase. Once most of Ms. Bendick's children had internalized one-to-one correspondence, they began to count with real understanding. She introduced various activities where she had children comparing, matching, and sorting groups of objects into sets. A favorite game was when Ms. Bendick wrote a number on the white board and then played "More or Less Than" by showing an array of objects on a tray. It didn't take children long to guess the correct answer.

The nine principles discussed earlier in the chapter and in Table 2.2 about child development and learning are central to your becoming an effective teacher. However, that alone will not be sufficient to ensure that your teaching will be of high quality (Mellor, 2007). The next step is to become very familiar with content in early childhood education and the content standards that provide an agreed-upon agenda for teaching and learning.

Early Childhood Educators Need to Know About Content

Where do butterflies go when it rains?

How many is this?

What does this say?

Children want to know all about the world and how it works. To guide them in their quest for new knowledge and understanding, you must know a lot about the world yourself so you can provide accurate information and relevant experiences. Thus, you need a broad grasp of content knowledge in the following disciplines:

- Language and literacy
- The arts
- Mathematics
- Health and fitness
- Science
- Social studies

In addition, it is likely that your center or school will have established **content standards** or quality guidelines, you will be expected to address in your classroom. For example, a common science standard for PK–2 is for children to recognize that animals and plants are living things that grow, reproduce, and need food, air, and water to survive. An early literacy standard is for children to understand the relationship between letters and sounds. These standards are grounded in the disciplines just described and, when carefully developed, provide teachers with a credible source for developing early childhood curricula (Seefeldt, 2005). The best standards come about through the collective thinking of experts in the field, giving practitioners access to an agreed-upon agenda for teaching and learning.

You can become familiar with the content standards published by various groups by searching on the web for those published by your state department of education, by individual school districts where you might teach, by Head Start, by various professional societies (e.g., National Council of Teachers of Mathematics or NCTM), and by the National Association for the Education of Young Children (NAEYC.org). A strong

content standards Level of quality or excellence related to educational content as identified by and agreed upon by experts in the field.

effort is currently underway to produce national standards for mathematics, language arts, science, and social studies, and some school districts are considering adopting these for their elementary and secondary programs. Most states and school districts have created downward extensions in these disciplines for their preschool programs, and many childcare centers have also developed written plans for what they want children to learn.

Children benefit when standards are used wisely. However, you will want to be aware of certain challenges you may face during implementation and how to address them:

1. *Too many standards.* As you will find, there is a dizzying array of early childhood standards from a number of sources. Sometimes they duplicate one another and sometimes they contradict one another. Sorting through all of these can be eye opening but also confusing and time consuming. In Chapters 9 to 15 in this text, you will see a listing of goals for each of the curricular domains. These are arranged in sequence from the most basic to more challenging. Each addresses expectations for what children should know and be able to do from 3 to 6 years of age.

2. *Standards that are inappropriate.* At times, standards are developed by content experts or by committees dominated by individuals focused on older children and without input from early childhood educators. As a result, some standards are not age appropriate. The standard may be too abstract or not fit the criteria of individual and cultural appropriateness that governs DAP, depending on children's backgrounds, special needs, and experience. You can assess the appropriateness of standards that are provided to you (or are being developed by your center or district) by asking the following questions (Seefeldt, 2005, pp. 22–23):
   - From the body of knowledge addressed by this standard, what seems to be most meaningful to children this age? What is most meaningful for the particular children in your classroom?
   - What facet of this standard might a beginner need to know?
   - What do the children already know about this standard?
   - What can children learn through firsthand experience related to this standard?
   - How can this standard be integrated with what children are already experiencing in your classroom?

3. *Standards that are expected to be implemented in a lockstep fashion and according to a rigid timetable.* Standards may be well written and even developmentally appropriate. However, there may be unrealistic expectations by program developers about how they are to be covered, not taking into consideration the individual needs of the children in the program or variations in their rates of development and learning. This can be highly stressful unless teachers understand ways to integrate standards throughout the day and are confident that well-planned activities that range over the curriculum will naturally support the required content. Remember that children do not accomplish any standard through a single activity or all in one day. Observe carefully to see how each child responds to activities you have planned, where he or she is in the learning cycle, and what other kinds of learning materials or experiences you can provide to bring each student closer to achieving the skills and concept that need to be learned. There are strategies that will increase your effectiveness with every child, and they are highlighted in this next section.

Early Childhood Educators Need to Know About Effective Teaching Strategies

Because young children develop and learn in many ways, the teaching strategies that support their learning also vary greatly. Core strategies that you will use regularly are highlighted in this section. You'll see that they vary in type, complexity, and degree of teacher direction needed. They will help you prepare the learning environment, encourage children's participation, and facilitate understanding.

STRATEGIES FOR PREPARING THE LEARNING ENVIRONMENT
SENSORY ENGAGEMENT

Because all of children's learning begins with perception (seeing, hearing, touching, tasting, and smelling), plan to include a high level of sensory engagement in your program. Find ways to give children direct contact with real objects, people, places, and events (Armstrong, 2006). If no firsthand experience is possible, seriously consider whether the activity is age appropriate. The younger the children, the more you should rely on firsthand involvement.

ENVIRONMENTAL CUES

You can use many physical clues to help children know what is expected of them in your classroom. For example, after showing it to children in large group, you may post a pictogram or rebus chart by the snack center, showing the steps for preparing individual carrot salads (see Figure 2.4). There may be four places at a table with play dough but only two rolling pins, signaling to the children that these are to be shared. A small center meant for only four children at a time might be managed by putting a sign with the number 4 and four dots. These nonverbal signals foster independence, cooperation, and self-regulation in the children.

pictogram or rebus chart Chart with pictures or symbols to provide a simple guide through a process.

task analysis Thinking in advance about necessary steps to achieve a specified outcome.

TASK ANALYSIS

The strategy of task analysis involves thinking in advance about a sequence of steps children might follow to achieve some multi-step behavior, such as getting dressed or planting a garden. For example, your goal may be to have children clear their places independently after snack and lunch. However, expecting 4-year-olds to know exactly how to do this without any instruction or modeling is unrealistic. The first thing to do is to consider the knowledge, skills, and procedures necessary to complete the task. Do the children know where the basket is to empty their plates? How should they be taught to carry their plates so that uneaten food doesn't spill on the floor before they get to the basket? How do you scrape a plate and make sure it goes in the basket and not on the floor? Where do they put their plates once they're scraped? What do they do with their cups? Do you expect them to wash their hands afterwards before they select a book? Do you teach only a couple of steps at a time or do you model the entire procedure to children? Thinking all of this through carefully *beforehand* will eliminate confusion and distress on the part of the children and, realistically, a lot of aggravation and backtracking for you.

STRATEGIES TO ENCOURAGE AND ENHANCE PARTICIPATION
INVITATIONS

Invitations to join you or their peers promote feelings of belonging among children: "Here's a place for you, right next to me." Or, "Jack was looking for you. Come play here with him." Children are quite different in the way they initially navigate a room, even if the activities you've planned are appealing. Some need no encouragement to take part; others will drift from place to place or only watch what other children are doing. Even then, they may be reluctant to join without a special role to play or

FIGURE 2.4 Pictogram of steps for making carrot salad

Carrot Salad

Wash and grate a

into a

Add a scoop of Raisins

Add 1/2 cup ½ of Yogurt

Stir it with a

Eat it with your

What could you add to this dramatic play center to further enhance children's concept of what goes on in a bakery or a restaurant?

materials to use ("Kendra, I need someone to stir this cake for our bakery. Come and help me."). It helps to plan what you might say in advance, just in case some children need a bit more support.

BEHAVIOR REFLECTIONS

Behavior reflections provide verbal feedback to children about actions they are taking (Kostelnik, Whiren, Soderman, & Gregory, 2011). They are nonjudgmental statements that describe children's actions and are intended simply to draw children's attention to certain aspects of an experience or enhance their receptive and expressive vocabulary. "You are building with blue blocks." Or, "You are making bubbles." Such statements do not interrupt children's activity or require children to respond in words. However, they do increase children's self-awareness and encourage children to maintain their focus. For example, Jorge has blue, yellow, and red paint available to him and is painting yellow over what is apparently a foundation of blue grass. His teacher remarks in passing, "Jorge, you've found a way to create green grass with no green paint. That took some thinking!" While Jorge doesn't respond verbally, the slight smile that appears on his face indicates he is pleased his teacher noticed his achievement.

PARAPHRASE REFLECTIONS

Paraphrase reflections restate in your words something a child has said. These reflections (often termed *active listening*) are similar to behavioral reflections in that they are also nonjudgmental; however, they are intended to expand the child's vocabulary and grammatical structures. There are a number of other benefits, as well. Think about a situation where Alma is watching two fish swimming together in a bowl and points, wanting her teacher to notice. "Fish," she says.

Her teacher responds, "You've been observing those two fish and have noticed that one seems to be taking the lead."

"The big fish," Alma agrees.

"Ah," says the teacher. "The big fish may be teaching something to the smaller fish."

Taking time to have a conversation like this with a child develops positive relationships between teacher and child and enhances the learning climate significantly in the early childhood classroom. It helps both the teacher and the child refine and clarify key concepts and messages. Teachers also learn more about children's interests and ways to shape instruction and future planning.

DO-IT SIGNALS AND CHALLENGES

Simple directions to children, such as "Watch me," "Tell me what you see," "Put together the blocks that are alike," "Listen for the word *dinosaur* as I read this book" are called do-it signals. You'll notice that they all begin with a verb, that they are brief, and that they are intended to prompt children to take action. Using them consistently, teachers can evaluate what children understand and where they still need help or additional experience.

Do-it signals should not be phrased as questions. They should be phrased as positive statements that give children a clear idea about what you'd like them to do. For example, questions such as, "Can you take this to your cubby for me?" "Take this to your cubby, okay?" or "Would you like to put this in your cubby?" may result in the child deciding not to do what you've asked and require another request from you. Be clear and direct: "Take this to your cubby, please."

Challenges are open-ended variations of do-it signals that motivate children to create their own solutions to teacher-suggested tasks. For example, instead of simply saying, "Walk quietly down the hall," a teacher may ask a group of 4-year-olds in a whisper: "Think of a way that we can be as quiet as possible so that no one can hear us while we're walking down the hall today. How can we do this?" In the block area, you might challenge the children to use a certain number of blocks and see how many different structures they can create with that amount.

"If you have only these blocks, what can you create?"

EFFECTIVE PRAISE

Did you know that some forms of praise are not always helpful to young children and that praise can even lower children's self-confidence and inhibit achievement (Miller, 2009)? If you want to promote positive behavior and encourage children to persist at a task, you will want to differentiate between the use of effective and ineffective praise. Saying something like, "Good job" or "Wow! Way to go!" is ineffective because it is general, repetitive, and not very genuine. Ineffective praise also evaluates children, compares them with one another in unfavorable ways, or may imply to children that they were successful because of luck. Thus, your "praise" may serve no other purpose than to interrupt their focus. Conversely, effective praise is very specific (e.g., "You finally found the right key to open that lock." "You stayed with it until you did!"), links their success to effort and ability, fits individual children and the situation, and may compare their progress with their past performance. It is nonintrusive in that it can be delivered in passing to acknowledge effort and outcome without requiring any response from the child.

STRATEGIES TO FACILITATE UNDERSTANDING AND PROMPT FURTHER LEARNING

TELLING, EXPLAINING, AND INFORMING

Giving children appropriate information involves more than simply lecturing. It involves looking at the experiences you plan and the age-appropriate information children need to learn and anticipating the questions they may ask spontaneously. This is why effective teachers take time to gain sufficient background before introducing new information. Planning a recent trip to the aquarium, Ms. Crawford visits it ahead of time, talking with aquarium staff about the kinds of sea creatures the children will see, how the museum obtained them, and a little bit about how they are taken care of. Still not satisfied, she learns still more on the Internet and downloads pictures of fish she knows the children will see. She shows the children a picture of Otto the puffer fish, who can grow to twice his normal size by swallowing air or water when he is afraid. She also shares a picture of Barney the barrel-eye fish that has a transparent head and two barrel-like eyes that rotate or turn when looking for food. To help the children understand what "transparent" means, she shows them a clear baggy filled with water and another one that is opaque.

As noted earlier in the chapter, children must be told the names of things and about conventional facts and behaviors that they would not discover on their own. When you want to convey this kind of information to children, explain new concepts in relation to familiar skills and situations they have already experienced. Whenever possible, take advantage of "teachable moments": those times when new information makes the best sense to children because it helps them with an issue, question, or problem they have at the present moment. For example, when children are using brushes and pails of water to write on the sidewalk under a sunny sky, it would be an opportune time to talk about evaporation and to experiment with how long it takes for certain amounts of water to turn into vapor and disappear. In doing so, a teacher would be conveying information through telling, but supporting her explanation with hands-on involvement by the children to enhance understanding.

CHAINING AND SUCCESSIVE APPROXIMATION

Sometimes, what you want to teach to children seems too complex to teach all at once. It may be age appropriate, but they may benefit when you build the task up a little at a time—called *chaining* (Malott & Trojan, 2008). After you have done a task analysis to sequence the series of steps necessary, introduce the steps one at a time, building patiently on one and then another until there is total completion of a task. For example, you would not expect children who are just beginning to write their names to be totally accurate. You might begin by drawing their attention to the shape of the letters on their name tags, dismissing them at large group with signs of their first name and other name-related activities. You could eventually introduce a "sign-up sheet" on the writing table with their first names printed individually and a space for them to copy it, accepting their initial attempts with encouraging comments. Later, you may call each child's attention to using upper and lower case and help them with reversals. Once they have had time to practice the first name and it becomes fairly automatic, introduce a model of their entire name on the daily sign-in sheet and have them try, asking them to write both names on all of their work every day.

Successive approximation is a bit different. It involves modeling the entire task all at once and then gradually shaping behavior so that children's responses become

Learning by watching and reflecting.

more and more accurate. For example, remember our example of children clearing their places after snack and lunch. That might be a time when you can model the entire sequence (it may take more than once, of course) and then assist children in becoming more and more successful each day as they go through the process. For example, you would encourage them to do all the steps you modeled to them as well as they could and narrow your focus each day on teaching one of the steps in more depth (e.g., making sure that everyone knows where the basket is to empty their plates) until everyone is able to do each of the steps well.

MODELING AND DEMONSTRATING

Think of something new that you have learned to do this year and how you learned to do it. Often, it is much easier (and quicker) to watch someone do what we want to learn—that is, to watch someone *model* and *demonstrate*—than simply to read about it or be told how to do it. Most of what we have learned to do in life has been through imitating others. This includes how we learned to take care of our self needs, how we learned to play games, use a computer, interact with others in social situations, write, and perform hundreds of others skills that we no longer have to think about as we do them.

Children have much to learn, and they profit enormously when adults show them new or more appropriate behaviors by:

1. Drawing children's attention to what we want them to learn or do.
2. Describing in simple language what we want them to do while showing them how to do it.
3. Having children repeat in words or actions what we want them to do.

GUIDED PRACTICE AND REPETITION

Real learning does not occur in a single episode. To have children internalize skills or concepts, they need many, many opportunities to practice what they are learning and to apply it in new situations. You can provide for this in your classroom by including the following experiences that allow for guided practice and repetition:

- *Rehearsal.* Children may watch the teacher model purchasing some things in the play store that has been set up and then have an opportunity to play store themselves. They can be helped to take various roles, moving through the process of being both a seller and a buyer for a couple of weeks before the dramatic play area is reassembled into something else.

Matthew planning and creating a menu for his restaurant.

- *Repeating an activity with variations.* The play store could be a grocery store initially, eventually turn into a jewelry store, and subsequently be a shoe store.
- *Elaborations.* The teacher may suggest that children make menus for the restaurant they have set up in the dramatic play area, provide "take out" for their customers, create pizzas to sell the next day, or keep track of the number of customers they have during the morning.

QUESTIONS

Questions are basic instructional tools in any educational setting. However, you need to be careful that the questions you ask are:

- Purposeful and tied directly to the objectives you are trying to teach
- Thought-provoking so that they go beyond the obvious to stimulate higher levels of thinking
- Clear and understandable
- Brief and to the point

Develop the habit of asking children open-ended questions that require more than one word or yes/no responses. There are many ways to do this, depending on your goals for children (see Table 2.4).

Closed-ended questions are appropriate in functional situations in which critical thinking is not necessary (Epstein, 2007). For example, at snack, when Ms. Gage asks Mandy, "Would you like some melon?" she is not expecting anything more from Mandy than, "Yes, please" or "No, thank you." The preference for asking open-ended questions in early childhood settings is an important one because it prompts children to offer opinions and to think in new and different ways (Charlesworth & Lind, 2010).

In addition to becoming expert at asking open-ended questions, you'll also want to keep a few other factors in mind (Kilmer & Hofman, 1995; Marzano, 2003):

- *Limit amount.* Ask only one question at a time and plan your questions carefully.
- *Provide time.* Give children enough time to respond to a question. Wait several seconds for children to answer. Do not appear impatient or undermine their

TABLE 2.4 • Open-Ended Questions	
TO ENHANCE CHILDREN'S ABILITY TO	**SAMPLE QUESTION**
Observe	What do you see/hear/smell/taste/feel?
Reconstruct previous experiences	What happened the last time we mixed two different colors?
Relate cause and effect	What happens when/if you do....?
Predict	What do you think will happen next?
Evaluate	Which of these is your favorite? Why?
Generalize	Now that we made these sets of the same, what happens if I add one more object to this set?
Compare	How are these the same? Different?
Reason	Why do you think we have that rule?
Discriminate among objects/events	Which one of these doesn't belong?
Solve problems	How can we keep the paint from dripping?
Quantify	How many? How long? How far?
Imagine something	What if we lived outdoors instead of in a house?
Propose alternatives	In what other way could we group these?
Utilize factual knowledge	Given what you learned about why objects sink or float, what do you think will happen if I push this ball under the water?
Infer	Why do you think it happened?
Become aware of their thinking processes	How did you know....? Why did you decide....?
Apply	How can you use what you learned?
Make decisions	What do you think we should do?
Communicate	How can you share with others what you think?

"How can we share this play dough with the other children?"

thinking by answering your own questions or always calling on children who readily volunteer answers.

- *Use do-it signals.* Phrase some of your questions as do-it signals to add variety: "Show me how you might divide this cookie into three parts."

- *Ask all.* Phrase questions to the entire group of children, not only to individuals: "Let's all think of a way we could share this play dough."

- *Listen and reflect.* Listen carefully to children's responses. Acknowledge their remarks by using behavior reflections and paraphrase reflections. Focus on the process of their thinking, not merely the correctness of their response.

- *Redirect.* If a child's answer indicates a lack of understanding, follow up: "Mmmm. Tell me more about why you think that." Or "Why do you think those two go together?" Children sometimes make connections that are reasonable to them but less obvious to an adult.

- *Address misconceptions.* If a child's answer to a question indicates a true misconception, handle the situation matter-of-factly. Paraphrase the child's idea and then offer more accurate information: "You think the cars go in the block bin because we played with the cars and trucks together here. The cars have their own special place so we can find them if we want to use them for something else. Put them in this basket, please."

SCAFFOLDING

What happens when a child becomes stuck and is unable to move forward with a particular skill or concept? In any learning process or continuum, the learner has what Russian psychologist Lev Vygotsky called a *zone of proximal development* (ZPD) or the difference between (1) a learner's ability to solve a problem independently and (2) the learner's "maximally assisted" problem-solving ability under the guidance and in collaboration with an adult or a more knowledgeable peer (Vygotsky, 1979). Providing this kind of guidance is called *scaffolding.* As the child and partner work together toward a common goal (for example, understanding patterns and how to change them), the child stretches to understand the new information. At the same time, the child is helped by the teacher pointing out the connection between what he or she already understands and the new skill or concept.

Vygotsky believed that it was important not to work outside of the child's ZPD. However, he was also certain that it was important not to have children spending time on what they had already mastered. Adults, he believed, needed to be constantly nudging children to move along on the developmental pathway toward more complex learning. Scaffolding is likely to be more successful if the following is true (Soderman, Gregory, & McCarty, 2005):

- Rapport has been established between the teacher and the learner.
- The coaching adult or peer is sensitive to the child's responses.
- The task is neither too tough nor too easy.
- The adult or more experienced peer knows when to back away and let the child take the next step.
- The coach lets the child control the activity as much as possible, gradually relinquishing support.

It is important that teachers recognize and respect the value of peers to act as scaffolders, for children are often quick to pay attention when another child attempts to show them how to do something (for example, how to tie shoes, make the letter B, or work the water fountain). Purposefully placing a child with a more knowledgeable classmate for a task or in a group where at least one other child has more advanced knowledge or skills multiplies a teacher's ability to be effective and a child's chances to be successful.

SILENCE

Sometimes, the best strategy to support children's involvement and learning is to remain silent. As previously noted, we want to give children time to think about open-ended questions. We also need to be sensitive about interrupting children who are having a discussion about something that is important to them, intensely involved in dramatic play where each child is playing a role, or deep in thought about what they are painting or constructing. Children view the learning environment as more supportive and respectful when teachers refrain from inserting themselves into the center of every interaction.

As you gain experience in applying these varied strategies thoughtfully and skillfully, your competence and confidence will also expand. Watch to see how knowledgeable educators use each of these tactics and in what kinds of situations they employ them with young children.

Meeting the Needs of Diverse Learners

In Chapter 1, you learned about considerations that would help you be successful in serving children with diverse cultural and linguistic backgrounds and those with a variety of abilities. Being able to adapt what we are doing in the classroom to support every learner is the essence in delivering high-quality DAP programs.

Strategizing to accommodate the needs of individual children calls for understanding what each of them can do independently and what they can do if they had additional support from a peer or teacher mentor. Stretching children's abilities and moving them toward mastery of certain skills represents higher-order learning. This will call for your assessment of where children are having difficulty in moving to the next step in applying what they have already learned or simply at a stand-still and not progressing. Your ability to do this will keep children from feeling overwhelmed by a task or unable to move on because they don't know what the next step is. Again, remember that children at a more advanced level of understanding may also be good teachers in helping their peers move forward.

Communicating with Families

One thing to keep in mind when teaching children is that parents appreciate and need ongoing reassurance that their children are safe, receiving a good education, and learning every day to work and play well with others. Some may be vocal and tell you about worries they have. Others may not. Keep on top of issues by finding ways to establish healthy two-way lines of communication with each family. Some questions families have may be taken care of by telephone or e-mail. Others may require a face-to-face meeting with enough time for family members and teachers to discuss topics of importance, to find areas of agreement, and to work toward resolution of concerns. In Figure 2.5, see how one teacher addressed a few parents' questions about why the preschool children were allowed so much time for play when 'they could just do that at home.' In a respectful way, she made sure to get a critical point across about the developmental issues involved in balancing free play and directed teaching time effectively.

In this chapter, you have learned about the foundations of teaching and learning within a developmentally appropriate framework. Now, you are ready to set the stage for children's learning, and the first step will involve using the effective child guidance strategies that will be discussed in Chapter 3.

NEWSLETTER/WEB READY COMMUNICATION

FIGURE 2.5 • Developmentally Appropriate Activities in Your Child's Classroom

Our goal here at Wexton Elementary School is to strike a good balance in each classroom between activities your child initiates and those more formally planned by our teachers. Research strongly suggests that this is the most successful way to teach young children new skills, expand their understanding of the world, foster language growth, and encourage self-control and friendship building. You'll notice that for our 3- and 4-year-olds, the balance is tipped in favor of more time for children to choose activities of interest. This helps accommodate their growing attention span, need for individual attention and language building, and motivation to learn through play. For our 5-year-olds, you'll find there is somewhat more teacher-directed activity. In both cases, however, teachers carefully construct the learning environment and are thoughtful about the kinds of materials they highlight in order to focus your child's attention toward exploring and experimenting with what is provided in the classroom each day.

Plan to visit our parent website to read about the themes your child's teacher has planned and ideas for connecting learning at home with what goes on at school. Teachers share information about favorite books being read in the classroom, and you might consider checking out some of them at your local library. Ask your child to teach you some of the finger plays or songs he or she is learning. Children love to be the teacher!

2 Applying What You've Learned

1. **Remembering the Principles.** In this chapter, nine principles of child development and learning were described. See how well you remember each of these and name specific practices you will implement in your own teaching to make sure each is acknowledged.

2. **Recycling.** Think about a new skill or concept you have learned in the last year or two. Connect it to the cycle of learning described in this chapter and reflect on each phase—awareness, exploration, acquisition, practice, and generalization. How confident are you that you have mastered the skill or concept?

3. **Exploring Content.** Visit a college, university, or community bookstore. What do they carry in terms of content-related ideas for teaching young children? Would suggestions for implementing these ideas support the content and standards approved by your program? What are the names of three books that seem to provide the highest-quality activities and engaging experiences for a classroom of 3- to 6-year-olds?

4. **Strategizing.** Go back to look at the various categories of strategies described in this chapter. Which one seems the easiest and most comfortable at this point in your own development as an early childhood educator? Which one would you need additional time and practice with? Where do you believe you can gain that practice before you actually have to carry the strategy out independently with a class of young children?

5. **Twenty Questions.** Do a self-survey to determine whether you are in the habit of asking mostly open-ended or closed questions. Keep track of the next 20 times you ask a question of someone in a conversation (remember that functional questions require only a yes/no or one word answer, so don't count those). How many times did you ask a closed question? Challenge yourself for the next 20 times to ask only open-ended questions. Did this have any effect on the *quality* of your conversations?

6. **Adaptations.** Observe an early childhood classroom and describe three ways you saw adults adapt their teaching strategies to the diverse needs of children with whom they were interacting.

References

Armstrong, T. (2006). *The best schools: How human development research should inform educational practice.* Alexandria, VA: ASCD.

Berk, L. (2009). *Child development* (8th ed.). Boston: Pearson.

Charlesworth, R., & Lind, K. (2010). *Math and science for young children* (6th ed.). Belmont, CA: Wadsworth/Cengage Learning.

Copple, C., & Bredekamp, S. (2009). *Basics of developmentally appropriate practice: An introduction for teachers of children 3 to 6.* Washington, D.C.: NAEYC.

English, H. B., and English, A. C. (1958). *A comprehensive dictionary of psychological and psychoanalytic terms.* New York, NY: David McKay.

Epstein, A. S. (2007). *The intentional teacher: Choosing the best strategies for young children.* Washington, D.C.: NAEYC.

Gardner, H. (1993). *Frames of mind* (Rev. ed.). New York: Basic Books.

Ginsberg, K. R. (2007). The importance of play in promoting healthy child development and maintaining strong parent-child bonds. *Pediatrics, 119*(1), 182–191.

Horowitz, E. D., Darling-Hammond, L., & Bransford, J. (2005). Educating teachers for developmentally appropriate practice. In L. Darling-Hammond & J. Bransford (Eds.), *Preparing teachers for a changing world* (pp. 88–125). San Francisco: Jossey-Bass.

Isenberg, J. P., & Jalongo, M. R. (2012). *Exploring your role in early childhood education* (4th ed.). Upper Saddle River, NJ: Pearson.

Kilmer, S. J., & Hofman, H. (1995). Transforming science curriculum. In S. Bredekamp & T. Rosegrant (Eds.), *Reaching potentials: Transforming early childhood curriculum and assessment* (Vol. 2, pp. 43–63). Washington, D.C.: National Association for the Education of Young Children.

Kostelnik, M. J., Soderman, A. K., & Whiren, A. P. (2011). *Developmentally appropriate curriculum* (5th ed.). Upper Saddle River, NJ: Pearson.

Kostelnik, M. J., Gregory, K., Soderman, A. K., & Whiren, A. P. (2011). *Guiding children's social development: Theory to practice* (7th ed.). Albany, NY: Delmar Learning.

Malott, R. W., & Trojan, E. A. (2008). *Principles of behavior.* Upper Saddle River, NJ: Pearson.

Marzano, R. J. (2003). *What works in schools: Translating research into action.* Alexandria, VA: Association for Supervision and Curriculum Development.

Mellor, S. (2007). *Australian education review no. 50.* Camberwell, Victoria: Australian Council for Educational Research.

Miller, D. E. (2009). *Positive child guidance* (6th ed.). Clifton Park, NY: Delmar Learning.

Parten, M. B. (1932). Social participation among preschool children. *Journal of Abnormal and Social Psychology, 27*, 243–269.

Robertson, B. (2007). Getting past inquiry versus content. *Educational Leadership, 64*(4), 67–70.

Seefeldt, C. (2005). *How to work with standards in the early childhood classroom.* New York: Teachers College Press, 144–197.

Soderman, A. K., Gregory, K. S., & McCarty, L. (2005). *Scaffolding emergent literacy.* Upper Saddle River, NJ: Pearson.

Stronge, J. H. (2002). *Qualities of effective teachers.* Alexandria, VA: ASCD.

Trawick-Smith, J. (2009). *Early childhood development: A multicultural perspective* (5th ed.). Upper Saddle River, NJ: Pearson.

Vygotsky, L. (1979). *The genesis of higher mental functioning.* In J. V. Wertsch (Ed.), *The concept of activity in Soviet psychology.* Armonk, NY: Sharpe.

Wenner, M. (2009, January 28). The serious need for play. *Scientific American.* Retrieved February 25, 2009, from www.sciam.com/article.cfm?id=the-serious-need-for-play.

3 More Than a Referee: Child Guidance in Developmentally Appropriate Classrooms

NO PULLING oDf ThE NOBS

Katherine Mulroney, the lead teacher in the 5-year-old class, did a little tape repair on the sign the children had made earlier in the week to govern spaceship play in the pretend area. Worried that their refrigerator box spaceship might "get wrecked" because the play was getting too rough, the children and teacher held a class meeting to decide what to do about the problem. The conversation lasted several minutes. With the teacher's help, the children decided on three rules for using the spaceship:

- No pulling off the knobs.
- Tell the astronauts when you want a turn.
- Only three astronauts inside at a time.

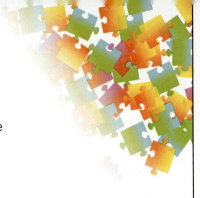

The children posted signs in the area to remind everyone about what they had decided. Katherine was pleased. She and the children had turned a problem situation into a learning experience that enhanced harmony in the classroom. She felt good knowing the children were learning to get along and that she was playing a helpful role in that process.

Just like Katherine, most early childhood professionals devote much of their time to guiding children's behavior. They teach children to care for one another; to respect their neighbors and themselves; and to keep the classroom healthy, safe, and conducive to learning. In doing so, they recognize that teaching young children how to act in socially responsible ways is an important part of their job.

Yet child guidance can be a thorny task. The teaching strategies that promote positive child behavior are not entirely self-evident, nor are they easy for you to acquire all on your own. Children vary in their temperaments, degrees of maturity, and in the experiences they bring to the classroom. As a result, many adults find themselves unsure of how to assist individual children or groups of children in behaving appropriately. This is especially true when children make mistakes or engage in challenging behaviors to express their needs and wants. In fact, early childhood teachers cite problems with behavior management as a top concern during their first years on the job (Kostelnik & Grady, 2009). This chapter is designed to ease this dilemma. It introduces important child guidance techniques early childhood professionals use to create happy, smoothly running classrooms in which children as well as teachers thrive.

LEARNING OUTCOMES

After you read this chapter, you will be able to:

- Describe how young children learn the dos and don'ts of the societies in which they live.
- Explain how differing approaches to child guidance influence children's conduct.
- Demonstrate proven state-of-the-art strategies for promoting positive child behavior.
- Adapt your guidance strategies to meet the needs of diverse children and families.

Essential Life Lessons

Wait your turn.
Be gentle with yourself and others.
Cross at the light.

Every society has rules like these to help people get along and to keep them safe. The role of adults is to pass this knowledge on to the younger generation. This occurs through the process of socialization, whereby adults communicate the norms, values, behaviors, and social skills they think children need to function as successful adults. In early childhood classrooms, we see this in action as teachers protect and nurture children while also guiding them to adopt a code of conduct that is acceptable to their community and culture.

Take a moment to consider what young children need to know to manage well at home, at the center, at school, and in life. In an essay titled *All I Really Need to Know I Learned in Kindergarten*, Robert Fulghum (2003) describes essential social lessons he learned as a child. Perhaps you thought of some of the same things he identified. See Figure 3.1 and compare your ideas with his.

socialization The process through which adults communicate the norms, values, behaviors, and social skills they think children need to function as successful adults.

FIGURE 3.1 **Kindergarten lessons**

In kindergarten, I learned to:

- Share

- Play fair

- Not hit people

- Put things back where I found them

- Clean up my own mess

- Not take things that weren't mine

- Say "sorry" when I hurt somebody

- Wash my hands before eating

- Flush

Source: Based on Fulghum, 2003, p. 2.

Child development experts agree with Fulghum. Here is a list of fundamental skills researchers throughout the world say young children must master to become successful members of their communities (Epstein, 2009; Ladd, 2008):

- Express their needs, wants, and feelings constructively
- Consider other people's wants, needs, and feelings
- Calm themselves when they feel upset
- Act in a safe and civil manner
- Follow rules, routines, and directions
- Take proper care of materials
- Share, take turns, help, and cooperate
- Distinguish acceptable from unacceptable behavior
- Carry out behaviors they think are right
- Avoid behaviors they think are wrong

Learning to put things in their proper places is a lesson in responsibility children can learn early in life.

Young children do not automatically know how to do all these things on their own. Adults must teach them what is expected and help them learn skills to meet those expectations. That is where you, as an early childhood teacher, come in. You will provide children opportunities to become more knowledgeable about books, art, music, physical activity, nature, and mathematics; you will also give them chances to learn how to interact with others and how to behave successfully. At first, children will require constant support to achieve these aims. In time, however, they will become more independent, thinking for themselves and monitoring their behavior without adult supervision. When that happens, children have achieved a milestone in human development—self-regulation.

Self-Regulation

self-regulation Making judgments about behaviors being right or wrong and then voluntarily acting in ways that match those beliefs.

Self-regulation happens when a person makes independent judgments that certain behaviors are right or wrong and then voluntarily acts in ways that match those beliefs. Such individuals do not rely on others to make these decisions for them and they do not rely on external rewards or punishments to determine what to do. Instead they base their actions on internal decisions about what is ethical, honest, and fair (Rose-Krasnor & Denham, 2009).

People who achieve high degrees of self-regulation are people with consciences. They can be depended on to do the right thing, even in tough situations. It takes years to come about, but eventually such individuals:

- Resist temptation (Marcia does not cheat on an exam, even though she could get away with it.)
- Curb negative impulses (Felipe does not take the last cookie, even though he really wants it.)
- Delay gratification (When talking in person to a friend, Lisa waits to look at a text message, even though she is anxious to see what it says.)
- Initiate positive social actions (Madeline consoles Simon when he doesn't make the team.)
- Make and carry out positive social plans (Kyle works with other students to plan a "Food Bank" rally.)

These advanced abilities enable people to contribute to the social order in many constructive ways. Moreover, self-regulating individuals do not need constant prodding or monitoring to help others, cooperate, or stand up for what they think is right. They can be depended on to do these things even when it is inconvenient or difficult and when no one else knows. Such behavior is at the core of a civil society.

Self-regulatory thinking is not inborn and does not happen overnight. It evolves gradually, starting in infancy and continuing through early adolescence, moving through four phases: *amoral*, *adherence*, *identification*, and *internalization*.

How Self-Regulation Emerges in Young Children

IN THE BEGINNING (AMORAL)

Initially, babies have no concept of right or wrong and no self-control. In other words, they are amoral. That is, they are unable to make internal judgments about their actions or consciously control their behavior in response to what others might want them to do. For instance, when baby Jack cries, his mother gently tells him to hush. But Jack continues to cry, unable to soothe himself or to respond immediately to his mother's efforts to calm him. In this situation, neither Jack nor his mother has the power to totally control Jack's response. Slowly, however, through maturation and experience, Jack's lack of self-regulation will change. He will start to recognize his mother's voice and gentle touch as physical signs of comfort and use these signals to help himself become less agitated. Based on more experiences like this, Jack will eventually move into the first real phase of self-regulation—adherence.

amoral The inability to make judgments about whether something is right or wrong.

ADHERENCE (EXTERNAL REGULATION)

When children respond to outside controls to guide their actions, we say they are operating at adherence. Adults such as family members and teachers supply these controls. Typical forms of external regulation include:

- Physical assistance (the teacher divides the blocks for children to share)
- Words (the teacher reminds the children about sharing the blocks)
- Rewards (the teacher acknowledges children's efforts to share)
- Admonitions (the teacher cautions the children that throwing blocks will lead to the blocks being put away for a while)
- Guidance (a child grabs a block; the teacher intervenes, helping the victim retrieve the block and helping the child who took it find a better way to express her wants)

adherence Relying on external controls such as physical intervention or tangible rewards in order to behave.

In these situations, children rely on adults to define and maintain the boundaries of socially appropriate behavior. Through many such encounters, children practice the basics of cooperative living and begin to figure out which behaviors are acceptable and which are not. Operating at adherence is much better than exercising no self-regulation at all. However, when children comply merely to gain a reward (a smile, praise) or avoid a negative consequence (having to put the blocks away), they do not comprehend the ethics (such as fairness or justice) involved in each situation. Because they don't understand, children at adherence are likely to behave in certain ways (in this case, share the blocks) only when an adult is present. Conversely, if Mom or the teacher are unavailable to monitor things directly, the children may find it difficult to share. They may even resort to hitting to protect their blocks because no one else is there to regulate the situation.

This is the drawback to adherence: Children who rely on external controls need constant support and supervision to behave as desired. When such controls are missing, they have few skills and little motivation to act appropriately on their own. Thus, adherence is an important step in the maturation process, but it is not the ultimate form of self-regulation.

IDENTIFICATION (SHARED REGULATION)

identification The child relying on imitating someone he or she admires as the primary rationale for behaving in a certain way.

A more advanced degree of self-regulation occurs when children imitate the conduct and attitudes of important people in their lives. This is called identification, or shared regulation. Typically, children identify with nurturing, powerful people—parents or other family members, teachers, childcare providers, and older children (Maccoby, 2007).

Identification plays a critical function in children's character development. The people with whom children identify validate the importance of appropriate social behavior and provide concrete examples of those behaviors in action. For instance, children learn valuable social lessons when teachers they admire advocate sharing, demonstrate ways to share, and express pleasure whenever children share or displeasure if they do not. Over time, children imitate the lessons they have absorbed, making identification a shared means of self-regulation. Children influenced by identification rely on external sources to help them control their actions (the model), but are beginning to use internal thought processes as well (remembering what the model said or did).

Carlos loves his grandmother and identifies with many of the social behaviors she values such as being polite to one's elders (*respeto*) and maintaining close family ties (*familismo*).

In all these ways, identification advances children's development. It moves them beyond the simple formula of rewards and admonitions that characterize adherence and provides them with many of the ideals and standards they carry with them into adulthood.

Unfortunately, there are limits to what identification can accomplish. Children who share the blocks to imitate the teacher do not necessarily recognize the inherent fairness in sharing or the real needs of the person with whom they are taking turns. In addition, if children find themselves in a situation unlike any they have seen the teacher model (such as witnessing bullying on the playground), they often find themselves at a loss for what to do. This leaves children not knowing how to respond and lacking enough tools to figure it out for themselves. So, although identification is a step up from adherence, it does not represent the highest level of self-regulation.

FIGURE 3.2 Three levels of self-regulation

Three Children Cleaning Up After Snack		
Martin	Wants a pumpkin sticker	Motivated by adherence
Carmen	Imitates the teacher's clean-up routine	Motivated by identification
James	Wants to do his fair share	Motivated by internalization

---

INTERNALIZATION (SELF-REGULATION)

The most advanced state of self-regulation comes about when children internalize values such as justice, honesty, and kindness and then act in concert with those values (Epstein, 2009). Now their thinking revolves around ethical judgments and their actions are aimed at avoiding self-condemnation rather than acquiring external rewards or emulating others. These are the children who will share because it "feels right," based on their understanding of others' needs and basic notions of fairness. Not sharing would prompt such children to feel uncomfortable, not because anyone else is monitoring their behavior, but because they would know they had not acted in accordance with their own ideals. Also, children who internalize notions of fair play or respect abide by those values long after their contacts with certain adults are over and in spite of the temptation or opportunity to act otherwise. This makes self-regulation both self-satisfying and long lasting.

> **internalization** The child relying on his or her own values and conscience to guide actions and behavior.

Three progressive degrees of self-regulation are depicted in Figure 3.2.

VARIATIONS IN SELF-REGULATION

Not all children march lockstep through the phases of self-regulation on the same timetable. Individual children (even of the same age) may operate at varying levels, depending on experience and maturity. For example, 4-year-old Jon may be at adherence for most things; his peer Celeste may have moved on to identification for some things too. In addition, the same child may exhibit differing degrees of compliance for different expectations (Kochanska & Aksan, 2006). This is why you might see Hyuk Jun put his backpack in his locker to avoid a scolding and adopt attitudes toward caring for animals similar to those held by his older brother. Later, he may say "sorry" when he accidently runs into someone on the playground because he genuinely regrets hurting another person. Such variations are typical. Regardless of the pace at which particular children mature, it takes many years for *every* child to reach the highest levels of social functioning.

What Adults Need to Know and Do to Support Self-Regulation

Guiding children's behavior involves teaching children many things about personal responsibility and ethical behavior. As with all teaching, you must take into account what young children are like and how their development and day-to-day experiences influence learning. See Figure 3.3 for a summary of critical variables to remember.

All of the developmental characteristics outlined in Figure 3.3 greatly influence how children behave and indicate to adults and teachers the social lessons that make the most sense to the children. Adult practices also contribute to children's understandings and their ability to translate those understandings into action. Think about the four phases of self-regulation. What supports do you think children need from adults to navigate them all? In Table 3.1, we list the conditions and strategies researchers have identified as key (Bronson, 2006; Thompson & Goodman, 2009).

FIGURE 3.3 How child development affects children's learning

A BEHAVIOR PROFILE OF THE YOUNG CHILD

I AM EAGER TO LEARN

I am learning new things every day.

I learn best when you create many opportunities for me to interact with other children and adults.

I WANT TO PLEASE

I care about what you think.

I learn best when you notice what I am doing right and when you treat my mistakes as learning opportunities.

I USE MY WHOLE BODY TO EXPRESS MYSELF

I often use actions rather than words to communicate needs.

I learn best when you help me translate my wants into words.

I AM IMPULSIVE

It is hard for me to sit still or put off getting what I want.

I learn best when wait times are short.

IT IS HARD FOR ME TO TRANSLATE NEGATIVE COMMANDS INTO POSITIVE ACTIONS

I have difficulty following rules or directions that start with the word *don't*.

I learn best if you tell me what to do instead of what not to do.

I HAVE A LIMITED UNDERSTANDING OF ALTERNATIVE BEHAVIORS

It is hard for me to imagine what else to do when my actions are unsuccessful or inappropriate.

I learn best when you help me substitute positive alternative behaviors for negative ones.

I DON'T ALWAYS REMEMBER WHAT YOU TOLD ME

I sometimes forget the rules.

I learn best when you remind me of your expectations matter-of-factly and often.

I CAN'T RESPOND TO TOO MANY THINGS AT ONCE

I have difficulty responding to too many rules or to multiple-step directions.

I learn best when rules are few and when you tell me to do one thing at a time.

I DON'T ALWAYS SEE THE CONNECTION BETWEEN ACTIONS AND CONSEQUENCES

It can be difficult for me to recognize why a certain behavior is right or wrong.

I learn best when you give me reasons for why I should or should not do something.

TABLE 3.1 • Self-Regulation and Adult Support

BECAUSE CHILDREN ARE INFLUENCED BY THIS PHASE OF SELF-REGULATION . . .	THEY NEED THESE THINGS FROM ADULTS . . .
Amoral	• Close warm relations • Physical support and direction
Adherence	• Manageable expectations • Clear communication of expectations • Physical and verbal assistance to carry out expectations • Rewards for positive behavior • Clear signals that certain behaviors are inappropriate • Redirection when engaged in mistaken behavior • Opportunities to practice and approximate desired behaviors
Identification	• Positive role models
Internalization	• Reasons behind expectations • Opportunities to explore values • Opportunities to reflect on personal behavior and ideals • Opportunities to put personal beliefs into action

These strategies are cumulative, meaning each stage incorporates the strategies that went before as well as new ones.

Looking at Table 3.1, you will see that there are many things adults do to help children learn to be happy, productive members of society. Guiding children's learning in this way is important as well as challenging. You have probably heard people say, "Children are not born with a set of directions." Of course, that's true. But we also know that some ways in which adults approach child guidance are more effective than others. Let's consider these variations next.

Differing Approaches to Child Guidance

Two preschoolers are "pretend" wrestling in the grassy play yard. What had begun as an active and playful interaction is becoming more strident and out of control.

Adult 1: Barely notices the children's activity.

Adult 2: Thinks, "They'll work it out. Kids always do."

Adult 3: Says sternly, "No more wrestling. Stop that now!"

Adult 4: Carefully pulls the children apart and says in a calm voice, "This started out as fun. Now it looks unsafe. I'm worried someone might get hurt. Let's think of something else you could play."

These adults are exhibiting four different approaches to child guidance.

Children need warm relationships and physical support from adults to develop self-regulation.

Most adults want children to learn to behave in certain ways and to do things "right," but not everyone interprets how to achieve this in the same fashion. Research over the past 40 years has identified at least four approaches to guiding children's behavior that seem most common: the uninvolved style, the permissive style, the authoritarian style, and the authoritative style (Baumrind, 1991; Maccoby & Martin, 1983). Although few adults adopt a single style completely, one style more than the rest tends to dominate their approach to teaching children right from wrong. As a result, these four variations continue to be the ones we talk about today (Berk, 2011).

Each adult socialization style is distinguished by certain attitudes and strategies related to these four elements: nurturance, expectations, communication, and control.

- **Nurturance**: How much care and concern adults express toward children.
- **Expectations**: The standards adults set for children's behavior.
- **Communication**: How much information and instruction adults give children about how to behave.
- **Control**: How much and in what ways adults enforce children's compliance with their expectations.

Differences among the four styles are reflected in how much each element is emphasized, how the elements are combined, and how they are interpreted. These variations are depicted in Figure 3.4. Adults low in every element typify the uninvolved style. Permissive adults are high in nurturance and low in everything else. Adults displaying an authoritarian style are low in nurturance and communication but high in expectations and control. Adults high in all four elements are called authoritative. Understanding more about each approach and their impact on children will help you to think about future directions in your own guidance practices.

nurturance The amount and type of care and concern adults express toward children.

expectations The standards adults set for children's behavior.

communication The amount and type of information and instruction adults offer children about how to behave.

control The amount and type of ways adults enforce children's compliance with their expectations.

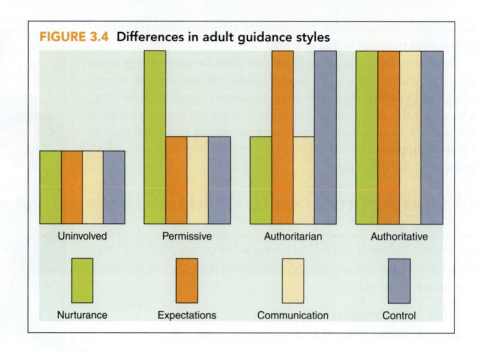

FIGURE 3.4 Differences in adult guidance styles

THE UNINVOLVED STYLE

uninvolved style Taking little notice of children and putting minimal effort into relating to them or teaching them how to behave.

In the **uninvolved style**, adults take little notice of children and put minimal effort into relating to them or teaching them the ins and outs of becoming successful members of society. What might prompt someone to act according to this style? Usually the answer is stress, depression, ill health, strained resources, or self-absorption. Whatever the cause, the uninvolved style conveys to children that they are unloved and unlovable. Children who feel unloved have no incentive to behave well because what they do does not matter. Moreover, children get few lessons in how to behave appropriately, leaving them without the means to connect with and get along with peers and other adults. Lack of involvement also reduces the number of nurturing grown-ups with whom children can identify productively. This combination of factors yields highly negative outcomes for children (Kochanska, Aksan, Prisco, & Adams, 2008; Steinberg, Blatt-Eisengart, & Cauffman, 2006). Some of these are:

- Aggressiveness
- Immaturity
- Impulsivity
- Insecurity
- Irresponsibility
- Low achievement
- Low self-esteem
- Low self-reliance
- Low self-control
- Non-compliance
- Unhappiness

Self-regulation is hard for children to develop when adults ignore them altogether. Because children do not have the human relationships and adult guidance that could help them move toward internalization, they tend to remain at the amoral or adherence stages of self-regulation. Of all the guidance approaches described, the uninvolved style has the least to recommend it.

THE PERMISSIVE STYLE

Adults who display a permissive style have warm loving relationships with children and enjoy children's company. However, they establish few boundaries on children's actions and do little to teach children how to comply with the rules of society. Some adults adopt this style out of the belief that "good" relationships lead to "good" behavior or because they think that behavior controls interfere with children's development. Other adults are permissive by default; they just don't know how to get children to listen (Mackenzie & Stanzione, 2010). Whatever the case, permissive adults provide little instruction about acceptable behavior. They do not talk to children about how their actions affect others or about other people's needs, and they seldom enforce rules. Under these circumstances children fail to develop effective social skills and codes of conduct. Peers and adults frequently view the unrestrained behavior of these children as immature, inconsiderate, and unacceptable. Such negative perceptions contribute to children's feelings of anxiety and low self-esteem (Steinberg, Blatt-Eisengart, & Cauffman, 2006). The behaviors and perceptual outcomes associated with permissiveness mirror those associated with no involvement:

permissive style Having loving relationships with children, but setting few limits on their behavior.

- Aggressiveness
- Aimlessness
- Immaturity
- Impulsivity
- Irresponsibility
- Low achievement
- Low self-esteem
- Low self-reliance
- Low self-control
- Non-compliance
- Unhappiness

Although these impacts are overwhelmingly negative to the child, the emphasis on nurturance within the permissive approach is a positive feature of child guidance. Unfortunately, other essential elements, such as establishing behavior standards, communicating these standards to children, and enforcing compliance in developmentally appropriate ways, tend to be ignored within this style. This lack of information detracts from children's abilities to become self-regulating.

THE AUTHORITARIAN STYLE

Adults who adopt an authoritarian style have high or unrealistic standards for children's conduct and devote most of their time to enforcing those standards. Because they value unquestioning obedience above all else, they deal with broken rules swiftly and forcefully. Reasoning and teaching alternative behaviors are not in their repertoire of guidance strategies. Not too surprisingly, they tend to have aloof, distant relationships with children (Dodge, Coie, & Lynam, 2006). As a consequence, children who interact mostly with authoritarian adults tend to display a variety of negative perceptions and behaviors (Kochanska, Aksan, Prisco, & Adams, 2008). Some of these are:

authoritarian style Demanding unquestioning obedience in lieu of all else.

- Aggressiveness
- Aimlessness
- Fearfulness
- Hostility
- Irresponsibility
- Low achievement
- Low self-esteem

- Low self-reliance
- Low self-control
- Suspiciousness
- Unfriendliness
- Unhappiness

Unfortunately, heavy-handed discipline tends to produce children who do as they are told, but who act out of fear or blind obedience, not out of concern for others (Brown, Odom, & McConnell, 2008). They obey in the short run, but only under direct supervision and not for long. These conditions prompt children to maintain an external orientation to their behavior, remaining at adherence rather than progressing toward internalization.

As you can see, the authoritarian style can yield many counterproductive outcomes. This is because certain disciplinary elements such as establishing unrealistic standards or harshly enforcing compliance may be carried to an extreme and because other elements of child guidance such as communication and nurturance are left out entirely. Having said this, it helps to remember that establishing appropriate standards for children's behavior and enforcing these standards are valuable variations on authoritarian approaches. These ideas will be revisited later in the chapter.

THE AUTHORITATIVE STYLE

authoritative style Having warm relationships and high expectations of children and enforcing rules in constructive ways.

Adults who exemplify the authoritative style combine positive elements of the permissive and authoritarian approaches and avoid the negative ones. They respond to children with warmth and nurturance; they have appropriate expectations and establish high standards for children's conduct, enforcing those standards firmly and appropriately. In addition, authoritative adults use communication strategies that the permissive and authoritarian styles overlook altogether. Among these are encouraging children to assume appropriate responsibility, acknowledging children's accomplishments, giving children reasons for behavioral expectations, and teaching children relevant social skills. The results for children are much more heartening than those associated with the other socialization styles (Hart, Newell, & Olsen, 2003; Milevsky, Schlechter, Netter, & Keehn, 2007). Some of these are:

- Cooperativeness
- Empathy
- Feelings of security
- Friendliness
- Goal oriented
- Happiness
- Helpfulness
- High achievement
- High self-reliance
- High self-control

When adults effectively address all four elements of guidance and discipline, children benefit. They tend to be happy and well adjusted, caring and responsible. Most important, they gain access to information and models needed to progress from adherence, to identification, to internalization. This is why the authoritative style is considered the most effective for promoting self-regulation. It is also the most closely aligned with DAP. You can see this in the following examples of DAP guidelines outlined in Figure 3.5.

Because there are so many positive outcomes associated with the authoritative style, the rest of this chapter is devoted to helping you adapt this style for yourself.

Authoritative adults demonstrate warmth and provide clear expectations for children's behavior.

FIGURE 3.5 **DAP guidelines for creating a caring community**

Teachers in classrooms using developmentally appropriate practices do the following:

- Help children develop responsibility and self-regulation
- Supervise, monitor, anticipate, prevent, and redirect behaviors that interfere with learning
- Teach positive behaviors

- Set clear and reasonable limits on children's behavior and consistently apply them
- Listen to and acknowledge children's emotions and frustrations
- Help children resolve conflicts
- Model skills that help children solve problems on their own

---

Source: Based on NAEYC, 2009, p. 16.

Authoritative Guidance Strategies

Everyone can learn to be more authoritative. It just takes education and practice. The following techniques provide the basic guidelines for this to happen and are distributed among the four elements of authoritative guidance: nurturance, maturity demands, communication, and control, which you read about earlier in this chapter.

NURTURANCE

Positive adult-child relationships form the foundation for authoritative child guidance. When children are close to their teachers, they feel emotionally safe and secure, which enables them to engage in the social world with confidence and to learn from their mistakes without undue stress. Some ways in which you convey nurturance to children follow.

- *Help children feel welcome and included.* Greet children by name and say goodbye to children individually at the end of the day. Tell children that you have been anticipating their arrival or that you look forward to seeing them again the next day. Smile at children often. Create a physical environment in which children have personalized spaces and things (e.g., cubbies, name tags, individual journals, names on the job chart, etc.) that tell them they are part of the group. Make sure classroom decorations and materials reflect the experiences and family backgrounds of all the children in the class. Children need to see themselves in the surroundings to feel comfortable there.

- *Make it a priority to get to know each child as an individual. Do the same with the important people in their lives.* Take time to observe and talk with children to find out more about their experiences in the program and at home. Have conversations with others in the child's life to gather information about the child and to make it more likely that children's experiences, interests, and family customs will be represented in the physical environment and in classroom activities.

- *Show genuine interest in what children are doing and saying.* Get down to children's eye level when talking to them. Look directly at children, not over them or through them. When a child tells you something, say to the child, "Tell me more." Invite children to spend time with you in an activity, on your lap, or next to you at group time.

Authoritative adults demonstrate respect by getting down to children's eye level and by listening carefully when children are upset.

- *Demonstrate respect for children.* Speak politely to children. Listen carefully to what they have to say. Do not interrupt children who are talking to you or each other. Ask relevant questions about what a child is telling you. Wait for children to respond to your queries. Do not jump in with your own answers when children do not reply right away. Take time to wonder with children, to "ooh and ah" over their discoveries, and to listen to *all* they have to say. Slow down your own pace in the classroom and avoid rushing children through experiences and conversations.

EXPECTATIONS

Child development and experience influence which behavioral expectations children can achieve and which are beyond their ability, at least for the time being. As with all learning, children need to successfully negotiate guidance-related tasks most of the time to stay motivated. Children who are overwhelmed or who fail more often than not tend to stop trying (Copple & Bredekamp, 2009). On the other hand, children who feel both challenged and successful keep working at mastering new skills and progressing to higher levels of self-regulation. Therefore, you must set expectations for children's behavior that are reasonable. *Reasonable* means that children have the ability and knowledge to do what is expected of them either on their own or with some support from you.

- *Observe what children can do and what they are trying to do.* Keep children in view from a short distance away. Make yourself available if children want your help, but let them work things out if they can. Intervene if children become unduly frustrated. Provide physical and verbal assistance as needed; for example, offer information, provide relevant scripts, demonstrate, or advise a child to take a break and then try again.

- *Establish reasonable expectations for children's behavior.* Take into account children's development, past experiences, current abilities, and what they must know and be able to do to meet the standard you have set. Individualize your expectations based on differences in ability and experience. Monica may be ready to sit still through the entire group time; Jeff may be able to sit for only a while. Adjust your expectations accordingly.

- *Revise unreasonable expectations.* If you become aware that children are unable to follow a standard you have set, revamp it so children are better able to comply. For example, at clean-up time you might ask the children: "Put away all the blocks by placing them on a shelf with a matching shape." This task involves two steps: first, finding matching shapes and second, putting all the blocks away. If you see children struggling to find the shelf with the matching shape or if you see many blocks left on the floor, it's a signal that the standard is not reasonable. You could change the expectation to, "Put the blocks away wherever they fit." This addresses one of the two steps, making it easier for children to do. Once children can do this with reasonable success, you could set a higher standard by adding the "matching shapes" portion of the expectation.

- *Add or take materials away to make expectations easier for children to manage.* A typical expectation of children is for them to share. However, if there are too few objects for children to use in the sandbox, it could make the sharing standard more difficult for children to achieve. Adding more funnels and pails might be all that is needed for children to play more cooperatively. In contrast, too many objects in the sandbox might make pouring and sifting without getting sand in people's hair and eyes challenging. In this case, removing a few items might be the better tactic for making the situation more manageable for children.

- *Reward children's approximations of desirable behaviors.* Break expectations into manageable steps and acknowledge the small steps children achieve. Do not expect 100 percent compliance 100 percent of the time. For instance, if the expectation is that children must wait quietly to be called on to choose a class job, you should not expect perfect silence as you dole out the jobs. At first, it is likely that as children wait their turn, they may call out or talk excitedly to gain your attention. Rather than focusing on the infraction of talking, it would be better to praise them for remembering to stay seated as they wait their turn. Gradually, with time and reminders, fewer children will call out as they wait to choose a job.

COMMUNICATION

Authoritative adults provide information to children about how to behave through:

- Modeling (showing children what is expected)
- Reasoning (explaining why some behaviors are desirable and others are not)
- Direct instruction (telling children what is right and what is wrong, informing children of expectations, or providing information about how child behaviors affect themselves and others)
- Restricting certain behaviors or penalizing them
- Encouraging certain actions and rewarding them

These lessons occur through hundreds of day-to-day interactions and are communicated physically and verbally to individual children and to groups of children. The most effective communications are unambiguous and calm. Most involve teaching children what to do versus simply letting them know that they have erred. Following are some effective ways to communicate expectations to children.

- *Say what you see.* Paint a verbal picture of what children are saying and doing. This helps children recognize and interpret what is happening. "It looks like two people want to use the glitter paint at the same time. That's a problem." Or, "You found a way that three people could use the bucket at the same time. That was a friendly thing to do."

- *Model appropriate behaviors.* Taking turns, sharing, helping, cooperating, comforting, encouraging, and waiting are all behaviors associated with self-regulation. Model these actions with children. However, don't assume that just modeling is enough. Draw children's attention to what you are saying or doing. This helps children recognize critical details of such lessons that they might otherwise miss. "Watch how I am petting the hamster gently. See how careful I am not to squeeze her too hard."

During circle time, these children agree on the rule "one child at a time can touch the bird's nest."

- *Invite children to help make classroom rules.* Hold open-ended discussions in which children create some of the rules everyone in the class will follow. Open the discussion by asking, "How can we make our classroom a safe and happy place to learn?" Write children's ideas on chart paper and post the results throughout the room.

- *State expectations clearly and positively.* Tell children what you want them to do versus what you don't want them to do: "Take two crackers." "Wear a smock to paint." "Wash your hands before you handle the books." Avoid negative rules, unless they are coupled with a positive statement, such as "Walk, don't run." Keep your expectations explicit, not implicit or vague. It is easier for children to comply with the expectation "Walk" than the more vague statement "Stay safe." Do not suppose children understand a particular expectation simply because you have talked about

TABLE 3.2 • Effective Expectations	
NEGATIVE STATEMENT	**POSITIVE STATEMENT**
"Don't peel the carrot toward you."	"Peel the carrot away from you."
"No sand throwing."	"Keep the sand low to the ground."
"Don't get paint on your shirt."	"Wear a smock when you paint."
"Don't lose track of the magnifiers."	"Put the magnifiers back on the shelf."
"Don't be so rough with the computer."	"Push the computer keys gently, like this."
"No standing during the story."	"Sit on your bottom."
"Don't be mean to your friend."	"Tell her you want a turn."

TABLE 3.3 • Expectations and Reasons	
EXPECTATION	**REASON**
"Peel the carrot away from you."	Health and Safety: "So the peeler doesn't slip and hurt your hand."
"Keep the sand low."	Health and Safety: "So sand doesn't get in anyone's eyes."
"Wear a smock when you paint."	Property: "So your clothes stay clean."
"Put the magnifiers back on the shelf."	Property: "So the magnifiers don't get lost or broken."
"Push the computer keys gently."	Property: "So the keys don't break."
"Sit on your bottom."	Rights: "So everyone can see the pictures."
"Tell her you want a turn."	Rights: "So she can finish using it and then you can have a chance to use it too."

it previously. Remind children of expectations both when they are not an issue and at other times when children forget. See Table 3.2 for more examples.

- *Give children reasons why some behaviors are acceptable and others are not.* Give children reasons every time you talk to them about their behavior. Do not assume that children can infer or remember the link between expectations and reasons, even if they have heard them before. It takes many repetitions for reasons to make sense and for children to use them to regulate their actions. The reasons that resonate the best with young children center around *protecting people's health and safety, protecting property,* and *protecting people's rights.* See Table 3.3 for examples of reasons associated with typical classroom expectations. Rationales such as "Because that's the rule" or "Because I said so" are not adequate explanations.

- *Remind children of limits in context.* Remind children of expectations when they are most relevant. For example, you might say, "Remember to walk in the classroom" when children are found running. When children forget or otherwise fail to comply, avoid accusatory statements such as "How many times have I told you not to run inside?" or "You know better than to run in here." Treat such incidents as teachable moments, not punitive ones.

CONTROL

For children to regulate their behavior, they must recognize that how they behave matters. Adults convey this message when they follow through on their expectations, rewarding appropriate actions and redirecting or limiting children's mistaken behaviors, which are undesirable things they do because they don't know any better or they lack the skills to behave appropriately on their own.

mistaken behaviors Undesirable things children do because they don't know any better or because they lack the skills to behave appropriately on their own.

In time, children rely less on the external controls adults apply and adopt more internalized means for monitoring personal actions. Following are some of the most important things you can do to help children in this process. Let's consider each one in the context of the children from earlier in the chapter who were wrestling.

Two preschoolers are 'pretend' wrestling in the grassy play yard. What began as an active and playful interaction is becoming more strident and out of control.

- *Physically intervene as necessary.* Always stop children's unsafe behavior first and then work on resolving the problem that prompted it. Separate two children who are pulling on a toy, then discuss their desires. If a child is waving a saw in the air, catch hold of it before addressing your concerns. In the case of the wrestlers, gently but firmly disentangle the children so they can hear your message more clearly.

- *Acknowledge children's perspectives and needs from the start.* Framing a situation in terms of the children's perspective before communicating your own reactions helps children tune in to what you have to say. It also signals to children that you recognize and care about the needs they are expressing. If Ian is running in the classroom say, "You're anxious to get outside." If Emma shares her blocks, say, "You wanted Jamie to have some blocks too."

The teacher acknowledges Kara's desire to play before enforcing the clean-up rule. "You wish you could play some more. I need help putting the toys away so we can go to lunch. Come help me."

In the case of the wrestlers you could say, "You're having fun wrestling." Or, "You started out having fun, but now you look upset."

- *Describe your own emotions—both positive and negative.* These statements serve as a bridge from adherence to identification. Give a reason for your feelings (linked to health and safety, rights, or property). When Ian runs in the classroom, say, "I'm worried that when you run you could knock into things. That would not be safe." When Emma shares, say, "I'm pleased you shared with Jamie. Now you both have blocks to use." With the wrestlers you might say, "I'm worried that you are starting to hurt each other."

- *Redirect children's inappropriate behavior by pointing out more acceptable alternative actions.* When children engage in mistaken behavior, assume children do not know what to do instead. Show them or tell them what to do. As children gain experience, invite them to generate ideas of their own. Remain close at hand to help children carry out alternate approaches. For instance, you might redirect the wrestlers to run across the play yard to deal with their energy in a more constructive way or ask them what they might like to do instead.

- *Combine guidance strategies to create personal messages.* **Personal messages** are adult scripts that acknowledge children's positive behaviors or redirect mistaken behavior. There are three parts:
  - Acknowledge the child's perspective
  - Describe your own emotion
  - Give a reason

  Examples are provided in Figure 3.6.

- *Use positive consequences to acknowledge children's appropriate behaviors.* Catch children being good. Notice and comment on children's appropriate conduct and give a reason (connected to health and safety, rights, or property) for this positive assessment. Recognize the effort required to display positive behaviors or compliance and note aloud these productive outcomes. If the children stop wrestling, you might say, "You decided to ride big wheels instead. That is a safer game to play."

personal messages Messages from adults that acknowledge children's positive behaviors or redirect mistaken behavior in three parts: Acknowledgement of the child's perspective, statement of adult emotion, reasons for reaction.

FIGURE 3.6 Sample personal messages

When John shares his blocks with Ali, the teacher says,

Acknowledge:	"You gave Ali some of your blocks.
Emotion:	I'm pleased you found some she could use.
Reason:	Now each of you has blocks to build the road."

When Ali knocks John's block tower down, the teacher says,

Acknowledge:	"You had fun knocking down the blocks.
Emotion:	I'm concerned John is upset.
Reason:	He wanted to keep his tower standing."

When behavior change is needed, teachers redirect mistaken behavior.

Redirect:	"Next time, ask before you knock down someone else's blocks"

Or

"Knock down only your own blocks."

Catch children being good and let them know you noticed their positive behavior.

rehearsal Having children approximate or practice a desirable behavior in place of some mistaken behavior.

restitution Having children make amends to try to rectify mistaken behavior.

• *Use logical consequences to address children's mistaken behavior.* Logical consequences teach alternate behaviors. A common form involves **rehearsal** (children approximate or practice a desirable behavior in lieu of some inappropriate action). For example, if the rule is "Walk; don't run" and Abigail runs down the hall, a logical consequence is to have her retrace her steps and walk. The act of walking approximates the rule and allows Abigail to rehearse it physically. This consequence provides a better reminder for the future than simply making her sit down. Sometimes rehearsals are not feasible, so **restitution** is a better choice. When children make genuine amends for their mistaken behavior, they are making restitution. For instance, if Kaylee draws on the wall, a logical consequence would be for her to wash off the marks. This action returns the wall to a more acceptable condition and shows Kaylee that the unacceptable act of defacing the wall is not allowed. In the wrestling example, if, during their play, one child hurts another, you might have the perpetrator soothe the victim's hurt with a damp towel. See Table 3.4 for more examples.

• *Enforce consequences consistently.* Follow through with expectations to help children make a connection between expectations and ways to comply. Describe the aftermath of the children's behavior when children comply and when they do not. Remain calm at all times. Treat compliance as a teaching opportunity, not a punishment. "You're having a hard time choosing something other than wrestling. I'll help you find another spot to play." Or, "You got a towel to help Gerald feel better. That was helpful." Be consistent. This makes it easier for children to predict what will happen if they comply or fail to comply, strengthening their self-regulating abilities.

TABLE 3.4 • Logical Consequences		
MISTAKEN BEHAVIOR	**LOGICAL CONSEQUENCE**	**TYPE**
Cassidy peels carrot toward herself	Adult guides peeler as Cassidy holds carrot	Rehearsal
Eleanor tosses sand that goes into Marc's eyes	Eleanor accompanies adult and Marc inside to help wash out Marc's eyes	Restitution
Chung-hee begins painting without a smock	Chung-hee must go back and put on a smock	Rehearsal
Child leaves magnifiers on the floor and one is stepped on and broken	Child 'repairs' the magnifier or earns the money to replace it	Restitution
Deon slaps the computer keys roughly	Deon uses computer with closer adult supervision	Rehearsal
Zoe stands in front of the storybook, and the other children can't see the pictures	Zoe sits next to the adult to be reminded to sit on her bottom	Rehearsal
Steven knocks down another child's blocks as he takes more blocks for himself	Steven helps the child to rebuild	Restitution
	Steven practices asking for a turn at building with the help of the teacher's aide	Rehearsal

Meeting the Needs of Diverse Learners

Used in combination, the previously described strategies promote greater self-regulation among boys and girls, among children of differing ages, and among children of varying ethnic and socioeconomic backgrounds (Rothbaum & Trommsdorff, 2007). They can also be adapted for children with special needs (Stephens, 2006). All children benefit from knowing your expectations. The adaptations presented in Figure 3.7 make it easier for children with special needs to be successful in meeting those expectations.

Dinah, a child with Down syndrome, does not respond to the signal to go inside. What can her teacher do to help her comply more successfully?

FIGURE 3.7 **Adapting rules for children of varying abilities**

- Observe the environment carefully.
  - Determine whether there are sights, sounds, smells, sensations, people, routines, or times in the day that trigger a child's misbehavior or make it more difficult for him or her to behave successfully.
- Minimize potential problem situations.
  - Reduce sensory overload such as too much noise, too many visual distractions, too many directions at once, and so on.
  - Make adjustments in environments and routines to avoid triggers that prompt mistaken behavior.
- Get children's attention before stating your expectations.

- Use repetition to enhance children's understanding of expectations.
  - Create predictable routines to help children become familiar with common expectations.
  - Repeat the same few expectations often.
- Give children ample time to respond to expectations.
  - Become familiar with each child's response pattern.
  - Avoid demanding instant compliance.
- Apply demands for compliance wisely.
  - Ignore some behaviors that are annoying but that do not threaten safety, property, or rights.

TECH TIP

Using Technology to Support ALL Learners

Are you looking for additional ideas about how to support children with special needs? Go to the *Beyond the Journal* portion of the NAEYC website for information about "Supporting All Kinds of Learners," www.naeyc .org. On this website you will find articles, checklists, and other recommended websites that you can access to expand your inclusion and teaching strategies, including ideas for helping children with special needs successfully adapt to school rules and routines.

logical consequences Consequences for mistaken behavior that teach children alternate behaviors.

TRY IT YOURSELF

Think of an activity in which you will participate with children and identify one expectation that fits that situation. Write it down and then analyze your expectation using the criteria presented in this chapter.

Expectation: _____

1. Is this expectation **reasonable** developmentally?   Yes   No
   If no, revise.

2. Is this expectation stated **positively**?   Yes   No
   If no, make it a 'do' instead of a 'don't.'

3. What is the **reason** for this expectation? (health and safety, property, rights?)
   If none fits, revise your expectation.

4. Here's my **script**. (How will you say your expectation to children?)

5. Got it! (What **positive consequence** will you use?)

6. More to learn! (What logical consequence will you use if children engage in mistaken behavior?)

Communicating with Families to Promote Children's Self-Regulation

Children benefit when the significant adults in their lives communicate with one another about important issues. In no arena is this more critical than in child guidance. As a teacher, you need to talk with family members about their expectations for their children and the guidance strategies they use at home. In turn, you should acquaint families with your expectations for children and how you will address them. Such information could be exchanged during home visits, parent meetings, or workshops. Written materials such as newsletters or handbooks also provide valuable information for teachers and parents to discuss. See Figure 3.8 for a newsletter/web-ready piece that conveys an authoritative philosophy to families of children enrolled in your program. A note like this one could be sent to new families or to families early in the year.

NEWSLETTER/WEB READY COMMUNICATION

FIGURE 3.8 • Communicating with Families About Classroom Expectations

One thing many families want to know is how children are supposed to behave at the center. Here are some basic expectations I have for children in our class. All of them are designed to keep children safe, protect the rights of everyone in the group, and safeguard belongings. We can talk about these in more detail at our orientation next week. In the meantime, I'd be happy to answer any questions you have and to hear your comments about our classroom rules.

Children will walk, not run, indoors.

Children will use materials in a safe manner.

Children will refrain from hurting other children and will express their feelings in words.

Children will participate in clean-up every day.

Children may knock down only their own blocks and may dispose of only their own artwork, unless the owner has said it's okay to do otherwise.

Throughout the year, the children and I will discuss these rules and others that they think are important. We will spend a lot of time working on ways to make our classroom a safe, happy, caring place to live and learn.

Such information opens the door to further conversations about child guidance. It gives family members a sense of your priorities, a chance to ask questions, and an opportunity to provide feedback. These exchanges set the stage for further understanding between family members and program personnel, as well as for developing mutual expectations among the main settings in which children function.

3 Applying What You've Learned

Based on what you now know about child guidance, try these activities to increase your skills.

1. **What Are the Rules?** Observe an early childhood classroom. Identify three expectations adults have for the children. What cues helped you decide what these expectations were?

2. **Looking Carefully.** Observe a group of young children interacting with their teachers or caregivers. What positive behaviors did the children display? What were some of the problems they encountered? What implications did your observation reveal for your approach to child guidance?

3. **Up Close and Personal.** Interview an early childhood educator. Ask him or her to describe the most common mistaken behaviors children exhibit. How does he or she address such problems when they arise?

4. **Connecting with Families.** Interview a family member of a child in your program. Ask him or her to describe a positive behavior he or she would like the child to demonstrate. How does the family approach this behavior at home?

References

Baumrind, D. (1991). The influence of parenting style on adolescent competence and substance use. *Journal of Early Adolescence*, II, 56–95.

Berk, L. (2011). *Infants and children.* Upper Saddle River, NJ: Pearson.

Bronson, M. B. (2006). Developing social and emotional competence. In D. F. Gullo (Ed.), *K Today: Teaching and learning in the kindergarten year.* Washington, D.C.: NAEYC, 47–56.

Brown, W. H., Odom, S. L., & McConnell, S. R. (Eds.). (2008). *Social competence of young children: Risk, disability, & intervention.* Baltimore, MD: Paul H. Brookes, 3–30.

Copple, C., & Bredekamp, S. (2009). *Developmentally appropriate practice in early childhood programs.* Washington, D.C.: NAEYC.

Dodge, K. A., Coie, J. D., & Lynam, D. (2006). Aggression and anti-social behavior in youth. In N. Eisenberg, W. Damon, & R. M. Lerner (Eds.), *Handbook of child psychology* (pp. 719–788). Hoboken, NJ: J. Wiley & Sons.

Epstein, A. S. (2009). *Me, you, us: Social-emotional learning in preschool.* Washington, D.C.: NAEYC.

Fulghum, R. (2003). *All I really need to know I learned in kindergarten* (15th anniversary edition). New York: Ballantine Books.

Hart, C. H., Newell, L. D., & Olsen, S. F. (2003). Parenting skills and social/communicative competence in childhood. In J. O. Green & B. R. Burleson (Eds.), *Handbook of communication and social interaction skills* (pp. 753–797). Mahwah, NJ: Erlbaum.

Kochanska, G., & Aksan, N. (2006). Children's conscience and self-regulation. *Journal of Personality, 74,* 1587–1617.

Kochanska, G., Aksan, N., Prisco, T. R., & Adams, E. E. (2008). Mother-child and father-child mutually responsive orientation in the first 2 years and children's outcomes at preschool age: Mechanisms of influence. *Child Development, 79,* 30–44.

Kostelnik, M. J., & Grady, M. L. (2009). *Getting it right from the start: The principal's guide to early childhood education.* Thousand Oaks, CA: Corwin Press.

Ladd, G. W. (2008). Social competence and peer relations: Significance for young children and their service providers. *Early Childhood Services, 2*(3), 129–148.

Maccoby, E. E. (2007). Historical overview of research and theory. In J. E. Grusec & P. D. Hastings (Eds.), *Handbook of socialization theory and practice* (pp. 13–41). New York: Guilford Press.

Maccoby, E. E., & Martin, J. A. (1983). Socialization in the context of family: Parent-child interactions. In P. H. Mussen (Ed.), *Handbook of child psychology* (4th ed., Vol. 4). New York: Wiley.

Mackenzie, R. J., & Stanzione, L. (2010). *Setting limits in the classroom.* New York: Random House.

Milevsky, A., Schlechter, M., Netter, S., & Keehn, D. (2007). Maternal and paternal parenting styles in adolescence: Associations with self-esteem, depression, and life satisfaction. *Journal of Child and Family Studies, 16,* 39–47.

National Association for the Education of Young Children. (2009). *Developmentally appropriate practice in early childhood programs serving children from birth through age 8: A position statement of the National Association for the Education of Young Children.* Washington, D.C.: Author.

Rose-Krasnor, L., & Denham, S. (2009). Social-emotional competence in early childhood. In K. H. Rubin, W. M. Bukowski, & B. Laursen (Eds.), *Handbook of peer interactions, relationships, and groups* (pp. 162–179). New York: Guilford Press.

Rothbaum, F., & Trommsdorff, G. (2007). Do roots and wings complement or oppose one another? The socialization of relatedness and autonomy in cultural context. In J. E. Grusec & P. D. Hastings (Eds.), *Handbook of socialization: Theory and research* (pp. 461–489). New York: Guilford Press.

Steinberg, L., Blatt-Eisengart, I., & Cauffman, E. (2006). Patterns of competence and adjustment among adolescents from authoritative, authoritarian, indulgent, and neglectful homes: A replication in a sample of serious juvenile offenders. *Journal of Research on Adolescence, 16,* 47–58.

Stephens, T. J. (2006). Discipline strategies for children with disabilities. Sioux Falls, SD: School of Medicine & Health Sciences, Center for Disabilities, University of South Dakota.

Thompson, R. A., & Goodman, M. (2009). Development of self, relationships and socioemotional competence. In O. A. Barbarin & B. H. Wasik (Eds.), *Handbook of child development and early education: Research to practice* (pp. 147–171). New York: Guilford Press.

4 Teacher, Teacher, What Do You See: Observing and Documenting Children's Learning

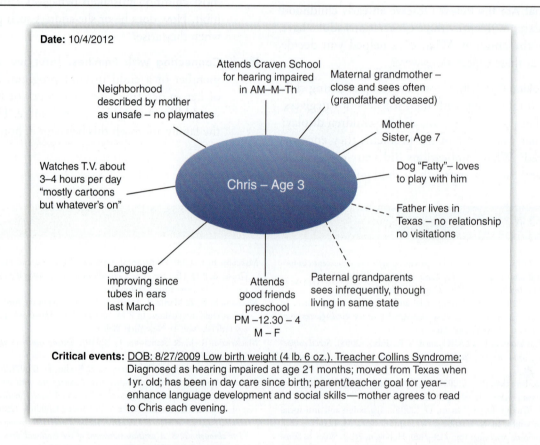

Date: 10/4/2012

Attends Craven School for hearing impaired in AM–M–Th

Neighborhood described by mother as unsafe – no playmates

Maternal grandmother – close and sees often (grandfather deceased)

Mother
Sister, Age 7

Watches T.V. about 3–4 hours per day "mostly cartoons but whatever's on"

Chris – Age 3

Dog "Fatty"– loves to play with him

Father lives in Texas – no relationship no visitations

Language improving since tubes in ears last March

Attends good friends preschool PM –12.30 – 4 M – F

Paternal grandparents sees infrequently, though living in same state

Critical events: DOB: 8/27/2009 Low birth weight (4 lb. 6 oz.). Treacher Collins Syndrome; Diagnosed as hearing impaired at age 21 months; moved from Texas when 1yr. old; has been in day care since birth; parent/teacher goal for year– enhance language development and social skills—mother agrees to read to Chris each evening.

ecomap A graphic representation of the significant people in a child's everyday world and a timeline of critical events that have occurred since birth.

It's time for fall conferences again, and Ms. Herbas has decided that she's going to try a new strategy she's heard about called an **ecomap**, a graphic representation of the significant people in a child's everyday world and a timeline of critical events that have occurred since birth. After greeting each individual family, she asks them to work with her to fill out an ecomap for their child. Drawing an oval in the middle of the paper and a timeline across the bottom, Ms. Herbas asks Ezra's parents about his world outside the classroom, such as best friends that he chooses to play with in his neighborhood, grandparents, extracurricular activities, and critical events that have happened since birth, such as any illnesses, moves, transitions within the family, etc. Using the process to interview each family, Ms. Herbas discovers that Kendra lives with a single mother working two jobs, that Peyton did not speak until after he was 3 years old, that Gilbert lives with his grandparents, and that Lucy has a beloved cat named Ringo. One parent whose child goes to child care in the afternoon following preschool in the morning remarks that she didn't realize how many transitions her child was making during the day until she actually saw it on paper.

Mr. Lei has been teaching the children in his classroom to count by 10s. They all join in readily and obviously enjoy working their way to 100. He wonders, however, does each child truly understand what 10, 20, 30, and 100 mean in terms of quantity? He thinks about how he can design an appropriate way to find out. He wants something that will fit naturally into the ongoing math activities that the children look forward to, not a "test" of their abilities. He begins to make plans about working with the children to convert the pretend play center into a bank and ways he can incorporate what he needs to learn into the activities.

LEARNING OUTCOMES

After you read this chapter, you will be able to:

- Describe the purposes for assessment in early childhood education.
- Discuss developmental considerations in assessing young children.
- Explain what is meant by authentic assessment.
- Develop strategies for documenting learning over time.
- Involve children and families in the assessment and evaluation process.

Each of these teachers understands that developmentally appropriate practice requires her or him to know where any particular child is in the learning cycle, which children may need extra support, and to document the learning that is taking place. This enables teachers to be accountable to the children, parents, and others interested in how much progress children are making.

Day after day, early childhood classrooms are filled with busy children involved in a variety of activities and learning experiences. To make sure that what you have planned for the children in your classroom is working effectively, you build useful assessment strategies into your everyday instruction. This chapter focuses on ways you can monitor, document, and communicate to others how well children are learning. We will discuss strategies that responsible teachers use to improve individual and group instruction, identify children's special needs, and make informed decisions about creating the most effective learning environment.

Purposes for the Assessment and Evaluation of Young Children

Assessment of young children should always be intentional. To design and implement good assessment, your purpose should be based on one of the following reasons:

- *Inform instruction.* For the classroom teacher, improved instruction is the primary rationale for assessment—and for evaluation, which attaches meaning or value to an assessment. As you deliberately watch children in various situations,

evaluation Including or adding meaning or value to an assessment.

"See, your page is just like mine."

at different times of the day, and as they interact with materials in carrying out the learning tasks you've designed, you will become a more effective and confident teacher. Documentation of how children are growing in all developmental domains will add to your certainty that the activities you've planned for them are making a positive difference—or need to be adapted or scrapped altogether. With the proof you will gather through periodic assessment of individual children and groups of children, your planning for what happens during each day, each week, and over the school year in your classroom will be more decisive. You will make better use of children's time and you will be more likely to address intended outcomes that are highlighted in the curriculum.

- *Identify and monitor children with special needs.* At times over your teaching career, you will become concerned about apparent gaps in a child's development. For example, it may be that the child is demonstrating learning difficulties with tasks that other children do not find overly challenging, exhibiting unusual behavior in getting along with others, or clearly falling behind in language development. When this happens, you must document carefully the particular behaviors that have been causing you apprehension, and you should do this before you bring your concerns to your administrator, the child's parents, or other professionals.

- *Assess strengths and needs of your program.* In your role as an early childhood educator, you will also have the responsibility of keeping track of the indoor and outdoor environments and evaluating how well you have designed them to facilitate children's physical, socioemotional, language, and cognitive development. How safe are children? How useful is the curriculum in your planning and for meeting the learning needs of children? How balanced is your daily schedule in providing active and quiet activities? Are the small-group and large-group experiences that you're planning for children meaningful and engaging? Are you choosing materials that are developmentally appropriate and free of racial and sexist elements? Program assessment should be an important and ongoing part of your total assessment picture (Wortham, 2010).

- *Provide data for families, other educators, and policy makers at the local, state, and national level for improving services and educational programs.* Parents and other family members who are responsible for young children want to know how their children are performing in a program. In addition to the planned conferences you have with them, informal communications, and sending home products that children create, one of the best ways you can document children's progress over time is to keep dated work samples in a portfolio intended to be shared with families. If you are working in a Head Start or other state- or federally-funded program, you may be asked to complete inventories of certain behaviors and accomplishments of children in your classroom and document your interaction with their families.

As a classroom teacher, you may be one of the first persons to notice that a young child is having speech, learning, or behavior difficulties; if so, you will want to request that a professional with greater expertise come in to observe and determine whether further diagnosis is necessary.

Occasionally, children may enter your program with specifically designed strategies required to help them progress in certain developmental areas. You'll remember from Chapter 1 that the written plan that outlines the special instructional needs of children 3 years of age and older is called an individualized educational program (IEP). That plan will usually require you to monitor the child closely and gather certain data to evaluate whether the current intervention is working to meet the child's needs. In addition, continued funding of programs is often related to the ability of educators to communicate to policy makers and funding agents that a program is genuinely making a difference in the lives of children and families being served.

Developmental Considerations in Planning for Assessment in the Early Years

When you are thinking about appropriate assessment of children between 3 and 6 years of age, keep in mind a number of developmental factors:

- Child development is uneven and it changes dramatically over a year. This makes single assessments unreliable.
- Young children are not good test takers—formal achievement tests and once-a-year paper-and-pencil tests are inappropriate for them. Also, such tasks do not capture some skills that are essential to school success, such as social competence, approaches to learning, or motivation.
- Young children have immature language skills. They have limited ability to follow oral directions, read printed instructions, or express themselves adequately in words.
- Children are sensitive to the setting, the timing, and the people involved in the assessment process. The more you can design your assessment to document what children are doing naturally in your classroom, the more it is likely that assessment outcomes will be accurate.
- Children tire quickly and are easily distracted.
- Children have no concept of the importance of assessment and may have little understanding or interest in doing well (Kostelnik & Grady, 2009).

Observing the child's performance is a key to assessment.

A number of benefits accrue when teachers develop an effective assessment and evaluation system based on learning goals and objectives. They have factual information to improve instruction for individual children and the overall quality of their programs. They are able to build strategic partnerships with families, other educators, and policy makers who want and need information about children's learning and their ability to be successful in school. Teachers are also more likely to teach what children need to know and do when they examine patterns in development over time with individual children and subgroups of children (e.g., those differing by language ability, gender, age, culture). This calls for assessment practices that have come to be known as authentic assessment.

authentic assessment Carrying out useful strategies in the regular classroom to see whether children are making progress.

Using Authentic Assessment Strategies

The National Association for the Education of Young Children (NAEYC) has indicated that to provide an accurate picture of children's capabilities, teachers must:

- Observe children over time
- Collect a reasonable amount of data
- Use their findings to adjust their curriculum and instruction

Some assessment practices that are currently mandated by federal legislation are considered inappropriate by educators who support developmentally appropriate practices, such as the evaluation of young children by testing and ranking them against a standardized group norm. In the early years, teachers should avoid emphasizing test scores as indications of a child's success or failure, using letter or numerical grades when reporting to parents, using timed assessments, or comparing children to others in the class. These are unsupportive practices that undermine children's success and confidence. They are also likely to be inaccurate. Instead, we can put into practice authentic assessment such as observation with annotation and work sampling, which are essential strategies for determining positive directions for instruction (Gestwicki, 2010).

Authentic assessment is useful assessment that is carried out in the regular classroom to see whether children are benefiting from what is planned for them. You are doing authentic assessment when you:

- Have a systematic plan for collecting and using periodic assessment information.
- Choose assessment tools and methods that:
  - Are appropriate to the age and experience of the children in your classroom.
  - Allow for individual variations in learning.
  - Take into consideration such factors as the child's language abilities and special needs.
  - Address not only what children can do independently but what they can do with assistance from other children or adults.
  - Measure the progress children have made as well as their current learning capabilities.
- Use input from families.
- Provide opportunities for children to evaluate their own work.
- Collect a variety of data across time. This eliminates the "snapshot in time" mentality about assessment that fails to help you see how children are developing. It looks at a range of behaviors and skills (e.g., documenting children's progress with certain skills such as cutting with scissors, counting, listening during large group).
- Evaluate growth in all developmental domains, not just the child's academic performance.
- Conduct your assessments in the natural learning context as a part of the regular day while children are working with everyday materials on everyday performance tasks.
- Base your assessment on children's best performance rather than documenting what they do not know or cannot do well.
- Use your findings to plan for classroom instruction and to organize and move children's learning forward.
- Share your findings with relevant others who are involved in the child's overall development and well-being (Copple & Bredekamp, 2010; Johnson, 2008; Soderman, Gregory, & McCarty, 2005).

In keeping with the principles of authentic assessment, you can use a number of strategies to determine whether or not children are benefiting from the kinds of learning activities that take place in your classroom. You can obtain data about children systematically or by informally observing them in the classroom, on the playground, in other places in the school, or during a home visit.

DOCUMENTING AND ORGANIZING INFORMATION

Let's look at some examples of selected strategies for documenting and organizing detailed information about the children in your classroom.

TEACHER AS OBSERVER

Your understanding of developmental benchmarks and knowledge about the curriculum content that you'd like children to learn will guide your observations, allowing your mind and eyes to become valuable assessment and evaluation tools. Because simply looking at children does not guarantee *seeing or understanding*, however, effective observation calls for identifying a particular situation, problem, or progress toward an identified goal you are interested in assessing (Soderman, Gregory, & McCarty, 2005; McAfree & Leong, 2010). Before considering carrying out any assessment, you will want to ask yourself the following questions:

- What exactly do I want to learn about this individual child or group of children?
- How will this be useful?
- When would be the best time and place to do this?
- What is the best way to document what I want to know and in what format?
- Who else will I want to share my findings with?

During an observation, the focus should be on the child's visible behavior rather than on making any interpretation of that behavior (see Figure 4.1). What you record (the annotation) should be objective, accurate, and thorough enough to shed some light on the child's behavior of interest, patterns of behavior, or some ideas for subsequent observation. Maintain your objectivity by recording only what you see, feel, hear, and smell (MacLean, 2009).

A question many teachers ask is how to work in these observations when they are so busy just managing the classroom. The answer is to simplify. Times for observing a small number of the children can be scheduled daily during learning center activities or free play when children are working independently, using helpful tools such as the grid displayed in Figure 4.2. When using the grid, plan to observe only one-fifth of the children on Monday, one-fifth on Tuesday, and so on. The next week, change these groups so that you are not always observing the same children on the same day. Observe the designated children during free play or at a particular task they have been given—keeping in mind the targeted behavior of interest. Make quick notes on the grid that can be kept on a handy clipboard. Also spend another 5 to 10 minutes before leaving for the day to note in an ongoing observation journal what you have seen about those particular children—how they participate in large group, on the playground, and in social interaction during the day. You may also choose to make notes about a child on a sticky pad, placing these in their individual portfolios for later reference.

No conclusions should ever be drawn about a child and no decisions should ever be made based on a single observation. If you suspect a learning or behavior problem, it is always important to make several

What kinds of social skills might be observed and annotated in watching these boys in the block area?

FIGURE 4.1 Examples of *objective* notation of behavior versus *interpretation* of observed behavior

Example of objectively written observation notation:

"Riley spent one minute near the block area, leaving when Lawton knelt down beside him."

Example of observation with inappropriate interpretation notation:

"Riley spent one minute near the block area. He left right away when Lawton knelt down beside him because Lawton has been overly aggressive whenever they have played together."

FIGURE 4.2 Observation grid

Date:_____

Monday	Tuesday	Wednesday	Thursday	Friday
Keri	**Alex**	**Adam**	**Sophie Z.**	**Monica**
First time asking for help to use toilet. Washed hands without reminder.				
Kevin	**Bebe**	**LeShan**	**Mehan**	**Damon**
Wandered during learning center time. Needs help in entering play frames.				
Gavin	**Isla**	**Connie**	**Michael**	**Tanisha**
Blocks: "I'm making a 'cow fence.'" Watched feet in stepping carefully over Michael's structure.				
Henry	**Donald**	**Wendy**	**Meghan**	**Sophie L.**
Chooses books to read during center time. Was first one to large group for story time.				

observations over a period of time, in various settings, at various times of the day (and by more than one person if possible) before you can consider a picture of a child complete.

When you make regularly scheduled observations and annotations a part of your teaching practice, you'll find that you gain in-depth information about each child and begin to notice patterns that will help with planning instruction and sharing information with parents. More important, you will gain knowledge of every child in your classroom over time rather than only those children who attract attention because they are more aggressive, more interactive, or more challenging (Soderman & Farrell, 2007).

If you are teaching preschoolers, you can also invest in a well-constructed tool created by HighScope called the Preschool Child Observation Record (COR), 2nd Edition. This instrument is used to observe young children's knowledge and abilities in six areas of development: initiative (e.g., making choices, solving problems, initiating play with others, taking care of personal needs), social relations, creative representation, movement and music, language and literacy, and mathematics and science. In each of these components, broad areas of development are indicated at five levels from simple to complex. Hard copy forms are available (www.highscope.org) or you can computerize your observations with other versions offered.

DATED WORK SAMPLES AND REPEATED PERFORMANCES

One of the most powerful assessments to see if children are making progress over time is comparing children's work samples from one time to another or to have them again perform a task they have done earlier. Are they growing in their ability to put ideas on paper in the form of pictures and/or symbols? Are they performing essential learning tasks with increased independence, ease, and confidence? Do you see cognitive growth in their use of classroom materials such as blocks, games, manipulative materials, writing tools, and art materials? Collect and date particular samples of what children are producing naturally early in the year and then periodically at certain junctures. Save work samples for future comparison (see the section on portfolios and student-led conferences later in this chapter). You can make brief videos or take pictures of performances and jot down evaluative comments about the learning that is taking place.

TECH TIP

Keep a digital device (e.g., smart phone, digital camera, tablet device) handy as you move about the classroom so that you can capture what children say about their work. Organize your documentation records by using photo-organizing software such as Snapfish web albums (Parnell & Bartlett, 2012).

NURSERY RHYME REPETITIONS

Nursery rhyme repetitions are useful for producing work samples that can be compared over time because you are using the same rhyme to replicate the task. The goal is to note whether the child's ability to depict detail in drawing about a particular rhyme (see Box 4.1 for suggested rhymes) or to write some of the words in the rhyme from memory is growing. Implement this by first acquainting children with a nursery rhyme such as Humpty Dumpty. Present the words on a chart with a drawing of Humpty Dumpty. Have children learn the rhyme and read it with you. Point out the rhyming words and how they are spelled. After sufficient repetitions over a number of days, remove the chart. Provide paper and ask children to draw a picture of Humpty Dumpty and to write as much of the rhyme as they can. Have them write their names and the date on their work. Encourage them to do their own work instead of copying from other children for this task (see Figure 4.3).

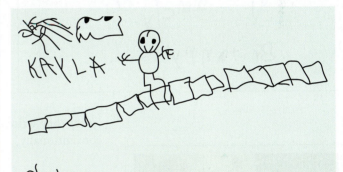

FIGURE 4.3 Nursery rhyme repetition, baseline sample for Kayla, age 4.10, September ("Humpty Dumpty sat on a wall. Humpty Dumpty had a great fall. All the king's ....")

Suggested Nursery Rhymes for Assessment

Humpty Dumpty sat on a wall
Humpty Dumpty had a great fall
All the King's horses and all the King's men
Couldn't put Humpty Dumpty together again.

Little Miss Muffet sat on her tuffet
Eating her curds and whey
Along came a spider who sat down beside her
And frightened Miss Muffet away!

Jack and Jill went up the hill
To fetch a pail of water
Jack fell down and broke his crown
And Jill came tumbling after.

FIGURE 4.4 Example of attribute naming by Britanny

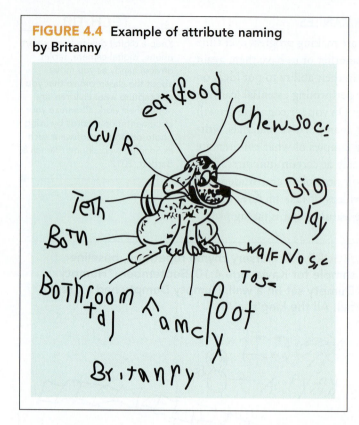

ATTRIBUTE NAMING

Attribute naming is an assessment strategy for comparing work samples of older preschool and kindergarten children over time. Place a picture of something familiar (e.g., house, garden, person) in the middle of an easel page or on the whiteboard. In a large or small group, have children see how many words they can generate that relate to the picture. Write each of the words they suggest and, as appropriate, ask for help from the children in spelling the familiar words. After children have watched you conduct the activity a number of times, implement the activity with a picture of Clifford as the stimulus (you can download it from the Internet). Remove what has been produced and tell the children, "I want to see if you can remember any of these words and can write some of them." Provide 8½″ × 11″ pieces of paper with Clifford centered in the middle and ask them to write all the words they can think of themselves, spelling the words as well as they can (see Figure 4.4). Encourage children who are able to write a sentence or two to write a story about Clifford. Use this same stimulus several more times over the span of a year to see if children are moving forward in the number of words they write and whether they are beginning to spell some words conventionally.

In what way is a mini-conference between a teacher and a child valuable as an assessment strategy?

MINI-CONFERENCES

Brief interactions with individual children that usually take less than a few minutes can yield valuable information. For example, Ms. Korhonen wants to know if the children in her room are able to identify four geometric shapes. During center time, she asks each child to work with her for a few minutes and places a circle, square, triangle, and rectangle on the table. "Ready?" she asks and then directs the child to choose the one she names. Before going on to another child, she records on her checklist which of the shapes were identified correctly by that child and the date. On another day, she wants to assess the expressive language of each child and presents each with the same picture, saying, "Tell me about what you see in this picture," noting the quality of the child's responses. Mini-conferences are useful for quick assessments of how a child is functioning currently in any developmental domain. They allow a teacher to provide prompts and hints in gaining specific information about what a child can do independently and where further assistance is needed to increase the child's abilities. Because mini-conferences are conducted one-on-one between teacher and child, they are highly effective in addressing the cultural and language differences that are sometimes problematic in other kinds of assessment (Soderman, Gregory, & McCarty, 2005).

USING CHECKLISTS

You will find that there are many commercial checklists available to help you keep track of the various skills you want children to develop over the course of a year. For example, one of the best is the set from birth to five years of age created from Syracuse University's CNY Early Childhood Direction Center. For preschoolers and children in kindergarten, milestones are listed in movement, hand and finger skills, language, cognition, and social development. For each age group from birth to five, developmental red flags are also listed. For example, with children who are 4–5 years of age, we would be concerned if a child exhibits extremely aggressive, fearful or timid behavior, lacks self-care abilities, is unable to separate from parents, shows a significant lack of concentration, and/or shows little interest in playing with other children. These and other warning signals suggested by CNY are helpful in documenting suspected *lags* in development and communicating concerns to parents or other professionals.

Teacher-developed checklists of desired curricular outcomes are easily created and will help you determine after periodic assessments how many children at any particular time are proficient in developing the skills you want to see. To produce your own checklists, examine the important skills listed in particular domain chapters in this text. Choose desired outcomes you want to foster with the activities and experiences you are building and determine a specific period of time for assessment. For example, you may want to develop a checklist of skills in a particular domain or include a few from several domains, listing important competencies you want all children to develop over the course of the year. Each item listed should be observable (e.g., knows five colors, uses the toilet independently, writes first name, shares materials with others). Using a variety of assessment strategies already described, make a check mark or insert a date when each child has satisfactorily demonstrated the skill; leave it blank for the next marking if the child has not yet done so. Keep a folder on each child in which to store all assessment data. This knowledge should help you shape future instruction or provide additional support to particular children. For example, if your curriculum guide and checklists include the cognitive milestone that a child can correctly name at least six colors or a language milestone that a child is using pronouns correctly, and you find you don't really know which children have these skills, you will want to create an appropriate assessment to find out and record the information.

■■ TRY IT YOURSELF

Imagine that you are interested in how children are progressing in their ability to wash their hands independently. Create a simple checklist to document children increasing their skills over time. Identify the behaviors you would look for (e.g., turns on water; puts soap on hands . . .). Use task analysis as described in Chapter 2 to help you decide what to include.

DOCUMENTING WITH DIGITAL CAMERA AND VIDEO

One of the easiest ways today to preserve both process and product over time in your classroom is to have a good quality digital camera handy. You can catch children working independently or with others and can save the results of their work to share

These children are exchanging information about dinosaurs.

with others later or to compare with future efforts. Similarly, a video camera is useful for recording how a child approaches and carries out a task early in the school year, again in the middle of the year or following direct instruction, and finally at the end of the school year after lots of practice.

Remember that you must always have parental consent before children are filmed or photographed. Most schools and centers obtain this permission as part of the intake process and include it in the forms that parents fill out when enrolling a child. Instead of just asking parents to indicate permission by a "yes" or "no" response, however, include a brief explanation of how the pictures and videos will be shared with them or for other legitimate educational purposes. Once these explanations are provided, almost all parents agree to the process. For any who are reluctant to do so, ask if they would like to meet to discuss concerns they have. Respect the right of parents to say no and be sure their children are not included in group pictures.

Videos are especially useful during fall orientation or other parent-education programs to demonstrate how expectations for academic performance might vary over the course of the school year or how development and capability change over time (e.g., "This is what you might expect from 3-year-olds in block play, with 4-year-olds, and with 5-year-olds."). If these devices are used frequently and without a lot of fanfare in the classroom, children eventually pay little attention to them, and behavior becomes "normal." It's best to simply catch children while they are working and playing rather than staging or posing a picture.

Pictures or videos can be sent home to parents or posted on the school's parent website to illustrate the kind of learning and interaction going on in the classroom, to illustrate concepts you want to highlight, and to share the developmental growth that occurs over the course of time in individual children or groups of children. The documentation can also be entered into children's portfolios or used to illustrate domain-specific concepts, skill-building, and progress in year-end evaluation reports.

SOCIOGRAMS

Caring teachers always have concerns about the social climate in their classroom and about children who seem to be isolated from the rest of the group. *Sociograms* are devices that can be used to determine and document children's perceptions of others in the classroom. We may find, for example, that boys and girls are quite separate in interacting with one another; that certain children are "stars," while some are unnoticed by anyone; or that some friendships are heavily determined by language or culture (Lemlech, 2009).

To create a basic sociogram for very young children, set up a six-column table (see Figure 4.5). In the first column, list the names of each of the children in your classroom. Interview each child individually and in as private a place as possible so that children are not privy to other children's responses. Displaying pictures of all the children in the group, ask each child: "Who is your favorite friend to

FIGURE 4.5 Basic sociogram showing children's friendship preferences

Name	First Choice	Second Choice	# of First Nomination by Others (Score 2 each)	# of Second Nomination by Others (Score 1 each)	Total Social Score
Keri	Mehan	Sophie	XXXX		8
Alex	Henry	Isla			0
Adam	Kevin	Gavin		X	1
Sophie	Mehan	Connie		XX	2
Monica	Keri	Connie		XXX	3
Kevin	Henry	Michael	XXX	XX	8
Bebe	Connie	Isla	X		2
LaShan	Kevin	Monica		X	1
Mehan	Keri	Monica	XX		4
Gavin	Michael	Kevin		XX	2
Isla	Keri	Sophie		XX	2
Connie	Bebe	Monica	XX	XX	6
Michael	Damon	Gavin	X	X	3
Damon	Kevin	Adam	X		2
Tanisha	Keri	LaShan			0
Henry	Connie	Kevin	XX		4

play with in this classroom?" Have the child point to the relevant picture. Record the child's choice in Column 2. Then ask, "If _____ were not here, who would be your *next* favorite friend to play with?" Write the child's second choice in the third column. In the fourth and fifth columns, tally the number of times each child is nominated by another child as a first choice and the number of times a child is nominated as a second choice. In column six, create a "total social score" by scoring 2 times the number of first choices and 1 times each second choice and adding them together. For example, Kevin is nominated by three other children as a first choice (3 x 2 = 6) and by two other children as a second choice (2 x 1 = 2), for a total social score of 8. Notice, also, that Alex and Tanisha are not mentioned by anyone as a first or second choice, resulting in 0 for a total social score—

Matthew is making a message for his friend Patrick.

a cause for concern and immediate planned intervention. It's obvious that Adam and LaShan need to be observed carefully to make sure that their social skills keep growing and that friendships are being maintained. Note which children need additional support in forming friendships.

ART AS AN ASSESSMENT TOOL

Art in the early childhood classroom is such a natural program component that we often fail to appreciate what it can tell us about how children are learning. We can assess children's growing competence in using tools and their ability to apply new techniques to produce art works. We can document growth in how a child depicts details, direction, size, shape, and color in what they choose to draw. We know that their cognitive perspectives of lines, circles, and shapes, as well as their visual motor integration and ability to represent abstract ideas, are linked in the early years to their emerging writing ability. Growth in a child's ability to recall mental images and events can also be documented.

Having children draw a self-portrait in the fall, again in January, and finally in late spring helps to document fine motor and cognitive growth and allows us to make comparisons from one time to another. Similarly, having children draw family portraits helps us understand more about how a child views his or her place in the family, as well as to understand who's important and not important by placement, size of the figures, and who is included or missing. For example, in Figure 4.6, we see that Emma depicts herself on the far right, her little brother in the middle, and her father at the far left. When asked where her mother is, Emma thinks for a moment and then responds, "She's working."

A sampling of the many artifacts that children produce during the school year can be dated and saved in their ongoing portfolios that will be described later in this chapter. These serve over time as illustrations of their evolving abilities to remember and produce symbols (Soderman, Gregory, & McCarty, 2005).

CHILDREN'S SELF-APPRAISAL

Although the major responsibility for the learning that goes on in any classroom is admittedly the teacher's, children should be brought into the process so that they develop increasing accountability for their own learning and become more analytical about it. A good way to do this is to involve them in the assessment process, using creative forms such as that shown in Figure 4.7 and self-appraisal checklists such as that shown in Figure 4.8. Have children who are unable to write dictate their responses to you. For those who are unable to read, you can tell them what each of the skills are, such as those listed in Figure 4.8, and then have them make a check mark (√) in the space provided or color it in. To do so, however, they must have demonstrated the skill in a mini-conference or by a work sample. Notice in Figure 4.8 that there are spaces added at the end of

FIGURE 4.6 Emma's family portrait

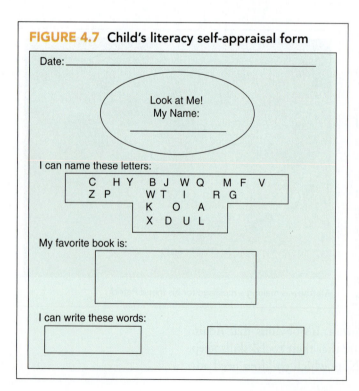

FIGURE 4.7 Child's literacy self-appraisal form

FIGURE 4.8 An early math self-appraisal checklist

MY MATH PROGRESS

NAME:_____

SKILL	OCT.	NOV.	DEC.	JAN.	FEB.	MAR.	APR.	MAY
I can count to 20.								
I can match same shapes that are different in size.								
I can identify a square, triangle, circle, and rectangle.								
I can use a nonstandard measure to see which object is longer.								
I can sort objects into three different groups.								
I can use the balance scale to find out which of two objects is heavier.								
I am able to recognize a simple pattern (e.g., long, short, long short) and extend it.								
I can draw four shapes when asked: circle, triangle, square, and rectangle.								

the checklist to add some new skills as others are achieved. Also, at the end of an assessment or self-appraisal, the teacher should always have the child choose one skill not yet obtained to work on until the next assessment.

Teachers may also create self-appraisal forms to use with children by using a simple "smiley-face" format for helping the child to document his or her perception of and attitudes about a task or situation. In Figure 4.9, the teacher wants to assess children's perceptions of snack and lunchtime. Children listen in an individual mini-conference as the teacher reads each item and then marks one of three choices: negative, neutral, or a positive face. The process generates some comments as well from the children that give their teacher additional information about the topic. When she

FIGURE 4.9 Sample of a "smiley-face" assessment format

SNACK AND LUNCH

Directions: Read each variable to the child and have him or her circle the face that most clearly matches the child's feelings about the item. Make sure the child understands the value and meaning of the three different choices (faces).

Variable	Negative Face 😞	Neutral Face 😐	Smiling Face 😊
Eating snack and lunch at school			
The taste of the food at snack and lunch			
Helping yourself at snack and lunch			
Clearing your place after snack and lunch			
Remembering to chew with your mouth closed			
Remembering to use a napkin			
Remembering to swallow what you're eating before talking with a friend			

asked Cooper how he felt about clearing his place after snack and lunch, he quickly circled the negative face. His teacher said, "Oh, not very good, huh?"

"No," he said emphatically, "'cause I eat it all at snack. At lunch, I have to scrape my lunch plate in the basket. It always goes on the floor."

"I'll see what we can do to make it easier for you to clean up when we have lunch today," said his teacher encouragingly.

DOCUMENTATION BOARDS

The well-known preschools in Reggio Emilia, Italy, primarily use teacher observation and notation to assess learning. Plenty of pictures are taken of projects in which the children participate, and learning is documented from the beginning to the end of these endeavors. The teachers post those pictures on three-sided, free-standing boards (see Figure 4.10) called *documentation boards* that can then be displayed for viewing by the children, parents, visitors, and others interested in what is being learned in the program. Teachers post brief narratives about what they believe children are learning, and they also post children's narratives about what is being learned by each picture, helping to relate learning objectives for activities as well as learning outcomes from the children's perspectives. These documentation boards have caught on in many U.S. early childhood settings, and we often see them displayed outside of classrooms in hallways or in school entryways at conference times. Family members and visitors enjoy stopping to view the colorful documentation of project activity and at the same time learn about how children's involvement and learning coordinate with intended curriculum outcomes for the program.

PORTFOLIOS AND STUDENT-LED CONFERENCES

As we have discussed, when children become involved in the assessment process, they become more invested in and analytical about their work. When they know that significant others in their lives will be looking at their work, they take increasing pride

FIGURE 4.10 Documentation board

Hector is observing that the red object is heavier than the blue one.

Peyton has found an object that is even heavier than the red one.

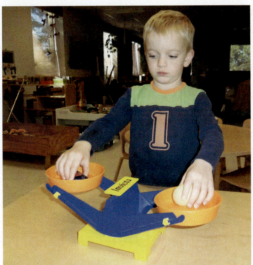

Gavin gets ready to test whether the 2 objects he has are equal in weight.

in what they are doing and are motivated to work harder at skill building. Learning to keep their work in a portfolio and then showcase it later at a planned conference for their families teaches children as young as 3 years old how to organize their work and take on more responsibility for showing how they are making progress. Most of all, this process empowers and motivates children to give greater value to their work and to the overall processes involved in their learning. It fosters creativity, respects each child's individuality, creates independent work habits, and improves children's self-esteem (Soderman & Farrell, 2008).

To implement this process, show the children in your classroom what a portfolio might look like (make up one of your own), some of the items you would like to have them include (e.g., a self-portrait, a family portrait, samples of any writing they can do, pictures of them with the friends they are making, self-appraisal checklists), and items they might like to include. Tell them on targeted days, "Today, we will be creating something for our portfolios that we will share later when your families come in. You won't be taking it home today but will be saving it for our March 19 conference. As always, do your best work." Teach children to use a date stamp to record the date on their work and have a special place somewhere in your classroom that is easily accessible for children to store their portfolios.

Once or twice a year (e.g., February and May), have children select at least five pieces of work from these individual portfolios to include in a "showcase" portfolio to share with family members. Sit with each child for a short time to help with this, and encourage the child to tell you why this particular selection would be a good piece to include. Add other pieces that you believe family members need to see, including some samples that show progress from one time to another, and tell the child why you've selected it. ("Look, here's where you wrote your name in all upper case. Here's a later one where you used both upper- and lower-case letters. That shows how you've made progress in your writing.") Have the children decorate a cover for this special grouping of work.

For the student-led conferences, work with your administrator to choose a date to have five to six families at a time come in for about half an hour for an event led by their own children. Work with children ahead of time to create invitations, clean and organize the room, select three to four activities to do with their parents to demonstrate what they are learning (e.g., do a math game, build a block city together, work a puzzle together, paint together at the easel, read the names of their classmates on a word wall). Have them choose some refreshments from several choices and select some music to play from several CDs you think would be appropriate. Help children make decorations for the tables.

On the appointed day, have each child introduce his or her family members to you (even if you've met them before) and then follow a routine that you've practiced with children in the classroom prior to the conference. Make sure that the adults take time to review the child's portfolio of work (remind them in a letter prior to the conference that you want them to focus only on evidence of the child's growth, not on what still must be learned). Thank each family for coming at the end of the scheduled time and provide a brief survey that will allow them to provide feedback to you about the value of the conference in terms of understanding their child's developing capabilities related to the program.

Identifying Diverse Learners and Children with Special Needs

It doesn't take long if you are teaching children who are between 2 and 6 years of age to conclude that they can be dramatically different from one another in the way they behave, how they interact with other children and adults, and how they respond to learning tasks. Physical, motor, and language development during these years are rapid, episodic, and highly influenced by how nurturing families are, the quality of care that children have received, and the various contexts in which children have spent time (Shephard, Kagan, & Wurtz, 1998; Kostelnik, Gregory, Soderman, & Whiren, 2011). Early childhood is a time when families and educators are most likely to notice differences in children's abilities, including developmental delays or advanced development. For example, consider Kaelyn and Connie:

Although she is one of the oldest children in the kindergarten classroom, Kaelyn is having a difficult time beginning the school year. She cries and clings to her mother at drop-off time, refuses other children's invitations to share materials or play, and rarely speaks to anyone in the classroom. A meeting with her parents yields information that is helpful: The family has moved frequently, and Kaelyn has had a variety of daytime caretakers, but none for very long. She has an older sister who is away at college and has had few playmates. Her parents suspect that her current nanny allows her to "watch more television than they consider healthy." Still, they felt they "couldn't control everything at home because of their heavy outside commitments" and admitted spending very little time with their daughter.

Connie is 3 years old and has surprised her teacher with her ability to sound out words. "She can actually read," the teacher notes. According to her parents, no one has pushed her to do so. Reportedly, she has "just always loved books and being read to." Currently, she enjoys drawing pictures and "writing messages" to her friends in the classroom (see Figure 4.11). Her parents want to know how her preschool teacher plans to preserve this "gift."

FIGURE 4.11 A message from 3-year-old Connie to her classmates about her lost stuffed animal, a pig

In addition to the natural variation that occurs in development in the early years, growing numbers of English language learners and children with special needs now make up our early childhood classrooms. Before you can begin to assess the progress of children who have difficulty, you will need to learn as much as possible about their current abilities as they enter your classroom. For children with language issues, when did they begin speaking in their primary language? How strong are their receptive and expressive vocabularies in English? For children who have other special needs, get as much information as you can from family members and other professionals about strategies likely to promote their success.

Even with a good store of basic knowledge about developmental benchmarks for young children, you will occasionally have questions about a child's developmental status that are beyond your own expertise and require observation or diagnosis by other professionals. You may receive requests from other professionals to observe a child in the classroom setting; if so, nothing should change about what usually takes place because it would affect the validity of the observation. Because intervention in the early years is so critical, you should not ignore a gut-level feeling that a situation requires more intensive support than you can provide. That should always entail obtaining a family's permission and alerting the head teacher or administrator of your program that you believe further evaluation is necessary.

Communicating with Families

Often, a family's level of satisfaction and comfort with a program (and with the teacher) are highly correlated with the manner in which the children's learning is documented and shared. Similarly, what you can gain from developing a close working relationship with families can make a distinct difference in your ability to work as effectively as possible with each child in your classroom.

One of the first and most valuable things you can share with families during an orientation at the beginning of the year is that you want to work with them as partners throughout the year in the best interest of their child. That means that you must rely on one another to share information about any events at home and in school that may affect the child's comfort levels, performance, and interactions with others. If you observe a dramatic change in a child's behavior in the classroom, alert the family about it and ask if any changes have happened at home. For example, you may notice and document that a child is exhibiting uncharacteristic sleepiness, reluctance to come into the classroom in the morning, unusual aggression toward others, or not wanting to be involved with certain children or activities. In talking with the child's family, you may learn that the family is going through a transition such as separation or divorce, that a parent is changing employment or returning to work, about changes in income resulting in financial difficulties, an illness, death of an extended family member, or new persons added to the household. Similarly, something may be taking place at school that may explain a change in the child's behavior at home. For example, a parent may call to have a conference about a child's comments at home about bullying by another child, something you would want to be aware of.

Newsletters or web messages about different aspects of the assessment process in school are helpful in letting parents know what kinds of information you collect regularly about their children, how it is used in determining instruction, and how it documents the progress children are making. See the example provided in Figure 4.12 where the teacher is inviting parents to share in the assessment process, providing helpful hints about participation, and asking for their feedback about the value of the conference for them.

NEWSLETTER/WEB READY COMMUNICATION

FIGURE 4.12 • Student-Led Conferences Coming Up

We want to share your children's successes with you and provide an opportunity for you to see evidence of the many kinds of learning that are taking place. Next week, the school is planning to hold its first annual student-led conferences where children will share their Showcase Portfolios. Your children have been saving work samples from the beginning of the year and are excited about showing you how much they have grown.

We will be sending home a scheduled time for you and your child to participate along with four other families for about half an hour in the classroom. If that is not a convenient time, please let us know and we will reschedule for earlier or later in the day.

The portfolio that you will view contains dated work samples that represent your child's best personal effort at this time. Please be very positive when viewing the contents, centering on how much growth has taken place and noticing details in the work that show confirmation of learning. Ask questions that let your child know that you are interested and want to learn more: "Which piece is your favorite?" "Why?" "How did you learn to do this?" "What was hard about doing this?"

Following your conference, you will find a brief survey to fill out before you leave. Please take a few minutes to let us know if you'd like to attend this kind of learning celebration with your child again in the future. We'd like to know if it gave you enough information about how your child is learning and if you and your child enjoyed the experience. We'll look forward to seeing you and your child together for this very special event.

4 Applying What You've Learned

Drawing on what you have learned about observing and documenting children's learning, apply that knowledge by carrying out the following:

1. **Purposeful Assessment.** Reflect on the four purposes for assessment described at the beginning of the chapter. Which of these do you believe is most important for the classroom teacher?

2. **Developmental Considerations.** Create a developmental checklist of 10 observable skills you would like all children in your classroom to master by the end of the year (e.g., zip their coats; wash hands without a reminder after using the bathroom). Meet with five children to go over the list with them and have them document how many of the skills they already have and one that they will be working on for the next assessment.

3. **Construct a Documentation Board.** Create a documentation board about a structured activity carried out with the children. On the board, include a stated objective for the activity and photos documenting children's participation. Display narratives from the children and from you alongside the pictures to document what they were learning. Place the board in a prominent place where families and others can view it.

4. **Family Matters.** Practice making an ecomap. Interview two different families, one with a child who is doing extremely well in the classroom and one who clearly needs additional support. What can you learn about these children in your discussion with their families that you would not know without using this process? In what way is the information helpful in working with each of these children in the classroom?

References

Copple, C., & Bredekamp, S. (2010). *Developing appropriate practice in early childhood programs: Serving children from birth through age 8* (3rd ed.). Washington, D.C.: National Association for the Education of Young Children.

Early Childhood Direction Center. (2006). *Developmental checklists birth to five.* Syracuse, NY: Syracuse University.

Gestwicki, C. (2010). *Developmentally appropriate practice* (4th ed.). Belmont, CA: Wadsworth.

Johnson, J. (2008). *Early childhood special education.* Australia: Thomson Delmar Learning.

Kostelnik, M. J., & Grady, M. L. (2009). *Getting it right from the start.* Thousand Oaks, CA: Corwin.

Kostelnik, M. J., Gregory, K., Soderman, A. K., & Whiren, A. P. (2011). *Guiding children's social development and learning.* Belmont, CA: Wadsworth.

Lemlech, J. K. (2009). *Curriculum and instructional methods for elementary and middle school* (7th ed.). Upper Saddle River, NJ: Pearson.

MacLean, D. (May 28, 2009). Learning to see . . . seeing to learn: The role of observation in early childhood development. ExchangeEveryDay@ccie.com.

McAfree, O., & Leong, D. J. (2010). *Assessing and guiding young children's development and learning* (5th ed.). Upper Saddle River, NJ: Pearson.

Parnell, W., & Bartlett, J. (May 2012). How smartphones and tablets are changing documentation in preschool and primary classrooms. *Young Children, 67*(3), 50–59.

Shephard, L., Kagan, S. L., & Wurtz, E. (1998). *Principles and recommendations for early childhood assessments.* Washington, D.C.: National Education Goals Panel. Online: www.negp.gov/reports/prinrec.pdf.

Soderman, A. K., & Farrell, P. (2007). *Creating literacy-rich preschools and kindergartens.* Upper Saddle River: Pearson.

Soderman, A. K., Gregory, K. M., & McCarty, L. T. (2005). *Scaffolding emergent literacy: A child-centered approach for preschool through grade 5.* Upper Saddle River: Pearson.

Wortham, S. C. (2010). *Early childhood curriculum: Developmental bases for learning and teaching* (5th ed.). Upper Saddle River: Pearson.

Roadmaps to Success: Lesson Plans as Teaching Tools

Child's Name	Make Random Cuts with Scissors on Paper	Cuts Straight Lines	Cuts Curved Lines
Jorge	X		
Isobel	X	x	x
Helen	x	x	
Emma	x		
Matilda	Held scissors in the right and paper in the left. Each time she closed the scissors on the paper, it closed horizontally and did not cut. When I held the paper firmly for her, she snipped about ¼". When she opened and closed the scissors independently, she did not make cuts.		
Jason	x	x	x

Interpretation: Jorge, Emma, and Matilda need additional practice with cutting; Helen may be ready to cut curved lines; Isobel and Jason are ready for more challenging cutting activities.

The teachers in the class for older preschoolers at the Hillcrest Child Development Center looked forward to Wednesdays. That was when the center, for two hours over naptime, provided adult coverage for the children so the head teacher, assistant teacher, and classroom aide could plan for the coming weeks. To support their planning, the teachers referred to observations they had made of the children as well as the early learning guidelines for children ages 3 to 5 established by their state. Their lesson plans for the next week were influenced by the following:

- Several children noticed a bird building a nest in the gutter outside the classroom window. They had many questions about birds and were intrigued by what the bird was doing.
- State guidelines say that children need daily access to planned activities that cover six domains of development and learning: aesthetics, cognitive, emotional, language, physical, and social.
- Jorge, Matilda, and Emma struggled with using the scissors at the art table last week.
- Children seem to be ignoring the puzzle table. Hardly anyone visited that area of the classroom during the past several days.
- At least half of the children in the class are printing letters in some form—on their artwork, on signs in the block area, and on labels for projects.

Based on information like this, as well as their knowledge of child development and learning, the teachers created a variety of lesson plans for the children in their class.

Just like these teachers, soon you will be planning activities and experiences for young children. Effective planning is key to creating developmentally appropriate lessons. Such lessons do more than simply keep children busy or entertained. They enhance children's learning by building on what children already know and by addressing gaps in their understanding. It takes skill and practice to create effective plans. This chapter will give you the background you need to get started.

Let's begin by considering the whole notion of why planning is important.

The Role of Planning

As a teacher, you need to know *why* you are teaching, *what* you are teaching, and *how* you are going to teach (Seefeldt, Castle, & Falconer, 2009). You probably would not start out on a thousand-mile trip without knowing where you were going, how you would travel, what resources you would need, and what adjustments might be necessary for those traveling with you. You would plan in advance so that you would most likely be successful in reaching your destination. Similarly, planning for children's learning will help you to do the following:

- Organize your thinking and actions
- Gather needed materials and equipment in advance
- Determine when and where a learning experience will occur
- Connect specific teaching strategies to program goals and state standards
- Consider the needs of the "whole child"
- Adjust for individual differences among children in ability, culture, and interests
- Communicate with colleagues about teaching goals and strategies
- Evaluate child learning and your own teaching

Effective planning leads to intentional instruction, which means that teachers act with specific goals in mind for children's learning (Epstein, 2009). Such instruction benefits children and conveys a message to families and administrators that your teaching is educationally productive. Through the planning process, you will gain useful information about individual children, materials, and teaching methods that work well with your group of children. This information will assist you in developing future activities.

What do you think the teacher had in mind when he put the wide brushes and lots of paint out on the table?

Ineffective planning leads to poor educational outcomes. It often results in disorderly classrooms and disengaged children who dabble in this or that, wander from one material to another, or behave inappropriately because goals and expectations are unclear or inappropriate. Often, children are either bored or overwhelmed in such an environment. Ultimately, poor planning leads to poor programs for children and dissatisfied families and supervisors.

FUNDAMENTALS OF PLANNING

What needs to be considered when developing dynamic lesson plans? In short, everything you know about child development and learning as well as instructional strategies will come together as you plan.

CHILD DEVELOPMENT

First, the plan should reflect your understanding of *child development*, the experiences and culture of the specific group of children, and the interests and abilities of individual children at a specific point in time. Plans written at a central headquarters or that appear on the Internet or in an activity book may be technically correct and useful as a resource, but they cannot possibly take into account the specific children in your group and their previous experiences. You must gather information about your own group of children by asking the following questions:

Yes, you have to look up content for all domains.

- What do the children already know and what can they do now?
- Are there individuals who have not had the opportunities to learn specific information (e.g., knowing the names of colors) or specific skills (e.g., how to cut with scissors)?
- Will the children's cultural, familial, or linguistic background influence what is meaningful to them? (For example, children who live in rural areas may have no understanding of public transportation vehicles but may have a lot of information related to local agriculture.)

CONTENT

Second, you must know the *content* of what is being taught. Various disciplines such as the arts, language and literacy, mathematics, science, health and fitness, and social studies all have basic **content** for children to learn. Content is also associated with each developmental **domain** (aesthetic, affective, cognitive, language, social, and physical) that make up the whole child. See Figure 5.1 for examples of content related to cognition and mathematics as well as content related to the social domain that are suitable for children ages 3 through 6.

GOALS

Third, the plan should contribute to specific **goals**. Sources of these goals are state **standards**, Head Start performance standards, local program or school district goals, and consideration of developmentally appropriate goals families have for their children. Functional goals that are developed for children with special needs in an individualized education plan (IEP) must also be considered (see Chapter 1). The goals listed in Chapters 9 through 15 are based on national

content The terms (vocabulary) and facts relevant to the lesson.

domains The six curricular areas related to child development and learning: aesthetics, affective, cognitive, language, physical, and social.

goal Desirable behaviors relevant to children's development and learning within a domain.

standard Something that has been established by experts as a measure of quality. A criterion or yardstick.

FIGURE 5.1 Sample mathematic and social content appropriate for young children

Sample Mathematical Content

1. Number refers to how many of something there are.
2. People count to find out how many things there are.
3. When counting, each thing is counted only once.
4. The number of objects is determined by how many objects there are, not by what they are, how they are arranged, or the order in which they are counted.
5. Numbers occur in an order that is always the same.

Sample Social Content

1. People are like other people in some ways.
2. People are different from other people in some ways.
3. People have thoughts and feelings that can be expressed to others.
4. People make choices.
5. People have relationships with other people.

---

standards developed by experienced leaders in many disciplines and can be used as a starting point.

PROCEDURES

Fourth, the plan should incorporate *strategies* for teaching that are *appropriate for the age* of the children, that are flexible enough to meet individual needs, and that will enable you to document the learning that takes place. For example, demonstrating what is meant when you ask a child "*to draw*", "*to circle*", or "*to place*" as you speak is a strategy that is very helpful for a dual language learner. **Procedures** include all that you plan to say and do when you implement an activity.

procedures A step-by-step description of how to implement an activity. Procedures may include multiple teaching strategies.

MATERIALS

Fifth, the plan must list all of the **materials** needed to carry it out, when and where it will be implemented, and any particular needs for clean-up. The plan should also include strategies such as how many can participate, how children will be attracted to or invited into the activity, and how they will transition to the next activity so that children are successful socially. In addition, any concerns for safety or adaptations for children with special needs should be identified.

materials All necessary props or equipment needed for an activity.

ASSESSMENT

Finally, every plan should have provisions to *assess child learning* and a plan for recording progress toward goals. Plans should also include provisions to assess the effectiveness of the plan as a whole and to identify areas where improvements could be made. See the summary of the fundamentals of planning in Figure 5.2.

Planning is a mental process, and a lesson plan is the written record of that process. If it is written step by step, then you can be assured that all of the details are there from start to finish, potential difficulties have been considered in advance, and you can approach each learning activity with greater confidence and security (Machado & Botnarescue, 2008). Written plans are a record of what you have done

FIGURE 5.2 Summary of fundamentals of planning

Development	Specific to your group of children and each child
	Culturally responsive
	Adapted to individual needs and interests
Content	Accurate information to convey to children in all areas of knowledge: subject matter
Goals and objectives	General: This text, state standards, program standards
	Individual: Based on assessed needs and targeting the particular needs of each child
Strategies	Varied strategies as discussed in this text
	Clear directions and demonstrations
Materials and management tools	Everything you and the children will need for success
	Resources for clean-up
	Invitation to and transition out of the activity
	Any safety needs and resources
Assessment	Documentation of successes for each child
	Plan to assess your own implementation and planning

with the children and can be reused at another time or by another member of the teaching team. At first, it will take you much time and thought to complete a single lesson plan. However, repeatedly going through the writing process of each part of the lesson plan gradually develops a habit of thinking more like that of experienced teachers. In time, you will write plans more quickly and in a shorter format. No matter their form, most programs for young children require some form of written planning.

Parts of the Plan

An activity plan, like the one shown in Figure 5.3, is useful for lesson plans in all disciplines and developmental domains, whether used for one child, a small group, or all the children at once. Formats may vary somewhat based on group size or other considerations, though all plans must consider these dimensions. Keep in mind that beginning teachers write out the details as they go through the process of learning how to plan; experienced teachers write shorter plans for themselves and for assistants.

Next we will consider each part of the plan in more detail.

DOMAIN

All of the parts of the plan make important contributions to your ability to prepare adequately for teaching. Even though multiple aspects of development are addressed in any learning experience, effective novice teachers focus on one developmental domain at a time. In this text, we refer to the six domains mentioned earlier. A *domain* is a curricular area that has one overarching purpose. You will learn about these in much greater detail in later chapters. For now, note that every child should encounter planned activities from each domain daily to address all aspects of whole-child learning. Each domain is listed in Figure 5.4 with its ultimate purpose.

FIGURE 5.3 **Activity plan format**

Activity Name The title of the activity.

Domain One of the six curricular domains: aesthetics, affective, cognitive, language, physical, and social.

Goal Goals are listed in Chapters 9 through 15 or from state or program guidelines. These goals identify desirable behaviors relevant to children's development and learning within the domain.

Objectives A list of specific instructional objectives leading to the goal and tailored to meet the needs of the children involved.

Content What will be addressed in the activity; identifies the terms (vocabulary) and facts relevant to the lesson.

Materials A list of all necessary props or equipment.

Procedures A step-by-step description of how to implement the activity. Procedures may include multiple teaching strategies.

Simplifications Ideas for reducing the complexity or abstractness of the activity. Ways to adapt the activity for children who have less experience or special needs.

Extensions Ideas for making the activity more challenging as children demonstrate the desire and ability to expand their knowledge and skills.

Evaluation Ways to assess children's learning and the teaching methods used.

Source: Kostelnik, M. J., Soderman, A. K., & Whiren, A. P. (2011). *Developmentally appropriate curriculum: Best practices in early childhood education* 5th ed., © 2011, p. 76. Reprinted and electronically reproduced by permission of Pearson Education, Inc., Upper Saddle River, New Jersey.

FIGURE 5.4 **General purpose of each domain**

Domain	The Purpose Is for Children to:
Aesthetic	Become aware of beauty in nature and art, to appreciate and participate in creative arts to achieve personally meaningful ends (p. 249).
Affective	See themselves as valued and capable (p. 294).
Cognitive	Acquire, apply, adapt, integrate, and evaluate knowledge as they construct new or expanded concepts: Math and Science (p. 324).
Language	Communicate their ideas and feelings and accurately interpret the communications they receive (p. 351).
Physical	Develop confidence and competence in the control and movement of their bodies and develop the attitudes, knowledge, skills, and practices that lead to maintaining, respecting, and protecting their bodies (p. 382).
Social	Develop social awareness and social competence in a culturally diverse, democratic society in an interdependent world (p. 414).

Source: Based on Kostelnik, Soderman, & Whiren, 2011.

In writing your plan, simply designate the domain by name and possibly a specific area such as "Cognitive: Math."

ACTIVITY NAME

Each activity should have a title that communicates the main idea accurately. This will make the activity easier to reference in the future and will communicate clearly to anyone else using the plan (e.g., assistant or volunteer). Avoid cute names or those that might be confusing. For example, *Sliding Fingers* does not communicate as much accurate information as *Finger Painting*. *Trash Recycling* is a better name for the activity of carrying materials to the recycle container than *Going Green*.

GOAL

A goal identifies desirable behaviors relevant to children's development and learning. Goals indicate the purpose of your specific plan and are listed in Chapters 9 through 15 by domain. You will pick one goal for each lesson plan. All the goals are based on national standards for the domain of learning.

OBJECTIVES

objectives Specific statements of desired child behaviors leading to individual goals and tailored to meet the needs of the children involved.

Objectives are the specific learning behaviors children might logically display in relation to a goal. They state precisely what children are expected to do and how they display knowledge or skill. Meaningful objectives have two parts: (1) the *conditions* under which learning will occur, and (2) a clear statement of the *behavior* children will exhibit as a function of their learning.

> *Given small pieces of construction paper and scissors and a demonstration*, the child will hold both paper and scissors correctly and snip the edges of the paper.

CONDITIONS

The materials and educational supports are stated in the conditions. Generally they start with the word *given* and are placed at the beginning of the sentence. Here is an example for a plan from the cognitive domain where children order by size:

> *Given four yellow pencils that are the same except for length, the child will....*

Notice how, in the next example, the statement of conditions changes though the task of getting something in order is the same.

> *Given six or more boxes that can be nested, the child will...*

See how the conditions are quite different to contribute to a goal in the affective domain:

> *Given a partner, a mirror, and adult coaching on comparing physical characteristics, the child will...*

The conditions may change from one objective to the next, even in the same lesson plan. However, in some simple plans, the conditions may be the same for a sequence of related behaviors.

BEHAVIORS

Objectives are characterized by actions that are observable. These actions signify that the objective is achieved. Sample behaviors are in bold in the following list:

The child will:

Order the pencils *by length.*
Give a reason *why each pencil is placed where it is.*
Insert *a new pencil into the sequence.*
State a reason *why it was inserted where it was.*

The child will:

Identify *at least two physical characteristics that are held in common.*
State *characteristics that are different from the partner's.*
Discuss *how people are alike and how each person is unique.*

FIGURE 5.5 Sample action words

Action Category	Examples
Demonstrating knowledge without speaking	Point, find, place, put, order, sort, organize, sequence, choose, select, measure, demonstrate, discriminate, separate, explore, touch, carry, circle, etc.
Demonstrating skills and knowledge without speaking	Paint, draw, cut, sew, screw, hammer, button, write, record, run, hop, jump, throw, show, build, make, pretend, cooperate, construct, etc.
Demonstrating abilities verbally	Compare, name, describe, discuss, explain, evaluate, predict, tell, narrate, count, read, sing, recite, converse, ask, give directions, list, count, etc.

Behaviors are seen or heard. They are designated through action words. A sample of action words is listed in Figure 5.5. All of the objectives relate to the same goal. They are listed in logical order from the simplest to the most complex. Sometimes, in basic activities, the objectives are listed in the order in which they would occur. A plan to teach young children how to wash their hands thoroughly would logically list wetting, soaping, scrubbing, rinsing, and drying in sequence, although one is not more difficult than the other.

COMPARING GOALS AND OBJECTIVES

Goals and objectives together give clear direction for an activity. How are they different?

- Goals come from an outside source (this text, program goals, state standards). *You do not make them up!* You do write out the objectives for activities that will contribute to the goal, using the format already discussed.
- Goals are broader in scope and will require many activities over a long period of time to accomplish. Objectives are very specific and you will be able to see if the child accomplishes the objective while the activity is in progress.
- Some goals have multiple parts that are related to a class of activities such as being able to carry out challenging cognitive tasks such as *sort, classify, and order.* Objectives are organized in a sequence of actions that will contribute to one task at a time.
- You will use some of the same or similar objectives more than once with different materials. For example, the specific objectives for classifying materials are the same regardless of the materials to be classified. Goals and objectives are used more than once to achieve desirable ends.

In Figure 5.6, you can see how the goals are met through implementing the objectives. Notice in Figure 5.7 that two activities using the same goal in the aesthetics domain and focused on the same part of the goal are provided so that you can see how the objectives change dramatically, while the goal does not. Usually materials are not specified in the objectives; however, they are in this case to add clarity.

FIGURE 5.6 Example of objectives meeting a goal

Affective Domain

Goal: Children will begin and pursue a task independently.

Objectives: Given verbal directions and a sequence of photographic reminders to remove (or put on) outerwear and to place it into the appropriate spot, the child will:

1. Take off hat and mittens and place them where they belong.
2. Unbutton or unzip the coat and hang it up.
3. Remove boots and place them where they belong.
4. Remove snow pants, if worn, and hang them up.

FIGURE 5.7 Sample different objectives meeting the same goal

Aesthetic Domain

Goal: Children will use a variety of materials, tools, techniques, and processes in the arts (**visual art**, music, dance, and drama). (The bold words indicate the target portions of this goal.)

Objectives: Given suitable materials (large piece of manila paper, scissors, and assorted smaller pieces of colored construction paper, a paste brush, and school paste) and a demonstration, the child will:

1. Cut or tear small pieces of colored paper to be used.
2. Dab a small amount of paste onto the paste brush.
3. Spread the paste on a selected piece of paper.
4. Turn the paper over and press down on it to adhere it to the manila paper.
5. Continue to paste small pieces on the larger piece to form a collage.

Goal: Children will use a variety of materials, tools, techniques, and processes in the arts (**visual art**, music, dance, and drama).

Objectives: Given the materials (aprons, trays, wet sponge, finger paint, spoons, and a 12 × 18 piece of paper) the children will:

1. Put on an apron and roll up sleeves.
2. Dampen the tray with a wet sponge so that there is moisture all over.
3. Spoon finger paint onto the tray.
4. Spread the finger paint across the tray using fingers, palms, or elbows.
5. Place a clean piece of paper on the painted tray and press down on it to make a print.

COMMON MISTAKES BEGINNERS MAKE

When writing lesson plans for the first few times, plan deliberately to avoid common errors, some of which are identified in Table 5.1. In writing good objectives, you must focus on the children, think through what they will need to do to perform the task, use action words for the objectives so that you will know if each child can do it, and focus on performance. Sometimes, young children can do something and do not

TABLE 5.1 • Common Errors in Writing Objectives and Corrections

ERROR TYPE	SAMPLE OBJECTIVE ERROR	CORRECTED OBJECTIVE
Focusing on what you will do rather than on what you want the child to do	Give the children crayons and paper.	Given crayons and paper and instruction, the child will draw on the paper.
Failing to think through all of the specific objectives necessary to achieve the targeted behavior	Given colored slips of construction paper, the child will name all eight colors (red, yellow, blue, green, orange, purple, black, and brown). (If you started with this, you are testing children before the instruction.)	Given colored slips of construction paper, the child will: • Hear the name of each color as the slip is held up. • Repeat the name of the color. • Point to a specific colored slip that is placed among several other hues when asked to do so. • Find a colored slip that is **not** the color named when asked to do so. • Tell the name of the color of a colored slip when asked to do so.
Using verbs for the behavior such as "to be creative" "to learn" "to know" None of these verbs describe what the child can do that you can see or hear.	Given rhythm instruments, the child will be creative. To know the states of water. To learn to be friends.	Given rhythm instruments and the request to listen while playing, the child will: • Test the sound of each instrument. • Select one. • Strike the instrument in a steady beat.
Using the phrase "be able to" in front of the action portion of the objective	Given appropriate instruction, the child will be able to jump from a standing position.	Given appropriate instruction, the child will jump from a standing position.

choose to do so. You will not be able to assess their learning unless you actually see or hear a target behavior.

CONTENT

The content of the plan is the information that the activity will address. **Terms** are the vocabulary that is used for activity-related objects and events. For example, *pitch* is how high or low a musical sound is; *volume* is how loud or soft the music is. Children acquire new terms as a function of the activity. **Facts** are something known to exist or to have happened. An example is that people match or reproduce musical tones using their voices or instruments. Another is that people all over the world play instruments and make music.

The content you select determines what you tell children to do and the explanations and demonstrations you give. Teachers made the following statements reflecting content to different children:

"A line is like a dot that takes a walk. It can change directions and move across the page and is still a line. Sometimes the line is curved or zigzag."

"A contour line is a mark around the edge of a shape. Sometimes it makes a ridge."

"Toy cars make lines when the wheels have paint on them."

"A line may be thick or thin. Lines are made by the edges of a shape."

Look at Figure 5.8 and determine which statement of content is best related to this child's drawing.

terms The vocabulary that is used for activity-related objects and events.

facts Something known to exist or to have happened.

FIGURE 5.8 Drawings reflecting different content related to lines

Accurate content is essential to good planning. You must research the terms and facts carefully and write them so that anyone else can understand them. We recommend including at least three terms, facts, or some of both for each lesson plan.

MATERIALS

Each plan includes all of the materials you will need to set up the activity, implement it with the children, and clean up afterwards. This list must be detailed and include necessary quantities for each item. You or someone else can quickly assemble the materials and arrange them appealingly at the beginning of your day. For example, if you plan to ask children to look at books and then tell a partner what the book is about, you will need several more picture books than there are children, as well as tubs to carry the books to the group area. Mrs. Clyde, who did this reading activity on a daily basis, had laminated pictures of lips for the children who would read and ears for the children who would listen. The children would trade the pictures when their role in the activity changed, which was also

All materials in the early childhood classroom can be used in planned learning, including lunch.

helpful in guiding appropriate behavior. Clean-up materials such as a broom and dustpan in the sand area, mop or sponge for the water play activity, or newspapers to cover tables when paints are used are examples of materials essential for success of the activity and must be included. Test runs with the materials will aid you in identifying potential weaknesses in the plan.

■■ TRY IT YOURSELF

Use the format suggested here to practice writing objectives. Include a simple list of materials that you would use. Making a list of the materials can help you think through the objectives. Give both parts of the objectives, the conditions, and the behaviors or what you want to see or hear the children do. One is done for you.

> *Goal:* Identify body parts by name and location.
>
> *Materials:* Only your own body
>
> *Objectives:* Given a demonstration where each body part is pointed to and moved, the child will:
>
> **1.** Observe the action, hear the name.
>
> **2.** Imitate the action and repeat the name.
>
> **3.** Given the direction to move a body part, the child will move it without additional cues.
>
> *Goal:* Care for the environments in which they live (including cleaning and taking care of own things in the classroom).
>
> *Goal:* Solve quantitative problems, such as counting objects in a set.
>
> *Goal:* Listen and view for pleasure.

PROCEDURES

The procedures are a step-by-step plan of what you say and what you do in carrying out the plan. Each objective must have procedures to implement it. You will use what you know about the children and how they learn in writing procedures. The instructional strategies outlined in Chapter 2 are all appropriate for young children. You must select the strategies best suited to the activity and to your group of children for each plan you write. The procedures also are used to convey the content. Children will not learn the new terms unless you use them. Children will not understand the facts unless they experience them or you explain them. Keep in mind that the instruction aspect precedes the assessment phase and avoids a series of questions for which the child as yet has no information with which to answer. The easiest way to write the procedures is in a stepwise

What did this teacher say to this child that would enable him to play the game?

fashion corresponding to the objectives, one at a time. Keep in mind that if you want children to point to something, you have to ask them to do it. You will find it helpful to write out both what you say (sample scripts) and what you will do (short descriptions of your behavior) for each objective. The procedures also contain an invitation to the activity (display, demonstration, or oral invitation) at the beginning and a transition statement at the end ("Tell me where you are going next." or "Wash your hands and join the others in the group area.").

You will make *assumptions* about what the group as a whole can do as well as what individual children can do. They are based on your observations and knowledge of development. We use them to gauge our teaching as we try to build new learning on the old. Sometimes, it is helpful to write out the specific skills that children need in order to do a particular activity. Inevitably there are some children who can't do what we have assumed they could and others who can do more and become restless and bored. Therefore, each plan has simplifications and extensions.

SIMPLIFICATIONS

simplifications Ideas for reducing the complexity or abstractness of an activity. Ways to adapt an activity for children with less experience or with special needs.

Simplifications are ways to modify the activity if the objectives identified in the plan are too advanced or too complex for some children to navigate. There are several reasons why you might need this:

- New children added to your group have not had the opportunities to learn skills and information that the ongoing children have acquired earlier.
- Younger children or less experienced children may need the repetition of prerequisite knowledge or skills.
- Children with special needs often can participate in a group of more typically developing children if modifications are planned in advance.
- Your teaching will be easier on those occasions when you assume the children can do something that they can't or know something that they don't. You will have planned a fall-back strategy.

Simplifications are of different types. Probably the easiest one to do is to change the amount of materials. For example, if you want children to put materials in order from heaviest to lightest, it is easier to do three than six. Another variation of adjusting the materials is to use different ones. For example, if you want children to discriminate red from other hues, it is easier when the comparisons are purple, brown, and green than when the comparisons are blush pink, bright pink, and burgundy. In the physical domain, it is easier to jump off a block or a step than to jump forward from a standing position.

Occasionally the content should be adjusted. The child might have the skill to do something but does not have the information. For example, a child might know how to paste, but not know which adhesive to use to make wood or cardboard stick.

Increasing the number of cues also makes a task easier. A cue increases the information provided to a child. It can be verbal: "Bend your knees when you jump"; it can be a gesture: using finger actions in a song; or it can be something physical, as in the following instance: When one teacher drew the letters of the child's name and asked the child to copy it, she found that the child did not know where to start. Her simplification was to put a big dot at the starting point and well-spaced light lines that the child could follow to form the letters. Once he could do that, the dots and dashes were no longer necessary.

Occasionally a shift in domain is necessary, especially for the youngest children. If a youngster has not learned how to unbutton or button (a physical coordination skill), that skill must be taught before the goal of independence in putting on or taking off clothing would be relevant (see Figure 5.6 for objectives). All plans should have at least one simplification.

EXTENSIONS

Extensions provide ideas for making the lesson more challenging. Keeping children who achieve all of the objectives engaged and interested is desirable. Just as there are 4-year-olds who enter programs unable to button their coats, there are others under 3 who can do so independently.

> **extensions** Ideas for making an activity more challenging as children demonstrate the desire and ability to expand their knowledge and skills.

You will need to think through the logical steps for your specific activity. A few strategies for extensions are suggested here:

- Increasing the amount of materials children work on at a time.
- Selecting alternative, often more abstract, materials and having them ready, such as using a pencil mark to tally the amount of something instead of an object counter.
- Adjusting content (moving from rote counting to counting objects).
- Providing information in greater depth such as providing detailed information about the illustrations in an information book rather than just naming the objects.
- Decreasing the number of cues provided. (It is more challenging for children to put together puzzles in which the shapes of the pieces are similar than if the pieces vary in both color and shape.)
- Increasing the number of alternatives for social problem solving from two that you might offer to several that nearby children could offer.
- Shifting domains but remaining with the same materials (rarely, used only as it will contribute to the success of the original goal). An example might be explaining, in an activity whose original purpose was an exploration of paints, how to generate new hues from the primary colors (creating orange from yellow and red) and why it works.

All of these strategies, and others, enable children to learn and grow in accordance with their needs and talents. Using advanced planning, you will be more likely to develop those strategies most suited to the task and the children. All plans should have at least one extension.

EVALUATING THE LESSON

Effective teachers reflect—that is, make an evaluation—on what they have done and think about what alternatives might be better. You must consider the quality of the

> **evaluation** Ways to assess children's learning and the teaching methods used.

plan (methods, content) as well as the appropriateness of the implementation. In addition, you must note which children dabbled with the materials, which ones performed which objectives, which were fully engaged and learning, and which children needed the simplifications or extensions. Using your observations and reflections and an organized approach for collecting information will enhance your learning while improving outcomes for children. Most important, the evaluation provides ideas for the future. What would you change if you repeated this plan? How can you use what you learned about the children?

Writing three or four questions in advance will help you to focus on specific issues to improve your own teaching as well as assess outcomes for children.

How would you plan to evaluate this physical experience?

You will answer some, members of the teaching team might answer others, and children might contribute as well. Daily focused evaluation where all contribute will keep your program dynamic and communal. Varying the questions from day to day and from one plan to another will provide you with the information you need. Information may be gathered through observations, anecdotal records, performance checklists, rating scales, samples of children's work, participation charts, and children's assessments of their work or progress. All of these tools were discussed earlier in Chapter 4. Some sample evaluation questions are listed in Figure 5.9.

FIGURE 5.9 Sample evaluation questions

Children's Interest and Participation

- What did I do to create interest in the activity?
- Which children showed interest but did not participate?
- Who engaged in the activity fully?
- How long did each child stay in the activity?

Children's Learning

- Which children met which objectives?
- Was the level of the activity appropriate for the children who participated? Did they have the necessary prerequisite skills and information to do the activity?
- Were the simplifications and extensions useful? If not, why not?
- What did the children do or say that indicated that they were learning? Were curious? Were interested? Were excited?
- What indicators did I notice that this activity was developmentally appropriate?
- Did I notice something to indicate interests, dispositions, information gaps, or skills that require future attention?
- What curriculum standards or IEP goals need further attention and what did I observe to make this conclusion?

Teaching Effectiveness

- How did my planning (or lack of it) contribute to children's success (or lack of it)?

  Sequence of objectives

  Completeness of materials, material suitability

  Comprehensive procedures including inviting children into the action and helping them to transition to other activities

  Adequacy of the plan for assessment of child performance

- Was the activity carried out as planned? What changes were made? Why? Did the changes contribute to children's success and learning? Why or why not?
- Was the implementation smooth? Did I provide sufficient support and guidance to children while encouraging their independence?
- How well did this activity meet the special needs of children? Were all adequately challenged? Was everyone successful to some extent?
- If I were to do this again, what would I change, if anything, and why?
- What did I learn from this activity? Planning phase? Implementing phase? Evaluation phase?

Putting All the Parts of the Lesson Plan Together

All parts of the plan must be congruent with each other, meaning they all fit together. Every part must relate to and support the other parts. For example, in building a plan to have children become more skillful in using scissors, the plan may contain the following: If the goal focuses on tool use, then objectives might be to use scissors to cut a straight line, a curved line, and a zigzagged line. The words or terms *straight, curved, zigzag,* and *line* should appear in the terms sections. Medium-weight paper that is no larger than 5 × 8 with those kinds of lines on them would be listed in materials along with the scissors. Additionally, the procedures should have specific directions that use those words that would aid the children in carrying out the activity. For example, you might demonstrate how to hold the paper and how to move both paper and scissors so that the line is followed. "Cut all the way to the point of the zigzag line" would be an appropriate direction, as would, "Turn the paper sharply when you get to the point." A simplification would likely be helping children to grasp the scissors correctly and hold the paper ready to snip a fringe. An extension might be to cut out a complex shape that has straight, curved, and zigzag lines or sharp points. The evaluation of the plan would be whether or not the children were able to use the scissors to cut on various lines. Paying attention to the congruence of the plan adds substance and provides a stronger educational message to the children.

Care must be taken to avoid straying from the goals and objectives in all parts of the plan. For example, directing children to name the color of the paper as a part of the plan is irrelevant. You may respond to any comment a child makes during the implementation, however. Tearing the paper is not a good simplification because it does not relate to the use of a tool, but shifting to simply cutting a fringe along the edge of the paper would be. Cleaning up, pasting the cut strips, and counting the cut pieces are not appropriate extensions of this activity because they do not pertain to the goal of tool use. A more appropriate extension might be to cut on tracing paper (light weight) or index cards (heavier weight); another alternative would be to cut a complex shape or outline such as a tulip.

Inexperienced planners profit from writing detailed plans. Eventually, as you become fluent in thinking through the details, your need to write everything will decrease. With practice, you will need to write only the details necessary for someone else (parent, aide, volunteer, substitute teacher) to follow. Your planning will shift from enhancing your own understanding to helping other adults to do what you intend.

Now that all of the parts have been explained, read carefully a plan from the cognitive domain in Figure 5.10. This plan is appropriate for children 3 to 5 years of age.

Seasoned teachers, ones who have planned in detail similar activities, think through the plans with detail but write less. For example, Mrs. Enright, who has taught for 8 years, has planned many observation experiences for her group of children and used a short form plan (Figure 5.11) for the observation of rocks. However, even an experienced teacher like Mrs. Enright wrote out a detailed plan for creative dance because she had not done that activity previously. She included all

The *goal* of demonstrating courteous listening behaviors is supported by the *fact* that people who listen quietly and look carefully while the story is being conveyed make it easier for everyone to enjoy.

FIGURE 5.10 A complete lesson plan

Activity Name	Examining Rock
Domain	Cognitive: Science
Goal	Examine the observable properties of man-made and *natural objects*, using their multisensory abilities.
Objectives	Given an assortment of rocks and teacher guidance, the child will:
	1. Select a rock from the container.
	2. Inspect the rock visually.
	3. Smell and feel the rock.
	4. Record his or her observation in some way (drawing, rubbing, notes dictated to an adult or peer or self-written notes/drawing).
Content	Rocks are hard pieces of stone found in nature.
	Rocks vary in composition, shape, texture, color, weight, and hardness.
	Scientists observe objects from nature.
	Scientists make a record of their observations.
Materials	A selection of rocks of approximately the same size, each one having at least one rock that is similar to another. (Four more than the number of people.)*
	5 small sheets of paper no heavier than copy paper (3 × 5 to 5 × 8)
	1 pencil for each person (5)
	1 container for rocks
	Paper towel or damp sponge
	Black construction paper as a placemat for each child
	5 magnifying lenses and a dish of water for extension
Procedures	Invitation: Arrange placemats to define children's workspace. Arrange the materials attractively within reach on the table and say, "Come look at these rocks."
	1. Place the rocks in array in the middle and say, "Look at these rocks. Rocks are hard and part of the earth. Pick out one that you like."
	2. "Examine it closely. Look for a pattern. Do you see different colors? Look at mine." Demonstrate close examination. Point to the layers of sediment or the pieces of aggregate in the particular stone you have. Comment on what you see. "Scientists look at rocks very carefully and record what they see. You can do that too."
	3. "Demonstrate sniffing the rock and rubbing it in your fingers." "Is your rock smooth or rough? Curved or pointed? Smell it."
	4. "Make a drawing on your paper to help you remember your special rock." (Depending on the rock selections, a rubbing that can record lines of different minerals might be appropriate.) Take dictation as needed.
	Transition: "Please put your rock in the container and wipe the table." "Tell me what you are planning to do next."
Simplifications	1. Alter the selection of rocks: (a) reduce the number; (b) use only rocks that are very dissimilar.
	2. For very inexperienced children, just examine the rocks closely (objectives 1 through 3) and verbally point out characteristics of the rocks.
Extensions	1. Add a dish of water. Ask children to look at their rock when dry and when wet. Ask them how it looks similar or different.
	2. Add magnifying glasses for children to examine in more detail.
	3. Encourage them to compare two rocks.
	4. Ask children to share their observations of rocks that they have seen elsewhere or to observe rocks nearby.

(continued)

FIGURE 5.10 A complete lesson plan (continued)

Evaluation (child)	Using the following checklist, identify which children completed which objectives. 1. Select a rock from the container. 2. Inspect the rock visually. 3. Smell and feel the rock. 4. Record each child's observation in some way (drawing, rubbing, notes dictated to an adult or peer or self-written notes/drawing). (Teacher constructed checklist)

Objective	1	2	3	4	Comments
Carol					
David					
Su Lin					

Evaluation (mine)	Did I have all the materials I needed to carry out the plan? If not, what else was needed? Did I follow the plan as written? If not, what changes did I make and were they effective in helping children achieve the objectives? In what ways did I adapt the plan to address children's varying abilities?

*Materials are for 1 adult and 4 children.

FIGURE 5.11 Short form lesson plan

Activity Name	Examining rocks
Domain	Cognition
Goal	Examine the observable properties of man-made and *natural objects*, using their multisensory abilities.
Objectives	Given the materials and verbal cues, the child will: 1. Select a rock from the array. 2. Inspect the rock visually. 3. Smell and feel the rock. 4. Record notes or make a rubbing on the paper.
Content	Rocks are hard pieces of stone found in nature. Rocks vary in composition, shape, texture, color, weight, and hardness. Scientists observe objects from nature. Scientists make a record of their observations.
Materials	A selection of rocks of approximately the same size, each one having at least one that is very similar to another. (Four more than the number of children.)* 5 Small sheets of paper no heavier than copy paper (3×5 or 5×8) A pencil for each person (5) 1 Container for rocks Paper towel or sponge Dish of water and magnifying lenses for extension Black construction paper for placemats
Procedures	Display the materials and invite children to participate. Demonstrate how to examine the rocks visually, by scent, and with touch using the objectives as a guide. Encourage each child to use paper and pencil to record observations.
Simplification	Take dictation from the group about what they see, smell, and touch.
Extension	Add water and magnifying glasses. Encourage comparisons.
Evaluation	Use an evaluation checklist numbered by objectives. Did I transmit the content effectively?

the details for moving furnishings to provide enough room as well as what she would say to children so that they would move in rhythm with the music, using all parts of their bodies, but refraining from dashing about. The efforts of the adults in the room were coordinated, and the activity progressed as planned.

You have learned how to write a lesson plan using both a long form and a short form. Now you are ready to communicate about the planned program to family members who may be volunteering in your classroom.

Communicating with Families

Adult family members want to know that their children are learning something in programs from the time they enter pre-kindergarten. They are concerned about what they are learning and are usually interested in how you are teaching them. When they are confident that you are using national standards and carefully planned activities, they are generally comfortable with the strategies that incorporate ample opportunities for play as a context for developing ideas and skills. Figure 5.12 shows a sample newsletter used to keep family members informed.

NEWSLETTER/WEB READY COMMUNICATION

FIGURE 5.12 • Sharing Broad Program Goals That Parents Understand and Value

Dear Family Members,

Many materials are displayed in the classroom. Each one has a specific purpose, and we have made plans to help your child learn while using these and other materials. As a part of our deliberate planning process, we think about what your child already knows and can do, related to nationally recognized goals and standards. Then we shape the activities using hands-on experiences and accurate knowledge content that will lead your child to improved skill or greater understanding. All activities are appropriate for the age and experience of the children, ensuring each child has the opportunity for success as well as being challenged and maintaining interest. Our planning is very detailed so that we may assist each child to:

- *See him- or herself as capable*
- *Acquire new ideas and vocabulary about many subjects*
- *Demonstrate increasing skill in learning how to learn and remember*
- *Increase his or her social competence through learning about sharing materials, waiting to use materials, and cooperating with adults and other children*
- *Acquire more knowledge and skills to keep safe, healthy, and fit*
- *Develop skill in movement of the whole body, including the eye and hand coordination needed to write*
- *Communicate his or her ideas and feelings and understand others*
- *Participate in creative arts and appreciate the beauty in nature*

Our ongoing goal is to provide for a well-organized program where individual needs are addressed and all children are successful learners. In addition, children acquire the knowledge and skills that content experts in many fields of knowledge see as important and necessary during the early years.

Sincerely,

5 Applying What You've Learned

Based on what you now know about lesson plans, try these activities to increase your skills.

1. **Planning in Theory.** Discuss the role of careful planning and how it affects the children, their families, and yourself. Compare the written planning of the novice teacher and a seasoned teacher.

2. **Planning in Parts.** Define the parts of a lesson plan, their purpose, and give an example of each one.

3. **Planning in Action.** Put your new understandings to work by doing the following:

   Write out the procedures (what the teacher must say and do) for the following objectives used in a long-form lesson plan in the cognitive domain:

   Given a set of colored blocks, the child will:

   - Listen to the color name as the teacher points to it and names it.
   - Repeat the name of the color.

   - Point to a specific colored block from among several different colors when asked to do so.
   - Find a colored block that is **not** the color named when asked to do so.
   - Tell the name of the color of a block when asked to do so.

4. **Using Old Plans in New Ways.** Using the complete lesson plan format illustrated in Figure 5.11 as a starting point, modify it so that the children are observing leaves or shells. Be sure that the content is accurate. Use different child assessment and self-evaluation questions.

5. **Shortening Up the Process.** Using the plan that you wrote from Question 4 above, modify it for a short form plan.

6. **Adjusting Plans.** Explain how the lesson plan is structured to be useful for children with special needs and abilities. Give some specific examples related to the plans you wrote in Question 4.

References

Epstein, A. S. (2009). *Me, you, us: Social-emotional learning in preschool.* Ypsilanti, MI: HighScope Educational Research Foundation.

Kostelnik, M. J., Soderman, A. K., & Whiren, A. P. (2011). *Developmentally appropriate curriculum: Best practices in early childhood education* (5th ed.). Upper Saddle River, NJ: Pearson.

Machado, J., & Meyer Botnarescue, H. (2008). *Student teaching: Early childhood practicum guide* (6th ed.). Albany, NY: Cengage Learning.

Seefeldt, C., Castle, S. D., & Falconer, R. (2009). *Social studies for the preschool/primary child* (8th ed.). Upper Saddle River, NJ: Pearson.

6 Up Close and Personal: Teaching Children in Small-Group Activities

Early childhood educators teach children one-on-one, in small groups, and in whole-group situations. In this chapter we will concentrate on what happens during the small-group portions of the children's day. Consider what children are learning and how their teachers are interacting with them in the following small-group activities:

The children are curious about seashells. Their teacher **invites** them to explore and handle real shells of varying kinds. She listens and watches carefully to see what interests the children about the shells.

During a sink-and-float activity at the water table, some children notice that two blue objects are floating. They decide that only blue things can float. Rather than telling children their idea is wrong, the teacher encourages them to test their idea. She has on hand a variety of objects from which children may choose. As children add more objects to the water table, the teacher **guides** them in describing what they see and in predicting what will happen to each object. They notice that some blue objects float, but so do some green ones and yellow ones. Two blue items sink. Together with their teacher, the children make a graph that shows the results of their investigation. They return to the water table for several days, adding to the graph and exploring more properties of objects, such as size and shape, that they think might influence whether objects will float or sink.

The children have been on a field trip to the post office. Upon returning to the classroom, the teacher **leads** the children in dictating a thank-you note to the people who hosted them. She writes the children's words on poster paper in front of the group and then goes back over their message, pointing out certain words and the punctuation she used to get their message across.

LEARNING OUTCOMES

After you read this chapter, you will be able to:

- Discuss six common types of early learning activities.
- Describe how to use the same materials in different activities.
- Adapt small-group plans to meet the needs of diverse children.
- Communicate with families about the different kinds of activities children will experience in your classroom.

The teacher has planned these activities with specific goals in mind for children's development and learning. Each activity involves some form of firsthand experience children use to make connections between what they know and what they have yet to learn. At the same time, all three activities vary in format and in the steps involved in carrying them out. They also differ in the extent to which children as well as adults influence activity content and direction. In early childhood circles, this variation is referred to as being more or less **child-guided** or more or less **adult-guided**. The seashell activity, in which children are primarily in charge of the exploration, is an example of a mostly child-guided experience. Other activities involve much greater amounts of teacher direction; although children's input remains important, adults determine the goals and specific procedures children will follow. The thank-you note lesson falls into this category. Some activities appear in between the two dimensions of child-guided and adult-guided instruction. The sink-and-float investigation exemplifies this dual influence. These variations are depicted in the continuum in Figure 6.1.

At one time some early childhood experts argued that teachers should focus exclusively on child-guided activities; others favored mostly adult-guided instruction. That has changed. Few people today believe

child-guided Children mostly control the content and direction an activity takes.

adult-guided Adults determine the content, approach, and direction of an activity.

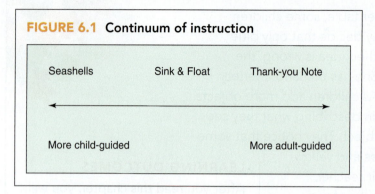

FIGURE 6.1 Continuum of instruction

Seashells	Sink & Float	Thank-you Note

More child-guided   More adult-guided

that activity planning and classroom teaching are either/or propositions. Instead, researchers propose that teachers who use developmentally appropriate practices (DAP) must know how to use an entire continuum of activities ranging from primarily child-guided to more adult-guided approaches (Epstein, 2007). Helping you gain this expertise is what this chapter is all about.

Learning Activities in Early Childhood Education

Now that you have a format for thinking about and writing lesson plans as well as a repertoire of teaching strategies to incorporate into those plans, you will find there are different types of activities you may choose to support children's learning. Six of the most common kinds are listed here:

- Exploratory play
- Guided discovery
- Problem solving
- Discussions
- Demonstrations
- Direct instruction

These are key learning experiences you will rely on to organize whole days, entire weeks, and even years of instruction for young children. Let's consider each of them in turn.

EXPLORATORY PLAY

The preschool children have been playing in the make-believe doctor's office all week. Today their teacher adds three stethoscopes to augment the play. Martin and Jemma pretend to be doctors taking care of sick babies. They use the stethoscopes to listen to the dolls' hearts and they take the dolls' temperatures with straws. Martin announces, "We need Band-Aids. We all need Band-Aids. Doctors have to have Band-Aids." He tries to wrap a paper towel around one of the dolls as a Band-Aid, but it falls off. Moving over to the art area, Jemma holds up a roll of masking tape and announces, "Here's some Band-Aids." She seizes some foam packing squiggles as well and says, "Doctors need some of this medicine too." The play continues, with the two doctors wrapping one baby's leg with the tape and giving the dolls their "medicine."

Raymond, age 4, enters the area and picks up a stethoscope, blows into the bell, looks at the earpieces, puts the earpieces in his ears, taps the bell, and then walks over to a doll and places the bell on its stomach. "I can't hear anything," he announces. "Let me hear you," he says to Martin and puts the stethoscope against Martin's arm. "Nothing!" Martin tells him," Right here," and points to his chest.

Raymond listens to Martin's chest in different places, asking each time, "Can you hear that?" He goes on to listen to the radiator, to the hamster, to the light switch, and to the refrigerator. He abandons the role of doctor and becomes absorbed in exploring sounds through the stethoscope. His teacher watches but does not interrupt or redirect him back to the doctor's office. She can see that Raymond is excitedly exploring something important to him.

You already know from previous chapters that exploration is where all learning begins and that exploratory play is children's natural means of finding out about the world and how it works. Through exploratory play, children carry out firsthand investigations of people, places, objects, roles, and events, constructing personally meaningful concepts and extending their knowledge in critical ways. An essential dimension of such play is self-determination—children choose what to explore and how to explore. They proceed at their own pace and make most of the decisions about the direction the play will take (Elkind, 2007). In this way, exploratory play is open-ended (there is no one possible outcome) and it is self-initiated by the child (something piques a child's curiosity, prompting him or her to want to find out or do more).

exploratory play Activities in which children carry out firsthand investigations of people, places, objects, roles, and events. Through these open-ended experiences, children determine what to explore, how to explore, and the pace of exploration.

The children in the pretend doctor's office are all exploring, but in different ways. Martin and Jemma are exploring the roles of doctors and patients. They have their own ideas about what such people do and the materials they need to carry out their work. Raymond is exploring, too. His teacher understood this essential fact and respected his need to investigate the stethoscope. Although the planned activity was the doctor's office, she recognized the educational benefit of Raymond's sensory experimentation and supported his learning by allowing him to pursue his interest in his own fashion.

Even though children assume primary responsibility for exploratory play, teachers do more than just make materials available for children to use. They select broad experiences from which they believe children will benefit and they consider the best ways to facilitate children's involvement in those experiences. They pay careful attention to selecting appropriate and interesting materials as well as to safety. Because the content of the activity is up to the children, teachers do not focus on a single curricular domain (e.g., cognition or social) or on a few specific objectives for children to pursue (e.g., learning to count or learning insect names). Instead, teachers plan around broad objectives that could address any domain:

1. To inspire children's interest in materials or events
2. To encourage children to investigate those materials and events in numerous ways

To support exploratory play, teachers rely heavily on the teaching strategies of sensory involvement and using environmental cues to stimulate children's interest. They use behavior reflections or paraphrase reflections to acknowledge children's actions and discoveries ("You made a color pattern—red, blue, red blue." Or, "You found a new way to make the blocks balance."), and they maintain attentive silence so children can focus on their own ideas and what interests them. To enable them to participate freely and safely, teachers also guide children in interacting peaceably and in using materials constructively (such as not breaking

Because this is an exploratory play activity, the teacher invites Gabriela to explore the combination of sand, water, and light on the light table. She does not ask Gabriela to make letters or other specific shapes.

things). However, they do not require children to use materials only in conventional ways. Because they want exploratory play to remain open-ended, teachers avoid potentially leading strategies such as do-it signals ("Find a red triangle."), challenges ("Make a tower using three different kinds of blocks."), or questions ("What shape is that block?"). These strategies direct children's thinking in a singular direction. In sum, in exploratory activities:

Children: Explore objects, words, and experiences
Choose what to explore and how to explore
Use multiple senses in their explorations
Collect information and develop ideas through firsthand experiences
Make personally meaningful discoveries
Refine their thinking through repetition
Refine their thinking through interactions with objects and people

Teachers: Offer children a variety of exploratory experiences and age-appropriate materials
Arrange props and the physical environment so children can explore freely and safely
Verbally acknowledge children's actions and investigations
Observe children and make adjustments to materials and activities to match children's needs and interests
Give children plenty of time to explore materials before asking children to use those materials in a prescribed way

With support from the teacher, this child is learning a lot about worms by watching the worms, handling them gently, and making drawings of his observations.

You can see many of these factors in operation in the exploration activity presented in Figure 6.2.

A complete exploratory play lesson plan is provided in Appendix A.

GUIDED DISCOVERY ACTIVITIES

Another type of activity early childhood teachers create is called *guided discovery*. The children playing a memory game in Figure 6.3 provide a typical example.

The children playing the memory game are discovering important math concepts such as *more* and *most*. They are also finding out that number is a function of the amount of objects, not simply how much space the objects fill. A stack of cards may seem like more in one instance and a line of cards like more in another. In this activity, the children and the teacher are actively involved in the learning. This mathematical encounter did not come about by chance. The teacher purposely provided materials to stimulate the children's number thinking and used questions, observations, paraphrasing, and challenges to guide the children's discoveries.

Guided discovery builds on exploration but goes a step further in terms of teacher-guided planning and implementation. Teachers create plans with specific curricular domains in mind, identify curriculum-based objectives for children's learning, and incorporate the additional teaching strategies of modeling, effective praise, telling and explaining, do-it signals, challenges, and questions in their instruction.

FIGURE 6.2 Exploratory play

Worm Explorations

The children in Mrs. Murphy's class of 3-year-olds are exploring worms. The teacher planned the activity based on the children's interest in worms they found outdoors following a rainstorm. The teacher **encourages** the children to gently examine several worms available in a tub of soil. She **provides** a variety of worms, magnifying glasses, small white trays on which children can place their worms for closer inspection, and several pictures of worms. When some children decide to draw pictures of their worms, she helps them find paper and markers to use. She moves in and out of the area, **inviting** children to participate, and occasionally **reflecting** on what they are saying and doing ("You found a really long worm." "You're looking for more worms in the soil." "Caleb, Jack wants you to see what he found."). She provides smocks so the worry of getting their clothes dirty will not hamper children's involvement. She also **shows** children how to handle the worms gently so as not to harm them and to minimize the need for further adult intervention. She does not direct children to do anything particular with the worms, such as looking for their body parts or figuring out what kinds of worms they are. Instead she creates a safe, open environment in which children are free to pursue personal interests. As the children explore, the teacher **observes** their investigations. She notices:

> What actions children are taking
>
> Which children are involved
>
> Whether certain children explore alone or with a friend
>
> What questions children are asking
>
> What ideas children are expressing

The teacher uses the information she gleans from these observations to shape future planning.

FIGURE 6.3 Guided discovery

Memory Game Guided Discovery

Three 5-year-olds have just finished a game of "Memory," making pairs among face-down cards on the table. "I won!" Angela proclaims.

Their teacher **asks** a question, "You're excited. How did you figure out that you won the most cards?"

"Well, because," says Angela, holding a mass of cards in one hand and placing them next to Lillian's pile in comparison. "See? I've got more!"

"Does everyone agree?" the teacher asks.

"Wait a minute!" Cameron calls out. "Let me look at something." He spreads his cards end-to-end in a line on the floor. His line contains so many cards that it extends from the math area out into the center of the classroom.

Observing this the teacher questions, "What do you think?"

"Look. See?" he answers. "My line is really long. I won. I have the most."

The teacher paraphrases, "Cameron, you found a different way to think about the cards. You're pretty sure you have the most. Does everyone agree with that?" the teacher asks the group. She **challenges** the children to develop more ideas: "What other ways are there to figure out who won?"

With the teacher's **guidance and encouragement**, the children continue to try different solutions until clean-up time (Frost, Wortham, & Reifel, 2008). By the end of the session they have generated several more ideas including comparing lines of cards side by side, measuring the lines and stacks of cards with string, counting the cards, and ordering them in piles from most to least.

These girls are figuring out who has the most memory cards. They tried counting and are now stacking the cards in a pile to see whose stack is highest.

guided-discovery activities
Activities in which children pursue answers, information, and strategies for "finding out," guided by a supportive teacher. Teachers determine the general direction of learning; children determine specific details.

These kinds of activities give children the freedom to discover some things on their own but also make sure they encounter certain curricular content and concepts along the way (Robertson, 2007).

The children's role in guided-discovery activities is to construct knowledge for themselves: making choices and decisions, experimenting and experiencing, raising questions, and finding their own answers (Maxim, 2006). The teacher's role is to serve as a guide: emphasizing how to find answers, providing information and strategies as necessary, and supporting children as they apply their learning (Copple & Bredekamp, 2009). Children as well as adults influence the direction of guided-discovery activities. Adults provide the broad parameters in which learning occurs; children determine the details of what is learned. More specifically, during guided-discovery activities:

Children: Build a reservoir of knowledge about the world and how it works
Observe and recall
Choose and decide
Experiment
Interpret, compare, and contrast
Order, group, and identify patterns
Raise questions
Pursue answers and refine their thinking
Represent their ideas in tangible ways (building, drawing, making)

Teachers: Select and arrange materials
Provide opportunities for children to investigate
Serve as resources
Model how to find answers
Provide information
Model and demonstrate strategies
Offer opportunities for practice (rehearsals, repetitions, elaborations)
Ask questions
Challenge children's thinking
Acknowledge children's ideas and findings
Encourage children to represent their ideas using pictures and/or words

Go back to the memory game in Figure 6.3 for evidence of these roles among the participants. Refer to Appendix A for a sample of a long-form guided discovery lesson plan.

PROBLEM SOLVING

Children are intrigued by all kinds of problems—movement problems (How many different ways can I bend my body? How can I get from here to there?), physical science problems (How can I get these blocks to balance? How can I build a faster ramp?), skill problems (How many different ways can these objects be grouped? How can I make different strokes with this brush?), social problems (How will we decide who gets to spin next?), and strategy problems (What will I do to get Raymond to share the paint? How will I get the glue to stick better?). An individual problem (e.g., choosing the block captain for today) may be resolved in a single sitting, whereas other problems may be revisited over and over again (e.g., What do plants need to grow? Why did the guinea pig die?).

Sometimes problems like these come up naturally and adults take advantage of them (How many crackers will we need for snack? How will you make your tower more stable?). At other times, adults plan problem-solving activities to enhance children's thinking and learning. The best problems for children to encounter are multisensory, allow children to gather information concretely, and have more than one possible solution. The more immediate, observable, and obvious the problem, the more easily children can evaluate their actions and come to their own conclusions. All good problems prompt children to observe, analyze, synthesize, and evaluate events, information, and ideas. This encourages children to make new mental connections and construct fresh ideas (Freiberg & Driscoll, 2005; Robertson, 2007). A typical problem-solving sequence and actions children take in response to each step are outlined in Table 6.1.

problem-solving activities
Activities specifically designed to enhance children's observing, analyzing, experimenting, and reporting abilities.

There are many opportunities to walk children through the problem-solving steps outlined in Table 6.1. The sink-and-float activity that opened this chapter is a good example. Generally, children don't go through every step in a single day. Sometimes teachers plan activities around an individual phase of the process, such as observing or predicting. This was the case in the sample lesson plan you read about in Chapter 5, in which children examined rocks. Sometimes activities stretch out for several days, as

The children predicted in what direction their bubbles would float. Now they are testing out their ideas.

TABLE 6.1 • Problem-Solving Basics		
PROBLEM-SOLVING STEPS	**CHILDREN'S ACTIONS**	**ADULT SUPPORT STRATEGIES**
	In this step, children:	In this step, teachers:
Observing	Notice, observe, wonder, question, identify a problem, explore	Set up simple tangible investigations Use sensory engagement Invite children to participate Ask children to describe what they see
Gathering Information/Predicting	Think about why things happen, gather information, make predictions, construct reasonable explanations	Ask open-ended questions about children's thinking Reflect on child's experiences Provide information Invite children to make predictions and provide explanations for why they think things happen
Experimenting	Take action, test ideas, observe results	Use do-it signals and challenge children to try out their ideas
Concluding	Reflect on outcomes, explore patterns and relationships, compare, make generalizations about why something happened, develop alternative explanations, make plans for further experiments	Ask questions and use reflections to prompt children to think more deeply about their experiences and to consider multiple possibilities Avoid solving the problem themselves or mandating a particular solution
Communicating Results	Talk about what happened, record data, represent experiences and data	Help children record their observations and conclusions

illustrated by the mud puddle investigators in Figure 6.4. In every case, teachers are interested in helping children explore the thinking involved in problem solving rather than trying to get children to come up with one right answer (Chalufour & Worth, 2004; Epstein, 2008).

FIGURE 6.4 Problem-solving activity

Mud Puddle Investigators

The children in Lucita Ortiz's class discovered a large mud puddle in their play yard. Its large size, squishy edges, and depth at the center intrigued them. The teacher took advantage of the children's interest to create a multi-day problem-solving activity.

Day 1: Ms. Ortiz asks the children to **observe** the puddle and **describe** what they see. Some of their observations include:

   Soft parts

   Wet parts

   Brown water

   Squishy edges

   Bubbles

   Wide across

   Looks deeper in the middle than on the edge

   Curvy sides

   Thick mud on the sides—makes a slappy sound when hit with stick

   Middle part splashes

Among the questions children want to answer are:

   How big is the puddle?

   How deep is the puddle, on the edges and in the middle?

   Will the puddle be here from now on?

The teacher encourages the children to **gather information** by using sticks to test the solidity of the mud and the depth of the water. They see it is deeper in the middle than on the edges. The teacher has the children mark the edges and the center of the puddle with tongue depressors as illustrated below.

She asks the children to **predict** what they think will happen to the size of the puddle. Some children think it will get bigger, others think it will stay the same, and some children think it will shrink.

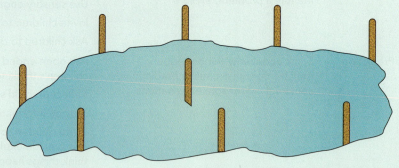

Days 2, 3, 4, and 5: Each day the children return to the puddle to **test** their predictions and **observe results**. The children mark the edges of the puddle daily with more tongue depressors. They measure the center each day, too. By day 5, the puddle is nearly gone.

Each day the children describe what they see happening to the puddle and **draw conclusions**:

   The puddle is getting smaller.

   The edges are cracking.

   The old soupy parts are not so soupy.

   The middle is not so deep as before.

The children and teacher **document** their findings in a series of pictures and dictated descriptions.

The activity in Figure 6.4 is a current real-life example based on an original activity described by Cliatt and Shaw (1992).

Go to Appendix A for a sample problem-solving activity plan.

DISCUSSIONS

Discussing is more than talking. Genuine **discussions** involve conversational give and take, listening as well as speaking, and opportunities for contributing ideas as well as reacting. Discussions also incorporate independent thinking and collaboration. They serve to inform, clarify, stimulate new thinking, and contribute to shared understandings within the group. In early childhood discussions, teachers talk to children, children talk to teachers, and children talk to one another. These interactions may take place among small groups of people or with the whole class at once (Warden, 2008). Teachers engaged in discussions with children use a wide variety of teaching strategies, ranging from sensory engagement to purposeful silence.

discussions Activities designed to promote children's conversational skills and to contribute to children's sense of community within the classroom.

Numerous topics interest young children. Here are some of the things children and their teachers discuss:

What is happening in the program? Who will feed the fish? Why are some people unhappy about what is happening in pretend play? Today we will begin a new clean-up routine.

What is happening to children away from the program? Logan has a new kitten at his house. Laura's grandma is visiting. Denise will be moving to Texas.

During snack, these children and their teacher discuss the differences between apples and pears.

What is happening in the community? There was a hard rain last night. A new park is being built across the street from our center. There will be a parade on Saturday.

Discussions are sometimes impromptu but often are planned, taking the form of a class meeting, a brainstorming session, conversations that involve planning for individuals or the group as a whole, and discussions in which children reflect on what they did during the day. Sometimes a record is made of the discussion, such as when the group develops guidelines for putting toys away, or comes to an agreement about how many people can go to snack at one time, or when the class votes on which visitor to invite to group time. At other times no written record is necessary. During discussions you might see and hear:

Children and Teachers: Talking
Listening
Commenting
Posing ideas
Providing information
Making inquiries
Coming to agreements
Summarizing
Building concepts
Adjusting their thinking to accommodate
    new information

Not every discussion involves all of these elements. Not every conversation leads to children developing final, accurate answers or common agreements. However, every discussion does give children opportunities to practice talking together and developing

---

FIGURE 6.5 Discussion

A Dinosaur Discussion with 4-Year-Olds

The children were sitting with their teacher in a circle. They had been studying dinosaurs and were now deeply involved in a discussion about paleontology.

Teacher: "How did those dinosaur bones get under the ground?"

Eze: "They died in the ground. The dinosaurs uh laid down in the mud, and then they just, uh, died in the ground."

Chris: "Quicksand—it was quicksand that got 'em."

Carlos: "Somebody put the bones there; I think it was the sand man."

Sara: "There was a big hole and the dinosaurs fell in and they got all buried up."

Nathan: "After the dinosaurs died, then the people came and buried up the bones."

Teacher: "It sounds like you know a lot about dinosaurs and how they became fossils. Remember, there were no people alive when the dinosaurs were on earth."

Nathan: "Oh yeah, That's right. That's right. I know! It was a front-end loader. That's it! A front-end loader buried 'em, but it didn't have no driver."

Source: Based on Kostelnik & Grady (2009), p. 142.

Hector and his brother and sister demonstrate how to use their arms to keep their balance walking on a pretend log.

demonstrations Activities in which children learn how to do something through purposeful modeling by someone else.

insights into one another's thinking as well as their own. See Figure 6.5 for a sample discussion among 4-year-olds related to fossils. Notice how the teacher provides accurate information while also letting children pursue their own notions of how fossils were formed.

Refer to Appendix A for a long-form discussion plan.

DEMONSTRATIONS

People learn many things by watching and imitating others. Children learn when they see the teacher use a woodworking tool, listen to someone think aloud, or observe how one person greets another. Commonly, adults demonstrate and children watch. However, sometimes the roles reverse, with children leading the demonstration—how to play a game, how to build a bridge from blocks, or how to hold a wiggling frog.

In early childhood programs, teachers use **demonstrations** to show children how to do things (e.g., capture air in a jar and invert it in water, peel a potato, put their name on their painting), or to pique children's interest in something that is coming up later (e.g., how to use a material that will be available during free-choice time). Demonstrations combine invitations, modeling, do-it signals, informing and explaining, and effective praise. In most demonstrations this is what happens:

Observers: Watch
        Summarize
        Imitate
        Practice

Demonstrator: Gains people's attention
        Shows something
        Prompts observers to respond in words or actions
        Gives observers opportunities to practice

TABLE 6.2 • Actions and Words for Demonstrations	
WHAT YOU DO:	**WHAT YOU COULD SAY:**
1. Gain children's attention	"Look up here." Or "Watch closely."
2. Show children something	Describe your actions while modeling them, such as, "See how I'm putting the little one on first."
3. Prompt a response	"Tell me what you saw." Or "What did I do first? Then what came next?"
4. Provide practice	"Now you try it!"

FIGURE 6.6 A planned demonstration

Planned Demonstration: Feeding the Hamster

Before adding "Feed the Hamster" to the job chart, the teacher **models** the process of opening the food container, pouring out the correct number of hamster pellets, putting the food in the dish, and then closing the container and putting it away. She **describes** each step while doing it. At group time, the children talk her through the steps as a rehearsal and reminder. The next day, Janos becomes the first child to **practice** carrying out the new job.

FIGURE 6.7 A spontaneous demonstration

Spontaneous Demonstration: Getting Play Dough Legs to Stick

Allie likes to work with play dough. She spends a lot of time at the art table shaping it. Today, she is trying to make a cat. She has rolled a sausage-shaped body and is trying to attach four chunky legs to make it stand up. However, the legs keep falling off. Allie is frustrated.

Her teacher comes over to the table and, using a separate ball of dough, **models** and **describes** how to score two pieces of dough and then push them together to make the pieces stick together better. Allie strives to duplicate the teacher's technique. Eventually she holds up her creation (four legs, shaky, but attached) and announces, "Look. It's a cat!" For the next several days, Allie **practices** the scoring technique on a variety of critters, making each one sturdier than the one before.

Actions and sample words you could use to conduct a demonstration are summarized in Table 6.2.

Some demonstrations are planned and some happen spontaneously, as noted in Figures 6.6 and 6.7. Despite this difference in origin, both involve the same steps.

You will find a lesson plan for demonstrations in Appendix A.

DIRECT INSTRUCTION

The names of the dinosaurs

What to do during a tornado drill

When writing, sentences begin with a capital letter

Mrs. Wagner uses direct instruction to teach Roy how to hold his hands correctly and when to add water to the clay.

The items in this list are all important things children cannot learn simply through self-discovery—they need direct instruction from someone else to learn what to do or how to use the information. Thus, there are times when teachers use **direct instruction activities** to teach children facts or routines they could not discover easily or safely on their own or to reinforce certain skills in short lessons. In these activities, adults follow a series of steps that gradually lead children toward a single correct response. It is this focus on a particular answer that distinguishes direct instruction from all the other activity types described so far. During direct instruction activities:

direct-instruction activities
Experiences in which adults primarily determine the goals, content, and process of the activity in order to teach children facts or routines.

Children:	Observe, pay attention
	Show or tell something
	Differentiate examples and non-examples of what they are learning
	Apply what they have learned
Teachers:	Gain children's attention
	Show or say something
	Prompt children to respond
	Reinforce correct responses
	Correct or ignore inaccurate responses
	Give children opportunities to practice

Although direct instruction is the most fully adult-guided activity described in this text, such lessons are still influenced by the children's responses, as illustrated in the activity highlighted in Figure 6.8 (Robertson, 2007).

When teachers plan direct instruction activities, they begin with task analysis and then use chaining or successive approximation to make big tasks easier for children to manage. Although information transfer is the primary objective, teachers do not simply tell children the information they need to learn. Teachers use do-it signals, explaining and informing, questioning, guided practice, and effective praise to gradually lead children toward a goal. To vary their lessons and capture children's attention, teachers also use gestures, intentional mistakes, surprises, pauses, and enthusiasm to enhance children's interest and understanding. Usually such lessons are short and are supplemented by other kinds of experiences so children can use the information they are learning in personally meaningful ways.

See Appendix A for a complete example of a direct instruction activity plan.

The Relationship Between Learning Activities and Materials

Most early childhood classrooms have blocks; art materials; picture books; pretend play props; materials for sensory, science, and mathematical investigations; and sand or water tables. Depending on how you plan, all of these materials could

---

FIGURE 6.8 **Direct instruction**

Differentiating Musical Sounds

The teacher in the preschool class is using direct instruction in this short lesson on musical sounds with a group of four children sitting on a rug. The curricular goal is to have children associate an instrument with a sound as a way for children to practice listening and develop sound association skills. Prior to this, children have had several opportunities to explore the real instruments and the sounds they make.

Teacher gains children's attention	"Look up here. I have some of the instruments we had a chance to play with this morning."
Children look and listen	The children look at the teacher as she holds up a tambourine, a castanet, two sand blocks, and two rhythm sticks.
Teacher shows and tells	"I'm going to make some musical sounds. Listen." (Teacher demonstrates each instrument.) "Now, we'll play a game. I will play a sound, but you won't see the instrument I use. You point to the instrument that makes that sound." (Teacher lines up instruments in front of a flannel board.)
Teacher prompts a response	The teacher plays one sound at a time, using a second set of instruments hidden behind the flannel board.
Children respond	The children point to an instrument in response to a sound.
Teacher reinforces and corrects children's answers as they differentiate among the sounds	If a child points to the correct instrument, the teacher responds by saying, "That's right, the tambourine makes that jangling sound." If a child points to an incorrect instrument, the teacher ignores the response until the child gets it right. Or, the teacher says, "You think the sand block makes that jangling sound. It makes a scratchy sound like this. Let's try again."
Children practice and apply	Later in the day the children have a chance to play with the instruments on their own. The teacher is pleased to hear the children referring to differences among the instruments and the sounds (mostly correctly).

---

support valuable learning experiences for children ranging from exploratory play to direct instruction. As an example, in Table 6.3 we provide descriptions of how each of the activities you have just read about could be carried out with blocks.

As you can see, materials alone do not dictate what children learn. Any material can support just about any lesson plan. It is what children do with the material that matters. Thus, knowing how to plan for different kinds of activities and knowing which teaching strategies to use in association with each one are important skills to develop. The leaf activities highlighted in the Try It Yourself activity presented here will give you an opportunity to get started.

Chin-Hwa is trying out his idea for building a tall tower.

TABLE 6.3 • Block Activities	
ACTIVITY TYPE	**BLOCKS EXAMPLE**
Exploratory Play	Children explore the blocks and accessories in their own way, combining various materials and incorporating different shapes, sizes, and configurations of blocks in their structures. Some children play alone; some play with others. Some children create designs; other children build objects. Some children build objects that "work" (ramps or chutes), some children build representational structures (e.g., a corral, a stove for the restaurant, a rocket ship) that support pretend play.
Guided Discovery	The teacher interacts with the children to encourage more elaborate block play. He asks, "These trucks need a place where people can work on them when they break down. What could you build for them?" "I've noticed that one of your favorite stories to act out is Rapunzel. Rapunzel lived in a tower. What kinds of blocks might you use to build a tower?" As the children build, the teacher says, "You found a way to use many different kinds of blocks." "Tell me how you decided which blocks to put on the bottom and which blocks to put on the top." The teacher makes sketches of or photographs the structures children build and writes down words children use to describe their structures.
Problem Solving	The teacher challenges the children to build tall towers in the block area. He asks, "Which blocks do you think will be best for making tall towers? Why?" The teacher and children brainstorm ideas for building tall towers. Children are encouraged to choose an idea from among those they brainstormed and then try it out. Children evaluate each approach and make representational drawings of their tall structures.
Discussion	The children and teacher discuss safe ways of building tall towers. Together they decide what defines *tall*. They agree that once a tower is as tall as a child, builders must wear hard hats to stay safe. They also agree that no one will crash tall towers on purpose. Tall towers will be disassembled a few blocks at a time.
Demonstrations	The teacher demonstrates how to make a representational model of a child's tall tower using collage materials (paper, boxes, foil, etc.), glue, tape, and scissors. As part of the demonstration, children give the teacher instructions about what materials might work best as he proceeds. The teacher provides similar materials near the block area for children to use in making their own models. The teacher follows up with observations and questions such as, "I noticed you put the big unit blocks at the bottom of your tower and now you've picked the biggest boxes to make the base for your model." "Tell me how you decided where to start in building your model." "What part of your tower was the hardest to fit? Was that part hard to fit in your model too? I wonder why?"
Direct Instruction	The teacher notices that the children have created a block building that includes a cornerstone. He draws the children's attention to the cornerstone in the building, points it out, and briefly defines it. He asks children to point out the cornerstone and to find other parts of the building that are not cornerstones. He invites the children to make more buildings that include a cornerstone.

Source: Ideas for exploratory play, guided discovery, problem solving, discussion, and demonstrations were based on ideas presented in Chalufour and Worth (2004).

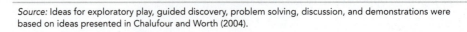

TRY IT YOURSELF
CHOOSE TEACHING STRATEGIES FOR AN EXPLORATORY PLAY AND A GUIDED DISCOVERY ACTIVITY

Karim, Nita, and Eric are 4 years old. They are examining several different kinds of real leaves that have been made available in an otherwise empty water table. Magnifiers, plain sheets of paper, crayons, markers, and nature books are located on the shelves nearby.

Assume you planned this leaf activity as an exploratory play experience for the children. Think of three things you will do or say to support children's explorations.

1. (Example) Invite children to the activity.

2.

3.

4.

Next, imagine you are using the same materials as part of a guided-discovery activity. Name three additional things you will do or say to guide children's discoveries.

1. (Example) Challenge children to find three leaves that look the same.

2.

3.

4.

Go back over the material you have just read to check or expand your choices.

How Early Learning Activities Relate to One Another

Exploratory play, guided discovery, problem solving, discussions, demonstrations, and direct instruction are all useful tools for teaching young children from early preschool through age 8. Each activity can be implemented in ways that are age-appropriate, individually appropriate, and socially and culturally appropriate. The main dimension that differentiates these activities from one another is in where they fall on the child-guided to adult-guided continuum we discussed at the beginning of this chapter. For some activities, how and what children learn is mostly determined by the children themselves (explorations and guided discovery); in other activities, children and teachers share equal responsibility for the learning process (problem solving and discussions); still other activities give adults primary control over what direction the lessons will take (demonstrations and direct instruction). These variations are illustrated in Figure 6.9. Consider the figure carefully. It depicts not only the continuum from child-guided to more adult-guided activities but also the relative amount of time devoted to each type of activity in classrooms characterized by DAP.

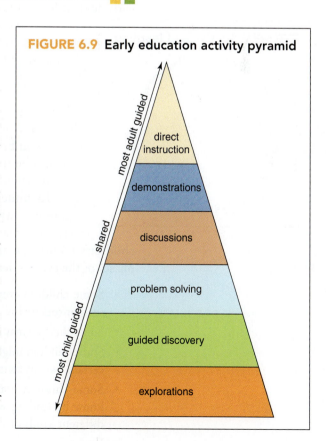

FIGURE 6.9 Early education activity pyramid

most adult guided

shared

most child guided

direct instruction

demonstrations

discussions

problem solving

guided discovery

explorations

It is no accident that Figure 6.9 is depicted as a pyramid. Because of what we know about how young children learn best, explorations form the foundation for all other activities. Going up the pyramid, guided discovery, problem solving, and discussion activities are more child-guided and therefore are more prevalent in early childhood programs than are predominantly adult-guided activities such as demonstrations and direct instruction. Thus, when you visit an early childhood classroom you will see many exploratory and guided-discovery activities available for children to pursue. Problem-solving and discussion activities will also be part of the day. You will likely see some demonstrations and direct instruction activities as well, but fewer of these kinds of activities than the others.

In combination, the activities outlined in Figure 6.9 provide a strong array of experiences common in early childhood education. Each is adaptable to all areas of the early childhood curriculum. Even so, not all children are alike and not every child will experience the same activity in the same way. To practice DAP effectively you must adapt to the needs of individual children as you work with them in small groups. Let's talk about how to do this next.

Meeting the Learning Needs of Individual Children in Small-Group Activities

Remember the cycle of learning introduced in Chapter 2? You will find yourself coming back to the cycle of learning over and over again in your planning and teaching (see Figure 6.10). It will be especially useful to you when you are working with three or four children at a time in an activity.

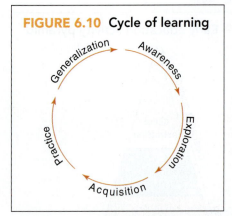

FIGURE 6.10 Cycle of learning

Very few children move through all five phases of the cycle of learning as the result of a one-time experience. Depending on the concept or skill, it could take days, weeks, or even years for children to progress from awareness to generalization. As with all other aspects of development, children move forward at varying rates. This means that even when all children in a group experience the same lesson at the same time, each child will be in a different place in the learning cycle for that lesson, depending on his or her backlog of experience and present understandings. This will be true for typically developing children as well as for children with special needs.

To understand how this works, let's revisit the children from Figure 6.2, who were exploring worms in Mrs. Murphy's class. If you were their teacher you might observe the following differences in the children's knowledge and behavior. These variations would represent different phases of the cycle of learning:

- Some children could just be entering the **awareness** phase—they have never seen or touched worms before.
- Some children may be aware that worms exist but desire more time for **exploration**.
- Some children might have enough past experience that they are ready to **acquire** certain "worm facts" such as where worms live and what they eat.
- Some children may practically be worm "experts." They **practice** what they know by finding worms in different places outdoors as well as by identifying different kinds of worms from pictures in books.
- You may even see children who know so much about worms that they are ready to **generalize** what they know from worms to other outdoor crawling creatures such as caterpillars or garter snakes.

To accommodate these differences among children, your planning and teaching must be flexible enough to address all five phases of the learning cycle at once. The following strategies will help you accomplish this:

- Design open-ended activities that allow individual children to participate in the learning cycle at the point that suites them best
- Involve children in a broad spectrum of firsthand, direct investigations
- Observe children carefully and make records of their learning
- Invite children to explore new objects and experiences
- Provide a wide array of materials for children to explore
- Follow up on exploratory play experiences with guided-discovery and problem-solving activities that match children's interests
- Offer information, ask relevant questions, and provide appropriate demonstrations in the acquisition phase
- Use discussions to gauge children's interest in various topics and to gain insights into which phase of the cycle of learning different children are experiencing
- Give children many opportunities to practice new skills throughout the year
- Provide many chances for children to generalize what they have learned to new situations
- Discuss children's experiences with family members to gain feedback and information about what children know or want to know

Developing lesson plans that incorporate more than one objective and including simplifications and extensions in your plans are additional strategies that help you accommodate the needs of individuals within the small-group activities you plan.

Mrs. Murphy exemplifies some of these strategies as she thinks carefully about how best to support Tasha, a child in her class who is developmentally delayed. The worms have been in the classroom for several days. Most of the other children have moved beyond simple exploration to the acquisition phase, recording their observations and looking up worm facts. Tasha holds back, uncertain what to do. The teacher takes a worm from the tub and shows Tasha how to hold it. She encourages Tasha to imitate her actions and uses short, simple sentences to describe what Tasha is doing. As Tasha becomes more comfortable with the worms, Mrs. Murphy has other children show Tasha what they are doing and encourages Tasha to imitate their actions. Tasha laughs as a worm squirms in her hand.

Communicating with Families About Learning Activities

As a teacher of young children, you appreciate how exploratory play, guided-discovery, and problem-solving activities contribute to children's development and learning. However, the instructive dimensions of these mostly child-guided activities may not be so obvious to individuals outside early childhood education. In addition, family members may not realize the important role they could play at home in promoting the same skills you are working on at the center or school. You can use family communications to convey the educational nature of these activities and to elicit family support in promoting child-guided learning in children's lives. An example of a newsletter/website-ready note that urges family members to promote children's problem solving using commonplace materials is presented in Figure 6.11. The teacher has included a brief rationale, simple instructions, and a few potential scripts for parents to use as children construct scrap structures (Chalufour & Worth, 2004). Note the request for feedback as well—this reminds us that family communication must always be two-way.

NEWSLETTER/WEB READY COMMUNICATION

FIGURE 6.11 • Reinforcing What Your Child Is Learning

Children spend a lot of time creating structures from a variety of materials such as blocks, boxes, wood scraps, foam shapes, and wire. As children build, they practice social skills such as sharing and working together. They explore the physical nature of the materials such as size, shape, and balance. Children use their imaginations to transform something they imagine into a tangible object such as a building or tower. Often, we see scientific problem solving with the building materials. This involves children:

Making observations

Sharing their thinking and ideas

Testing out strategies

Making records of their discoveries (through drawings, written notes, and photographs)

You can foster this same important learning at home by encouraging your child to build with scrap materials you have at hand. Although commercial building toys such as Legos® are educational too, they do not provide the same scientific problem-solving challenges relative to balance, stability, and design that loose materials do. Your child will be delighted to incorporate many different materials into his or her building at home. Here are some strategies we are using at school that you can also use to guide children's scientific problem-solving abilities.

Invite your child to talk about his or her building (Tell me about your building. Tell me about this part on top.)

Encourage your child to reflect on his or her thinking while building (How did you decide what should go at the bottom? What did you do first?)

Help your child think about the characteristics of his or her structure (What are the shapes that you used? How did you get this part to balance?)

We'll be sure to keep you updated on the children's building at the center and we'd love to hear how the building is going at home.

6 Applying What You've Learned

Based on what you now know about teaching children in small groups, carry out these activities to increase your knowledge and skills.

1. **Activity Resources.** Review one or more activity books/activity collections for preschool-age children. Find at least one activity that seems to fit each of the six kinds of activities described in this chapter. Take one of these and rewrite it so it fits another activity type on the early education activity pyramid.

2. **Clay Power!** Using clay as your prop, describe how you could use clay or modeling dough to teach a lesson using at least three different activity types described in this chapter.

3. **Adapting to Differences, Part 1.** Observe a small group of young children interacting with their teachers or caregivers in a planned activity. What do you notice about where children seem to be in terms of the cycle of learning? How does the teacher adapt to differences in where individual children might be in the cycle? What implications did your observation reveal for your approach to working with children in small groups?

4. **Adapting to Differences, Part 2.** Observe the exploratory play of a young preschooler and of an older preschooler using some type of open-ended material such as blocks, water, or sand. Describe similarities and differences between what the children say and do in their explorations. What implication does this have for your planning and teaching?

5. **Communicating with Families.** Select one activity type described in this chapter. Develop a one-page handout for families describing the activity and what children might learn through their participation.

References

Chalufour, I., & Worth, K. (2004). *Building structures with young children.* Washington, D.C.: NAEYC.

Cliatt, M. P., & Shaw, J. M. (1992). *Helping children explore science.* New York: Merrill/MacMillan.

Copple, C., & Bredekamp, S. (2009). *Developmentally appropriate practice in early childhood programs serving children from birth through age 8* (3rd ed.). Washington, D.C.: NAEYC.

Elkind, D. (2007). *The power of play: How spontaneous, imaginative activities lead to happier, healthier children.* Cambridge, MA: De Capo Press.

Epstein, A. S. (2007). *The intentional teacher: Choosing the best strategies for young children's learning.* Washington, D.C.: NAEYC.

Epstein, A. S. (2008). An early start on thinking. *Educational Leadership, 65*(5), 38–43.

Freiberg, H. J., & Driscoll, A. (2005). *Universal teaching strategies* (4th ed.). Upper Saddle River, NJ: Pearson.

Frost, J. L., Wortham, S., & Reifel, S. (2008). *Play and child development.* Upper Saddle River, NJ: Pearson.

Kostelnik, M. J., & Grady, M. L. (2009). *Getting it right from the start: The principal's guide to early childhood education.* Thousand Oaks, CA: Corwin.

Maxim, G. W. (2006). *Dynamic social studies for elementary classrooms* (8th ed.). Upper Saddle River, NJ: Pearson.

Robertson, B. (2007). Getting past "inquiry versus content." *Educational Leadership, 64*(4), 67–70.

Warden, C. (2008). *Talking and thinking floorbooks.* Keynote address, NAEYC, Lincoln, NE.

7 Centered on Learning: Creating and Maintaining Learning Centers Indoors and Outdoors

Young children are very aware of their physical environment and use all of their senses to respond to and interact with it. Sometimes they reconstruct their experiences by actually drawing out maps or pictures of the spaces where they live and play.

Look at Michael's drawing of his preschool classroom. Can you find the kitchen? The light table? The rug? The sink? And the goo? These are all important features of Michael's world.

Sam turned toward the sound of falling blocks and hurried to join Tom and Jorge in the block center. Craig paused as he entered the room, looked around, and sniffed as he glanced at some new flowering plants near the window. He moved slowly into the room, checking out each learning center carefully before choosing any to enter. Jean clung to her mom for a last hug before she accepted the hand of Miss Baldwin, who walked her over to a table where puzzles had been arranged.

These children responded to the environmental design of the classroom and the climate created by their teachers. Knowing that children learn from everything they see, hear, smell, feel, and taste, the teachers in this classroom created a space that would support engagement, learning, and motivation and where children would feel safe and secure.

LEARNING OUTCOMES

After you read this chapter, you will be able to:

- Create an environment that is comfortable, safe, and responsive to the needs of all young children.
- Select and arrange materials for learning.
- Set up a variety of learning centers.
- Implement learning centers related to program goals and identify related pitfalls.
- Adjust centers to meet the diverse and changing needs of all children.
- Communicate with parents about space, materials, and children's learning.

Creating an effective learning environment like this is something you must learn to do too.

A good place to begin your environmental planning is by considering the materials children use day to day.

Materials

Among the things you provide children will be purchased items and materials you have found. Thus, the things you use to teach children will come from many sources. Here are just some examples of items and materials and their sources:

- *Commercial toys.* Blocks, puzzles, games, balls, climbing frames, and tricycles
- *Household goods.* Measuring cups, nuts and bolts, buttons, pieces of fabric, dress-up clothes, food containers
- *Commercial discards.* Containers of various sizes and shapes, bits of wood, paper cut to unusual dimensions and with varying textures
- *Natural materials.* Flowers, shells, rocks, sand, water, sticks, soil, clay, food, and feathers
- *Office supplies.* Recycled office items as well as purchased items such as glue, tape, paper, and writing implements
- *Teacher-constructed materials.* Teacher-made games, pretend play kits, recordings of stories you have read aloud, recycled materials, special collections in support of science, math, or art
- *Books and other literacy-related materials (owned by the program or borrowed from the library).* Big books, regular library books, audio books, stories illustrated in videos, video and computer games
- *Special supplies and tools.* Art supplies; science materials such as magnifiers, magnets, pulleys, and clamps; recorded music and rhythm instruments
- *Kits purchased by the program to be used for instruction.* A variety of materials and instruction books (often expensive)

Regardless of the source, the selection and use of materials share some common characteristics.

SELECTION OF MATERIALS

Every teacher likes to spend time looking through toy and equipment catalogues. It is fun to order new things and exciting when the boxes arrive! Yet equipping a classroom involves more than leafing through catalogues and choosing the latest offerings. It involves careful planning and making choices related to the criteria in the discussion that follows.

GOAL RELATED

Select materials with specific program goals in mind. Avoid "cute" things that might appeal to you initially but do not lend themselves to furthering your program goals. The best materials are those that can be used across domains. For example, in Figure 7.1, the same collage materials (art scraps, glue, fabric scraps, pompom balls, ribbons, magazine pictures, markers, foil, construction paper, and tape) are used for different educational purposes. Those purposes are determined by how the materials are used (Kostelnik, Soderman, & Whiren, 2011, p. 150).

SAFETY

First, keep the children safe. All materials should be structurally safe and sturdy. For example, a tricycle built for group use is less likely to lose a wheel than is one built for an individual's use. Consider risk factors of ordinary objects. Anything larger than a dime and smaller than a quarter is a choking hazard. Some things have sharp edges or points (push pins), or the potential for pinching or falls.

AGE APPROPRIATE

Childcare centers are often recipients of toys that members of the community no longer need at home. Select only those toys and materials that the children in your group will find challenging and rewarding. A few materials to meet the needs of the

---

FIGURE 7.1 Collage materials in several domains

Affective activity. 1-2-3-4-5 Collage

Purpose. To work through a task from beginning to completion

Procedure: Tell the children. "Select several items for a collage. Make your collage, show it to a friend, and talk about it. Put extra materials away, and announce 'The end.'"

Aesthetic activity. Color Collage

Purpose. To contribute to the aesthetic environment of the school

Procedure: Tell the children. "Make a collage in colors you like best. When you are finished, hang up your work for everyone to see and enjoy."

Physical activity. Snip or Tear Collage

Purpose. To practice fine-motor skills

Procedure: Tell the children. "Choose some large paper. Either cut or tear it into little pieces to make your collage.

Language activity. Texture Collage

Purpose. To increase children's descriptive vocabulary

Procedure: Tell the children. "Choose some materials from the box that feel different. Create a collage of many varied textures. Tell someone else as many words as you can think of to describe the textures."

Social activity. Buddy-Up Collage

Purpose. To practice negotiation skills

Procedure: Tell the children. "Each of you will receive a bag containing different collage materials. If you need or want something from someone else's bag, find a way to ask, trade, or share to get what you want."

Cognitive activity. Number Collage

Purpose. To practice number skills

Procedure: Tell the children. "There are four pans of materials from which to choose. Select four items from each pan and glue them onto your paper. You will then have four sets of four."

developmentally delayed or the gifted may be stored and used when the need arises. However, when materials are not age appropriate, children may misuse them.

SIZED CORRECTLY

A larger boy's shirt, tie, and hat are closer in size to young children than is menswear for use in pretend play. Bigger scissors are very hard to use and potentially dangerous for young children. All toys and materials should be of a size suitable to the age group.

COMPLETE AND READY TO USE

Make sure that all the pieces of a game are together. A puzzle with three pieces missing is simply frustrating for children. Check to see that books have all the pages. All material displayed should be usable.

CULTURALLY DIVERSE

Materials should represent the children in the group and the community. The interests of boys as well as girls should be reflected. Unbiased images and materials can help children understand diverse populations (Derman-Sparks & Edwards, 2010). For example, if there is a photo of an ill or disabled aged person, there should also be some photos of healthy, active aged people. Music, art, games, and photos are available that depict diverse populations:

- Men and women in a variety of work and family roles
- Families of various compositions, ages, and economic conditions
- Workers in business, homemaking, agriculture, education, and service occupations
- People of all races, abilities, and religions displayed respectfully

Materials in the classroom should represent the families of children attending, the larger community in which they live, and the nation.

PROVIDING FIRSTHAND EXPERIENCES

Young children learn best with concrete materials and real things. Their ability to handle abstract ideas varies widely, but between the ages of 3 and 6, most children need to form ideas with real objects. In Table 7.1 you can compare potential learning materials. When firsthand experiences are not safe or practical, then using video images and photos are the next best choice. Clearly, not every child can experience a real bear, for example, but models of bears and teddy bears can be handled, and bears are

TABLE 7.1 • Examples of Materials Varying from Concrete to Abstract

CONCRETE	INCREASINGLY ABSTRACT	ABSTRACT
A yellow coffee cup	A life-size photo of the same cup	A drawing of a cup
Colored beads with a life-size colored pattern of the beads on poster board	Colored beads with a reduced-size colored pattern of beads on poster board	Colored beads with a colored pattern of dots on poster board
Unit blocks	Unit blocks with a simple floor plan drawn on large paper	Unit blocks with a floor plan of a house from a magazine
Field trip to the zoo	Realistic models of zoo animals	Abstract sculptures of animal forms
A garden tended over time	Photographs of gardens	Stories about gardens or words related to gardens written on large paper

often in zoos where they can be viewed from a distance. The younger the children are, the more they are dependent on firsthand, concrete experiences.

LITERACY-RELATED MATERIALS

When considering literacy materials, you might think of picture books, reading schemes, and wide-ruled paper as literacy materials. They are, but there are so many more, such as cookbooks, magazines, shopping lists, blueprints, envelopes, and advertisements. Ms. Marinez took a clipboard and pen with her on a walk with the 3-year-old children and asked them to tell her what they noticed as they moved from one place to the next. She wrote each child's observation down and used her notes to summarize what they saw when they returned to the classroom: "Clinton noticed the bird feathers near the tree, and Isaac pointed out the bird nest above them." Children acquire many basic concepts about literacy if they see materials used in every center every day.

VARIED MATERIALS FOR EACH DOMAIN

Materials should be changed regularly in each domain. For example, there are many memory games available, one about birds of the Rocky Mountains, another about Disney characters, and a third about shapes. Selecting a variety of materials related to the same goal and rotating them in and out of the center will increase use. A variety of commercial and homemade percussion instruments and a vast array of picture books are available. Leaving some for comfort or that are a favorite of specific children is fine, but a variety in the selection over time will enhance learning.

INCLUDING LOOSE PARTS

loose parts Anything that is small and can be manipulated by children; often what adults call junk (e.g., stones, seeds, sticks or other natural materials, or small tools or recycled material such as Styrofoam peanuts).

Sand, water, leaves, stones, sticks, plants, and other loose parts such as containers and shovels provide for more challenge and interest in outdoor play (Herrington, 2011). Industrial and commercial discards or even shipping peanuts and holiday wrapping paper can be used to enhance interest and variety without much cost. Children frequently see potential that adults miss.

USING MATERIALS

Children react differently to materials depending on how they are displayed and how accessible they are. Materials in a heap on a shelf elicit a different reaction from children than do materials that are displayed in separate containers or on shelves labeled with what they are. Consider the following dimensions as you support children's use of materials in the classroom.

PROVIDE PROPER STORAGE

Use clear plastic containers for storing small items such as one-inch cubes or counters. Cardboard file boxes might be useful for storing pretend-play kits until the materials are brought into a classroom. Store things where they are used first. For example, put scissors, paste, paper, and crayons all in one storage area in a creative arts center. Consider how and where something will be stored so that children can get it easily and take care of it independently when it is in active use and you can store it out of the way when it is not in use. Show children how to maintain their environment and encourage them to keep it organized. Label storage containers to facilitate children in cleaning up the materials and returning them to where they belong.

ROTATE MATERIALS

Displayed materials should be exchanged from week to week as the needs of children change or for new themes and projects. Materials also can be rotated during the day when children are in session for 8 or more hours. Mrs. Wilkinson had a cart where she stored some materials displayed only after nap. Children are more likely to explore materials that have not been out earlier.

PROVIDE QUANTITIES OF MATERIALS APPROPRIATE FOR THE NUMBER OF CHILDREN

There must be enough materials for the number of children who share them. One child can successfully use a 12-piece puzzle or a small picture book. Three or four children can share a large bowl of play dough or a collection of nursery-sized blocks. Avoid asking several children to share materials more suited to one or two children, as no one will have an opportunity to experience success.

KEEP SHELVING NEAT AND ORDERLY

Provide adequate space around materials on shelves; young children have difficulty locating objects crammed together. Use colored paper or cloth to draw attention to some materials or drawings to indicate where to return playthings to the shelves. Remove materials once children have completed the learning objectives related to them. Avoid clutter.

GIVE REASONS FOR THE STANDARDS FOR CHILDREN'S USE OF MATERIALS

The maintenance of the physical environment by the children is one of the instructional strategies that can support goals in the affective and social domains. It also helps children feel like contributing members of the group. For example, Mrs. Sawyer asked Janet to wash paint brushes so they will be ready to use another time. She also asked David to wipe up spilled milk so Mike would have a clean spot to eat. These daily occurrences help children to develop standards of cleanliness.

DEMONSTRATE THE USE AND CARE OF MATERIALS

Jeremy flipped a wooden puzzle over, scattering pieces on the table and the floor. When Mr. Sherbo showed him how to lift the pieces one by one and lay them beside the puzzle, he willingly did so.

Children are not likely to know how to use all of the materials commonly found in programs. Children who are shown how to use paints so they are not mixed up in the paint jars, are taught to place blocks on shelves according to size and shape, and who are encouraged to sort small parts of materials that have been mixed learn intellectual skills as well as being more responsible members of the classroom community.

■■ TRY IT YOURSELF

Gather a collection or supply of natural materials (stones, leaves, sticks, shells, bugs, feathers, soil, clay, etc.) from a public park, open space, or your yard. Do not damage the area. Select a container to store the material and a place to display it indoors or out. Arrange the materials appealingly where children can examine them. Observe the children's responses to the materials, the display, and storage cues. Identify what you might change or repeat. Repeat using manufactured materials such as bottle caps, keys, screws, buttons, and so on.

Learning Centers

Learning centers are well-defined interest areas that provide children with a wide range of materials and opportunities to engage in hands-on learning across the curriculum (Stuber, 2007). As an early childhood educator, you will create a variety of learning centers from which children will choose. Sample outdoor centers are swings, sand, riding toys, climbers, and water play. Some indoor centers might be blocks, creative

learning center Well-defined interest area where children engage in hands-on learning.

arts, pretend play, math, and science. When participating in learning centers, children self-select their activity, the pace, the order, and the specific means through which they approach different learning tasks. Thus, learning centers give children the chance to:

- Make choices
- Move about as needed
- Build on previous experience in meaningful ways
- Choose activities that fit their particular learning styles and needs at the time
- Progress at their own rates within and among activity areas
- Sustain self-directed activity
- Integrate knowledge and skills from one activity to another
- Develop concepts and consolidate their learning across the curriculum
- Develop skills in working with other children and adults (Kostelnik, Soderman, & Whiren, 2011, pp. 132–133)

Centers are arranged in three-dimensional rooms with the materials and equipment ready to use.

Learning centers have some common characteristics. First, they are *spaces with clear boundaries*. For example, a curb or an edge of a box outdoors usually surrounds the sand center. Sometimes a paved path functions as a center for wheeled toys while forming the boundary for a climbing structure. The space that encloses the pretend play center is defined by the placement of storage units, a table, and the kitchen appliances so that it looks like a little room. The painting center may be on a hard-surface floor bound by shelves holding supplies. Learning centers are three-dimensional and are connected by pathways where children move freely.

Second, a learning center will *contain all of the materials that are needed* to implement an activity. Often the materials are stored in that specific center. An empty table with no learning materials available is not a learning center. Activities may be self-sustaining or initiated by an adult. Learning centers usually have many materials from which the child can choose an activity in addition to the specific one planned for the day. Planned activities also are often repeated so that all children may participate over time. Every center should include literacy-related materials such as cookbooks in the housekeeping area or paper and pencils in the block area to draw constructions.

Third, learning centers must remain *flexible*. The same center may have different functions over time. For example, the art center may be used to meet social goals when children work together, cognitive goals when they learn about the effects of mixing paints, or affective goals as children learn the satisfaction of finishing what they have begun. The same tables may later be used for eating lunch. Centers also have activities available that will challenge the most skilled children and activities that can be successfully completed by those with special needs.

Fourth, learning centers *encompass a range of activity types*—exploration, guided discovery, problem solving, discussions, demonstrations, and direct instruction—with exploration, guided-discovery, and problem solving predominating. Children use centers with minimal adult guidance once they understand what they are to do and how to do it. Additionally, children display knowledge and skills while using centers that you will observe and document to assess children's learning (Kostelnik & Grady, 2008).

Last, all centers combined, both indoors and outdoors, should *provide a balanced curriculum* that includes every domain every day. Some plans are for the whole group, others for individuals or small groups. Some center activities last only one day or two; others last a month or are continuous. Sometimes the same domain is addressed several times in full-day programs. For example, Ms. Rothbart may have several aesthetic centers operating at one time: creative dramatics, pretend play, and a collage activity, with singing as a part of large group center and musical instrument exploration planned for outdoors.

Centers in early childhood settings vary in number, materials, equipment available, and the creative ideas of teachers as well as children. The same centers may be indoors or outdoors, depending on the climate. In addition, a center such as a literacy center may be broken down into several subcenters such as a listening center, a writing center, and a read-

What activities would you expect to occur in this outdoor center?

ing or book center. Special interest centers may be of short duration, one day to one week, based on special interests such as having a cardboard box space ship in the room. Others, such as a cooking center, might be recurring. Some key centers, however, form the basic structure of early childhood programs: language arts; the creative arts and construction center (two- and three-dimensional art of modeling); the science and collections center; the math, manipulative materials, and table games center; a dramatic play center; and a large space for the block center. A large open space where whole group gatherings are held may also be the place where dance, gross motor activities, music, and group storytelling occur during other parts of the day.

LANGUAGE ARTS CENTER(S)

The language arts center supports children's emerging language skills and abilities in speaking, listening, viewing, reading, and writing. Programs may have several centers that are devoted to these skills open throughout the day.

As 3- and 4-year-olds enter their full-day program, they find their name card, with parental help, on a small table near the door and place it in a holder under the "question of the day" (e.g., "Are you wearing red?") that is posted. Later, teachers and children will read the question together and count how many yes answers there were. There is a reading/ listening center with pillows and a covered baby mattress near shelves of books displayed where one or two children can enjoy looking at books or listening to a volunteer read to them. A small desk with earphones, books, compact disc player, or iPod is nearby with two chairs available. An adjacent bulletin board serves as a message center where teachers respond to children's drawing in writing, and read these messages aloud to them. Eventually, older children will begin to leave messages for the teacher and each other.

Children listen to stories daily during group experiences and sometimes enact a favorite story such as *Caps for Sale* or *Three Billy Goats Gruff.* Story reenactment is often an independent center where kindergarten children enact a well-known story with appropriate props that define the characters and are essential to

This writing center is part of a larger area that includes a listening area and books.

display the action in the story. When designing and implementing an activity in your language arts center, use the following nine guidelines:

1. Provide materials for all aspects of language arts (listening, reading, writing, viewing, speaking) every day.
2. Display the front covers of picture books and encourage children to share their ideas with others.
3. Display the alphabet at the children's eye level.
4. Print upper- and lower-case letters legibly when identifying children's work and when recording dictation.
5. Provide some excellent high-interest, culturally diverse, and nonbiased books that will remain in the classroom so children can reread them. Also provide supplementary books to support themes or new interests.
6. Include nonfiction books and books made by the class or individual children.
7. Take dictation related to children's drawings and display them within the room.
8. Provide reference materials related to current themes and projects.
9. Include age-appropriate technologies: computers, audio books, and videos of children's literature.

CREATIVE ARTS AND CONSTRUCTION CENTER

Children are attracted to the arts center, where they can explore materials and display their ideas visually. The teacher's role is to encourage exploration, demonstrate the skills the children will need to use the equipment and the materials, and stimulate children's ideas. You should value children's creation and reinforce their personal expression and interpretations. In this center, the process of production is most important. The end product should not be an imitation of someone else's product or held to adult standards of reality. Pink cars may float over blue roads with brilliant rainbows under chartreuse suns. Children may explore the effects of drops of paint on a coffee filter or they may represent events or objects important to them. To support them, organize the center using the following five guidelines:

1. Place the storage of art materials and furnishings near a water source and be sure that traffic does not flow through the center.
2. Provide a rack, clothesline, or flat surface where products can dry.
3. Display products of all children in the group and send the art home regularly.
4. Facilitate independent cleanup by providing newspapers to go under messy projects, wet sponges for wiping spills, paint smocks, and paper towels.
5. Set up furnishings so that children may work alone, in pairs, or in small groups.

What would you add to this art center to make it more appealing?

SCIENCE AND COLLECTIONS CENTER

Children observe intently as they sniff, examine, touch, pinch, and sometimes taste natural and manmade materials as they compare what they already know to new ideas they glean from their most recent experiences.

Your role is to organize the materials, ensure safety, and provide information. Whether the center is focused on basic tools (e.g., wheel, wedge, pulley), astronomy, birds of prey, or water, the essence of the science center is for children to find out something. Therefore, you will ask them to scan, explore, observe, sort, vary conditions, compare, predict, describe, label, and evaluate outcomes. Questions such as "What do you see?" or "How are they alike/similar/different?" or "How can you find out?" or "Why did that happen?" or "What do you think will happen when (new conditions)…?" are most important. Good science centers have something for children to do and a way for them to communicate what they have done. Be alert to the young child's tendency toward "magical" thinking, such as when Kent thought that floating was a function of the color of the boat that floated. Instead of telling him he was wrong, Mrs. Ishikawa simply provided materials that would sink and others that would float in that color and enabled him to discover his own error in thinking.

What do you think children will do with these materials in this space?

Young children benefit most from exploring real things, particularly in topics they encounter every day, such as why cars roll faster on hard floors than fluffy carpets. However, they also benefit from photographs of distant ecosystems, videos of animals, and appropriate simulations and models as they show interest in topics too distant or unsafe for firsthand experiences. Here are five guidelines for setting up the science center:

1. Locate the science center according to the science topic. Put plant observation near a window, comparing rolling cars on different surfaces in a large open area, and viewing a video of birds of prey near an electric outlet.

2. Gather and attractively display the materials, including reference books and photos that will extend knowledge.

3. Arrange tools for easy access, and ensure ahead of time that everything works.

4. Demonstrate the use, care, maintenance, and storage of tools and materials.

5. Provide digital cameras, writing/drawing materials, or tape recorders so that children can record their experience and communicate their ideas, and make sure to train children to use these materials appropriately.

scaffold To organize into incrementally more difficult steps while providing cues for success.

MATH AND MANIPULATIVE CENTER

Children need a lot of experience in comparing things as a foundation for mathematics. Carefully select materials to facilitate observation. Scaffold children's ability (that is, organize it into incrementally more difficult steps while providing cues for success) to note differences and similarities: patterns with varied colors, sizes, shapes, textures, and materials (wood, plastic, metal). When the materials selected to be sequentially difficult are placed in this center, children construct some mathematical ideas as they play. For example, activities that encourage simple matching pairs of duplicate objects are easier than an activity that requires a child to sort a large group of objects. Many of the objectives in the cognitive/math chapter (Chapter 12) can be carried

Identify the concepts a child must explore in order to make objects balance.

out through organized center activity. The following five guidelines will help you set up this center:

1. Provide materials for all aspects of mathematics. Highlight materials by placing them on tables before children arrive. Store materials with plenty of space around them for easy identification.

2. Provide a balance of open-ended materials (Bristle Blocks®, pegs, Legos®), self-correcting materials (plastic doughnuts on a cone, puzzles, nesting cubes), simple games (Memory®, Candyland®, Go Fish®), and collectibles (bottle caps, buttons, sea shells).

3. Provide novel and familiar materials, some that are easier and others more challenging, some that can be used by individual children and others to be used in groups.

4. To maintain interest, rotate similar materials over time. For example, a program may have 36 puzzles and display only 12 at a time, switching them out occasionally. For full-day programs, some materials should be set aside for late afternoons only.

5. Provide paper and pencils, number and shape books, and printed or hand colored pattern cards to use with actual materials (e.g., pictures or drawings of cubes and beads to match with real items).

Blocks are sorted by size and shape and placed in easily accessible shelves with related materials.

BLOCKS CENTER

Blocks are versatile and can be used across many domains, as shown in Table 7.2.

When literacy materials are included, the block center may also provide reading and writing experiences (Schickendanz, 2008). Save sketches or photos of constructions as an excellent starting point for taking dictation or detailed oral description (Neuman &

TABLE 7.2 • Using Blocks Across the Domains		
DOMAIN	**SAMPLE GOALS: CHILDREN WILL . . .**	**ACTIVITIES**
Affective	Demonstrate care and responsibility for classroom materials.	Replacing unit blocks to match posted shapes in cupboards; annual block cleaning.
Aesthetic	Recognize and respond to basic elements of art (pattern, shape).	Constructing patterns using block shapes.
Cognitive	Recognize, describe, and extend patterns.	Continuing a pattern of construction once begun.
	Explore firsthand a variety of cause-and-effect relations.	Spacing blocks vertically so that they will sequentially fall when only one is slightly pushed (domino effect).
Language	Put their thoughts on paper, first through simple pictures and then incorporating print into their drawings.	Sketching out a block structure so that the builder can reconstruct the structure or can communicate to others how it is constructed.
Physical	Engage in a variety of activities that require coordinated movements with large and small muscle systems.	Pushing, pulling, lifting, placing, adjusting, manipulating, balancing.
Social	Develop play skills: initiate play, join a group, make suggestions, take suggestions, play productively alone or with others.	Negotiating space and materials. Cooperating when two or more work on the same structure; discussing and agreeing or the play disintegrates.

Roskos, 2007). Children frequently make signs labeling their structures. The following nine guidelines will help you construct a block center:

1. Arrange a storage unit near a corner so the end touches the wall and forms a three-sided enclosure. This should be away from traffic or doorways to prevent constructions from being knocked down accidentally.

2. To control noise, locate this area in the most active or noisy part of the room on a rug or carpet.

3. Place the block area near the pretend play area if possible to enhance play in both areas.

4. Label the storage areas with silhouettes of blocks that should go on each shelf, and provide bins for storing other props.

5. Establish rules to encourage safety and cooperation. For example, ask children to build at least 1 foot from the storage unit to allow others access to blocks. You could mark this zone on the floor with masking tape to help children remember the rule. Blocks should remain clean and unmarked so other children will enjoy them.

6. Provide sign-making materials for older children, as well as blueprints or house plans or other related literacy materials.

7. Provide a variety of other loose parts to be used with blocks, such as small shells, bottle caps, and scraps of cloth and paper.

8. Using Velcro fasteners, attach fabric to the block storage unit so that it can be closed when the large space is used for other purposes.

9. Provide accessories such as small people, cars and trucks, animals, and stop signs in appropriate storage baskets placed with or near the blocks.

PRETEND-PLAY CENTER

Children reenact roles that are familiar (family, store clerk), distant (space person), and imaginary (animals that talk). The roles they assume are varied and numerous, often relating to the content of themes. They integrate what they know happens in various community settings such as a post office or restaurant into their play as they build varied perspectives on their world. Pretend play is the first area where abstract thinking is obvious in very young children.

Relevant props are necessary to encourage theme-stimulated pretend play, so you will need to gather materials that support community helper roles, family roles, work roles, and character roles based on literature. Effective teachers assist children in moving beyond media-dominated pretend play based on action figures by providing the props and information children need to expand their pretend narratives to a broad range of roles and themes. Housekeeping is usually the beginning pretend situation explored because it is what children know the most about. However, with information, children explore their ever-expanding worlds to include television stations, a variety of retail stores (shoe stores, clothing stores, hardware stores), professions, and services such as car washes and beauty parlors. The pretend-play center provides opportunities for children to be creative, interact socially, understand complex economic and social relationships, and practice oral skills. When

Pretend-play centers work best if arranged in enclosed spaces or rooms.

menus, grocery list pads and pencils, telephone books, and other literary materials are available, children learn how to use them. The following four suggestions will assist you in setting up the center:

1. Enclose the center so children can easily tell when they are in or out of the center. Use a wall as a boundary and furnishings placed on the opposite side or extending into the room from the wall to form a three-sided room. Placement adjacent to the block center enables you to use the back of the block storage unit to hang dress-up clothes or other props. It also encourages interactive play between the two centers.

2. Exchange new props for old ones once or twice a week to expand understanding and maintain interest. Younger children need the same setup for a longer time than do older children because they are just learning to develop their play scenarios with others.

3. Adjust the pretend-play center to support projects and themes. Remove theme-related props at the end of the theme.

4. Include books and literacy materials such as food advertisements, cookbooks, and so on.

LARGE-GROUP CENTER

Children and adults gather together in the large-group center, which fosters a spirit of unity within the classroom. The large group center may be used to implement goals from a variety of domains such as aesthetic (e.g., dancing and singing), language (e.g., singing, finger plays, story telling), and physical (e.g., climbing frames or guided exercises). Group discussions, demonstrations of new materials and equipment, and presentation by visitors are likely to occur here as well. To develop a space for the whole group, follow these five suggestions:

1. Provide sufficient space to seat children and adults comfortably, usually on a rug or carpet.

2. Close open cupboards, cover shelves, and remove distractions.

3. Place audio equipment, big-book easels, or other tools nearby for easy access.

4. Locate the center near an electrical outlet, usually behind where you sit or behind equipment.

5. Mark seating spots with floor tape where children are expected to sit. A circle, a fan shape, or rows of varying length will work as long as each child can easily see you in the focal point.

Adults and children in the large-group area are comfortable, and everyone can see.

SENSORY CENTERS

Children have complete control of sand and water when used with selected accessories. They learn about the flow of fluids, volume, measurement, comparison, observation, and evaluation. They develop eye-hand coordination during pouring, scrubbing, grasping, and squeezing activities. In addition, these are favorite soothing activities, as children enjoy the sensory stimulation of the materials. Sand and water centers are found indoors and out in many programs and are particularly adaptable for guided activities across the learning domains. Snow, pebbles, cornstarch goop (cornstarch and a little water), and other small or fluid materials may also be used. Follow these six guidelines in setting up these centers:

1. Place a covered sand or water table near the source of water on hard-surface flooring. A heavy plastic sheet may be used to cover a carpet. Some programs use large washtubs and hang them on walls when not in use.

2. Provide a covered 5- to 10-gallon pail for storing sand when the table is being used for other things. A large pail will also be needed to drain the water.

3. Use washed sand or special sandbox sand because it is cleaner and does not cause allergic reactions.

4. Rotate accessories used with the sand and water regularly in support of specific program goals.

5. If space and resources allow, offer both a sand table and a water table.

6. Provide clean-up materials (sponges, broom and dustpan).

Teachers vary the materials in the water table to achieve a variety of goals. The concept here is that some materials float.

NATURE STUDY CENTER

The nature study center is generally a long-term setting where children can observe and participate in the care of plants and animals. Fish and rodents do well indoors. Occasional visits of other animals such as cats or dogs provide great interest in the study of pets. Caution and care should be taken with program animals and visitors to ensure safety, sanitation, and the health of children. Nonpoisonous indoor plants contribute to the aesthetics as well as the air quality of the room. "Grow" lights enable herbs and houseplants to flourish indoors when window light is inadequate.

Vegetable gardens that children plant, weed, and harvest make excellent outdoor nature study. When sections of playgrounds are not mowed, they become meadows with a variety of small animals such as insects, reptiles, mice, and birds as well as a variety of plants native to the area. Such natural areas are of great interest to children, and many firsthand learning experiences occur, providing opportunities for observation and discussion (National Arbor Day Foundation, 2007). Children also develop a sense of respect and responsibility for the natural environment (Woyke, 2004; Keeler, 2008). The eight guidelines for developing this type of center are very general:

1. Place the indoor nature center near natural light or electricity. If possible, put it near water.

2. Keep animal food and bedding near the center but store cleaning supplies and other chemicals away from children.

3. Provide drawing materials or cameras to record change over time.

4. Select an outdoor nature center away from traffic, usually in back of the school, and where there is plenty of sunshine.

5. Cultivate the soil, conditioning it in the autumn with worms, compost, dry leaves, and other vegetable material, to be ready for spring planting.

6. If the schoolyard is large enough, plant butterfly bushes or other shrubs to attract birds, butterflies, and other insects.

Children learn about nature by interacting with it.

7. Hang and maintain birdfeeders over the winter within view of classrooms.

8. Consult with the Cooperative Extension Service in your region, which has materials related to naturalized gardens and can identify poisonous plants.

Implementing Learning Centers

If center activities are new to children, such as at the beginning of the year, introduce them by using familiar materials that have a clear purpose and need less constant direct supervision for children to be successful. Over time, centers can be elaborated upon, expanded, and new ones developed. Children need 2 to 4 weeks to learn the routine of using centers and classroom expectations. The following five guidelines will help you set up self-sustaining centers:

1. Introduce the activity, explaining its purpose and demonstrating the use of materials. Show children how to clean-up materials before they leave.

2. Introduce new centers and more complex activities only after general center activity has begun. Work with small groups and encourage them to teach other children how to use the materials.

3. Use reminders, such as drawings or photographs of a child doing the task or recorded audio instructions, to help children know what to do in the center.

4. Provide center activities that support the need to practice previously taught skills.

5. Structure activities so that children can complete the project independently. Demonstrate processes and provide close supervision as you rotate through the classroom. Check on progress regularly.

DECIDING HOW MANY CENTERS TO MAKE AVAILABLE

Children should have enough options during learning center time to have some choices about what to do and to be able to move from one activity to another without interfering with others. Generally, plan at least 1.5 activity spaces for each child in the group; for 20 children, there would be 30 activity spaces. This strategy assures that there will be enough choices. However, if there is substantial interest on a particular day, an additional game, more puzzles, or increased manipulative toys may be added to the array to accommodate interested children. You count activity spaces by counting the number of children that can be involved at one time with the materials made available. For example:

Math and Manipulative

Board games such as Candyland	2–4 children
Puzzles (6)	2–6 children
Legos	1–2 children
Blocks	2–4 children
Pretend play	2–4 children

Language arts

Listening center	1–2 children
Writing activity	1–2 children
Story books	1–2 children

Creative arts	2–4 children
Easel	1–2 children
Collage activity	2–4 children
Science and collections	
Examining the parts of a plant/tulips	1–2 children

Teachers often use pictographs of stick figures or clothespins to indicate how many children can participate at a time, particularly when children are learning to use centers. Teachers may adjust center numbers based on the specific activities planned, the age of the children, the ability of children to work independently, and the limitations of space.

MONITORING CHILDREN'S USE OF CENTERS

In most early childhood programs, some centers are open daily (pretend play or blocks); other centers are open occasionally (water or sand). The particular selection is driven by the goals and activities you planned. You may be carrying out a guided activity in one center with a small group of children while other youngsters are engaged in self-sustaining activities. Usually, you or a team teacher will move about the room, checking in with children and offering instruction as needed. Observe, listen, instruct, guide, support, and encourage your students. Likewise, children will question, suggest alternatives, express interests, and develop plans (Kostelnik & Grady, 2008).

In some classrooms, youngsters may have "have-to" centers that they must complete during the week that support skills that they have not yet achieved (see Table 7.3). Painting, puzzles, and pretend are available but not required of anyone on this day. As a required task is completed, children choose another activity. Mrs. Cheny has used a yellow marker to indicate that she wants to see their work in particular centers, or discuss it with them before they leave. Children are asked to raise their hands or call for her to come when they need her.

EVALUATING CHILDREN'S SKILL DEVELOPMENT DURING CENTER TIME

Strategies for assessing children's progress can be implemented readily during center time, when advance planning is done. For example, Mrs. Cheny plans to take photos of James and Joseph's block buildings, collect a sample of writing from Mary and Mathew, and make notes on how the children playing the game were able to initiate and maintain their play. She intends to hold a mini-conference with Paul, William, and Patrick and write down some of their dictation about the collage they constructed. Thus, assessment is embedded in the ongoing flow of instruction and an ordinary part of classroom supervision. To be successful, Mrs. Cheny has her camera on the block cupboard and a pen and large sticky notes in her pocket for making

TABLE 7.3 • Have-To Centers

GAME	PUZZLES	BLOCKS	LEGOS	PRETEND PLAY	WRITING	STORY	COLLAGE	PAINT	PLANT	LISTEN
Hui-ren	Jean	James	Rose		Mary	Jan	Paul		Amir	Meredith
Robert	Dena	Joseph	Beth		Mathew	Doris	William		John	Katherine
Ben							Patrick			

observational notes, which she can expand later. Keeping records of these observations and other assessments, Mrs. Cheny will plan her "have-to" activities and assess every child's progress in each area over several days.

MAKING CHANGES TO THE ENVIRONMENT

indirect guidance Altering the physical environment to clarify expectations you have for children.

Altering the physical environment to clarify expectations you have for the children is called **indirect guidance** (Hearron & Hildebrand, 2009). You add, adjust, or delete materials and equipment so as to highlight learning possibilities, enhance safety, protect materials and equipment, and maintain a peaceful social environment for everyone. These adjustments are necessary when children lose interest, when materials are misused, when interpersonal conflicts arise, or when activities appear to be inaccessible to some children. Examples of how you might add to the environment include:

- Putting a colored cube in a plastic bag outside a clear plastic box that holds the cubes, or gluing a photo of the cubes to the box so children will know where to store them.
- Adding another damp sponge to facilitate cleaning a messy activity.
- Adding a chair to a table where there is room and the supply of play dough is sufficient.
- Adding more props to the pretend play area, enhancing the complexity of the play.
- Adding orange cones to the outdoor play yard to separate the children who are playing a chase game from those who are experimenting with water and ice.

Deleting materials from the environment temporarily may also be necessary until children are able to effectively interact within the more complex environment. For example, you might consider:

- Reducing the number of puzzles that are available when children dump them all out at once without putting them together.
- Removing all wheeled toys from the block area when children persistently drive them rapidly across the room, disturbing others.
- Reducing the numbers of hats and dress-up clothes available at one time if they seem to distract from the ongoing pretend play.
- Removing clutter from the cupboard top and adult storage area to set a better example of caring for the environment.

Further adjustments within the environment may include:

- Altering the consistency of tempera paint by adding sand or liquid soap.
- Using floor tape to mark pathways as no-clutter zones so that a child using crutches temporarily can move more easily from one center to another.
- Shifting some furnishings so that more space is available for a large-group dance activity.
- Substituting an electric pencil sharpener for a manual one so that children can sharpen pencils without using them up.
- Taping a wooden dowel to the sink handle so that a child with short arms can wash independently.

PITFALLS TO AVOID

As you select materials and set up learning centers, try to avoid some of the common mistakes beginning teachers make.

FAILING TO PLAN FOR ALL CENTERS

Children learn from materials and from peers, but these are not substitutes for an adult who has prepared materials and guides children systematically toward important goals. Block, pretend play, and collections centers are sometimes neglected. Outdoor centers also provide opportunities for learning. Plans can be repeated or reused later as needed, but teachers should not assume that children will learn optimally without preplanning and active guidance.

USING ABSTRACT MATERIALS PREMATURELY

Even primary children learn best from firsthand experiences with concrete materials and events. Begin all new instruction with familiar objects and very concrete activities, using more abstract materials later, after children begin to understand the concept.

TOLERATING CLUTTER

Young children respond best to a well-organized, clean, uncluttered environment. Store materials in file boxes or closets and keep the room orderly. Discard or find alternative uses for materials that are not age appropriate, are broken, or are otherwise unusable. Avoid putting all the program materials on the shelves for children the first day and then leaving everything out all year long.

ASSUMING CHILDREN KNOW HOW TO USE CENTERS

Introduce new materials during large group. Discuss expectations of behavior as a group. Provide instruction on how to use new tools or equipment to a few children at a time in centers where group introduction is less appropriate (e.g., sewing activity or the computer).

ENGAGING IN ADULT-FOCUSED ACTIVITY DURING CENTER TIME

Every adult should be interacting with children, observing for assessment, or actively supervising children during center time. Other activities such as cleaning or planning should be minimized in favor of active engagement with children.

TOO MANY OR TOO FEW CENTERS

Having too many centers means teachers have difficulty monitoring them and children are too dispersed to interact with each other. Too few centers means children will be crowded or have to wait, making the potential for conflict high.

UNREALISTIC BEHAVIORAL EXPECTATIONS

Children should walk between centers and speak in normal tones. Rigid time schedules for moving from one center to another and a silent classroom are not appropriate. Children should have the opportunity to pursue their learning and move at their own pace and complete tasks they have begun, gaining satisfaction in the work.

Meeting the Needs of Diverse Learners

In her class of 5-year-olds, Sarah Williams had two children whose physical needs required special consideration in learning-center design. One was Santos, a child whose broken leg temporarily affected his ability to move about the room easily. The other was Shirley, whose short stature was the result of an inherited and permanent condition. This condition influenced her ability to access materials and activities fully.

When Santos came to school with a broken leg and had to use crutches, his teacher increased the width of some pathways between centers, added a chair in the locker area to make it easier to put on his boots, and provided a stool for him to sit on at the water table so he could play in the water without having to prop himself up the whole time. Other temporary adjustments were made as needed to ensure his full participation on the program.

Shirley is a little person who at 5 years old is the height of a 2-year-old. She has unusually short arms and legs and other skeletal differences from typical children but is otherwise healthy and competent. Following a review of the classroom space with Shirley's parents, it was determined that Shirley needs a cushion secured to the back of her chair and a stool to put her feet on to provide proper support when she sits at an activity table. She also needs mobile stools in the classroom near storage areas so she can reach materials. The toilet needs to be modified with a larger seat so she does not fall in and with a raised platform so she can reach the seat. A small, sturdy set of wooden stairs will be built so she can reach the water fountain and sink. She needs a wagon for field trips because she gets tired walking a long way and she needs a toddler child seat on the school bus.

Some modifications, like the ones for Shirley, are made in advance. Others require adjustments as you plan activities. Both Santos and Shirley are successful in their programs. Their teachers continue to make on-the-spot adjustments regularly to meet the children's day-to-day learning-center needs.

Communicating with Families

When adults first encounter a developmentally appropriate classroom, they may perceive it as a big playroom, not understanding that play is the primary vehicle of learning in the early years. Inevitably, they wonder what learning could take place in an environment filled with exciting things such as sand, blocks, and toys. The newsletter in Figure 7.2 is a sample of questions and answers you might use to address these concerns.

NEWSLETTER/WEB READY COMMUNICATION

FIGURE 7.2 • Questions and Answers About Play

The classroom that your young child is entering may look different from the classrooms you remember as a child. The following are some common questions families sometimes ask about early childhood classroom space and sample answers.

Q. *They seem to be moving around all the time. Shouldn't they sit still?*

A. Children set their own pace in learning. Some children will engage in one activity over and over until they are satisfied, while another child might learn this particular skill more quickly. When they are finished with one activity, they can choose another. All young children learn best by handling real objects. Center work provides lots of practice with real things.

Q. *Are they just playing all day long?*

A. Children engage in center time a portion of the day. Usually the center learning lasts about an hour at a time. Outdoor center time varies according to the weather. They also have whole-group activities, guided small-group activities, and they have time for meals and naps. When you come into the classroom, take a few minutes to watch your child. You will see him or her talk to other children, solve problems, examine written materials, or otherwise participate in important learning tasks as they play.

Q. *What if a child spends all her time in blocks and never looks at a book?*

A. Every center is planned to meet specific learning goals. Some children take longer than others. In addition, some children have greater interest in some centers. Therefore, I first assess what the children have accomplished and what they still need to accomplish and may assign a center or centers that must be completed during a week. Children are not rushed or pressured, so that they can complete these centers and return to revisit favorite ones.

Q. *How can you tell what they are learning?*

A. Evaluating children's learning is built into every plan for every center. You might notice a clipboard with a checklist or an observation sheet on a storage unit or a camera on the counter. These are tools that I use to record what children are learning. Over time, these records of daily performance are gathered and summarized so that they can be shared with you.

7 Applying What You've Learned

1. **Seeing Is Believing.** Observe a program with center-based instruction when children are not there.

   - Sit on the floor near the doorway. Describe what you see from this perspective. Is the room appealing, attractive, orderly?

   - Move from center to center and note what strategies the teachers use to communicate expectations or directions when they are not present.

   - Describe what you think children would do if they entered each center just as it is.

   - What has the teacher done to create a safe, responsive environment?

2. **Photo Op.** Photograph the centers of two or more classrooms. Using the photographs, identify at least two strengths of each center. Think about what you might add, take away, or otherwise adjust in the centers to make them more attractive or useful in the learning process. Based on what you have read in this chapter, identify areas for improvement.

3. **Make a Change.** While participating in a center-based classroom, add, remove, or adjust something in the physical environment. Explain what you did, why you did it, and the effect it had on the children.

4. **Check It Out!** In selecting materials for a classroom, you must consider many criteria to determine whether a particular material is suitable. Answer the following questions as applied to 1-inch stringing beads with strings, play dough, or scissors and paper. Then select any other material and answer the questions again.

   a. If a child used this material, what goals and domains could be addressed?

   b. Is there a safety issue? If yes, how would you structure the activity for enhanced safety?

   c. Is the size of the material appropriate for younger, older, or all children? How would you judge this?

   d. Is the material sturdy for independent use? Can it be used on its own or do you have to have additional materials for it to be effective?

   e. Does the material have any cultural or ethnic content inherent in it?

   f. How suitable would the material be for a child who has autism, Down syndrome, or attention-deficit/hyperactivity disorder (ADHD)? What adjustments, if any, would you need to make?

5. **Check the Web.** Companies who sell equipment and supplies have catalogues on the web. They also provide information about the size of furniture, and some provide planning guides that include a model room plan and product lists. Explore one or two and compare the recommendations with those in this chapter.

6. **Center Stage.** With a classmate, write out what you would need to create a woodworking center and the guidelines for its use.

7. **Parent Involvement.** Generate three ideas that you could use to involve parents in enhancing a center on the playground or in the classroom, contributing to materials for the classroom, or otherwise enriching the physical environment.

References

Derman-Sparks, L., & Edwards, J. O. (2010). *Anti-bias education for young children and ourselves*. Washington, D.C.: National Association for the Education of Young Children.

Herrington, S. (2011). Taking back the playground. Retrieved March 17, 2011, from www.whitehutchinson.com/news/learners/2011_march article 105.shml.

Hearron, P., & Hildebrand, V. (2009). *Guiding young children* (8th ed.). Upper Saddle River, NJ: Pearson.

Keeler, R. (2008). *Natural playscapes*. Redmond, WA: Exchange Press.

Kostelnik, M. J., & Grady, M. L. (2008). *Getting it right from the start: The principal's guide to early childhood education*. Thousand Oaks, CA: Corwin.

Kostelnik, M. J., Soderman, A. K., & Whiren, A. P. (2011). *Developmentally appropriate curriculum* (5th ed.). Upper Saddle River, NJ: Pearson.

National Arbor Day Foundation. (2007). *Learning with nature idea book*. Lincoln, NE: Author.

Neuman, S. B., & Roskos, K. (2007). *Nurturing knowledge*. New York: Scholastic.

Schickendanz, J. A. (2008). *Increasing the power of instruction: Integration of language, literacy, and math across the preschool day*. Washington, D.C.: National Association for the Education of Young Children.

Stuber, G. M. (2007). Centering your classroom: Setting the stage for engaged learners. *Young Children, 62*(4), 58–60.

Woyke, P. (2004). Hopping frogs and trail walks: Connecting young children to nature. *Young Children, 59*(1), 82–85.

8 All Together: Teaching Children in Whole Groups

September 12 — Marcy's group time notes—Yesterday was such a frustrating day! I tried to read *The Very Hungry Caterpillar* for group time but it was just a mess. First, I had to wait for Raj and Kali to finish up snack before I could start. By the time they joined us on the rug, most of the children were already wiggling and squirming! Then Jeremy and Raj began to push each other because they couldn't see the book. Cameron started pulling things off the toy shelf, and then everyone wanted a toy. No one was interested in hearing the story. Finally, I just gave up and let them go play. Maybe 3-year-olds are just too little for group time!

September 11 — Kate's group time notes—Group time went splendidly today! When I sang the *Welcome Song* Deidre and Elsie knew all the words. By the time we had sung the song twice everybody was on the rug. I taped Charlie's picture to his rug so he knew right where to sit. We moved on to *Ten Little Caterpillars* (they love that finger play!) and then I read *The Very Hungry Caterpillar*. I used a big book and that seemed to work really well because everyone could see. After the story, it was time to head outside and we crawled like caterpillars to the door! That was fun for everyone. Jameson told me he was going to look for caterpillars on the playground. Group time is just one of my favorite parts of the day!

From these notes, you can see that these two teachers had very different group time experiences. Marcy's group time was clearly not as successful as she had hoped, while Kate's group time seemed to progress quite smoothly. You may be wondering why some group times go well and others go so poorly.

This chapter will help you learn how to plan and implement an effective group time for children ages 3 through 6 years.

Whole-Group Times in Early Childhood Programs

whole-group time Those portions of the day in which all or most of the children in a class gather in one place to share the same learning experience simultaneously.

Nearly every early childhood classroom includes portions of the day when all or most of the children gather in one place to share the same experience. These moments are referred to as **whole-group time**. Half-day programs may include one or two group times each day; full-day programs may include as many as three or four. The central focus of a specific group time might be in any developmental domain or across domains, and as a result include a wide range of activities (Henniger, 2009). On any given day, the whole class may come together to do the following:

- Participate in movement activities
- Problem-solve classroom issues
- Plan together as a group
- Interact with a special guest
- Review the day's events
- Learn about new materials
- Hear a story or act out a familiar story
- Experience or create music
- Discuss important events (upcoming field trip, fire drill procedures)
- Sing together, dance, or play group games

Carried out appropriately, group times benefit everyone involved. Group times are ideal for sharing important information everyone needs—new materials available in the classroom, the upcoming field trip, or a change in the day's schedule. Group times facilitate communication because everyone hears the same thing at the same time. These gatherings also provide a set of common experiences for all children in the class. Most important, group times foster feelings of connectedness within the classroom community. Looking around the circle, children see the faces and hear the ideas of all the children in the class, not just a few, as is the case in small-group activities. Children gain satisfaction and pleasure from one another's company as they sing and dance together or create stories to which everyone contributes. Children who share their work, talk about their day, or otherwise take part in group discussions construct shared meanings and explore together the give-and-take of group membership. Group time allows children to share and demonstrate their ideas to others and also learn from their peers. These experiences all contribute to a sense of community.

On the other hand, when whole-group instruction is carried out inappropriately, it can be an unpleasant experience where children may lack attention, exhibit distracting behaviors, or receive adult reprimands (Maag, 2004; McAfee, 1985). This results in frustration for all. The difference between positive and negative whole-group experiences is careful planning and preparation.

Planning Effective Group Times

For group times to be effective, careful planning and preparation are needed. For each large-group gathering, teachers select a variety of activities and carefully plan how to sequence the activities to keep children interested and engaged. Successful group times include four parts: (1) the **opening**, focused on gathering and engaging children in the group; (2) the **body**, focused on the main purpose of the group time; (3) the **closing**, when the teacher summarizes the activity and guides children into the next portion of the day; and (4) the **transitions**, the times linking each activity within the group time and between group time and the other parts of the day. You must consider each part both separately and in relation to other parts to plan effective whole-group experiences for children. Now let us examine each part of the group time plan.

LEARNING OUTCOMES

After you read this chapter, you will be able to:

- Describe different kinds of group times.
- Create plans for whole-group times.
- Identify developmentally appropriate practices associated with effective group times.
- Adapt group times for children with varying abilities.

opening of group Strategies used to signal the beginning of group time and capture children's attention.

body of group The main purpose of the whole-group instruction time.

closing of group When the teacher summarizes the activity and guides children to the next portion of the day.

transitions Strategy that links an activity with the next activity or step.

THE OPENING

The *opening* of whole-group time captures children's attention and signals that group time is beginning. Experienced teachers draw children to group by implementing intriguing, easy-to-join activities such as finger plays or movement activities. Some teachers may choose to begin group time each day with the same song, such as *The More We Get Together* (see Figure 8.1). The comforting familiarity of using the same song can ease the transition into group time (Schickedanz, 2008). Effective group leaders know that because young children do not wait patiently, group should begin as soon as two or three children are ready. Starting group with a few familiar songs or finger plays attracts children to the group time area. It is easier for children to join a group that is already engaged in an interesting activity. For example, you might begin chanting, "One, two, three, four, five. Once I caught a fish alive" (see Figure 8.1). Children who are engaged elsewhere in the room can easily join the group in progress.

You need to secure children's involvement before moving on to the body of group time. You could do this by singing a familiar song a few times, varying in some way each time. For instance, you might sing "Head, Shoulder, Knees, and Toes" using a normal tempo, then at a fast pace, and finally, in slow motion. Another strategy is to move smoothly from one song or finger play to another, being careful not to interrupt the flow by talking between songs. Either way, you will plan in advance the sequence of activities and the transition from one to another.

THE BODY

When most of the children are participating in the opening, you will move into the *body*, which is the main purpose of the group time. What you plan will vary depending upon the goal you choose for your group time. For example, you may have children act out the story of the *Three Billy Goats Gruff* if your goal is to have the children take on roles and act out interpretations of these roles to tell a familiar story. On the other hand, you would plan a very different group time if your goal is to have the children become familiar with different types of dance. Children's successful participation is supported when they understand what will happen during each portion

---

FIGURE 8.1 Songs for signaling whole-group time

The More We Get Together

Oh, the more we get together,
Together, together,
Oh, the more we get together,
The happier we'll be.
For your friends are my friends,
And my friends are your friends.
Oh, the more we get together,
The happier we'll be!

Once I Caught a Fish Alive

One, two, three, four, five.
Once I caught a fish alive.
Six, seven, eight, nine, ten.
Then I let it go again.
Why did you let it go?
Because it bit my finger so!
Which finger did it bite?
The little one on my right!

of the group meeting and what is expected of them at that time (Hendrick & Weissman, 2010). "Now is a time to listen." Or, "Look up here. I have a book for you to see." Or, "Everyone will get a chance to dance with the scarves." The body of group time is introduced by telling children about the focal activity and then inviting their involvement through strategies such as open-ended questions or posing a problem. Props may be used to stimulate children's curiosity and interest. For example, before reading the story of the *Three Little Pigs*, you might show the children a brick, some straw, and several sticks and discuss how the materials could be used to build houses. Identifying teaching strategies such as posing challenges, asking questions, explaining, using do-it signals, and modeling will help you support children's learning and make your group time plans more effective. Experienced teachers use facial expressions, varied voice tone, humor, and gestures throughout group time to capture and hold children's attention.

THE CLOSING

The *closing* indicates to children that group time is coming to an end and sets the stage for them to move to the next part of their day. Key ideas are summarized and children are directed into other learning activities. Experienced teachers always send children *to* the next portion of the day rather than *away* from group time. You might do this in a number of ways. Some teachers explain which activities are available and ask children to choose one. Another strategy is to use a song or finger play such as the one in Figure 8.2 to release children from group one at a time. Figure 8.3 has additional examples of transitions you might use to help a child move from group time to

---

FIGURE 8.2 Jack-in-the-box

Begin the chant by having each child crouch down, pretending to be in a box.

[*Child's name*] in the box,

[*Child's name*] in the box,

Sitting so still,

Won't you come out?

(Child jumps up and responds) Yes, I will!

FIGURE 8.3 Basic types of transitions out of group time

Type of Transition	Example
Musical	(To the tune of *I Had a Little Turtle*) I like peanut butter. I like when pop goes fizz. I like Jacob, just the way he is!
Social	Choose a friend to walk with you and go wash your hands for snack time.
Physical	Let's stomp to the playground door like a great big elephant.
Cognitive	Everyone who is wearing red can get up and choose a center to work in. Now everyone who is wearing green can get up.

> **FIGURE 8.4** Finger play *Grandma's spectacles*
>
> These are Grandma's spectacles (*use forefingers and thumbs to make glasses and hold over eyes*).
>
> This is Grandma's hat (*place hands on head*).
>
> This is the way she folds her hands and (*fold hands*)
>
> Lays them in her lap (*place hands in lap*).

the next part of the day. You will want to have another adult already stationed in the area to which children are moving. For example, if sending the children to wash their hands for snack time, have an adult positioned in the restroom to assist the children.

How would you bring this group time to a close and transition the children to the next activity of the day?

TRANSITIONS

Group time is made up of a series of short activities linked together by *transitions*. For example, a traditional group time might include an opening song, a movement rhyme, a short story told using the flannel board, another song, and an exit from the group. How well the group flows from beginning to end depends on smooth and interesting transitions. It is at transition points that children become intrigued by what is coming next or their attention begins to wander. For example, you might transition children from participating in finger plays to listening to a story by using *Grandmother's Spectacles* (see Figure 8.4). By using a finger play such as this, you have not only kept the children engaged but now have them with their hands in their laps ready to hear the story!

You need not use elaborate transitions, but you will need to plan them in advance. You will want to vary the transitions you use in order to maintain children's attention over time. In effective group times, the opening, the body, and the closing flow smoothly, one after the other in a way that makes sense to children and helps them focus on group-time content. Having transition strategies planned in advance will also allow you to switch activities smoothly when things are not going as well as you would like or children's attention is fading. Transitions require the same careful planning that goes into selecting the music, stories, and games that make up each portion of group time.

Different Group Times for Different Purposes

Not all group times are the same. You will plan different types of group times to address different purposes. Specialty group times have a more specific purpose than the general group times presented thus far. Discussions of some common variations follow.

GREETING TIME

Where, oh where, oh where is Kelly?
Where, oh where, oh where is Kelly?
Where, oh where, oh where is Kelly?
Here she is at circle time!

A brief group time held at the beginning of the day welcomes children and helps them transition from home to the early childhood program. During greeting time, children have an opportunity to welcome one another and share daily news before engaging in more individualized activities. Greeting time may also be used to introduce activities and materials available during the day. This introduction could simply involve telling children what their choices are or include demonstrations of materials that children will have a chance to use later in learning centers, individually, or in small groups. Some teachers may use greeting time for daily routines such as reporting on the weather or asking children to volunteer for classroom jobs such as watering the plants or carrying around the clean-up sign. Greeting time is generally brief and is often followed by free-choice or learning-center time. A second, more traditional, group time usually follows later in the day.

PLANNING TIME

Planning time is used to encourage children to make decisions and set goals. After activities that are available during the day are introduced, children choose two or three to do and (sometimes) the order in which to do them. Children may make these decisions individually or collaborate with peers or adults in making their choices. Younger children might mark an X on the activities they plan to do; older children may number their choices in the order in which they will engage in the activities. Children could also complete this type of form in retrospect, showing which activities they actually completed. Some plans include "have-to" activities (those that the teacher requires) as well as "choice" activities, from which children may freely select. As the day progresses, children periodically refer to their plans to determine how well they are following them. Plans may be oral or written, using pictures or words. A sample picture plan is presented in Figure 8.5. Some programs end with a group time, during which children describe the extent to which they followed plans made earlier in the day. In other programs, this reflection on the day is carried out one-on-one with an adult or in small-group time.

Plan different types of group times to address different purposes.

REPORTING TIME

Group time may be held as an opportunity for children to review what they have been doing during centers or other activities. As one child describes something he or she has done, others listen and ask questions for clarification. Some children complete a reporting form, such as that presented in Figure 8.5, as a way to record how they spent their time during the day. Reporting time provides closure to the day's activities and fosters a sense of group involvement in each other's efforts.

STORYTELLING TIME

Everyone enjoys hearing a good story. Telling stories with flannel boards, puppets, or props, and enacting stories through dramatic movement are all activities well suited to whole-group instruction. Effective storytellers use various techniques to capture children's interest and hold it from the beginning of the story to the end (Machado, 2009). They do the following:

- Choose stories related to the children's interests
- Tell familiar stories as well as new ones

FIGURE 8.5 Sample picture planning/reporting form

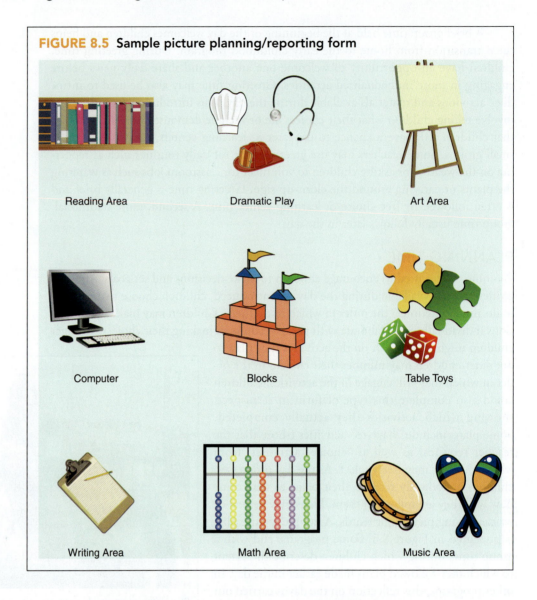

Reading Area   Dramatic Play   Art Area

Computer   Blocks   Table Toys

Writing Area   Math Area   Music Area

- Know their story well (practicing the story beforehand)
- Use dramatic voices and facial expressions to get children's attention
- Maintain eye contact with individual children by continually scanning the group
- Change the speed, pitch, volume, and rhythm of their voices to correspond to the meaning of the story
- Articulate each word clearly
- Use dramatic pauses to build suspense or facilitate transitions between events in the story
- Change their voices for each character in the story
- Provide an opportunity for children to participate in the story by making sounds or appropriate gestures or having them say repeated phrases in chorus (such as "Little pig, little pig, let me come in! Not by the hair on my chinny-chin-chin!")
- Show enthusiasm while telling the story
- Position themselves and the children so that each child can see the pictures as the story unfolds
- Transitions to the next activity if children are no longer interested

TRY IT YOURSELF

Choose a story that you might tell a group of young children. Make a video clip of yourself telling the story. Using the suggestions for effective storytelling described in the text, think about how you could improve your storytelling abilities as you watch the video.

MUSIC TIME

Singing, experimenting with rhythm and beat, and moving to music are typical activities during music time. These specialty-group activities emphasize mutual enjoyment and interactive learning. Chapter 9 provides guidelines related to several kinds of music activities.

READ-ALOUD TIME

During read-aloud time, adults read to children. The purpose is to provide adult reading models and to share good literature with the group (Neuman & Roskos, 2007). Literacy goals such as oral language, print concepts, and story sense may also be addressed during read-aloud time. Picture books with large, colorful illustrations make appropriate reading material for sharing with groups of children. When showing illustrations, the adult turns the pages from the bottom so that children have a clear view of the pictures. Often the adult sits in a chair so that children can see and hear more easily. Holding the book up high enough for everyone to see is another essential strategy. Books with complex illustrations or small pictures are better read to children individually rather than in a large group. In most early childhood programs that espouse developmentally appropriate practices, read-aloud time is a daily activity.

CLASS MEETINGS

Class meetings provide an opportunity to address matters that directly affect the group as a whole, such as changes in the room arrangement, what to do when children tease each other, or the fact that a classmate is moving away. These meetings are primarily discussion activities in which adults as well as children become actively involved. Class meetings contribute to children's sense of community and help engage children in discussions about classroom issues. Children learn how to work as a group and make compromises through class meetings (Gartrell, 2007; Hyson, 2008). During these times, children work together to explore problems, suggest solutions, and develop plans. As with any group time, class meetings have a clear purpose and established guidelines for behavior (e.g., one person talks at a time, children listen respectfully, participants have a choice to speak or not). Children as young as 3 years old can successfully participate in short meetings involving the whole group. Such meetings enhance a sense of community among children, leading to increased cooperation and ownership of classroom decision making. Over time, teachers often find that classroom conflicts are reduced (Hyson, 2008). Figure 8.6 illustrates how one teacher incorporated a class meeting before a field trip, and then again following the trip, to extend the learning experience for the children and help them relate the trip to happenings in the classroom.

BRAINSTORMING GROUPS

K = What do we **know**?

W = What do we **want** to know?

H = **How** do we want to find out?

L = What did we **learn**?

H = **How** did we learn?

FIGURE 8.6 **Utilizing class meetings as part of a field trip**

The children in Mrs. Miller's class are planning to visit a grocery store located across the street from their school. Before they leave, she holds a brief group time to discuss the trip. "Did you remember that today we are going to visit Applebaum's across the street?" Many of the children enthusiastically respond, "Yes!" She continues, "Next week we are going to change our dramatic play area into a grocery store. I thought we could use this trip to help us decide what we want to put in our classroom grocery store. Maybe we should also find out what different jobs there are in the store. How could we do that?" Samuel suggests, "We could ask the checker person at the front counter. Maybe he could tell us." Mrs. Miller replies, "That's a good idea! I think I better write our ideas down so we will remember the questions we want to ask." She writes *Ask the checker about jobs people have at the grocery store* on a large piece of paper posted on the wall.

"What else do we want to find out?" Children offer other questions such as "Where does the food come from?" and "Do the workers live at the store or do they have houses?" and Mrs. Miller adds each one to the list. Children decide who will ask which questions and Mrs. Miller transitions the group to leave. "Let's bring our clipboards with us so you can make notes about what you find out. Take your clipboard over the door by Mrs. Naga and we'll be ready to go."

The following day Mrs. Miller conducts a short discussion of the field trip during group time. They review the questions they asked and answers they discovered. On a large sheet of paper, she records each child's comments about his or her favorite part of the store. They then create a list of items they want to include in their classroom grocery store. Mrs. Miller is pleased that the children are so eager to create their own grocery store.

TABLE 8.1 • Children's KWHLH Lists for Exploring Water

WHAT WE KNOW	WHAT WE WANT TO KNOW	HOW WE WILL FIND OUT	WHAT WE LEARNED	HOW WE LEARNED
We drink water.	Where does water come from?	Look in books about water.	Snow, ice, and rain are all forms of water.	We read books about water and saw a video about different kinds of weather.
Rain is water.	How does water get from the sky into our house?	Ask Marcia's mom—she works at the utility company.	Water moves through pipes. Water gets cleaned at the water treatment plant.	We talked to Marcia's mom. We visited the treatment plant.
	Where does the rain go?		Some of the water runs into the drain and goes back to the treatment plant. Some of the water evaporates.	We read books about the water cycle.

The KWHLH formula describes the content of specialty-group times that early childhood professionals use to increase children's understanding and involvement in their learning. Such instruction times are usually tied to a theme or a project that the children are studying. Initially, the children brainstorm together a list of what they know about a specific topic (Mindes, 2006; Obenchain & Morris, 2007). During this phase, the adult does not comment on the accuracy of what children describe. As a result, the first list often contains faulty ideas along with accurate information. Next, the children create a list of what they want to find out and a third list of how they may obtain answers to their questions. The information on these three lists influences the teacher's and the children's planning. The children add to the lists or revise them as they investigate the topic. Finally, the group comes together to discuss what they learned and the strategies that led to their increased knowledge. Comparing their original ideas with what they discovered is one way children analyze their learning strategies and the outcomes of their involvement with the topic (see Table 8.1).

MINI-LESSONS

Occasionally you need to convey particular information to the whole group. Providing instructions about how to carry out a fire drill, demonstrating how to pluck the strings on a sitar added to the music area, or teaching rules for a new game are examples. Effective mini-lessons are brief and incorporate all the characteristics of active learning associated with DAP; they are not simply lectures. This kind of whole-group instruction usually precedes small-group or individualized learning experiences that build on what was presented to the entire class.

Planning Group Times: Strategies to Keep in Mind

The success of your group time is directly related to the amount of preparation and planning you do. Creating written plans prompts you to think through each aspect of whole-group instruction and sequence group time activities in a logical progression. Written plans also serve as a record of the learning goals and teaching strategies you have used, helping you vary your approach over time. In addition, written plans make it easy to identify what resources and materials are needed to implement the plan. Many elements of the written plan presented earlier in this book still apply when you are writing group time plans. However, in this chapter the format has been adjusted to address the sequence of each lesson (opening, body, and closing) and the transition from group time to the next activity in the day. Similar to what is true in writing small-group plans, you will benefit from writing out each part of the plan in detail. As you gain experience, you may choose to use a more abbreviated form. A sample whole-group plan is presented in Figure 8.7.

LOCATION FOR WHOLE-GROUP TIME

In real estate, experts say the key is "location, location, location." Effective group-time leaders realize the importance of location as well. There are several things to consider when choosing where to hold whole-group instruction. It is best to locate your group time area away from toy shelves and equipment or temporarily cover attractive items to minimize distractions. The area should be spacious enough for movement activities or whole-group dramatics. Children should be able to easily see the group leader and sit close enough together to hear one another's voices. Children can be seated in a circle, a clustered group, or a horseshoe-shaped configuration, with the adult facing the group at the open end. Some teachers use a large rug for group time; others mark the group area with tape on the floor in a continuous line or as a series of *X*s. This approach gives each child a specific spot on which to sit. Making sure everyone has enough room to see, hear, and move comfortably without disturbing others is critical. Children who are crammed together pay more attention to protecting personal space or touching their neighbors than to focusing on the whole-group activity. Figure 8.8 illustrates possible seating arrangements for group time.

Choose a group-time area that is large enough for children to move freely without bumping into each other.

FOCUS

Central to planning effective whole-group instruction is identifying what you want children to learn and then selecting activities to support this purpose. Failing to identify a clear purpose leads to confusion, superficial treatment of content, and a

FIGURE 8.7 Sample whole-group plan

Activity name: Throat, elbow, shin, and heel body parts song

Goal: For the children to identify body parts by name and location

Content:

- Every body has parts and each part has a name.
- The place where two bones are connected is called a joint.
- One joint in the body is the elbow.
- The heel is the back part of the human foot, below and behind the ankle.
- The shin is the front part of the human leg between the knee and the ankle.
- The throat is located in the front part of the neck.

Materials: Large drawing of a person with body parts labeled, posted in group time area.

Opening:

- Sing the songs "Hello Everybody" (incorporating the names of the children into the song) and "The More We Get Together."
- Transition to the body by telling the children "We are going to sing a song you know, but we are going to add some new words."

Body:

- Introduce the song: "Let's stand up and sing *Head, Shoulders, Knees, and Toes.* This time we're going to sing with the words we already know." Sing the song one time through using the typical words and body parts, making sure to touch each body part named in the song.
- Introduce throat, elbow, shin, and heels by pointing to each part on the picture and labeling each one

aloud: "This time we're going to use some different body parts. Look here and I'll show you what they are."

- Review body parts by having children touch the part on themselves as you name them: "Let's practice finding these new body parts." Say each new part, touching it as you name it.
- Practice the song using the new body parts: "Let's sing our song with these new body parts. Let's sing slowly this time so we can remember to touch each new part."
- Repeat the song several times until children can successfully locate each part by touching it as they sing.
- Transition to the closing by having the children clap for themselves.

Closing:

- Introduce Simon Says using various body parts: "Simon says touch your head." Begin with parts the children know well (head, arm, foot) and then include less familiar parts (shin, elbow, heel).

Transition to Next Portion of the Day:

- Dismiss children to wash their hands for snack by singing *Willaby-Wallaby* using body parts, touching one child at a time. "Willaby-wallaby welbow, I'm touching Jacob's elbow. Willaby-wallaby woulder, I'm touching Jose's shoulder."

Evaluation Questions:

1. How accurate were children in locating body parts?
2. What changes might I make to this plan if I were to implement it again?
3. What additional activities might I plan to extend children's knowledge of body parts?

FIGURE 8.8 Possible group-time seating arrangements

Horseshoe seating

Staggered seating

haphazard approach to skill development. Trying to address too many objectives in one group time can have the same result. You will choose one or two goals around which to plan, relating each activity to the next. Varying the focus of your whole-group instruction will help keep group time fresh and interesting to the children and enable you to address different learning objectives across time. On Monday you might choose to focus on the physical domain; Tuesday's focus might be language-related activities; Wednesday's group might center on science.

PACE AND VARIETY

Changing the pace and variety of each whole-group activity keeps group time interesting. Consider the sequence of activities within the group time; alternate quiet segments and more active times, balance listening with doing, and intersperse familiar activities with new ones. Activities such as learning a new song or watching a demonstration are best addressed early in the body of the circle time, when children are still alert and able to concentrate (Hendrick & Weissman, 2010). As the group time winds down, children sing familiar songs and engage in relaxing activities such as stretching or listening to soothing music before starting something new.

MATERIALS

Young children have short attention spans. Using a variety of interesting props will help you capture and maintain children's attention during group time. Such props may include books, flannel boards, puppets, musical instruments, audiotapes or compact discs, sections of videotape, nature items, real objects, pictures, charts, posters, and storybooks large enough for children to see. Select your materials in advance and be thoroughly familiar with the stories, songs, poems, or instructions you plan to use. Pulling a book from the shelf at the last minute or failing to practice a demonstration ahead of time can result in a frustrating group time for both you and the children.

When you select materials, keep in mind the objectives of the circle time as well as ongoing emphases, such as appreciation of diversity. Mr. Roberts illustrates this as he demonstrates a variety of musical instruments during group time. When choosing which instruments to use, he took care to include instruments from around the world as well as instruments more familiar to the children. The array of instruments is useful in addressing the goal of using a variety of materials, tools, and techniques in music and also supports Mr. Roberts' focus on multicultural inclusion. Effective teachers gather all group-time materials ahead of time, keeping them close at hand but out of children's sight until needed. Varying the types of materials used will help keep group time fresh and exciting. See Figure 8.9 for examples of materials you might use during group time.

What props or materials can you use to capture and maintain children's attention during your group time?

PREPARATION

Careful planning and preparation are crucial to successful group times. Practicing new stories or songs ahead of time will increase your confidence and poise. Practice may not make perfect, but it will help you feel at ease and organized. Think carefully about any potential problems before group time and plan for how these problems can be addressed. For example, providing visual cues for seating to ensure that everyone can see, or arranging the flannel board pieces in the correct order to prevent fumbling

---

FIGURE 8.9 Examples of group-time props

- Providing blueberries to the children when reading *Blueberries for Sal*
- Using binoculars or "special glasses" (e.g., empty frames) to play a game of *I Spy*
- Holding a teddy bear when reading *Corduroy*
- Providing scarves or ribbons to add a new element to movement activities
- Wearing a boa and glamorous hat while reading *Fancy Nancy*
- Examining a variety of leaves while discussing fall changes in nature

with them during the story, prevent potential distractions. Rehearse the words you will use for the transition from one group activity to another. Careful preparation and practice will increase the likelihood that group time will progress smoothly and enjoyably for everyone.

ACTIVE INVOLVEMENT

Consider the experience from the children's perspective when planning group times. Young children have difficulty sitting still and passively listening for any length of time. Avoid planning activities that require children to wait for long periods. Planning activities that include active involvement helps to keep children focused and attentive. For example, choose books with repetitive, predictable text so that children can join in as you read. Movement activities and simple games also add interest to group times.

Balance quiet and active segments of group time to keep children involved and attentive.

Teaching Strategies for Whole-Group Time

Although the goal of your group time will vary, your plans should reflect the age and attention span of the children present and include many well-planned activities that allow for active participation. Remember that firsthand experience for the children is as important for whole-group learning as it is for other learning activities. Make certain every activity has a purpose and ensure children know what is expected during group time. When you prepare children for what is coming next, they understand what is happening and are better prepared to participate. Experienced teachers tell children what to do instead of what not to do. For example, telling a child to "put your hands in your lap" is much clearer than saying "don't touch your neighbor." This allows children to develop the knowledge and skills needed to be successful at group time. Skilled teachers use a variety of teaching strategies during whole-group instruction. For example, you might use do-it signals, questions, effective praise, or any of the teaching strategies described in Chapter 2 for whole-group instruction. Likewise, all activity types presented in Chapter 2 (exploration, guided discovery, problem solving, discussion, and direct instruction) are applicable for group time. Figure 8.10 lists additional strategies that effective group leaders use regularly.

Review the group-time plans contained in Figure 8.11. Look for evidence of how each plan is similar and different. Consider how the plans incorporate active learning, a variety of strategies, and a balance of listening and doing.

INCLUDING OTHER ADULTS IN GROUP-TIME LEARNING

In many classrooms, adults work as a team to plan and implement activities throughout the day. For group times to be successful, it is important that everyone involved understand the expectations for group time. As one adult leads the whole-group instruction, other adults sit among the children and participate in all activities. When supporting adults position themselves close to the children and model the activities, they help to focus the children's attention on the task at hand. You will find that group times are more successful when expectations have been clearly defined and discussed ahead of time with adults as well as children.

FIGURE 8.10 **Group-time teaching strategies**

❏ Include group time as a predictable part of the classroom routine every day

❏ Clarify expectations for children's group-time behavior

❏ Balance active and quiet activities during group time

❏ Include age-appropriate materials and props

❏ Ensure that you can see the children and they can see you

❏ Continually scan the group to determine if a change in plans or approach is needed

  ○ Shorten, change, or eliminate activities that are not working

  ○ Extend or repeat activities that children enjoy

❏ Have materials ready

  ○ Pass out the materials only when needed and collect them before moving on the next activity

Source: Based on Dodge, Colker, Heroman, & Bickart, 2008; Neuman & Roskos, 2007; Stephens, 1996.

Addressing the Needs of Diverse Learners

All classrooms include children with diverse abilities and needs. In planning for whole-group instruction, you consider the duration of activities and what behaviors are required of all the children in order for them to participate. By carefully reviewing the skills needed to take part in each activity, you will be able to determine whether certain adjustments or supports are needed to successfully include children with special needs.

Most young children benefit from consistency and a stable routine, but for many children with special needs this is particularly crucial. Developing a regular circle time routine allows children with special needs to feel comfortable and in control of the world around them (Gould & Sullivan, 2005). For example, it is helpful to use familiar words or phrases to get children's attention and to use these phrases in the same way so that children understand what to expect. Introduce changes to circle time slowly, allowing children to learn each new part and adjust to the changes. You may want to use a picture schedule of the events taking place in group time so that children can visualize the sequence of activities. It is also important to demonstrate any new activities included in group time, taking care to break down the activity into component steps. Providing extra cues for each step of the activity will help children successfully participate in the new activity. Children with autism typically have delays in social skills and communication and often resist change in their routine. Figure 8.12 shows how one teacher adapted her group time to better include Justin, a child with autism.

Pitfalls to Avoid in Whole-Group Activities

WAITING TOO LONG TO BEGIN

One pitfall that many teachers fall into is waiting to start group time until all of the children have arrived. When you wait for children who are finishing cleaning up, using the restroom, or engaged elsewhere in the classroom, you run the risk of losing the attention of the children who *are* present. Begin group time as soon as a few

FIGURE 8.11 Sample group-time plans

Activity name: Creative Dancing

Goal: For the children to experience various art forms (dance).

Content:

- Dancing is a performing art that can be done to many types of music.
- Dancers can be men, women, boys, or girls.
- Some dances are spontaneous creations of the performer(s).

Materials:

- Several selections of different kinds of music (jazz, hip-hop, classical, and rock)
- Large poster paper with each type of music listed
- Markers

Opening:

- Stretching poem

    Once there was a dancer who was tiny and small (crouch down).

    She had a dancer friend who was very, very tall (reach up high).

    They danced together graceful and proud (stretch to each side).

    And when they were done they bowed to the crowd (bow deeply from the waist).

- Demonstrate different ways to move (slow swaying, tapping feet, twisting) while singing *Do What I Am Doing, Follow, Follow Me*, encouraging children to join in.

Body:

- Say "We just moved in many different ways. We're going to practice being dancers. Listen to the music, it will help you know when and how to move."

- Play music, and encourage children to move creatively. Say, "Think about how you are moving, change your moves to match the music." Dance with the children but do not encourage them to copy your moves. Use behavior reflections to point out different movements used by the children.

- Play another type of music and encourage children to move creatively using different types of movements. Before playing the final selection, announce, "This is our last dance for today."

- Following the last selection, announce, "That's the end of our performance today." Transition to the closing by having the children take a bow.

Closing:

- Briefly discuss the dances and music children enjoyed the most and why.

Transition to Next Portion of the Day:

- Have each child vote for his or her favorite song to dance to by placing a mark next to that song on the chart as he or she leaves the group to go to the learning centers.

Evaluation Questions:

1. If I were to implement this plan again, what would I change and what would I keep the same?

2. Did the types of movements used by the children vary with the rhythm and tempo of the music being played?

3. What others types of music or dance might I introduce to extend the children's learning?

Activity name: Whole-Group Storytelling

Goal: For the children to dramatize their version of a familiar story.

Content:

- People sometimes create stories on their own and sometimes in cooperation with other people.
- The people and/or animals portrayed in a story are called the story characters.
- Relating a story to others is called storytelling.
- Storytellers are people who retell or recite stories.

Materials: None or animal masks on sticks.

Opening:

- Sing *Hello and How Are You?* and *Old McDonald Had a Farm.*
- Transition to the body by talking about the animals in the song, then lead into animals in the story.

Body:

- Introduce whole-group storytelling. Say "You have really enjoyed the story of *Anansi and the Moss-Covered Rock* [by Eric A. Kimmel]. Today we are going to act out that story together."

- Briefly review the characters in the story and set the scene. Explain that each person will be a character and that you will be the storyteller.

- Begin the story by saying "Once upon a time . . ." and continue through the story.

- Announce "The End."

- Transition to the closing by having the children clap for themselves.

Closing:

- Discuss with the children the ways in which they portrayed various animals in the story. Explain that they will have the opportunity to enact the story again soon.

Transition to Next Portion of the Day:

- Dismiss from the group by having each child choose an animal from the story and walk to the playground door like that animal.

Evaluation Questions:

1. To what extent were the children interested in the activity?

2. How did the children show their understanding of the story as they enacted their roles?

3. Did I communicate directions and expectations clearly? How do I know? What might I change to better communicate these to the children?

FIGURE 8.12 **Meet Justin**

Justin is a 4-year-old boy with autism who attends Mrs. Baum's morning preschool class. She realizes structure and predictability are comforting for Justin, so she makes sure circle time follows an expected pattern. For example, she uses a visual agenda for group time so that Justin knows what is coming next. As she finishes each portion of group time, she removes the accompanying visual from the schedule. She uses dramatic vocal effects such as whispering and speaking in high and low tones to capture the attention of Justin as well as the other children. Mrs. Baum often includes puppets, pictures, or other visuals to promote children's understanding of group-time activities. Although the other children sit in chairs during group time, Mrs. Baum has Justin sit in a child-sized rocking chair. This allows him to be seated at the same height as the other children but permits him to rock, providing comforting sensory input that he needs. Mrs. Baum's careful consideration of Justin's needs has resulted in his successfully participating in group-time activities.

---

children arrive, using an intriguing, easy-to-join activity. Not only will this keep the interest of the children who are present, but it will attract the attention of the other children.

ALLOWING GROUP TIME TO DRAG ON TOO LONG

When group times run too long they tax children's ability to attend to what is happening. Select only activities that are relevant for the group time at hand. If there are several activities you want to include with the children, consider having two shorter group times instead of one long group. Group times for very young children should last only 10 to 15 minutes; children in kindergarten may be able to enjoy and benefit from group times as long as 20 to 30 minutes. Of course this is true only when the criteria for appropriate group times, such as active involvement and purposeful activity, are followed. It is better to end group time while children are still interested than after it has fallen apart.

What visuals would you use to engage Justin in your favorite children's story?

INTRODUCING DIFFICULT ACTIVITIES LATE IN THE GROUP-TIME ROUTINE

Waiting until the end of group time to introduce new or difficult activities is a pitfall that can be easily avoided. Think about which activities will require the most focus or effort from the children and present them early in the group time. Presenting such activities while the children are still fresh and attentive will maximize their ability to concentrate and successfully participate in the activity.

Communicating with Families About Whole-Group Time

The early childhood classroom can be a mystery for many families. They see children playing and enjoying themselves as they engage in various routines and activities and may wonder why you include the things you do in the children's day. Helping family members understand the importance of routines such as whole-group time can be accomplished by providing information such as that in Figure 8.13.

NEWSLETTER/WEB READY COMMUNICATION

FIGURE 8.13 • Creating Classroom Community Through Group-Time Activities

Young children are just learning to get along in groups. You may wonder, "How can we help children understand how to care for and about each other?" Early childhood teachers work to establish a sense of classroom community, helping children move from a sense of "me" to a sense of "we."

This takes time; young children need opportunities to learn how to be considerate, responsible members of a group. The classroom is an ideal setting in which to help children feel that everyone matters and is treated fairly. Most early childhood classrooms have group times scheduled throughout the day. During group time, children and adults may sing and dance together, share a good book, discuss a classroom challenge, or celebrate their accomplishments. The important thing is that they do these things together. These times together help children to develop a sense of camaraderie and take pleasure in each others' company. Group time gives children the chance to see one another and hear each others' opinions. They learn that there are different perspectives and no one view is more important than another. No matter what the activity, each person has something to contribute. This is an important step in learning to care for one another.

 **8** Applying What You've Learned

Based on what you now know about teaching children in whole group, carry out these activities to increase your knowledge and skills.

■ 1. Describe the different types of group times.

■ 2. Create plans for whole-group times. Write a detailed storytelling plan for a specific group of children. Include all portions of the group-time plan specifying what you will do and say for each part. Consider the following questions:

- Have I considered the attention span of the group as I planned the activities?

- How does my plan reflect the age, ability, and interests of the children?

- What opportunities do the children have throughout the group time to actively participate?

■ 3. Identify developmentally appropriate practices associated with effective group times.

Observe a group time

Watch a group time in an early childhood program. Look for the items contained in the checklist that follows as you observe. Based on what you see, identify two strengths of the group time and two areas that could be improved.

Group-Time Checklist

Did the leader…

✓ Choose a time and place to minimize distractions?

✓ Begin group as soon as a few children were present?

✓ Give simple, clear directions about group-time activities?

✓ Focus on what to do versus what not to do (shake the tambourine versus don't bang the tambourine on the floor)?

✓ Alternate active and quiet activities throughout group time?

✓ Change or eliminate activities that were not working?

✓ Plan transitions to send children to the next activity at the end of group time?

✓ Have a clear purpose or focus for the group activity?

Create a prop for group time

Make a prop such as a flannel board or puppet to use with the story time plan you have written. Practice using the prop as you tell the story.

■ 4. Review the group-time plan you wrote. Thinking about a group of children with whom you have worked, ask yourself the following questions:

- Are there adaptations needed for children with special needs in my group?

- How will I accommodate these needs? Do I need to:
  - Use different materials?
  - Adapt the flow or pace of my plan?
  - Add or change the structure of my group time?

References

Dodge, D. T., Colker, L. J., Heroman, C., & Bickart, T. S. (2008). *The creative curriculum for preschool* (3rd ed.). Washington, D.C.: Teaching Strategies.

Gartrell, D. (2007). *A guidance approach for the encouraging classroom* (3rd ed.). Clifton Park, NY: Delmar.

Gould, P., & Sullivan, J. (2005). *The inclusive early childhood classroom: Easy ways to adapt learning centers for all*. Upper Saddle River, NJ: Pearson.

Hendrick, J., & Weissman, P. (2010). *The whole child: Developmental education for the early years* (9th ed.). Upper Saddle River, NJ: Pearson.

Henniger, M. L. (2009). *Teaching young children: An introduction* (4th ed.). Upper Saddle River, NJ: Pearson.

Hyson, M. (2008). *Enthusiastic and engaged learners: Approaches to learning in the early childhood classroom.* New York: Teachers College Press.

Maag, J. W. (2004). Behavior management: From theoretical implications to practical applications (2nd ed.). Belmont, CA: Wadsworth/Thomson.

Machado, J. M. (2009). Early childhood experiences in the language arts (9th ed.). Albany, NY: Delmar Cengage Learning.

McAfee, D. (1985). Circle time: Getting past five little pumpkins. *Young Children, 40*(6), 24–29.

Mindes, G. (2006). Social studies in kindergarten. In D. F. Gullo (Ed.), *K Today: Teaching and learning in the kindergarten year.* Washington, D.C.: NAEYC.

Neuman, S. B., & Roskos, K. (2007). *Nurturing knowledge.* New York, NY: Scholastic.

Obenchain, K. M., & Morris, R. V. (2007). 50 social studies strategies for K–8 classrooms (5th ed.). Upper Saddle River, NJ: Pearson.

Schickedanz, J. A. (2008). *Increasing the power of instruction: Integration of language, literacy, and math across the preschool day.* Washington, D.C.: National Associate for the Education of Young Children.

Stephens, K. (1996, May). You can make circle time developmentally appropriate. *Child Care Information Exchange*, 40–43.

9 The Aesthetic Domain: Celebrating the Artist Within

May 29—Our sculpture project began when several children became interested in the sculpture located across the street from our school. This photograph shows Holly, Anna, and Luisa exploring the feel of the sculpture. Some children seem intrigued by the rough texture of the sculpture, others were fascinated by the size, and still others were curious as to how the artist made the piece. We learned the sculpture is made of bronze, but the artist first used cloth and plaster to create the shape.

Y ou may be wondering if including the arts in a child's early education is truly necessary. Some people believe aesthetic learning is less fundamental than cognitive or language learning. However, if you watch young children for any period of time, you will notice that the arts are basic. Children naturally seek out opportunities to express themselves artistically. Consider the following scenes of children at play:

- Emmett bounces up and down to the beat of the music playing on the radio.
- Emilie sketches with her fingertip on a steamy mirror.
- Denise and Rafaela don sparkly shoes, hats, and feather boas in the dress-up area, reenacting a scene from *Fancy Nancy*.

Each of these children is engaged in aesthetic experiences. This chapter will explore why involvement in the arts is important for every child and how aesthetics can be included as a fundamental part of the early childhood curriculum.

Aesthetics Defined

Aesthetics can be defined as the love and pursuit of beauty as found in art, movement, music, and life (Schirrmacher & Fox, 2009). Basically, aesthetics is a person's ability to perceive, be sensitive to, and appreciate beauty in nature and creations in the arts.

The term **arts** is used to describe both the creative work and the process of producing the creative work. The arts fall into four broad categories: visual arts, performing arts, usable arts, and literary arts (Kostelnik, Soderman, & Whiren, 2011). **Visual arts** include drawing, painting, sculpture, mosaics, collage, and numerous others. **Performing arts** include singing, dancing, playing instruments, dramatics, storytelling, and many others. **Usable arts** (or crafts) include weaving, ceramics, pottery, knitting, jewelry making, and many others. **Literary arts** include writing stories, poems, plays, jokes, skits, essays, novels, and several others. As you can see, the aesthetic domain covers a broad spectrum of experiences related to appreciation of natural beauty and art forms. This chapter will focus on designing curriculum for young children, concentrating on the visual and performing arts.

The Importance of the Aesthetic Domain

Involvement in the arts has many benefits for children. Creating and viewing art can enhance children's cognitive, social-emotional, and perceptual abilities (Epstein, 2007). The aesthetic domain also provides opportunities for children to work together and, in doing so, learn to appreciate each other's ideas and artistic preferences. Creating art is an emotionally satisfying experience and can enhance children's self-concept and positive feelings about self (Schirrmacher & Fox, 2009). Through individual art activities children develop ideas of what they want to do and how to carry out actions to meet their goals. This can lead to self-satisfaction and pride in their

LEARNING OUTCOMES

After you read this chapter, you will be able to:

- Describe the elements of the aesthetic domain.
- Describe key aesthetic concepts, processes, and skills for children to learn.
- Identify strategies for teaching in the aesthetic domain.
- Plan engaging experiences and activities in the aesthetic domain.
- Explain ways to address the needs of the diverse learners in your classroom.
- Create opportunities for families to support aesthetic learning.

aesthetics A person's ability to perceive, be sensitive to, and appreciate beauty in nature and creations in the arts.

arts The creative work and the process of producing the creative work.

visual arts The creation of art that is primarily visual in nature, such as painting, drawing, or sculpture.

performing arts Art carried out through the artist's face, body, or presence, such as singing, dancing, or puppetry.

usable arts Creation of art that is functional or practical in some way, such as weaving, ceramics, or quilting.

literary arts Creative writing such as writing stories, poems, plays, jokes, or skits.

accomplishments. In addition, providing hands-on aesthetic experiences makes learning more memorable and helps children to link ideas and concepts in a meaningful way (Koster, 2009). This happens as children experience or imagine something and then recreate it aesthetically. Thus, children communicate what they know about the world through drawing, creative movement, and music. Open-ended aesthetic activities, ones in which children pursue the activity in their own way, foster children's creativity and problem-solving abilities. For these and other reasons, aesthetic experiences are crucial to a young child's education. Effective teachers make a deliberate effort to include aesthetic education as an integrated part of the overall curriculum. This includes not only providing children direct experiences in creating art but also opportunities to develop an appreciation of art and skills in discussing and evaluating art forms.

Types of Aesthetic Experiences

A thorough aesthetic education for young children includes opportunities to experience and respond to various art forms as well as the chance to create their own art. Therefore, aesthetic experiences may be either responsive or productive.

responsive aesthetic experiences Experiences that involve learning appreciation for the arts, recognizing beauty in art and nature, and forming judgments about art.

Responsive aesthetic experiences refer to the way the child reacts to art or nature. Teachers provide children responsive experiences when they purposefully nurture awareness of the arts, foster appreciation of the arts, and develop skills in evaluating art forms. These experiences involve the child recognizing the beauty of nature, appreciating art and nature, and forming judgments about what they like and do not like. Responsive experiences include discovery, exposure, and evaluation activities.

Discovery activities provide children with opportunities to respond to natural beauty.

Discovery activities provide opportunities to respond to natural beauty. Young children explore the details of natural objects through their senses. They may study the frost on a window or a beautiful spider web or enjoy the scent of a rose or the texture of sea shells. They discover by looking, listening, smelling, touching, and sometimes tasting. Activities such as these can result in greater appreciation of nature and recognition of beautiful things.

Exposure activities broaden children's familiarity with the arts. These activities provide opportunities for children to listen to a variety of music, experience dance or dramatic performances, or view the visual arts in many forms.

Evaluation activities encourage children to discuss and make judgments about a variety of visual art, music, dance, and drama forms. Children may decide how to judge the art (such as "It has many bold colors." or "It delivers a message.") and express their preferences on the basis of those criteria. Through such activities, children learn that different art appeals to different people and that each person's view is valid.

productive aesthetic experiences Experiences that involve the creation of an artistic expression such as painting a picture, performing a dance, or singing a song, among others.

Productive aesthetic experiences involve the child in *creative art activities,* which engage the child actively with a variety of materials, props, instruments, and tools useful for making visual art, music, drama, or dance. These activities stimulate creativity and provide opportunities for self-expression. Painting a picture, gluing collage materials into a pleasing design, or experimenting with movement to music are examples of creative art activities.

Young children are naturally curious; because of this curiosity, they enjoy exploring nature, are motivated to create art and music, delight in the movement of dance, and spend hours in meaningful dramatic play. At first, the process of manipulating materials is more important to them than the product created. A child's early art, music, dance, or drama is made without regard to the effect of their work on others. Later, children feel a greater need to communicate ideas, and meaning becomes more important. Children also begin to evaluate their work according to emerging standards. These evaluations are based on developing tastes and combined with messages they have received from others. As an early childhood teacher, you will influence the extent to which children value the arts and aid them in becoming creative producers and tasteful consumers of the arts as adults. How can we accomplish this? Effective teachers (1) provide consistently high-quality creative art experiences, (2) share their enthusiasm by talking about beauty in nature and the arts with children, (3) provide opportunities and support for creative dramatics, (4) integrate art and music into the curriculum, (5) encourage individual expression, and (6) strive to become more creative themselves.

Table 9.1 contains examples of responsive and productive experiences and activities for each type.

Now let's turn our attention to creating a classroom that nurtures aesthetic learning.

TABLE 9.1 • Examples of Responsive and Productive Activities

TYPE OF ACTIVITIES	GOAL AND EXAMPLES
RESPONSIVE AESTHETIC EXPERIENCES	
Discovery activities	*Goal:* Show awareness of beauty in nature *Examples:* • Observing butterflies in the garden • Watching trees sway in the wind • Discovering beauty in spider webs • Smelling flowers, fruits, or spices
Exposure activities	*Goal:* Engage in different types of each art form *Examples:* • Examining details in paintings or photographs • Touching a sculpture • Watching a ballet or folk dance • Listening to an orchestra • Watching a dramatic performance
Evaluation activities	*Goal:* Participate in aesthetic criticism *Examples:* • Comparing several baskets (color, weave, materials, shape) • Selecting one's most colorful collage for a portfolio • Choosing a favorite painting • Telling which characteristics they liked best in a song
PRODUCTIVE AESTHETIC EXPERIENCES	
Creative activities	*Goal:* Use a variety of materials, tools, techniques, and processes in the arts *Examples:* • Playing an instrument • Dancing • Sculpting with clay • Singing a song • Taking on a role in a group storytelling activity

Setting the Stage for Children's Art Experiences

There are many general considerations to keep in mind when planning aesthetic experiences for young children. For example, locating the art area close to a sink to allow for easy hand washing after messy activities will prevent children from dripping paint across the room. The area should be well organized so that children can easily find what they are looking for and contain necessary items for cleaning up as well. Children should know where to place works in progress or items that need time to dry. Smocks to protect clothing should be easily accessible.

A well-organized art area enables children to plan and carry out their own ideas.

Access to basic art materials such as paper, crayons, and markers is needed on a daily basis. In addition to these regular art experiences, you will want to plan additional activities to introduce new concepts. You will find plans are most successful when you have carefully thought through each step of the activity. Consider the time of year and developmental levels of the children in your group. It may be best to plan simple activities early in the school year when children have had little or no experience using materials. Think about the amount of supervision needed, not only in the art area but in other areas of the classroom as well. New materials that are unfamiliar to children may require more adult guidance and supervision. Therefore, you would not want to introduce new items in several areas of the classroom at the same time unless you have adequate adults to supervise. Knowing the individual characteristics of the children in your group is also important. If necessary, think through ways you can modify the activity to meet the developmental needs of each child in the group.

Ensuring the safety of all art materials used in the classroom is of utmost importance. For this reason, it is important that you purchase materials from reputable vendors who conduct safety testing of materials before they are marketed. Carefully read the label of any new product to make certain it is appropriate for use by young children. Check for age appropriateness of materials, but also carefully consider the particular children in your group. Be alert to any allergies the children have and ensure that materials do not include allergens. Use only materials that are safe even when ingested. For example, use only water-based paints, natural vegetable dyes, and water-based glue. Check for any ventilation requirements before using materials that are not familiar.

Of course, even safe materials can present hazards if used inappropriately. It is important that you know the skill and developmental level of the children with whom you are working. Often, unsafe behaviors such as putting materials in their mouths happen as a result of the children's immaturity or lack of skill. The following guidelines will assist you in promoting safe behavior during art activities.

- Keep unsafe materials out of sight and reach. Children should not have access to items that require adult supervision or cannot be used independently. By keeping these items safely out of sight, children will not be tempted to use them on their own.

- Provide adequate space. Children may resort to inappropriate physical behavior if they do not have the space to work without being bumped or jostled.
- Keep group sizes small. This will make it easier to provide children sufficient space and adequately supervise the use of materials. This is especially important when children are first learning how to use specific materials or tools.
- Provide enough supplies to prevent children from fighting over items and place items where they are easily accessible to children.
- Teach safe use of materials and tools. Make certain that children know how to use materials safely and always model this behavior yourself.
- Supervise closely. Redirect unsafe behaviors. Remind children how to use materials appropriately.

These guidelines have focused on art activities; however, similar principles also apply to music and creative movement materials.

Addressing the Needs of Diverse Learners

Including children with special needs in art experiences may require modifying activities or materials or utilizing specific teaching strategies to assist children in being successful. It is important to know the skills and preferences of the children in your classroom, including those with special needs. You will want to monitor children's use of materials in order to match their developing skill and understanding. Open-ended materials that allow for a wide range of exploration and use are ideal for including children with varying abilities. Natasha is a 3-year-old girl with Down syndrome who attends Eric Marshall's preschool class. Mr. Marshall is mindful to break larger projects into smaller steps and give Natasha many opportunities to practice and refine her skills. He realizes Natasha has a limited attention span, so he provides open-ended art experiences that can be completed in a variety of ways. Mr. Marshall utilizes simple modifications to encourage Natasha's independent use of materials. Examples of these modifications include:

- Providing adapted tools such as loop scissors and short, chunky writing implements to assist with Natasha's weak grasp.
- Placing colored tape approximately an inch from the brush or pencil end to cue Natasha where to place her fingers when using them.
- Adding textures (e.g., sand, glitter) and scent (e.g., vanilla extract, cinnamon) to paint and play dough to enhance the sensory experiences of the activities.
- Providing alternatives to tape and glue (which are difficult for Natasha to manipulate) when making collages. For example, sticky contact paper can be used for the collage base.

As you can see, with some careful preplanning, Mr. Marshall is able to design art activities that can include Natasha.

Supporting Musical Experiences

Throughout human history, people have valued hearing and participating in musical experiences. Music has the power to excite or to soothe, to signal a celebration or to mark times of sorrow. For these reasons, music is an integral part of our lives.

This makes music an important part of an aesthetic education. Including music in the curriculum helps children to develop an appreciation of music and an understanding of music making. There are four crucial components of a comprehensive music education curriculum in early childhood programs: listening to music, moving to music, singing, and playing instruments (Schirrmacher & Fox, 2009). The following are suggestions for incorporating these four components into your classroom.

How could you support this child's interest in making music with the guitar?

- Provide a variety of music for children to listen to: jazz, contemporary, classical, folk, country, and music from around the world.

- Discuss music with children. Ask them how the music makes them feel. Encourage them to talk about images brought to mind by the music.

- Assist children in developing listening skills—listening for particular sounds, tempos, or words. Ask children which instruments they could discern in the music selection. Was the tempo fast or slow? Does the selection remind them of other music that is familiar to them? How are certain selections similar to or different from other pieces they have heard?

- Introduce new songs by singing them slowly and clearly. Repeat the song and invite the children to join in. Invite children to listen for certain words or phrases with each repetition to add variety to the singing and to help them make sense of what they are hearing. Sing the song several times with the children before introducing any actions so that children will have the chance to learn the words before combining the words with movements.

- Sing throughout the day, during transitions, and throughout various routines. Sing in the block area, on the playground, or while waiting to go outside. Don't confine singing to group time only. Use simple songs to remind children of the task at hand and make chores such as clean-up more enjoyable. See Figure 9.1 for examples.

FIGURE 9.1 Sample songs for various routines

We Are Picking Up Our Toys (To the Tune of the Farmer in the Dell)

> We're picking up our toys,
> We're picking up our toys.
> Heigh-ho the derry-o
> We're picking up our toys.

Welcome to School Today (To the Tune of Mary Had a Little Lamb)

> We welcome you to school today,
> School today, school today.
> We're glad that you are here today
> So let's begin our day!

FIGURE 9.2 **Musical instruments to include in your classroom**

Basic Rhythm Instruments
- Rhythm sticks (wooden dowels, wooden spoons, heavy straws, or heavy paper towel rolls)
- Castanets
- Maracas
- Triangles
- Jingle bells
- Sand blocks
- Tambourines
- Cymbals
- Drums

Basic Pitched Instruments
- Xylophones
- Tone bells
- Small keyboards
- Simple wooden or plastic recorders
- Basic stringed instruments
- Kazoos

- Include a variety of rhythm and melodic instruments for children to use. (See Figure 9.2 for suggestions.) Demonstrate proper usage of instruments. Teach children to treat musical instruments with respect and care.

- Provide children ample space for moving to music. Show them how to extend their arms to determine personal space and help them respect the space of others.

    For example, you can help children visualize personal space by placing a hula hoop for each child on the floor and explaining that they can dance and move within the hoop.

- Encourage children to move in creative and unique ways. Reinforce that there are many ways to move. Include props to promote novel types of movement. See Figure 9.3 for examples of props to use during music and movement activities.

- Model enthusiasm for singing and musical activities. It is not necessary that you be a talented singer or musician; children will respond to your attitude and the atmosphere you create. If you enjoy yourself and make the experience fun, children will happily join in!

Creative Movement and Dance

Young children are kinesthetic learners and they move for the pure joy of movement. Including creative movement activities as a part of your curriculum will help children develop control over their bodies and become aware of their physical abilities. One way to introduce creative movement to a group of young children is to listen to a carefully chosen selection of music. Simple music that has a strong and easily recognizable beat and moderate tempo is a good choice with which to begin. Encourage the children to listen carefully to the music and describe what they hear. Some children may instinctually begin to move or sway to the beat. At first, the movements of the children may be uncoordinated, but with repeated practice you will see them gain control of their bodies as their movements become more refined. As children become comfortable moving to the music, you can encourage

Simple music that has a strong and recognizable beat is a good choice when introducing creative movement activities to children.

FIGURE 9.3 **Props for creative movement and dance**

- Plastic hoops
- Bean bags
- Scarves of various colors and sizes
- Streamers or flags (e.g., crepe paper or strips of tissue paper attached to short, safe handles such as wide craft sticks or straws)
- Rhythm sticks
- Tambourines
- Paper towel rolls
- Pom-poms
- Batons
- Parachute
- Large mirrors so children can watch themselves move

---

their discoveries by challenging them to "find a different way to move" or "move the same way, but make it stronger." Poetry can also be used for inspiration for creative movement activities. Simple poems with rhyming verses and vivid imagery are good choices for very young children (Mayesky, 2009).

Here are some considerations to keep in mind as you plan creative movement activities:

- Begin with exploration. Tell the children that they can move any way the music "tells" them. Avoid directing the children to move in specific ways so they can experience the freedom of movement and the relationship of their movement to the others in the group.
- Establish special signals for starting and stopping such as holding up your hand palm forward. Practice these signals with children so they will know how to respond.
- Suggest moving body parts in addition to the hands and feet (e.g., sway your hips).
- Assist children in focusing on the music by repeating instructions such as, "Listen to the music carefully while you dance."
- Look to nature as inspiration. Encourage children to observe leaves blowing in the wind or clouds moving across the sky, and then use these experiences as inspiration for creative movement.
- Add rhythmic accompaniment. Clap a steady beat or use a tambourine or drum as the children move.
- Incorporate simple props to motivate creative movement exploration. Children will be inspired to move differently when dancing with scarves than when dancing without any props. Figure 9.3 contains a list of suggested props for movement activities.
- Learn dances and rhythmic movements of various cultural groups and include these in your planned activities.

Creative Dramatics

Young children enjoy acting out events and roles that are familiar to them. This often begins by children using real-life objects to enact familiar caregiving routines such as feeding a baby or cooking a meal. As they grow older, the amounts of pretend play

---

FIGURE 9.4 Finger play with motion

Five Little Hot Dogs

Five little hot dogs frying in a pan (Hold right hand up showing five fingers),

the grease got hot (Hold left hand palm side up, rub with right palm in circular motion),

and one

(Hold up one finger) went bam!

    (clap hard)

(Repeat words counting down four, three, two, and one)

No little hot dogs frying in a pan (Hold right hand up showing closed fist),

The grease got hot, and the pan went BAM! (End with BIG CLAP!)

FIGURE 9.5 Poem for creative dramatics

Once there was a giant who was tall, tall, tall.
Then there was an elf who was small, small, small.
Now the elf who was small would try, try, try
to reach the giant who was high, high high.

---

and imaginative role-playing greatly increase. You can introduce creative dramatics by presenting simple songs and finger plays with motions (see Figure 9.4 for an example). Once children are accustomed to these types of finger plays, you could encourage them to act out simple poems or songs such as the one found in Figure 9.5. Whole-group dramatics involve children role playing together in order to tell a story. In the beginning, you will find it best to have all the children act out each part together. For example, in acting out the story of the *Three Billy Goats Gruff*, you would have all the children pretend to be the smallest goat, then all the children pretend to be the troll, and so on. As they gain experience in creative dramatics, you can introduce the idea of individual children taking on different roles. Use the following hints for success when incorporating whole-group dramatics:

- Select a place for the dramatization that has enough space for the children to move about freely. Clearly identify the boundaries of the space so the children will understand where the action is to take place.
- Choose a story that the children know well. One with a simple plot and several characters will work best. Nursery rhymes can be ideal first stories for children to enact.
- Explain that role-playing is a particular type of pretending and help the children get into character. Encourage children to identify the characters and the things they said and did in the story.
- Provide realistic props for younger children. Older children may enjoy creating their own props or costumes to use while acting out the story.

- Actively include all the children. Model words and actions for children, providing simple scripts for children who are unsure of what to do or say.
- Keep the story moving from event to event. Begin with relatively short stories (around five minutes) extending the time and complexity as children gain experience.

Curricular Goals—Aesthetic Domain

You will find planning activities in the aesthetic domain easier when you consider specific goals. Goals for the domain are drawn from and consistent with those published by The National Standards for Arts Education, published by CNAEA (1994), along with the Music Education Standards from the Music Educators National Conference (MENC, 1994).

PURPOSE

The purpose of the aesthetic domain is for children to become aware of beauty in nature and art and to appreciate and participate in creative arts to achieve personally meaningful ends.

The following goals address this purpose.

GOALS

As children progress toward the goal, they will:

1. Show awareness of beauty in nature
2. Experience various art forms (music, dance, drama, and visual art)
3. Engage in different types of each art form (e.g., types of dance such as ballet, tap, folk, and square)
4. Use a variety of materials, tools, techniques, and processes in the arts (visual art, music, dance, and drama)
5. Identify and respond to basic elements of visual art (e.g., line, color, shape, texture, composition, pattern)
6. Identify and respond to basic elements of music (e.g., beat, pitch, melody, rhythm, dynamics, tempo, mood)
7. Talk about aesthetic experiences
8. Participate with others to create music, dance, drama, and visual art
9. Communicate with others using music, dance, drama, and visual art
10. Acknowledge themselves as artists
11. Participate in aesthetic criticism (describe, analyze, interpret, and judge)
12. Contribute to the aesthetic environment.

Teaching Strategies for the Aesthetic Domain

Here are useful teaching strategies that will assist you in designing meaningful aesthetic experiences for children:

- *Intentionally include the arts as a part of your curriculum.* Aesthetics are an integral part of a well-rounded education and should not be left for only when time allows. Plan a range of experiences to incorporate throughout the day, including some activities for children to explore with their senses with little teacher direction and others involving learning new skills.

- *Provide adequate time for children to explore and experiment.* Avoid the temptation to rush children into "making something." This can be a frustrating experience for children who may be engrossed in exploring the materials or experimenting with techniques. Before beginning an activity with children, ensure that there will be adequate time for them to become immersed in the activity.

- *Emphasize process over product.* Avoid the use of pre-made models (e.g., a panda face made from paper plates that the children must copy). These limit children's ideas and communicate that there is only one right way to use the materials. Children need time to freely explore materials and experiment with how to use them. They will also need the opportunity to revisit materials over time. By allowing children to use materials in original and unique ways, they maintain ownership of their creations. Show children you value their creative experimentation and encourage their own ideas in aesthetic activities, especially if these ideas differ from yours or others. Use words such as, "Your picture doesn't have to look like Anthony's. It is much more interesting when each person uses his or her own ideas!"

- *Demonstrate new tools and techniques.* Children do not intuitively understand how to use all art or music materials. Show them ways to manipulate the tools and substances to achieve particular effects. For example, show the children how to use a glue stick or how to twist two pipe cleaners together (see Figure 9.6 for examples of techniques to teach children). When demonstrating, it is best to avoid making a particular picture or a recognizable product. Doing so may inadvertently communicate to children that you expect them to create the same thing. Allow children to generate their own ideas by using the techniques you demonstrate. Comment on their technique using behavior reflections: "You twisted the pipe cleaners to keep them together." "You tapped the tambourine against your leg to make it sound louder."

FIGURE 9.6 Techniques to teach young children in the aesthetic domain

Keeping the ages and abilities of the children in your group in mind, the following are techniques you may demonstrate.

Visual Art Techniques

- Painting
- Cutting
- Folding
- Gluing or adhering surfaces
- Printing with objects
- Rinsing the brush between colors
- Kneading
- Weaving
- Twist-attaching pipe cleaners
- Using a brayer

Music Techniques

- Starting and stopping
- Being an audience
- Directing and following
- Clapping a pattern
- Handling instruments appropriately
- Concepts such as fast and slow or quiet and loud

Creative Dramatic Techniques

- Using the body to communicate thoughts
- Using facial expressions to communicate feelings
- Imitating actions
- Using props to tell a story
- Moving the head or arms of a puppet

Creative Movement/Dance Techniques

- Finding personal space
- Moving without bumping others
- Movements such as swaying, bouncing, or skipping
- Movement concepts such as high and low or fast and slow

- *Provide many choices.* Variety can be the spice of life. Different activities and materials appeal to different children. By providing children many choices of what materials to use and how to use them, children will become more deeply engaged in aesthetic activities. However, you will want to keep in mind the ages and abilities of the children in your group. Too many choices can be overwhelming. You can add choice to activities such as easel painting or drawing by providing various options for paper, brushes, or drawing tools. Early in the school year or with less experienced children, offer limited selections, expanding options over time.

- *Balance the novel and familiar.* Children need the opportunity to revisit materials and techniques in order to be comfortable and confident in their use. Basic art materials should be consistently available for regular use (see Figure 9.7). At the same time, interest in activities can be renewed by offering new twists on old favorites. For example, you could spice up easel painting by using different types of paper (e.g., grocery bags, pieces of cardboard, fabric, wrapping paper), substituting other materials for brushes (e.g., sponges, twigs, potato mashers), or adding materials to paint to change the scent or texture (e.g., mint extract or clove oil for scent, sand or sawdust for texture). Introduce a scented play dough in place of regular dough (see Figure 9.8 for sample recipes) to spark new interest. You could also combine aesthetic experiences by inviting children to paint to music.

- *Supply high-quality materials.* Few things are more frustrating than dried out markers or scissors that won't cut. Try out new materials before you introduce them to the children. This enables you to determine the best ways to use them and prevent any unexpected problems later. All materials should be age appropriate. Store materials that require close supervision or adult guidance out of sight until it is time for their use. Young children can be quite prolific artists; therefore, art materials should be plentiful. Provide recycled or donated materials in order to reduce the cost of keeping a well-stocked art area.

- *Arrange art materials in an organized and attractive manner.* This communicates to children that the activities taking place in the art area are important.

FIGURE 9.7 Basic art materials for young children

- Tempera paints (at least the primary colors—red, yellow, blue—and white and black)
- Watercolor paints (paint boxes with refillable colors, or larger paint cakes)
- Finger paints (at least the primary colors) with finger-paint paper
- Drawing materials (crayons, pencils, markers)
- Paper (manila paper, newsprint, construction paper—in white and a variety of colors, and a variety of recycled paper and paper products)
- Art chalk (like pastels, softer than blackboard and sidewalk chalk)
- Glue (white, nontoxic), paste, glue sticks
- Modeling clay
- Modeling dough (homemade is easy; see Figure 9.8)

Basic Tools for Art

- Paintbrushes—various sizes and shapes
- Paint containers (cups with covers)
- Rollers, sponges, other objects used to apply paint
- Tape (transparent, masking)
- Scissors (select appropriate for age of children)
- Staplers
- Paper fasteners
- Hole punches
- Recycled plastic containers of various sizes
- Wood tongue depressors or craft sticks
- Rulers
- Supply of newspapers

FIGURE 9.8 Scented play dough recipes

Chocolate Scented Play Dough

1¼ cup flour

½ cup cocoa powder

½ cup salt

½ tablespoon cream of tartar

1½ tablespoons oil

1 cup boiling water

Mix dry ingredients together and then add oil and water. Knead well, adding extra flour if dough is sticky. Store in an airtight container.

Fruit Scented Play Dough

2½ cups flour

½ cup salt

2 packages unsweetened, powdered drink mix (e.g., Kool Aid)

2 tablespoons oil

2 cups boiling water

Mix dry ingredients together and then add oil and water. Knead well, adding extra flour if dough is sticky. Store in an airtight container.

Cinnamon Scented Play Dough

2 cups flour

1 cup salt

5 teaspoons cinnamon

¾ – 1 cup very hot water

Mix dry ingredients together and then add hot water, mixing well. Store in an airtight container.

Materials should also be readily accessible to children so they can use them as needed. However, in order to keep shelves from being crowded and appearing cluttered, it may be best to offer limited supplies at one time and refill containers as needed. Having amounts of materials that are too large may prompt children to waste supplies as it appears there is an overabundance.

- *Challenge children to use materials in new ways.* Wonder aloud with the children by using comments such as, "I wonder how we could make this wire stand up" or "What tools do you think the artist used to create this picture? What could we use that would create a similar effect?"

- *Use language that is specific to aesthetics.* Be sure to introduce carefully chosen content related to your aesthetic goal. Words such as *landscape*, *portrait*, *tango*, or *dialogue* will be memorable to children when used in a context that makes their meanings clear. (See more about sample aesthetic content later in the chapter.) Children will need repeated exposures in order to fully understand new terms and concepts, so you will want to include numerous opportunities for children to experience their meaning.

- *Provide props that support creative dramatics.* Include props that children can use to enact familiar stories, such as three different-sized chairs, bowls, and pillows to act out The Three Bears or props that stimulate imaginative stories, such as masks, capes, or crowns.

- *Expose children to a variety of different types of art and music.* Include visual art and music from different cultures. When possible, take children to see music, dance, and drama performed. Visit museums to see a variety of visual art. Experiences such as these not only educate children; they inspire children to create art of their own!

- *Integrate the aesthetic domain with other curricular areas.* Art activities present opportunities to develop and refine both fine and gross motor skills. Music helps children expand language skills by developing new vocabulary. You might introduce new vocabulary to children by creating different words for a familiar tune; for example, substituting the words *head*, *thorax*, and *abdomen* in the song *Head, Shoulders, Knees* and *Toes* as children are learning about insects.

- *Create an aesthetically pleasing classroom.* Provide aesthetic experiences by displaying children's artwork at their eye level. Occasionally play music for pure enjoyment during other activities. Model singing for pleasure at various times of the day, such as transition or departure times, and encourage children to do the same. Remove clutter and use low shelf tops as places for displaying plants, sculpture, a beautiful basket, or items of natural beauty such as driftwood, a flower arrangement, or colorful rocks. Rotate interesting reproductions of famous artists' work in the classroom as a decoration, and use it in art appreciation discussions.

Sample Aesthetic Content

Children can learn many things in the aesthetic domain. Effective teachers think carefully about what they want children to learn and thoughtfully choose content to include in the aesthetic activities they plan. Some examples of content are provided in the following lists.

Content Related to Visual Art

- *Design* refers to the organization of a piece of art.
- *Texture* is the way something feels to the touch.
- Texture can be found in many types of art, including collage and sculpture.
- A *line* is a mark made by a tool moving across a surface.
- Lines can be straight or curvy, thick or thin.
- Lines are present in visual art and in the environment.
- People of many different ages create art.
- Art can be made from a wide variety of materials.
- There are many different styles or ways of creating art.

Content Related to Music

- Music is a combination of agreeable sounds.
- People all over the world play instruments and make music.
- *Tempo* refers to the speed or rate of beats in music.
- *Timbre* refers to the quality of sound.
- An *orchestra* is a large group of instrumentalists playing music together.
- Some instruments are played by striking or shaking them to make the sound: drum, maraca, triangle, clapper, xylophone, bells.

Content Related to Dance

- *Creative movement* is movement that reflects the inner state or mood of the individual.
- Dancing is enjoyed in every human society and at every age.
- There are many types of dance, including ballet, tap, swing, polka, and waltz.
- *Choreography* is the art of creating and arranging dances.
- Dancers can be men, women, boys, or girls.

Content Related to Dramatics

- *Drama* is literature written to be performed.
- *Dialogue* involves the lines spoken by the characters.
- People who act out stories are called *actors*.
- Actors use words, gestures, and movement to help tell the story.

- *Props* are objects actors use when performing a story.
- The *audience* is made of people who watch, listen to, and respond to the performance.

TALKING TO CHILDREN ABOUT THEIR AESTHETIC EXPERIENCES

Children are proud of their aesthetic accomplishments and are eager to share them with important adults in their lives. Consider the following scenes:

- Denzel, a 4-year-old who has been working for the past 20 minutes on a three-dimensional collage, grins broadly and says, "Look what I did!"
- Carmen, a kindergartner, recites a rhyme she has composed.
- Three-year-old Ruby exclaims, "Watch me!" as she twirls and sways to the music playing on the CD player.

How you react to Denzel, Carmen, and Ruby will influence their attitudes toward their creations. Therefore, it is important that you respond in a manner that demonstrates acceptance and encourages each child's creativity. Initially it may be best to smile and pause, taking a moment before you say anything. This provides you the opportunity to really notice what the child has done. Often, adults think children require a verbal response when a smile or nod would be sufficient. At other times, a child may request a response by asking, "Do you like my picture?" In these instances, it is best to stay away from judgmental comments ("That's a fabulous elephant; it looks just like the one in the book we read!") that may communicate a preference for realistic art over more abstract forms. Reflect on the design, color, or form of visual art or the imagery created by a child's poem or story. By focusing on one of the elements of the arts (e.g., line,

Talking with children about their art communicates that you are interested in their efforts. How might you encourage this little girl to tell you about her art?

texture, rhythm), you encourage aesthetic awareness and provide an opportunity for the child to discuss his or her work. Think about what you see in the child's work. Comment on line, symmetry, composition, or perspective in the work. How did the child create the work? Comment on the materials, medium, or tools used by the child (e.g., "You used a wide brush to make strong, thick lines in your painting." "The colors in your picture blend together."). Listen to what the child says, and respond in terms of what is said, remaining interested but nonjudgmental. This is an excellent time to utilize the teaching strategy of paraphrase reflections. Adult criticism and corrections can inhibit children's creativity and the pleasure they receive from participating in aesthetic activities. Children recognize when teachers truly value individual differences. Teachers who reward (in spoken or unspoken ways) only pictures that are realistic and recognizable, ignoring more abstract expressions, severely limit young children's creative expression of thoughts, feelings, and events. Young children often experiment with materials without intending to relate their finished product to reality. They may be fascinated by the way the colors change when they touch each other, or how the sand sticks to the glue and not to the paper. Adults who insist that they "see something" in children's pictures impose the value of realism that can force children into this singular mode of expression and the frustration of such limits. Focus on the effort invested by the child ("You worked hard on that sculpture."), how materials were used ("You used many shades of blue in your painting.") or the meaning of the work to the child ("What a big smile! I can see you are very proud of your dance.") When we focus on the artistic elements of the work or the effort expended by the artist, children see that they are free to use whatever means of expression they want, without worrying that their work will be devalued.

Communicating with Families About the Aesthetic Domain

Parents are often rushed at drop-off and pick-up times and may not have the chance for a leisurely talk with the teacher. You will want to use a variety of ways to share useful information with families about many topics. One such topic is talking with children about their art. Parents may not be sure what to say about a child's creation and will find your suggestions helpful. Figure 9.9 provides an example you can share through a newsletter or website.

Fostering Aesthetic Appreciation

Exposing children to the art of others helps them understand how and why art is created and how people may perceive art differently. When you encourage children to reflect on their art and the art of others, you assist them in developing an understanding and appreciation of art. In time, children develop personal preferences. Children learn that one person may prefer a particular painting; another person does not find that piece of art appealing. Some people prefer to listen to classical music; others favor country western. Being able to articulate personal preferences and explain why you are drawn to the selection are important in helping children develop an appreciation of the arts. As children experience a wide range of art, they are able to practice the cognitive skills of describing and responding to what they see or hear. Help children to notice how different artists use different elements such as line, texture, rhythm, or mood in their work. Focusing on such details encourages children to develop a more sophisticated understanding of art.

In order to facilitate art appreciation, it will be necessary for you to expand your own knowledge of the aesthetic domain. Expose children to a wide range of art forms, not just those with which you are most familiar or that best match your personal artistic preferences. By exposing children to a wide array of art, we help them learn to appreciate and accept others' creativity. Our goal is to assist children in valuing the

NEWSLETTER/WEB READY COMMUNICATION

FIGURE 9.9 • Talking with Children About Their Art

Young children can be prolific artists, bringing home page after page of scribble drawings, finger paintings, and collages. You may wonder what your child gains from these endeavors. As children draw, sculpt, or paint they get to see how their actions create different results. The sensation of smearing thick paint across the page is quite pleasurable and doing so helps to demonstrate the concept of cause and effect. Children discover that smearing the paint with their fingers creates a different outcome than does applying the paint with a brush. They learn language and develop concepts as they discuss shape, color, texture, and other terms related to art. Art activities provide children the opportunity to think creatively, express themselves, and problem solve, all skills that will help them be successful in life. The young artist becomes engrossed in the process of creating and isn't concerned with the outcome of her efforts. It seems logical to ask children, "What is it?" when you view their artwork. However, questions like these suggest that art should be recognizable, focused on the outcome rather than the process. Instead, invite your child to discuss the work by using comments such as, "Tell me about your picture." Describe what you see. "You used lots of colors." or "The blue looks bright next to the dark purple." Art is a vital and vibrant part of a young child's education, contributing to every aspect of development. Show your child that you value what he or she created by taking the time to talk about ideas and techniques. These strategies nurture the artist that lives inside every child!

very essence of artistic expression. As teachers, we must take the time to learn about the pieces of art that we introduce to children. What is the history or story behind that painting or musical selection? What was the artist trying to communicate? The more you know about a particular piece of art, the more confidently you can present it to the children.

■ TRY IT YOURSELF

Visit a local museum or art gallery. As you view different selections, focus on basic elements of visual art. Notice the way various artists use line, shape, form, or space in their art. Choose a piece that particularly appeals to you. Think about what captured your attention and why. What about the piece is pleasing to you? Does it convey any feelings or thoughts? How would you describe the piece to someone who has not seen it? Challenge yourself to learn about the piece and the artist. Consider purchasing a print of the work that you could introduce to children.

USING CHILDREN'S LITERATURE FOR AESTHETIC EXPERIENCES

Children's literature provides a readily accessible source of beautiful visual art. Every year, new and wonderful children's books are published that contain stunning illustrations. Sharing these with children helps them (1) discover the joy of art available to hold in your hand, and (2) explore and recognize techniques used by the illustrator. Epstein (2007) offers several suggestions to keep in mind when using a book to promote art vocabulary and appreciation.

- Choose a book that is already familiar to the children. This will allow them to focus on the illustrations instead of the narrative.
- Select the illustrations you wish to discuss ahead of time. Choose pictures related to things children have shown interest in or to specific concepts you plan to explore with the children.
- Choose large pictures with uncomplicated illustrations that will appeal to very young children. The examples should highlight color, shape, and texture. Use more subtle and complicated illustrations as children gain experience.
- Discuss how the illustrator's choice of medium contributes to the picture and enhances the story.
- Choose illustrations that reflect a wide array of artistic styles, mediums, and forms. Include work representative of various cultures as well.

OTHER ACTIVITIES USING BOOK ILLUSTRATIONS

- Use the art-related ideas in picture books to help children explore their own aesthetic ideas. Use books such as *Mouse Paint,* by Ellen Stall Walsh (1995), or *I am an Artist,* by Pat Lowery Collins (1994). See Figure 9.10 for suggested titles.
- Explore the various ways in which a particular subject is depicted by different artists—for example, grandmothers—as portrayed in picture books such as *Charlie and Grandma,* by Sally Ward (1986); *Gifts,* by Jo Ellen Bogart (1994); *My Grammy,* by Marsha Kibbey (1988); and *Bigmama's,* by Donald Crews (1998).
- Notice and imitate an illustrator's use of materials or technique, such as painted papers in any book by Eric Carle; collage in any book by Lois Ehlert; use of colored clay as in *Over in the Ocean in a Coral Reef,* by Marianne Berkes (2004); or use of a watercolor technique as in pictures by Leo Lionni.

FIGURE 9.10 Children's books related to aesthetics

Include a variety of books on music, dance, and musical performance in your reading area. The following are suggestions you may choose to include.

- *Harold and the Purple Crayon* by C. Johnson (1955). Harper Collins Publishers
- *The Art Lesson* by T. dePaola (1997). Puffin Publishers
- *Katie and the Sunflowers* by J. Mayhew (2001). Orchard Publishers
- *I Am an Artist* by P. L. Collins (1994). Millbrook Press.
- *I Ain't Gonna Paint No More* by K. Beaumont (2005). Harcourt Children's Books
- *Mouse Paint* by E. S. Walsh (1995). Sandpiper Publishers
- *Little Blue and Little Yellow* by L. Lionni (1995). Harper Collins Publishers

- *Degas and the Little Dancer* by L. Anholt (2007). Barron's Educational Series
- *Song and Dance Man* by K. Ackerman (2003). Knopf Books for Young Readers
- *Bat Jamboree* by K. Appelt (1998). Harper Collins Publishers
- *Piggies in a Polka* by K. Appelt (2003). Harcourt Children's Books
- *Charlie Parker Played Be Bop* by C. Raschka (1997). Scholastic
- *Zin! Zin! Zin! a Violin* by L. Moss (1995). Simon & Schuster Books for Young Readers
- *The Jazz Fly* by M. Gollub (2000). Tortuga Press
- *Itsy Bitsy Spider* by K. Toms (2009). Make Believe Ideas (or other books that can be sung)

TRACKING AESTHETIC DEVELOPMENT THROUGH PORTFOLIOS

Artists typically create portfolios of their work. You may find keeping individual art files for the children in your class a useful tool as well. Such a file will provide visible evidence of children's developmental progression over time. It will be necessary to be selective in choosing what to include in the file. Enlisting children to assist in choosing items to include will help develop a sense of ownership in the file and ensure that a child's favorite selections are included. Be sure to label and date each selection. Doing so will allow the viewer to see change over time. For this reason, it is important the file be as complete as possible, containing selections from throughout the year.

- Utilize a storage system that allows you to keep materials organized. There are multiple methods that could be used. Some teachers use file folders, whereas others use clean, unused pizza boxes.
- Make additions to the file regularly and throughout the year. Include a variety of media.
- Date and label each entry. Make note of the medium/materials used and any special significance of the piece. For example, you might note "Katelyn chose this piece because of the variety of colors used." or "First time oil pastels were used."
- Take photographs of three-dimensional or larger works of art that would be unwieldy to store.
- Include audio or video recordings to showcase musical or creative movement experiences.
- Share files with family members during conference time. The file can provide visible evidence of a child's progress over time and stimulate discussion.
- Review the items with the child, noting what the child has to say about the pieces included in the portfolio.

You may find reviewing children's aesthetic portfolios a rewarding experience yourself. Recognizing that a child has grown in his or her ability to create music, art, dance, or drama helps teachers realize the power of the arts to enrich lives.

Planned Activities in the Aesthetic Domain

The following are examples of possible activities related to the aesthetic domain. Goals referred to in each activity correspond to the goals listed earlier in the chapter.

Exploratory Play Activity: Examining Natural Objects

Ages 3-6

Goal 1: For the children to show awareness of beauty in nature

Content: *Beauty* is a combination of qualities such as shape, color, or form that pleases the aesthetic senses. Some people think that an object(s) is beautiful that others do not find beautiful.

Materials: Assorted natural items such as leaves, rocks, or sea shells

Magnifying glasses

Procedure: Prepare the activity by placing the gathered items in a sensory table or large tub. Tell the children that you have many beautiful things for them to examine. Model enthusiasm while studying the items. Encourage children to handle the items and examine them closely. Ask which ones are the most beautiful and why they think so.

To Simplify: Provide fewer items for the children to explore.

To Extend: Bring in additional items for the children to examine. Encourage them to look closely by providing magnifying glasses.

Guided Discovery Activity: We Are Dancers!

Ages 3-6

Goal 6: For the children to identify and respond to basic elements of music.

Content: *Rhythm* is a regular occurrence of strong and weak beats.

People experience rhythm through their bodies.

Freestyle dancing is moving to music with no fixed structure.

Materials: Large open space where children can move freely

Music (CDs and CD player)

Procedure: Tell children that you are going to play a song and want them to listen carefully to the rhythm. Encourage children to nod, sway, or clap to the rhythm as they listen. Play the song again and encourage children to move freely to the beat of the music. Emphasize the rhythm of the music throughout the activity. Remind children to listen as they move.

To Simplify: Select a song with a strong beat so that the rhythm can be easily identified. Clap the rhythm as the children listen to the music.

To Extend: Introduce additional pieces with a variety of rhythms. Allow children to move to the new music. Continue to emphasize rhythm.

Problem-Solving Activity: Creating Three-Dimensional Sculptures

Ages 3-6

Goal 4: For the children to use a variety of materials, tools, techniques, and processes in the arts.

Content: A *sculpture* refers to a three-dimensional work of art.

To be *upright* means to stand straight upward (not lay flat).

There is more than one way to create art.

Materials: Strips of construction paper

Stapler and staples

Glue

Large sheets of construction paper or cardboard (for sculpture base)

Assorted pipe cleaners and chunks of Styrofoam for simplification

Paper and pencils for extension

Procedure: Introduce the activity by reminding children of sculptures that they have seen. Explain that they will use the strips of paper to create a three-dimensional construction. Encourage children to share their ideas about how they will use the paper to create their sculpture. As the children test their ideas, encourage them to share what they have discovered with their peers.

To Simplify: Provide materials that lend themselves more easily to a three-dimensional project (such as pipe cleaners with a Styrofoam base).

To Extend: Have children draw a picture of their sculpture and share their sculpting technique with a peer.

Discussion Activity: Deciding What You Like

Ages 3-6

Goal 11: For the children to participate in aesthetic criticism.

Content: People often have preferences for various visual arts. What is pleasing and interesting to one person is not always pleasing and interesting to others.

Materials: Two art prints, large enough for a small group of children to easily view

Additional prints for extension

Procedure: Enthusiastically introduce the prints to the children. Encourage the children to tell you what they notice about the pictures. Emphasize that children should listen to one another without interrupting. Encourage children to discuss what they do and do not like about the prints. Have children tell the group which print they prefer and why.

To Simplify: Ask only one or two questions, keeping the discussion brief. Hold the discussion with fewer children in the group.

To Extend: Introduce other prints and encourage the children to discuss what message they feel the artist was trying to communicate through the artwork.

Demonstration Activity: Creating Clay Pots

Ages 3-6

Goal 3: For the children to engage in different art forms (usable art).

Content: Some art or crafts are used by people in their everyday lives. Each artist chooses the techniques to create art that is personally pleasing. In order to improve, artists practice techniques needed to create their art.

Materials: Several balls of clay, enough so that each child has his or her own

Smocks to keep clothes clean

Procedure: Demonstrate how to make a simple pinch pot. Have children carry out the technique with their own ball of clay. As they gain skill in shaping the clay, encourage them to make all sides of the pot even. Encourage the children to continue practicing the technique until they are pleased with their creation.

To Simplify: Make sure clay is pliable by kneading the clay well before the children begin. Allow children to mold the clay as they wish without pressuring them to create a pot.

To Extend: Demonstrate another technique to use with clay, such as using the coil method to create a pot. Introduce more advanced pinch techniques such as attaching a handle to the pot.

Direct Instruction Activity: A Visit from a Ballerina

Ages 3-6

Goal 2: For the children to use a variety of materials, tools, processes and, especially, techniques in the arts.

Content: Some dances are designed by a person and learned by the dancer.

Ballet dancers pay attention to how they move their arms, feet, and head as they dance.

Dancers practice their moves in order to perform the moves well.

There are words to describe certain positions in ballet dancing, such as *Arabesque, Bras bas,* or *Pirouette.*

Materials: Large open area where children can easily move

Procedure: Invite someone who has studied ballet to demonstrate a few ballet positions and moves to the children, introducing the names for each one as they are demonstrated. Encourage the children to watch and listen carefully. Point out to the children the way the dancer's arms, legs, feet, and head are held. Ask them to repeat the name with you. Try some of the positions or moves yourself, and ask the children to identify which one you are trying to perform. Ask them how they can tell. Intentionally and obviously perform a position or move incorrectly, then ask the children to tell or show you how to do it correctly. An alternative is to use the wrong name to describe a position or move. Ask the children to correct the name. Invite the children to try some positions or moves for themselves.

To Simplify: Choose only a few positions for the dancer to demonstrate. Choose moves that will be the easiest for the children to perform (e.g., the five basic positions of the feet, the five basic positions of the arms). See dance.about.com/od/ball2/f/Position for photos of the basic foot and arm positions.

To Extend: Once the children are able to perform several of the demonstrated moves, have them combine multiple moves to create their own short dance.

9 Applying What You've Learned

Based on what you now know about the aesthetic domain, carry out these activities to increase your knowledge and skills.

1. Describe the elements of the aesthetic domain.

2. **Key Science Concepts and Skills.** Arrange to visit an early childhood classroom. Take a few minutes to observe the overall aesthetic climate of the room. What is the climate from a child's perspective? What would you add or take away to make the room more aesthetically pleasing? Do you see evidence of aesthetic instruction in the classroom?

3. **Strategies for Teaching Aesthetics.** Choose at least 10 songs appropriate for use in an early childhood classroom. Write each song on a separate index card, including lyrics, melody, and actions (if applicable). Over time, continue to build your collection.

4. **Planning Experiences and Activities in Aesthetics.** Visit a book store and review several selections of children's literature, paying close attention to the illustrations. How might you use the books to introduce concepts related to the visual arts? What content terms or facts could you illustrate with the books? Develop a detailed plan to introduce some of the content you identified.

5. **Addressing the Needs of Diverse Learners.** Create a collection of multicultural prints to use with children. Museum gift shops can be an excellent source for inexpensive prints or postcards featuring art from a variety of cultures. Consider how you might use the prints to foster aesthetic experiences for young children.

6. **Supporting Aesthetic Learning at Home.** Identify several suggestions that families could use to create a prop box at home to support their child in creative dramatics. For example, you could suggest that families develop a "Baker's Box" containing play dough, cookie cutters, a rolling pin, pans, spoons, and dish towels to encourage their child in acting out the role of a baker.

References

Berkes, M. (2004). *Over in the ocean in a coral reef.* Nevada City, CA: Dawn Publications.

Bogart, J. E. (1996). *Gifts.* New York: Scholastic Trade.

Collins, P. L. (1994). *I am an artist.* Minneapolis, MN: Millbrook Press.

Consortium of National Arts Education Associations. (1994). *Dance, music, theatre, visual arts: What every young American should know and be able to do in the arts: National standards for arts education.* Reston, VA: Author.

Crews, D. (1998). *Bigmama's.* New York: Greenwillow Books.

Epstein, A. S. (2007). *The intentional teacher: Choosing the best strategies for young children's learning.* Washington, D.C.: National Association for the Education of Young Children.

Kibbey, M. (1988). *My grammy.* New York: First Avenue Editions.

Kostelnik, M. J., Soderman, A. K., & Whiren, A. P. (2011). *Developmentally appropriate curriculum: Best practices in early childhood education* (5th ed.). Upper Saddle River, NJ: Pearson.

Koster, J. B. (2009). *Growing artists: Teaching art to young children* (4th ed.). Clifton Park, NY: Thompson Delmar Learning.

Mayesky, M. (2009). *Creative activities for young children* (9th ed.). Clifton Park, NY: Thompson Delmar Learning.

Music Educators National Conference. (1994). *Opportunity to learn standards for music instruction, preK–12.* Task force chair P. Lehman. Reston, VA: Addison-Wesley.

Schirrmacher, R., & Fox, J. E. (2009). *Art and creative development of young children* (6th ed.). Clifton Park, NY: Thompson Delmar Learning.

Walsh, E. S. (1995). *Mouse paint.* New York: Sandpiper.

Ward, S. G. (1986). *Charlie and Grandma.* New York: Scholastic Trade.

10 The Affective Domain: Developing a Sense of Self

Celeste's and Rosalie's block people self portraits, K classroom

Rosalie, 5 years old, chooses her art materials carefully. She gathers black yarn, red and blue paint sticks, and two wooden blocks. She plans to use all of these items to make a figure of herself—one block for her face and one block for her body. She picks up a blue paint stick, looks down at her purple pants, sets the blue paint stick aside, and searches until she finds a purple one. She notices some yellow yarn and hands it to Celeste, saying, "Here, this is for you. See, I have black." She holds the black yarn close to her dark hair. "You have yellow." Blonde-haired Celeste nods yes and takes the yellow yarn. The girls begin working on their self-representations. Rosalie colors one block with a tan paint stick and adds facial features, including a turned up mouth. "See, I'm happy." Celeste laughs and says, "Me, too—happy, happy, happy." She adds a grinning mouth to the face she is drawing on her block.

This interaction reveals important information about Rosalie and Celeste. Both girls have a mental picture of what they look like. Both recognize materials that match their self-image and those that better fit their friend. Both are also aware of internal feelings. In time, their self-understandings will expand to include many other attributes as well. Self-knowledge like this is the subject of the affective domain.

Children are not born knowing everything about who they are—affective understanding evolves over time. As a teacher of young children, you will play an important role in this aspect of children's learning. The material included in this chapter will help you carry out this responsibility more effectively.

Let's begin by examining children's emerging sense of self and what elements make up the affective domain.

Key Dimensions of the Affective Domain

Who am I?

What am I like?

What can I do?

What makes me special?

Finding answers to these questions is a major developmental task of early childhood. As children interact with other people and explore the world around them, they gather information that contributes to greater self-understanding. Over the years they gradually develop a concept of "me" and "not me." They also explore the "me skills" needed to establish a place in the world. The knowledge and behaviors associated with **affective** (having to do with self-understanding, emotions, and emotional expression) learning fall within three categories:

- Self-awareness
- Emotional competence
- Self-efficacy

affective Having to do with self-understanding, emotions, and emotional expression.

We will examine each of these dimensions in more detail, beginning with self-awareness.

SELF-AWARENESS

As children interact with people or objects, they find out more about who they are and who they are not.

"I poured the juice myself—I can do things."

"I am a girl, he is a boy—we are different."

"I like chocolate, he likes chocolate—we are the same."

Children use such information to define themselves as individuals and to differentiate themselves from everyone else. These distinctions emerge a little at a time from children's earliest days through adulthood (Barr, 2008). Taken altogether, such attributes shape a child's **self-identity**. Self-identity is the descriptive component of the self. It

self-identity The set of characteristics, abilities, attitudes, and values that a child believes defines who he or she is.

involves all the characteristics, abilities, attitudes, and values children see in themselves and use to define who they are.

Based on their experiences, these kindergartners are building an increasingly complex sense of self.

HOW SELF-IDENTITY TAKES SHAPE

In preschoolers and kindergartners, self-identity is tied to observable personal attributes: *I am a boy. I have brown hair.* Gradually, children add activities, possessions, and preferences to their list of personal characteristics: *I can hop. I have a hamster. I don't like beets.* Personal relationships also figure into young children's self-descriptions: *I have a sister. I am a big brother.* With greater maturity come comparisons with one's earlier self and between oneself and others: *I run faster than I used to. I run faster than Jim. Amy runs faster than me.* These social comparisons are children's way of differentiating themselves from others and of establishing a relative sense of self. By the mid-elementary years, children's self-definitions expand to include internal and abstract qualities: *I am honest. I am a good friend* (Derman-Sparks & Edwards, 2010; Harter, 2006). It is this combination of attributes that ultimately make up a person's self-identity.

You have been drawing similar conclusions about yourself all your life. Take a moment to describe some attributes that make up your self-identity by completing the Try It Yourself exercise.

TRY IT YOURSELF

First, make a record of several words you would use to describe yourself in six categories associated with self-identity. Next, list some variables that are NOT characteristic of you.

	ME	NOT ME
Observable attributes		
Activities and possessions		
Preferences		
Relationships		
Comparisons		
Internal		

SELF-ESTEEM

As self-identity becomes more defined and complex, children assign positive and negative value to the traits that characterize themselves:

It is good to have red hair.	*It is not good to have red hair.*
I am smart.	*I am not smart.*
People like playing with me.	*People don't like playing with me.*

self-esteem The positive or negative judgments a person makes about his or her self-identity.

Self-evaluations such as these contribute to children's **self-esteem**. Self-esteem is the evaluative component of self-awareness and involves how much children value and like themselves. It is based on children's daily experiences with others.

Initially, children use familiar adults as mirrors through which they see and judge themselves. Eventually peers contribute too (Epstein, 2009). If feedback is favorable, children make positive self-evaluations. If the image is negative, children assume they have little worth (Kostelnik, Gregory, Soderman, & Whiren, 2012). No single event determines whether a child's self-esteem is generally favorable or unfavorable. Accumulated experience is what counts, both positive and negative. For instance, being the target of occasional criticism will probably not cause permanent damage to children's self-esteem; however, children subjected to relentless faultfinding could develop lasting feelings of inferiority (Brown, Odom, & McConnell, 2008). Moreover, a single attribute—say, speaking Spanish at home— may lead to a negative self-judgment in Manuel but a more positive self-evaluation in Isabella, based on their different experiences. When Manuel speaks Spanish at school, his teachers tell him they won't listen unless he uses English. There is no evidence of Spanish anywhere in the classroom. The adults call him Manny, not Manuel, because they say that Manny is easier to pronounce. Through interactions like these, Manuel concludes that Spanish is neither welcome nor valued at school, and that his teachers reject this part of his self-identity. The opposite is true for Isabella. What is reflected back to her is that Spanish is valued not only at home but also at the center. She has a caregiver who speaks Spanish, the class has learned some Spanish rhymes, and the children are learning to count—uno, dos, tres! The center's website includes both English and Spanish, and materials sent to families are bilingual.

In both cases, Manuel and Isabella see themselves reflected in the adults' actions and attitudes and form individual notions about their value based on these mirrored images (Denham, Bassett, & Wyatt, 2007). See Figure 10.1 for a summary of what the children might eventually believe and do as a result of their differing self-judgments.

As you can see from Figure 10.1, children's self-esteem influences their lives greatly. Many things, including emotional competence and self-efficacy, contribute to whether individuals feel mostly positive or mostly negative about themselves.

FIGURE 10.1 Characteristics associated with favorable and less favorable self-esteem

When children's self-evaluations are generally positive, they:	When children's self-evaluations are mostly negative, they:
See themselves as competent and likeable	See themselves as inadequate and unlikeable
Anticipate positive reactions from others	Anticipate negative reactions from others
Believe they can influence some of what happens to them	Believe that they have no control over what happens to them
Believe they will succeed in challenging situations if they keep trying	Believe they will likely fail no matter what
These children usually: • Feel good about themselves • Demonstrate self-confidence • Establish positive social relations • Engage in pro-social behavior • "Stick with it" in challenging situations	These children usually: • Feel incompetent or rejected • Demonstrate lack of confidence • Fail to establish close relationships • Engage in antisocial behavior • Give up in the face of adversity

EMOTIONAL COMPETENCE

Martin's face lights up: brownies for lunch!
Carl shouts, "I AM big!"
Annabelle dissolves into tears when Mara says, "You can't play!"
Lillian backs away as the teacher holds out a hermit crab for her to touch.

Children experience hundreds of different emotions every day. Emotions involve a combination of physical sensations, thoughts, and actions and may be more or less intense depending on the circumstances. They are part of everything children do and are prompted by incidents large and small. The extent to which children recognize emotions and how well they manage and express their emotions are key elements of **emotional competence** (Epstein, 2009).

emotional competence
Recognizing your emotions and using constructive means for expressing and managing emotions in daily interactions.

WHY EMOTIONS ARE IMPORTANT

Some emotions are pleasurable and some are not. *All* emotions play essential roles in children's lives (Ekman, 2007). Most of the feelings children experience stem from one of the four core emotions common to people worldwide:

1. Happiness
2. Anger
3. Sadness
4. Fear

Every one of these affective states tells children something about themselves and their well-being. Happiness tells children things are good. Anger alerts children to injustice. Sadness signals loss. Fear warns children of danger. These emotional messages prompt children to act. Happiness, for instance, makes children want to prolong a pleasant state of affairs or advance toward something pleasurable, whereas fear may cause children to retreat if a situation seems threatening. We see this when Celeste begs her teacher to "Do it again!" as he pushes her on the swing, but later hides behind his legs when a large dog approaches them. In every case, emotions help children interpret what is happening and prompt them to adapt within the varying situations in which they find themselves.

EMOTIONAL LESSONS LEARNED IN EARLY CHILDHOOD

Young children learn from others where, when, and how to express emotions. They hear people talk about emotions, see how others handle emotions, and experience reactions to the emotions they themselves display (Thompson & Lagattuta, 2008). In the process, children learn powerful affective lessons. Think about what the children are learning in the following situation.

There is shaving cream for children to spread on large trays in the art area today. Nadia watches from the side as Marvin and Lynette swirl the shaving cream into abstract shapes. She notices their smiles and laughter. Her teacher approaches and says, "Marvin and Lynette, you're excited we have shaving cream today. Nadia, you look like you want to try too. Here's a tray." Nadia begins to back away from the table. Noticing the child's reluctance, the teacher says, "You're not so sure. Here try just a little. See, it's squishy." Nadia gingerly touches the small blob of shaving cream. It squirts to the side. She looks startled. Lynette laughs and says, "See, it's fun." The teacher waits as Nadia cautiously explores the shaving cream. After several minutes, Nadia is happily smearing a slightly bigger glob on her tray.

Consider Nadia's affective experience. She saw that Lynette and Marvin were enjoying the shaving cream. She was curious, but reluctant too. Her teacher was encouraging and patient. She accepted Nadia's reaction and also gave her a strategy for trying the activity at a lower level of perceived risk. In time, Nadia experienced pleasure in participating. Alternately, she might have continued to avoid the activity or simply enjoyed watching the others. By following the child's cues, the teacher conveyed important emotional information to Nadia and the other children at the table:

- Everyone has emotions
- People can have different feelings about the same experience
- There is no one right way to feel
- There are things people can do to make their emotions more manageable

Imagine how these lessons would have differed if the teacher tried to shame Nadia into using the shaving cream ("Come on. Don't be such a baby. It won't hurt you.") or if she told Nadia how to feel ("Everybody likes shaving cream painting. You should too."). In either case, all three children may have come away thinking, "Certain feelings are wrong," and "It's not okay to show people your true feelings." Lessons such as these contribute to children's negative self-perceptions. Figure 10.2 lists guidelines to help you avoid harmful outcomes such as these.

HOW EMOTIONAL COMPETENCE DEVELOPS

Learning to recognize, express, and manage emotions are key components of emotional competence. Emotionally competent children express a broad variety of emotions, understand their emotions, and deal with their emotions without incapacitating themselves or others in the process (Galinsky, 2010). These abilities are influenced by children's temperaments as well as by their cognitive and language development.

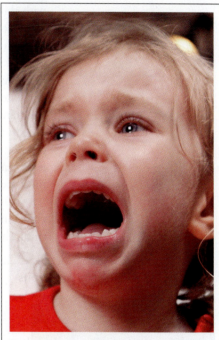

Young children may express their emotions with great intensity.

Temperamentally, some children are inherently more intense in their emotional reactions than are other children. Likewise, certain children are quick to register an emotional response, whereas others are slower to react (Epstein, 2009). In addition, some children are more sensitive to negative emotions (anxiety, anger, despair); others are more attuned to the positive (optimism or contentment). These are genetically based reactions, which children can modify but seldom eliminate entirely. As an early childhood educator, you need to recognize these differences among children and take them into account as you work with them.

Cognitive, language, and emotional development are all intertwined. Initially, young preschoolers think of their emotions in very simple terms: *happy, mad, sad*, and *afraid*. Emotional expression at this age is often intense,

---

FIGURE 10.2 Key points about children's emotional development

Remember:

Children experience many different emotions.

All emotions are useful.

Children's emotions are real to them.

There are no right or wrong emotions.

Your job is **NOT** to change children's emotions.

Your job **IS** to help children better understand and manage what they are feeling.

with children relying on bodily reactions more than words. This explains why preschoolers who are angry are totally angry and why those who are sad are momentarily inconsolable. These strong emotional interpretations alternate rapidly. One minute Lana may scream, "No!" and a few minutes later she may laugh watching the hamster run around its wheel (Gonzalez-Mena & Eyer, 2009). Gradually, as children learn new words to describe their emotions, they begin to think about and express those emotions in more sophisticated and differentiated ways. Eventually, rather than relying on vocal outbursts to express every variation of anger, children may shout in fury, pout in disappointment, whimper in frustration, or express their upset feelings in words. In fact, by ages 5 or 6, many children have a variety of labels to describe their emotions. They derive satisfaction not only from talking about being angry but also from more precisely describing their feelings, using words such as *irritated*, *disgusted*, or *frustrated*. The more words children have to talk about feelings, the more socially competent they become.

temperament The distinctive personal characteristics that children are born with and that remain constant over each child's lifetime.

Emotion Talk   Regardless of **temperament** (that is, the distinctive personality characteristics children are born with) or current skill level, children's emotional understanding increases when adults talk to them about their emotions (Calkins & Williford, 2009). Consequently, the single best way to promote children's emotional competence is to talk with children about what they are feeling. This can happen any time during the school day.

To engage in effective emotion talk, adults tune in to the emotions children convey through their facial expressions, gestures, and words. We saw this when Nadia's teacher noticed Nadia pulling back from the shaving cream and adjusted her message accordingly. As children's emotions become evident, effective teachers observe, listen, clarify, and extend children's affective understandings. Nadia's teacher demonstrated this when she translated Nadia's emotions into words, "You're not so sure." Thus, Nadia experienced a mini-lesson on feelings within the context of the ongoing art activity. Her teacher did not wait for a designated time to provide this lesson, nor did she make a big deal of it. Instead, she communicated important information in just a few moments when it was most meaningful. Much (though not all) affective teaching happens this way.

On a recent field trip to the Butterfly House, Mia experienced a wide range of emotions in just a few moments. These are depicted in Figure 10.3. What do you think she was feeling each time?

FIGURE 10.3 Butterfly emotions

Because children learn best from firsthand experience, they benefit when their emotions are named and described as they happen (Thompson & Twibell, 2009). For instance, when Marc becomes excited about something, you identify his emotion and put it into words, "Marc, you look excited." This gives Marc a hands-on experience with the abstract concept of excitement. Not only does Marc find out that his emotional state is describable (an element of language) but he also becomes aware of the internal and contextual cues related to that emotion (key cognitive concepts). Taking advantage of teachable moments like these has many plusses:

- Helping children better understand what they are feeling
- Making it easier for children to draw on past emotional learning
- Assisting children in differentiating one emotion from another
- Enhancing children's vocabulary and the ability to express themselves

This kind of affective talk promotes children's emotional understanding and contributes to children's healthy self-esteem. It also provides the foundation for helping children become more resilient—a vital facet of emotional competence.

RESILIENCE

Using cardboard boxes of different sizes, Mara and Sonya place one box on top of another until the top reaches 4 feet high. Three times, when the tower reaches this point, it falls down. After the third spill, Mara wails, "I'll never get this to stay up!" She leaves the area in distress. Sonya has also tried different approaches—none is working. She looks over at another child's structure, then says, "I know..." and tries something else.

Mara and Sonya have both experienced frustration, but each reacted in a different way. Mara tried then gave up. Sonya persisted in spite of difficulty. In this situation, we could say that Sonya demonstrated more resilience (greater emotional competence) than Mara did. **Resilience** is the ability to adjust constructively to adversity and to stressful situations (American Psychological Association, 2011). It involves that inner reservoir of self-perceptions and skills that enables a person to bounce back from disappointment and to deal more effectively with life's challenges.

Because every child's life is touched by achievements and setbacks, heartache and joy, failure as well as triumph, children benefit when they learn how to approach life with resilience. Not surprisingly, children who demonstrate greater degrees of resilience are less likely to resort to antisocial behavior. They also tend to experience higher levels of personal happiness and school success (National Association of School Psychologists, 2010).

As important as it is, resilience is not an all-or-nothing proposition. Individuals may be a little resilient, somewhat resilient, or very resilient. Also, people may be more resilient in some situations than in others. Resiliency is influenced by some internal factors such as personality and temperament, but specific strategies associated with resiliency (for instance, how to communicate with others or how to handle negative emotions) can be learned (Pizzolongo & Hunter, 2011). This means everyone has the potential to become more resilient and therefore more emotionally competent.

resilience The ability to rise above adversity and stressful circumstances.

STARTING YOUNG

No one, including young children, goes through life without some **stress**—the body's reaction to change that requires a physical, mental, or emotional adjustment or response. The stressors in children's lives often come about as a result of change (moving

stress The body's reaction to change that requires a physical, mental, or emotional adjustment or response.

to a new neighborhood, getting a long-awaited kitten), feelings of overload (too much excitement or too much worry), boredom, situations in which children feel thwarted or uncertain about what may happen, and experiences that prompt them to feel anxious or out of control (Kostelnik, Gregory, Soderman, & Whiren, 2012). There is no escaping such feelings while growing up. They happen as a result of hundreds of experiences large and small. Consider Thomas's start to the day. He wanted pancakes for breakfast, but got toast instead. His favorite orange sweater was in the wash. The carpool driver was late and spoke sharply to him as he got in the car. He forgot his show-and-tell dinosaur and there was no time to go back for it. When he arrived at the center, the hallways were loud and crowded, other children bumped into him, and people kept telling him to hurry. To make matters worse, his favorite teacher was at home, sick! Such incidents are typical in a child's day. Depending on how they are handled, situations like these either offer children opportunities for growth or serve as highly negative experiences that diminish children's emotional well-being. Moreover, although nothing that happened to Thomas was imminently dangerous, the cumulative effect of these incidents day after day could overwhelm a young child who is just learning to cope. For all these reasons, early childhood educators need to know how to interact with children in ways that contribute to emotional competence rather than detract from it. This is most likely to happen when teachers do these things (National Association of School Psychologists, 2010):

Thomas needs an understanding teacher to take his emotions seriously and to provide comfort and support.

- Provide affection and support to children
- Create an optimistic classroom climate
- Hold high expectations for children
- Promote children's full inclusion in classroom life
- Give children opportunities to influence what happens in their classrooms

The links between these lessons and children's resiliency-related beliefs are depicted in Figure 10.4.

Feeling valued, hopeful, confident, connected, and influential gives children the internal resources they need to keep trying when things are going poorly and to

---

FIGURE 10.4 Lessons in resiliency

When adults . . .	Children believe . . .
Develop caring relationships with children	I am valued.
Foster optimistic attitudes and nurture positive emotions	I have hope.
Hold high expectations for children	I can do it.
Give children opportunities to participate fully in classroom life	I belong.
Encourage children to make decisions and experience the consequences of their actions	I can control some things that happen to me.

seek alternate approaches in difficult circumstances. Taking advantage of on-the-spot interactions and through the activities they plan, early childhood educators teach children to believe in themselves, acquire coping skills, discover ways to recover from hardships, and develop strategies for meeting challenges effectively. One other way teachers help children develop greater resilience is to promote their feelings of self-efficacy.

SELF-EFFICACY

I think I can... I think I can... I think I can...

From *The Little Engine That Could*
By Watty Piper, Grosset & Dunlap, 2009

The Little Engine That Could has been a favorite storybook of young children for 80 years. It is all about optimism and hard work, setting goals, persistence, and believing in oneself. In other words, it is all about self-efficacy. **Self-efficacy** is the personal belief that one can accomplish what one sets out to do (Epstein, 2009). Children who exhibit a high degree of self-efficacy see themselves as competent and as potentially successful in most things they attempt. They apply themselves constructively, believing that practice and persistence will eventually lead to success. If they make a mistake or experience failure, they learn from the experience, adjust their actions, and try again. Efficacy is illustrated in Figure 10.5.

It is no surprise that children whose self-efficacy is strong are likely to enjoy healthy self-esteem. Such self-evaluations are based on realistic assessments of personal competence (Egertson, 2006). They come about through daily experiences that help children take stock of their strengths and explore ways to address limitations. Children expand their capabilities through play and through work, through fantasy and real tasks, and through feedback from peers and adults. Self-efficacy is not the result of inflated praise or adult exaggerations that a child is wonderful all the time or great at everything. It develops because children realistically see themselves as doers and decision makers, people who are capable of learning new skills, and as individuals who can put plans and ideas into action.

In the 1950s, Erik Erikson described the developmental process through which children expand their affective competencies. His observations remain relevant today. You have probably read about Erikson's stages in your child development classes. Those stages have implications not only for child development but also for the kinds of experiences teachers provide to promote self-efficacy. Let's consider them in that light.

Erikson identified eight emotional tasks people work through from birth through old age. These tasks occur in developmental stages, with each one serving as a foundation for the next. Three of them occur during the preschool and kindergarten years:

- **Trust** versus **mistrust**
- **Autonomy** versus **shame and doubt**
- **Initiative** versus **guilt**

Although all children have experiences that contribute to both ends of the continuum for each stage, optimal development happens when the weight of experience is toward the positive. That is, children develop greater self-efficacy when their experiences result in strong feelings of trust, autonomy (a sense of oneself as a separate individual), and initiative (a sense of ambition and responsibility). A brief summary

self-efficacy A person's belief that he or she can accomplish what he or she has set out to do.

trust Trust in oneself, trust in one's caregivers, trust in the world.

mistrust Sense of hopelessness and suspicion.

autonomy A sense of oneself as a separate, self-governing individual.

shame and doubt Feelings of helplessness and lack of control.

initiative Sense of ambition and responsibility.

guilt Feelings of shame resulting from rejection.

FIGURE 10.5 Marc builds a tree-ring tower

Marc carefully balances his tree ring tower   Momentary success

The tower falls   Marc starts over

of these three stages and sample experiences that lead to self-efficacy are presented in Table 10.1.

As you can see from the table, teachers support children's self-efficacy in numerous ways.

Now that you have a developmental grounding in affective development, you are ready to plan learning experiences for children in the affective domain. Since all planning begins with goals, we will start there.

TABLE 10.1 • Self-Efficacy and Erikson's Stages				
ERIKSON'S STAGE	**APPROXIMATE AGE**	**DESCRIPTION**	**TEACHING EXAMPLES**	**LESSONS LEARNED**
Trust versus mistrust	Birth–1 year	Trust evolves from warm responsive relationships with adults. Mistrust comes from harsh or unresponsive interactions.	Establish strong personal relationships with individual children. Provide prompt, responsive physical care. Create predictable routines.	The world is a good place for me.
Autonomy versus shame and doubt	1–3 years	Autonomy emerges as children establish "me and mine" and declare, "I can do it myself." Children benefit from making choices and experiencing reasonable limits. Shame and doubt result when children's attempts at independence are met with criticism, ridicule, or resistance and when adults do things for children that children can and should do for themselves.	Give children choices. Encourage independence: child pours own juice or zips own coat. Encourage children to experiment with materials.	I can make decisions. I can do things on my own.
Initiative versus guilt	3–6 years	The affective focus is on experimentation and mastery. Children experiment with objects, fantasy play, language, ideas, new skills and behaviors, as well as with their bodies. As children strive for mastery of themselves and their environments, they push boundaries and make mistakes. If such actions are treated as bad, or if children are made to feel that they are a disappointment, guilt dominates the period. When adults support and guide children, encourage them to explore, and tolerate mistakes, children develop a sense of purpose and ambition. This outcome translates into initiative.	Plan for physical mastery play such as climbing, running, and balancing. Repeat activities often to provide practice leading toward mastery. Teach children to use real tools of all kinds, such as science tools, wood working tools, kitchen tools, and so on. Focus more on the process of doing than on a final product. Invite children to make and follow plans.	I can put plans into action. I can do things I couldn't do before.

Curricular Goals—Affective Domain

PURPOSE

The purpose of the affective domain is for children to see themselves as valuable and competent.

The following goals address this purpose and are based on research and best practices related to children's development of positive self-awareness, emotional competence, and self-efficacy.

GOALS

Self-Awareness

As children progress within the affective domain, they will:

1. Identify attributes that define who they are (e.g., name, gender, physical appearance, abilities, family composition, race, ethnicity, language(s), religious affiliation (if any), and the place where they live).

2. Distinguish stable personal attributes (e.g., gender) from temporary ones (e.g., short hair).

3. Explore similarities and differences between themselves and others.

4. Identify attributes and qualities that make them unique.

5. Increase knowledge, understanding, and appreciation of their cultural heritage.

6. Positively evaluate personal attributes.

Emotional Competence

7. Acquire and use words and signs to express emotions.

8. Make connections among emotions, facial expressions, body language, and actions.

9. Discuss how circumstances and events influence emotions.

10. Control their emotions in day-to-day interactions.

11. Make reasonable attempts to master situations that are difficult for them.

12. Recover from setbacks and disappointments.

13. Accept constructive criticism and use it to improve themselves.

Self-Efficacy

14. Demonstrate a growing ability to care for themselves, their personal belongings, and to meet their own needs.

15. Demonstrate independence in using age-appropriate materials and tools.

16. Begin and pursue a task independently.

17. Make choices and experience the consequences of personal decisions.

18. Evaluate their accomplishments, failures, and choices.

19. Demonstrate care and respect for classroom materials.

20. Complete a task they have begun.

21. Know when and how to ask for and refuse help.

22. Demonstrate knowledge of what influences quality work; that is, time, care, effort, and responsibility.

Sample Affective Content

Teachers use a combination of on-the-spot teaching strategies and planned activities to address the affective goals listed in the previous discussion. In doing so, they also convey important affective content to their young pupils. Some examples are presented in Table 10.2.

Teaching Strategies for the Affective Domain

1. *Talk about what children are doing and saying.* Use behavior and paraphrase reflections to make nonjudgmental observations about children's actions and words. Try open-ended questions to help children think about themselves in new ways. See Table 10.3 for examples of these strategies.

2. *Help children recognize personal progress.* Describe children's progress in simple terms. "Remember when you couldn't reach the sink? Now you can." Or, "You used to know some of the words to that song. Now you know them all." Use documentation boards and dated work samples to record what children do throughout the year. Invite children to talk about what they did then and what they are doing now.

TABLE 10.2 • Sample Affective Content

DEVELOPMENTAL TASK	SAMPLE CONTENT FOR CHILDREN TO LEARN
Self-Awareness	• I have a name. • How I look, what I do, how I feel, what I like, and what I don't like all contribute to who I am. • I am a member of a family. • I am a member of a cultural group; I have a cultural heritage. • I am like other people in some ways; I am unique in some ways.
Emotional Competence	• Emotions have names. • People feel many different emotions. • There are different ways to express emotions; some ways are helpful, some are not. • If a job seems too hard, I can take a break, get help, start again, or try another way. • If a job seems too big, I can do a little at a time, ask for help, do some now, and do more later.
Self-Efficacy	• People make choices about many things. • Some choices turn out well, some choices turn out less positively. • People learn to do new things by watching, trying, and experimenting. • I can do some things for myself. • I can help keep my home and school safe and clean.

TABLE 10.3 • Enhancing Children's Self-Awareness Through Teacher Talk

CHILDREN DEFINE THEMSELVES BASED ON	ADULTS PROMOTE CHILDREN'S SELF-UNDERSTANDING WHEN THEY	VERBAL EXAMPLES
Observable attributes	Use nonjudgmental statements to describe children	You have brown hair. You are wearing a red shirt.
Activities and possessions	Describe children's actions and the objects they are using in objective terms	You are building a tall tower. You brought a book for us to read today.
Preferences	Identify aloud children's discoveries of what they like and don't like	You'd rather have the red cup. Your favorite name for the hamster is Chip.
Relationships	Talk about children's roles in their social relationships	You are a big brother now. I see three friends: Ted, Raymond, and Martin.
Social comparisons	Remind children of what they can do now that they couldn't do before Draw noncompetitive comparisons among children	See these pictures of your block buildings—this one is from the summer, this one is from today. How do they look different? You noticed your skin has some freckles and so does MaryAnn's.
Internal	Talk with children about their emotions and internal qualities.	You look *sad*. You *wish* we could keep on playing.

3. *Note the wide range of emotions children experience.* Children exhibit many emotions. Some are extreme, some are more moderate; some are positive, some are negative. Take advantage of naturally occurring situations to address whatever emotions arise.

4. *Talk to children about the emotions you observe.* Name or label the emotions you see. "You look sad." "You are happy we are having pizza today." "You're angry that all the glue is used up." Don't evaluate the rightness or wrongness of the child's emotions. Avoid saying, "You shouldn't be angry with her." Or, "Don't be afraid."

5. *Use a variety of feeling words.* Employ numerous words to describe children's emotions. Move beyond *happy, sad, mad,* and *afraid.* See Table 10.4 for examples.

   If you use a feeling word you are not sure children understand, follow up with a second sentence using other words to define what you mean. For instance, "You look disappointed. You wish we had more snack."

TABLE 10.4 • Developing a Broad Feeling Word Vocabulary				
COMMON FEELING WORD	**HAPPY**	**MAD**	**SAD**	**AFRAID**
Variations	Contented	Irritated	Disappointed	Concerned
	Pleased	Frustrated	Dismayed	Uncomfortable
	Satisfied	Annoyed	Upset	Uncertain
	Hopeful	Displeased	Distressed	Worried
	Glad	Disgusted	Discouraged	Terrified
	Proud	Disgruntled	Dejected	Anxious
	Delighted	Jealous	Embarrassed	Alarmed
	Excited	Angry	Sorry	Fearful
	Thrilled	Envious	Unhappy	Shy
	Elated	Furious	Ashamed	Wary

6. *Offer children sample scripts for expressing emotions.* Sometimes, children do not express their emotions verbally because they lack vocabulary or are too emotionally aroused to think of what to say. If this happens, do one of the following things:
   - *Suggest possible words children can use to describe their feelings.* For instance, coach Ellen to say: "Melinda, I *wanted* to sit by you," or "Lillian, I *don't like it* when you put away the paint before I'm done."
   - Once children can easily repeat scripts you provide, **help them think of their own words**: "You're *upset* with Lillian. Tell me words you could use to let her know how you feel."
   - *Ask questions that prompt children to describe their feelings.* Begin with simple yes-or-no questions ("Gregory took your cooking pot. Did you *like it* when he did that?"). Eventually, you can advance to open-ended inquiries ("Gregory took your cooking pot. How did that make you feel?").

7. *Create an optimistic environment.* Offer children a positive, realistic sense of what they can do now and what they could do with a little more effort.
   - *Build on children's strengths, then prompt them to stretch* beyond their current abilities: put one more piece in the puzzle, take one more bite, or add another ending to their story.
   - *Use encouraging statements* to help children push forward and to gain confidence as they try difficult tasks: "Keep going, I'm sure you'll make it," or, "Wow! You figured it out!"
   - *Reframe mistakes as learning opportunities.* Reassure children that mistakes are a natural part of learning. Help them think of alternate ways to approach difficult tasks. Avoid doing things for children that they are capable of doing themselves.

8. *Teach children coping strategies.* Remain alert to children who are experiencing frustration or anxiety. Help them think of different ways to react to tough situations. Some of these are:
   - Breaking task into smaller parts
   - Asking for help—physical help, information, emotional support
   - Taking a break
   - Trying another way

9. *Make it possible for children to find, use, and return materials on their own.*
   - Establish specific locations for certain materials so children know where to find them and put them away. Label these with pictures and words.

- Demonstrate appropriate care of materials: washing paint brushes, putting puzzles away with all the pieces, or hanging up the dress-up clothes.
- Invite children to create personal pictographs to guide them in choosing materials, using them, or cleaning up.

10. *Create opportunities for children to practice completing classroom tasks from start to finish.* Begin with simple three- to four-step tasks (e.g., at the art center: (1) Put on a smock, (2) choose a paper to paint on, (3) make a picture, (4) hang up your picture to dry.). Gradually increase the number of steps. Use pictographs or verbal cues to outline the steps. Remind children of what comes next or ask them to figure out the next step in their work. Help children recognize where they are in the process; for instance, say, "You remembered to put on a smock. That's the first step in this activity." Or, "Tell me what comes next." Or, "You hung up your picture. You are all finished."

11. *Encourage children to develop and carry out plans of their own.* Incorporate children's planning into daily routines: ask children to create a plan for what they intend to do during the day and later ask them to report on their plan. Create specific activities that involve children creating plans: "Let's make a plan for building in the blocks today. What will come first? What should you do next? How will you know you are finished?" Take advantage of spontaneous opportunities to encourage children's planning. For instance, if the children are pretending to be explorers on the playground, you might say, "Explorers often have a plan for where they are going. What is your plan?"

TECH TIP

Creating Documentation of Learning

- Using your phone or a digital camera, take a sequence of three photos of a child carrying out a multistep task from start to finish.
- Print the photos or show them to children out of sequence on a tablet device or computer.
- Invite children to put the photos in order.
- Ask children to help you add a caption to each one.
- Post the photos in the relevant learning center, in an electronic scrapbook, on the classroom door for families to see, or on the school website or teacher blog. See Figure 10.6 for an example created by LaTosha and her teacher.

FIGURE 10.6 LaTosha fills the tube!

Empty!

Halfway there!

Filled to the top!

12. *Give children chances to make choices.*

- *Offer many small choices each day.* These choices may include what color of paper to use, where to sit at snack, what role to play in the house, or whether to put away the big blocks or the small blocks first.

- *Use positive statements.* Tell children what to choose versus what not to choose: "You can use the blocks to make a road, a house, or a rocket." Not, "You can make anything except a gun."

- *Offer only choices that are acceptable to you.* If you say, "You can either water the plants or feed the fish," you should be satisfied with either choice. If what you want is for the child to water plants, do not make plant watering optional. Instead, offer a choice *within* the task, such as watering the plants in the morning or just after lunch.

- *Allow children sufficient time to make a choice.* Children need time to think. Without rushing them, give them a time frame within which to decide, saying: "You decide, red or blue" (pause). Or, "I'll check back with you in a few minutes to see what you've decided"

- *Support children in accepting the consequences of their choices.* Sometimes children make a choice and then regret that they did not choose something else. If this happens, acknowledge their disappointment and remind them that they can make a different choice another time. For instance, "You chose to build with blocks today, but you wish you had time in the pretend store. Tomorrow you may choose again."

Meeting the Needs of Diverse Learners

The affective teaching strategies you have just read about are useful for children of varying ages, temperaments, and abilities. See Figure 10.7 for an example of how Sam's teachers used several of them to help Sam develop greater emotional competence and resilience.

FIGURE 10.7 Sam's story

Four-year-old Sam participated in a special program for gifted and talented children each day. He had many fears and often said he was afraid. Anticipation played a big part in Sam's fears. He worried about what was going to happen and how to avoid anything he thought might be bad. His teacher found that the following strategies helped Sam cope with his fearful emotions:

- Explain things to Sam in advance
- Give Sam scripts to express his feelings
- Give Sam strategies for making his fears more manageable

Here are sample excerpts from notes his teacher sent home during the year to keep Sam's family informed about Sam's progress in relation to his fears:

Jan. 25—Sam cried during the story *Maia* (a chapter book about a dinosaur). He was afraid of the dinosaurs in the story. I had him sit close to another adult and although he covered his eyes, he made it through the whole chapter.

Jan. 27—We did the Dinosaur Dance in the gym. Sam thought he'd be afraid, saying dinosaurs are big and scary. I told him he could stand near me if that happened, but it didn't. He had fun.

Feb. 24—Outside, Mike P. was growling at Sam. Sam was scared at first. When Mike and I reminded Sam that Mike was playing dinosaurs again, he stopped being afraid and played dinosaurs with Mike most of the morning.

March 3—Sam is a little afraid of Erik, a loud child in our class who is very active. Erik also intrigues him. To help Sam manage his anxiety, we formulated a plan for him to use words to let Erik know when Erik was getting too loud. Outside today we practiced saying firmly, "Stop it. I don't like that." Of course, after one successful use, Sam wanted to say it often—not always when called for. The whole group talked a little about thumbs up and thumbs down as another signal to help each other know when something was getting to be too intense or uncomfortable. We all agreed to try this. Sam said it was a good plan.

Source: Based on Kostelnik, Onaga, Rohde, & Whiren (2002). *Children with special needs: Lessons for early childhood professionals.* New York: Teachers College Press (pp. 100–119).

Planned Activities in the Affective Domain

In addition to adopting the teaching strategies just described, you will create planned activities to support children's affective development. Here are six activity ideas to get you started. The goal numbers referred to in each activity correspond to the numbered goals listed earlier in this chapter.

Exploratory Play Activity: I See Me! Reflections of Self

Ages 3-6

Goal 1: For children to identify physical attributes that define who they are.

Content: How I look is part of me.

> Physical features I can see are hair, eye and skin color, face and body shape, gender, and clothing.

Materials: Several mirrors of different sizes and shapes, including at least one full-length mirror

> Markers and crayons

> Paper for the extension activity

Procedure: Set up several mirrors in a single activity area or in multiple spots around the room. Encourage children to look at themselves. Use open-ended questions to support children's explorations: "What do you see?" Use behavior and paraphrase reflections to echo what children seem to notice: "You see you have brown hair." "You have two bumps on your chin where you fell."

To Simplify: Use hand mirrors only. Invite children to concentrate on their faces.

To Extend: Add more crayons, markers, and paper. Encourage children to create a self-portrait based on the personal features they see in the mirror. See Figure 10.8 for examples of this extension carried out by the 4-year-olds at the Camelback Desert School in Scottsdale, Arizona.

FIGURE 10.8 Four-year-old self-portraits

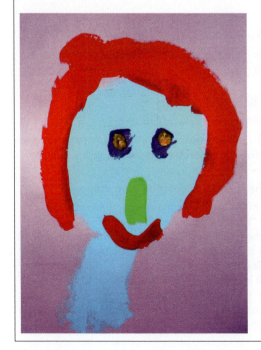

Guided Discovery Activity: All About Me Book

Ages
3-6

Goal 2: For children to identify personal attributes that help define who they are.

Content: How I look, what I do, how I feel about things, what I like, and what I don't like all contribute to who I am.

Materials: 8½ × 11-inch paper in various colors

Markers or crayons

Stapler (or paper punch and grommets to fit)

Procedure: Assist children in describing themselves on paper, one attribute per page, and then bind the pages together into a book. Depending on their age and ability, children may create the writing themselves or dictate their words to an adult or older child.

Sample pages:

Page 1	My name is….
Page 2	Here is my hand/foot (hand/foot tracing).
Page 3	This is me (self-portrait).
Page 4	Some things I can do (dictated list).
Page 5	Some things I like (dictated list).
Page 6	My favorite foods (dictated list).

To Simplify: Draw a self-portrait or a picture of "my family."

To Extend: Compare when I was a baby to what I am like now; discuss internal as well as external qualities (e.g., Sometimes I feel…); go back to this activity throughout the year, adding attributes and comparing what children are like now with how they were then.

Problem-Solving Activity: Self-Identity Graphs
Comparing Individual Similarities and Differences

Ages
3-6

Goal 3: For children to explore similarities and differences between themselves and others.

Content: I am like other people in some ways (everyone in the class has hair); I am unique in some ways (color, style, and textures of people's hair varies).

Materials: A large white plastic tablecloth or white shower curtain on which a 6 × 8 box grid has been drawn

Wipe-off markers

Damp paper towel for wiping the grid clean. See Figure 10.9

Procedure: This activity is most meaningful if children have had previous opportunities to group objects by attributes and to use a graph or other symbolic means to record or report their findings.

Lay the cloth or curtain on the floor, grid side up.

Follow the steps involved in the problem-solving process:

Observation: Invite the children to look carefully at all the children and to tell you what they notice about individual children's hair (colors, styles, texture, length, accessories, etc.).

Information Gathering: Ask the children to describe what they see.

Experimentation: Choose one of the attributes the children have observed (e.g., hair color or hair texture). "You noticed people have different-colored hair. Let's make a graph about the hair colors in our class." Invite the children to identify what colors are present among the children in the class. Put that color name at the top of the graph. Repeat this process until four or five different colors have been identified. Ask individual children to take turns identifying where their own hair color fits in the grid. An alternative strategy is to invite the children to stand up one at a time and for others in the group to categorize their hair. Ask the child if he or she agrees with the group's assessment.

FIGURE 10.9 **Graphing our hair**

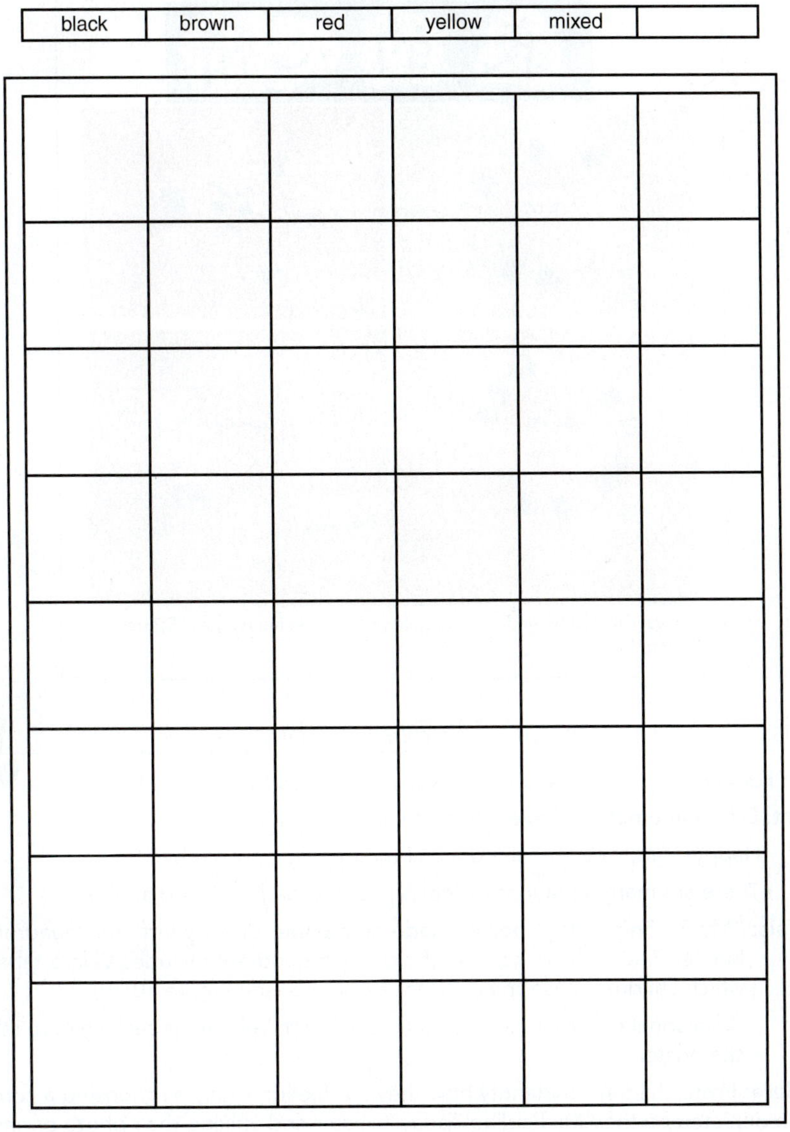

black	brown	red	yellow	mixed	

Drawing Conclusions: Ask children to look at the hair graph they have created and tell you what they notice. Discuss similarities and differences among individuals and groups. By comparing the length of the columns, children can tell which hair color occurs most often or less often. Invite children to tell you where their own hair fits best, as well as how their hair may be different from others.

To Simplify: Choose a subgroup of children so that fewer children are involved at a time. Identify a single predetermined category to focus on, such as hair color.

To Extend: After children gain experience with tangible attributes such as eye color, ear shape, hair color, or skin color, move on to activities children enjoy doing, preferences, and internal characteristics. Keep a record of the children's self-identity graphs over multiple days.

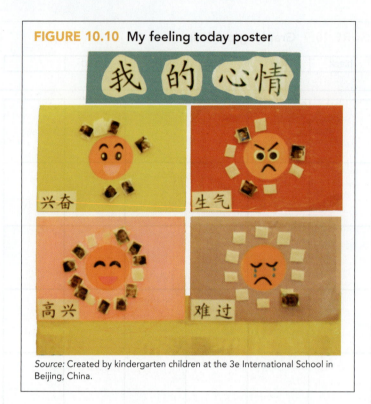

FIGURE 10.10 My feeling today poster

Source: Created by kindergarten children at the 3e International School in Beijing, China.

Discussion Activity: What's My Feeling Today?

Ages 3-6

Goal 7: For children to acquire and use words and signs to express emotions.

Content: Different emotions have different names.

Happy, mad, sad, and afraid are common ways people feel.

There are many variations of feeling happy, mad, sad, and afraid.

Materials: "My Feeling Today" poster made on a paper divided into four quadrants labeled happy, mad, sad, or afraid. Each quadrant includes Velcro tabs on which children place their photos or names (see Figure 10.10).

A personal photo or name card (backed with Velcro) for each child to stick to the poster

Procedure: Invite children to identify how they are feeling today by choosing a core emotion depicted on the "My Feeling Today" poster and affixing their photo or name to a place on the poster to show how they feel. Prompt discussion by saying something such as, "Think about how you are feeling this morning. Is anyone feeling worried about something? What made you feel worried?" "Where would worried fit on our mood poster?" Use paraphrase and feeling word reflections to expand children's understandings and vocabulary. "You are feeling happy today." Or, "You are excited we are going outside next." Discuss children's emotions and what prompted them. Encourage children to listen to one another and to contribute at least one idea to the discussion.

To Simplify: Focus only on primary emotions: happy, mad, sad, and afraid.

To Extend: Follow up on children's core emotions with related words associated with feelings. Draw comparisons among the similar and differing emotions children describe: "Harriette was pleased we had green beans for lunch. Maureen was disappointed." Compare children's emotions from yesterday to today.

Demonstration Activity: I Can Do It! Self-Help Tasks

Ages 3-6

Goal 15: For children to demonstrate independence using age-appropriate materials and tools.

Content: I can do some things for myself.

I can learn by watching others.

If I make a mistake, I can try again or use a different approach.

Materials: Depends on task

Procedure: During small group time, demonstrate how to carry out a simple classroom job such as pouring one's own juice, putting the blocks away, or washing hands. Follow these steps: (1) Model the task as you describe it aloud, (2) ask the children to talk you through the task, (3) make mistakes, so the children have to correct you, (4) invite a child to try it, (5) reinforce correct steps, coach toward increased proficiency.

To Simplify: Work with children one-on-one.

To Extend: Invite the children to help you create a sign or pictograph as a reminder of the steps involved.

Move on to less familiar tasks, such as using a hammer and nails.

Direct Instruction Activity: "Help Me/Don't Help Me" Skits

Ages 3-6

Goal 21: For children to know how to ask for or refuse help.

Content: I can do some things for myself.

I can get help when I need it from a friend, a teacher, or someone in my family.

I can tell people if I need help or not.

Materials: Two puppets clearly distinguishable from one another

Toy objects to illustrate a situation in which a character is doing a big task (e.g., lifting a big block, carrying many toys, or putting many objects away)

Procedure: Create a script a person might use to ask for help ("Please help me." Or, "This is too much for me. I need help."). Create a script a person might use to decline help ("I want to try by myself." Or, "No, thank you." Or, "Let me try it first."). Create a skit involving the six steps identified in Table 10.5. Keep each skit short.

To Simplify: Focus on one only script or strategy at a time.

To Extend: Ask children to add new scripts to the ones they have learned.

TABLE 10.5 • Affective Skits		
STEPS IN CARRYING OUT A SKIT	**TEACHER SAYS**	**TEACHER DOES**
Gain the children's attention	"Look up here. Some things you can do for yourself, sometimes you need help. Who might help you? How will they know you need help? Let's find out what Fred and Sam do to solve this problem."	
Demonstrate the script	"This is Fred. This is Sam. One day Fred was trying to put many blocks away by himself. There were so many, he started to get tired. He saw Sam. Fred said, 'Please help me.' Sam came over to help. The end!"	Point to characters Act out scenario with figures and props
Explain why the script worked and what happened	"Fred needed help. He asked Sam for help. Sam helped."	
Discuss this script with children and relate it to their own experiences in the classroom	"Tell me about times when you might need help in our classroom."	
Demonstrate poor use of the script or not using the script	"This is Fred. This is Sam. One day Fred was trying to put many blocks away by himself. There were so many, he started to get tired. He saw Sam. Fred didn't say anything. Sam walked away. The end!"	
Explain why this was a problem	"Fred needed help. He didn't say anything. Sam didn't know Fred needed help. The end!"	
Give children an opportunity to use the props to either recreate this story using the script, or make up their own stories in which the script is used	"Now you can tell a story about helping with Fred and Sam."	Offer puppets to children

FIGURE 10.11 **Materials that support affective learning**

Typical Materials: Affective Domain

- Photographs and paintings depicting people expressing emotions and carrying out tasks
- Mirrors, papers, paints (including assorted "skin-color" paints and crayons) and other art media for self-portraits and body tracings
- Job chart for choosing classroom jobs
- Name tags and labels for children's possessions and personal spaces (e.g., cubby, art storage, etc.)
- Pictographs of typical classroom tasks from first step to completion
- Real tools; for example:
  - Staplers
  - Scissors
  - Scrapers and peelers
  - Paint brushes of varying sizes
  - Three-hole punch
  - Screwdrivers and screws
  - Hammer and nails
  - Computer
- ✔ Assorted picture books (fiction and nonfiction) depicting emotions, characters striving to do something, and characters overcoming challenges. Here are some examples:
  - Bauer, Marion Dane. (2010). *Thank you for me!* New York: Simon & Schuster Books for Young Readers.
  - Nolan, Allia Zobel. (2009). *What I like about me!* East Rutherford, NJ: Readers Digest Press.
  - Tyler, Michael. (2005). *The skin you live in.* Chicago, IL: The Chicago Children's Museum.
  - Berendes, Mary. (2008). *Feelings = las emociones.* Mankato, MN: The Child's World, Inc.
  - Snow, Todd, Peggy Snow, Pamela Espeland, & Carrie Hartman. (2007). *Feelings to share from a to z.* Oak Park Heights, MN: Maren Green Publishing.
  - Adams, Diane. (2009). *I can do it myself.* Atlanta, GA: Peachtree Publishers.

Materials for the Affective Domain

Almost any object or piece of equipment could be used to support affective goals. A few examples related to affective planning are listed in Figure 10.11.

Assessment in the Affective Domain

All the assessment strategies you have learned about can be used to evaluate children's affective learning. Sometimes you can also enlist children's help in keeping track of personal progress. For instance, in Ms. Johnson's classroom, every learning center includes a small plastic bucket in which colored clothespins are stored. Each clothespin is marked with a child's name. When children complete a given task for the day, they clip their clothespin to a card marked "ALL DONE." This makes it easy for children and teachers to see who has completed the task and who may need more time or additional support to do so.

Communicating with Families About the Affective Domain

One of the reasons families enroll their children in preschool and kindergarten is to help them make a smooth emotional transition from home to school. When asked about the skills they want children to develop between the ages of 3 to 6 years, many parents identify self-confidence, the ability to control emotions, and learning to do more things independently as important lessons they hope their children will learn in early childhood (Galinsky, 2010). All of these fall within the affective domain. When families and teachers carry out similar strategies at school and at home, children find it easier to learn new affective skills. Letting families know how you address affective goals in your classroom and what they might do at home is one way to enhance children's learning. Another strategy is to ask families what they do to promote self-awareness, emotional competence, and self-efficacy. The insights you gain and the techniques you learn will expand your repertoire of skills and provide a bridge from home to school from which children may benefit. See Figure 10.12 for a sample of an affective "news bite."

NEWSLETTER/WEB READY COMMUNICATION

FIGURE 10.12 • Supporting Children's Independence!

"I can do it myself!" We hear these words a lot at school. You probably hear them at home, too. They are children's declarations of independence!

Most young children are eager to do many things for themselves—snapping their coats, pouring their juice, or making their own snacks. As they gradually take on more responsibility, children develop attitudes and skills they need to be successful later in school and in life—independence, self-confidence, and the ability to make decisions. To promote this kind of learning, we have developed routines and activities at school that allow children to practice basic self-help and decision-making skills every day. Some of these include encouraging children to:

- Pour their own juice at snack and serve themselves at family-style meals (we provide child-sized pitchers and serving spoons, we don't worry too much about spills, and we keep sponges handy just in case).

- Snap, zip, and button doll clothes and their own jackets, sweaters, and shoes (we build extra time into our going-outside and coming-inside routines to avoid rushing children and to provide the support children need).

- Get things from the shelves and put them back when they are through (we label shelves and containers with pictures and words to make these tasks easier).

- Make choices throughout the day such as where to sit at group time, whether to use the blue or red paint, and whether they want two or three crackers at snack (these are mini-decisions that give children good practice in decision making).

- Live with the consequences of their decisions (child finds he doesn't like the blue paint so much after all). However, we stand ready to help if children have chosen something that is just too difficult or if they can't figure out what to do next.

Strategies like these are effective because they are simple. They work best when adults use them intentionally and often, not haphazardly or infrequently.

Are there self-help tasks you are working on at home that you would like us to work on too? Tell us what those are. We look forward to hearing from you.

10   Applying What You've Learned

1. **Dimensions of the Affective Domain.** With a partner, describe the three dimensions of the affective domain. Provide an example of each that you have seen in the young children with whom you have come in contact.

2. **Key Affective Concepts and Skills.** Tour the classroom in which you are working or volunteering now. Look at the materials on the walls and shelves. What messages about self-identity do you see? Are all children represented? What would you add or take away to make the messages more effective?

3. **Strategies for Teaching in the Affective Domain.** Arrange to visit an early childhood classroom. Take a few minutes to observe the overall affective climate of the room. Then, look for at least two examples of a teacher promoting children's emotional competence.

4. **Planned Activities in the Affective Domain.** Write a detailed lesson plan that involves reading the book *The Little Engine That Could,* by Watty Piper, to a small group of children. Focus your objectives on self-efficacy. Carry out your plan. Read the story to children. Discuss the story with them. What messages of self-efficacy do the children talk about?

5. **Meeting the Needs of Diverse Learners.** Consider how you would support the affective development of a child who had limited English, a child with a hearing impairment, and a child with limited visual skills. Identify at least two modifications you could make to your *Little Engine That Could* plan to meet the needs of each of these children.

6. **Communicating with Families.** Refer to the family communication materials presented in Figure 10.12. Adapt the content to match the needs of families in the classroom in which you are participating. What changes did you make? How would you use the materials on a bulletin board, via text messaging, on a website, in a newsletter?

References

American Psychological Association. (2011). *Resilience guide for parents and teachers*. Retrieved from www.apa.org/he;pcenter/resilience.aspx.

Barr, R. (2008). Developing social understanding in a social context. In K. McCartney & D. Phillips (Eds.), *Blackwell handbook of early childhood development* (pp. 188–207). Malden, MA: Blackwell Publishing.

Brown, W. H., Odom, S. L., & McConnell, S. R. (2008). *Social competence of young children: Risk, disability, and intervention.* Baltimore, MA: Paul H. Brookes.

Calkins, S. D., & Williford, A. P. (2009). Taming the terrible twos: Self-regulation and school readiness. In O. A. Barbarin & B. H. Wasik (Eds.), *Handbook of child development and early education: Research to practice.* New York: Guilford Press.

Denham, S. A., Bassett, H. H., & Wyatt, T. (2007). The socialization of emotional competence. In J. E. Grusec & P. D. Hastings (Eds.), *Handbook of socialization theory and practice.* New York: Guilford Press.

Derman-Sparks, L., & Edwards, J. O. (2010). *Anti-bias education for young children and ourselves.* Washington, D.C.: National Association for the Education of Young Children.

Egertson, H. A. (2006). In praise of butterflies: Linking self-esteem and learning. *Young Children, 61*(6), 58–60.

Ekman, P. (2007). *Emotions revealed.* New York: Times Books.

Epstein, A. S. (2009). *Me, you, us: Social-emotional learning in preschool.* Ypsilanti, MI: HighScope Educational Research Foundation.

Galinsky, E. (2010). Skill one: Focus and self-control. In *Mind in the making: The seven essential skills every child needs.* New York: Harper Collins.

Gonzalez-Mena, J., & Eyer, D. W. (2009). *Infants, toddlers, and caregivers* (8th ed.). Boston, MA: McGraw-Hill.

Harter, S. (2006). The self. In N. Eisenberg, W. Damon, & R. M. Lerner (Eds.). *Handbook of child psychology.* Hoboken, NJ: John Wiley & Sons.

Kostelnik, M. J., Gregory, K. M., Soderman, A. K., & Whiren, A. P. (2012). *Guiding children's social development and learning* (7th ed.). Clifton Park, NY: Delmar/Cengage Learning.

Kostelnik, M. J., Onaga, E., Rohde, B., & Whiren, A. P. (2002). *Children with special needs: Lessons for early childhood professionals.* New York: Teachers College Press.

National Association of School Psychologists. (2010). The seven ingredients of resilience: Information for parents. *Communique, 38*(6), 1–3.

Pizzolongo, P. J., & Hunter, A. (2011). I am safe and secure: Promoting resilience in young children. *Young Children, 66*(2), 67–69.

Thompson, R. A., & Lagattuta, K. H. (2008). Feeling and understanding: Early emotional development. In K. McCartney & D. Phillips (Eds.), *Blackwell handbook of early childhood development.* Malden, MN: Blackwell Publishing.

Thompson, J. E., & Twibell, K. K. (2009). Teaching hearts and minds in early childhood classrooms: Curriculum for social and emotional development. In O. A. Barbarin & B. H. Wasik (Eds.), *Handbook of child development and early education: Research to practice.* New York: Guilford Press.

11 The Cognitive Domain: Nurturing Young Scientists

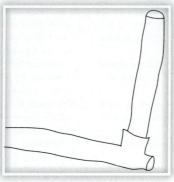

Sam's pipe drawing

Sam and Jared, both 4 years old, work together to connect two pieces of PVC pipe. "Let's make the pipe go sideways so we can roll the marble over there," Jared says as he points to his left. He reaches into the bucket of assorted PVC pipe lengths and connectors and pulls out a horizontal connector. He attaches the connector and adds another length of pipe to the construction. Realizing the pipe is now longer but just as straight, he says to Sam, "How can we make the pipe bend? It just keeps going straight!" The boys try taking the pieces apart and reconnecting them in a different order, but recognize the end result is the same: one long, straight pipe. They try to physically bend the pipe, but are not successful.

As Sam digs through the bucket, he finds a T-shaped connector and says, "Let's try this one!" He takes off the horizontal connector and attaches the T-shaped connector in its place. He fits a length of pipe onto one side of the connector. Both boys begin to jump up and down exclaiming, "We did it! We made the pipe bend!"

Mrs. Canon kneels beside the two boys and comments, "You both worked hard on that problem and you found a solution! Why don't you draw what you did so that you can show the other children how to make the pipe bend?" She hands each boy a clipboard and a marker.

"Yeah, let's write that you need to use the piece with three sides!" exclaims Sam as he points to the T-connector.

Sam and Jared are doing much more than simply playing with the materials in the scenario above—they are acting as scientists.

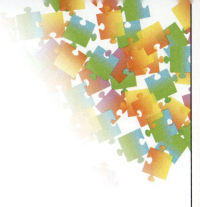

They identified a problem, making their pipe construction "bend." They tried several ways to solve the problem: reconnecting the pipe pieces in a different order, trying to manually bend the pipe, and finally, using a connector that allowed the pipe to connect to the construction from a different angle. Their teacher then provided the boys with a way to communicate what they learned to the rest of the class by drawing their pipe construction on paper.

Young children naturally try to make sense of their world. They are full of questions and expend a great deal of their energy on discovering how the world is organized and how and why things happen. As a result, they are intensely curious about many things—for example, how objects such as drawers, pliers, and flowers open and close; where bubbles go when they pop; how seashore waves "melt" sand castles; and why leaves change color in the fall. As teachers, we can assist children in developing an understanding of science by capitalizing on this natural inclination.

LEARNING OUTCOMES

After you read this chapter, you will be able to:

- Describe the importance of the cognitive domain as it relates to science.
- Describe key science concepts, processes, and skills for children to learn.
- Identify strategies for teaching science.
- Plan engaging experiences and activities in science.
- Explain ways to address the needs of the diverse learners in your classroom.
- Communicate with families about science learning.

The Importance of Science

Preschool- and kindergarten-age children act on their powerful curiosity by observing, experimenting with materials, and questioning adults. They develop ideas about the world and strive to test these ideas. To help children build a consistent and accurate picture of the physical world, effective teachers consider what children already know and relate new learning experiences to this knowledge. They watch and listen to determine what children are interested in and what they already understand. As they observe children in action, they evaluate any misconceptions children have about particular phenomena. For instance, it is common for young children to assume that certain events (such as how ice forms or how plants grow) happen spontaneously or happen by magic, which can lead to misunderstandings. Rather than representing a mistake that teachers correct simply through telling, such misunderstandings provide great opportunities for developing science-related activities that assist children in achieving more accurate ideas. For example, Mejing, a young preschooler, chases her shadow in an attempt to "catch" it, and is surprised when it disappears as she runs into the shade. Mejing tells her friends, "My shadow ran away. It doesn't like it when I chase it." Julie, her teacher, sees that Mejing has some misconceptions about shadows and recognizes this as an opportunity to provide a meaningful learning experience. Julie decides to plan activities to extend Mejing's understanding of light and shadow.

For Mejing to further her knowledge, Julie will need a basic understanding of scientific concepts related to light and shadow. Young children benefit when their teachers have a view of science as an active process that involves science inquiry (Lind, 2005). Children also need access to carefully chosen materials and many opportunities to work with and observe science-related phenomena. Teachers like Julie know that children will continue to expand their understanding of concepts when they are allowed to revisit, represent, discuss, and demonstrate the experiences they have with specially selected materials.

"SCIENCING" IN THE EARLY YEARS

Can young children really do something as complicated as science? When children in preschool and kindergarten classrooms observe, think, and reflect on actions and events, they are doing science. When they organize factual information into more meaningful concepts, solve problems, and act on their curiosity, they are doing science. As they endeavor to understand how the work of scientists is related to their lives and investigations, they are doing science. They would *not* be doing science if they were merely listening to the teacher talk about science or simply watching the teacher conduct a science experiment. As you provide meaningful opportunities for the children in your classroom to be actively involved in the scientific process by forming hypotheses, collecting data, and formulating and testing their conclusions, you offer them the basic skills they will need for lifelong "sciencing."

Effective teachers carefully listen to and closely watch children to gain understanding about the concepts young children are forming, and subsequently use this information in their instructional planning. This helps children realize that science is more than a collection of activities and facts. Science is made up of two central components: the **scientific process** (also called *scientific inquiry*) and **science content** (National Academy of Science, 2011). Teachers help children acquire scientific attitudes by encouraging children to think creatively in both identifying and solving problems. These are critical cognitive skills for living in a complex world.

Age-appropriate science concepts are those we would typically expect children to understand at particular ages, based on our knowledge of child development and experience with young children. With this in mind, ask yourself, "What do I want the children to learn about science? What science concepts, facts, or vocabulary am I hoping to teach? What concrete, hands-on experiences can I provide to help children discover this information? What do the children already know about this science topic and how can I build on their knowledge?" By asking yourself such questions, you can begin to plan meaningful and challenging experiences that will extend children's scientific learning. One way to do this is by using inquiry as an instructional approach.

Key Science Concepts, Processes, and Skills for Children to Learn

USING INQUIRY AS AN INSTRUCTIONAL APPROACH

As noted, assisting young children in thinking and behaving like actual scientists requires teaching both process and content. You will learn more about each of these elements in this chapter. For now we will focus on the process or inquiry portion of science instruction.

You were introduced to a variation of inquiry in Chapter 6, under the heading of problem-solving basics (see Figure 6.3). Adopting an inquiry approach involves providing children with multiple, high-quality experiences in which they investigate a problem or question using the following sequential process.

1. *Observation.* Every scientific discovery begins with observation and first-hand experience. For this reason, teachers using an **inquiry approach** start by teaching children to be effective and systematic observers of their world. As young children use their senses to explore the materials and events around them, they are using the same skills used by actual scientists to expand their knowledge of the world. Observation becomes the method for understanding relationships, making predictions, and figuring out why things happen. As children observe, they begin to formulate questions and can then use inquiry to gather information to answer those questions. Developing observation skills involves being selective in what is observed, focusing only on

scientific process Also known as scientific inquiry, the process used by scientists to gather information and answer questions.

science content Factual body of knowledge developed by the scientific community.

inquiry approach Teachers guide children in examining objects and events, posing questions, investigating, solving problems, drawing conclusions, and communicating findings.

FIGURE 11.1 **Encouraging students to observe carefully**

Maria Velarde explains to the students in her kindergarten class that they are to look at a tree on the playground and, in their journals, draw what they observe. As the children begin their observations, Maria notices that most of the drawings are quite vague and include little detail. She wants to encourage the children to observe carefully and note details they might normally overlook. To help the children focus their observations, she gives each child an empty slide frame to look through and tells the children to draw what they see. Richard places his frame against the trunk of the tree and notices the deep ridges in the tree's bark. He carefully draws the lines on the tree in his journal to indicate the ridges. Hector puts his frame on top of a leaf and studies the space inside the frame. He nudges Richard and says, "Look, there are little brown spots on this leaf and lots of green bumps. I didn't see that before." Maria kneels next to the boys and states, "You noticed some important details about your tree. Later you can show your drawings to the other children and tell them what you noticed."

---

those aspects that are important. As children gain skill, they decide what to observe and how to record their observations. Teachers promote inquiry skills by modeling observation, offering children tools and strategies to focus observations, providing scaffolding to generate active thinking, and structuring opportunities for practice. See Figure 11.1 for an example of how one kindergarten teacher encourages her students to observe carefully.

2. *Identifying a question based on observation.* Next in the sequence, children are encouraged to ask questions and explore ways to find the answers to their questions. Because children have limited experience and are prone to magical thinking, it is natural for them to reach incorrect conclusions. As a result, teachers encourage children to be cautious about accepting things at face value. This type of thinking is supported when you ask questions such as: Why do you think . . . ? How could you . . . ? What would happen if . . . ? Such open-ended queries help to focus children's attention on inconsistencies and new facets of the problem, particularly when accompanied by additional hands-on experiences. Answering such questions requires children to observe and collect information. This gives them a basis for reflecting on their experiences and for developing new theories and ideas.

3. *Developing ideas and making predictions.* Inquiry also involves developing ideas and predicting what will happen when those ideas are tested. This skill takes time for children to develop and requires good modeling on the part of the teacher. It also requires trial-and-error experiments and classroom experiences that foster exploration of cause and effect. Predictions are not simply guesses at what the right answer might be; instead, they are based on observations and information the child has gathered. Children become better at making predictions as they gain experience in doing so. As a teacher, you will encourage children to experiment, make choices, and explore ways to correct mistaken conclusions. Showing interest in children's ideas and demonstrating that their opinions are important and respected gives children the go-ahead for making reasoned predictions without focusing exclusively on simply "getting it right."

4. *Testing ideas.* When children have ownership of a question, they are invested in finding the answer. Providing children the opportunity to try out their ideas

What questions do you think these boys are trying to answer?

to see if they were correct is another necessary component in the inquiry process. This requires an adequately stocked classroom with tools and materials that encourage children to explore, investigate, classify, and compare. Goal-directed fieldwork such as field trips or visits with local experts can also be used to extend children's knowledge base and foster additional ideas or methods to test their theories.

5. *Analyzing and drawing conclusions from collected data.* Once children have collected data, the data need to be organized to help children make sense of their observations. This is a critical step in drawing conclusions. After the children have completed their investigations, provide them with time and guidance in analyzing their findings. What did they find out and what does it mean to them? What conclusions can be drawn? It is as important to find out what does not work as what does. Children might find their ideas confirmed or that the evidence does not support their original thoughts. Even when children find that their hypotheses were wrong, they have extended their learning and furthered their understanding of a concept. This provides the opportunity to gather additional information and revise their theories based on the evidence they have discovered.

6. *Sharing findings with others.* Following an investigation, a scientist summarizes what was discovered and shares these results with others. Similarly, children can be encouraged to explain their thinking and compare it to other people's ideas (Enfield & Rogers, 2009). Children need guidance in how to talk about what they found and why they believe their findings are important. They will need to organize the information in some useful way and communicate their outcomes to peers and adults. Children may share their findings through spoken language, gestures, or by putting their thoughts on paper using drawings and words.

Inquiry is not a lock-step process. Not all children will go through the preceding sequence at the same time or in the same way. Some children may take a long time to observe; others will move along more quickly to posing questions and testing their ideas. Also, different steps will provoke different questions and different responses among the children. The teacher's job is to guide the process according to each child's needs, not to try to get everyone through the steps in unison or to arrive at the same conclusion.

Inquiry is science in action. With practice, children become more competent in applying an inquiry approach to science. This approach requires you to go beyond merely setting up a science display or demonstrating simple experiments in which children watch but have no active means for following up or posing their own questions. The process skills associated with the inquiry approach can be put into motion again and again to support children in advancing their understanding of the "big areas" of science, such as these:

- Earth sciences (weather, space, ecology, major features of the earth)
- Physical sciences (change in matter; forces affecting motion, balance, direction, speed, light, heat, and sound; magnetism; electricity; physical properties; and characteristics of phenomena)
- Life sciences (characteristics of living plants and animals; life cycles and processes; basic needs, habitats, and relationships)

INTEGRATING SCIENCE ACROSS THE CURRICULUM

Children are showing an interest in inquiry when they:

- Raise questions about objects and events in their world.
- Explore and act on objects to see what will happen.

- Make careful observations.
- Use tools to enhance their observations.
- Describe what they have observed.

Teachers can easily integrate teaching basic concepts in science throughout the early childhood curriculum. For example, the children in Kelly Adler's kindergarten class became interested in a bird nest built outside the classroom window. Ms. Adler encouraged their interest and provided opportunity and materials to assist the children in learning more about the bird. She strengthened their observation skills by having the children draw and write about what they saw. The children compared their observations to one another and to the information they found in books and field guides related to birds that Ms. Adler brought into the classroom. Ms. Adler included different genres of children's literature, including picture books and selected pages from information books. She was always careful to make sure the nonfiction books were accurate or to point out any inaccuracies to the children. The children's excitement about their investigations was enhanced by the number of engaging pictures and interestingly displayed books that appeared throughout the classroom. The children tallied the number and types of birds they saw each day and graphed their results. The math center contained an assortment of bird feathers in various shapes, sizes, and colors for the children to examine, group, and order. The teacher listened carefully to the children's explanations of why certain feathers were grouped with others, making notes about the criteria children used to place the feathers in categories. During group time, Ms. Adler introduced recordings of different bird songs and the children clapped out the rhythm of each song. Later, they created a way to draw these rhythms on paper. Individually and as a group, they dictated poems and stories about birds. They learned that certain birds are predators but others are often prey. A local game and wildlife expert visited the classroom, bringing a live bird for the children to observe up close. The children studied several John James Audubon prints of birds and worked to create bird pictures of their own using a variety of media.

Activities can be integrated across the curriculum to strengthen children's understanding of science concepts.

As you can see, all curricular activity could spring from science; at the least, successful science teaching includes integration of activities and experiences from all other learning domains. The depth and breadth of children's learning will depend on hands-on opportunities to accumulate information about a variety of interesting and worthwhile topics and guidance in integrating what they discover with their existing knowledge. Using a more in-depth, integrated approach toward science education can lead to the development of higher-order problem-solving skills and should be a priority in good science teaching (Worth, 2010). Skilled teachers help children make connections between science and problems encountered in daily life. Once children have developed the basic skills of observing, inferring, and experimenting, they should be encouraged to engage in scientific inquiry, a process that requires them to think about and interpret what they are learning through the many sensory-experience activities in the early childhood classroom.

Teaching with a hands-on approach to science does not automatically teach problem solving and inquiry. Also necessary is the teacher's ability to ask good, open-ended questions and to provide well-planned activities involving guided discovery, problem solving, and social inquiry. For example, when Ms. Hamel asks children to add some white paint to each paint cup to create a pastel hue, she is simply using a hands-on approach. However, when she shows them several swatches of pastel-colored fabric and says, "I really like these colors, but we don't have any paint that matches my fabric. I wonder if there's a way to make each color lighter. Let's see if we can do that!" and then provides the children with a variety of paint to add to the paint containers, she is engaging the children in inquiry. The first approach simply has children carrying out a process she designed. The second encourages children to develop scientific skills that will become enormously useful to them—discovering a way to gather data when they need to problem solve and testing their ideas. When she encourages several children to tell the others what they did to make the new colors, she is facilitating the children in mentally organizing the information and effectively articulating it to someone else.

TRY IT YOURSELF

How many drops of water will fit on a coin before the water runs off? Practice using the scientific method to find the answer to this question. You will need several coins such as a penny, quarter, and dime; an eye dropper; water; and a place to record your predictions and results. First, predict how many drops you think will fit on each coin. To test your prediction, carefully drip water from the eye dropper onto the coin, counting each drop. Continue to add drops until the water runs off of the coin. How many drops were you able to place on each coin? Were your predictions correct? Did you change your predictions for the other coins after you observed the first coin? What factors may have influenced the number of drops?

WHAT TO DO WHEN CHILDREN COME TO THE WRONG CONCLUSIONS

Young children are immature thinkers. Their perceptions influence their understandings of what they see. This means that at times children will construct incorrect explanations regarding how things happen and why. When children have misconceptions about the world around them, teachers need to recognize these are a reflection of their current level of thinking and are developmentally appropriate. If we rush to correct children's thinking, we may inhibit their explorations. Providing the answer to children instead of encouraging further exploration may lead children to rely on adults for answers and undermine their confidence in themselves as learners.

This does not mean that we let children's incorrect conclusions stand without further guidance. Instead, effective teachers help children to frame additional questions related to the topic and provide additional experiences to further children's understanding of the concept. Knowing why an idea is wrong can be more valuable than knowing the right answer while having no idea why the answer is correct. As children act on objects and observe the results of their actions, they gain further experience and understanding and revise their ideas to reflect their new knowledge. For example, Mr. King planned a sink-and-float experiment and placed several items next to the water table for the children to use. Inadvertently, all of the items he chose that sank were dark in color. Martha, a 3-year-old, concluded that "pretty colors" make things float. Mr. King decided to provide Martha with some additional materials, making certain to include some brightly colored, clear, and multi-colored objects that would sink. As Martha placed these items in the water, she watched with surprise as they drifted to the bottom of the water table. Mr. King used comments and questions to focus Martha's attention on the fact that some items floated while others sank, regardless of their color.

Model the attitude that it is okay to try something you don't know and to make mistakes. Being original and different is a valuable and admirable trait. Invite children to explain their thinking to you by asking open-ended questions such as "What did you notice?" or "How did you decide to . . . ?" Encourage children to close their eyes and think about the question for a few seconds before they answer. This will provide them the opportunity to reflect on the question and formulate their response. Reflect children's ideas without criticism or judgment. Paraphrase children's words using comments such as "Derrick thinks. . . . What do you think Cameron?" How we respond to children's immature thinking or misconceptions affects their attitude toward their thinking and inquiring. If we respond with discussion, additional resources, or experiences, children learn that testing their ideas is valued and worthwhile, and being incorrect is just part of the process. As teachers, our attitude is key in children's development of inquiry skills and building confidence in them as learners. Hands-on experiences alone do not guarantee that children will learn the content that you have identified as important. When children would not be able to discover the answer on their own, such as the name of an object, teachers must provide the knowledge for them.

CHILDREN'S LITERATURE THAT IS SCIENCE BASED

One way to extend children's knowledge is to provide rich literature with science-related concepts in your classroom. Reading, discussing, and building on the content of children's science books can incorporate inquiry in your curriculum (Sackes, Trundle, & Flevares, 2009). You can include information books that children can use as resources (such as field guides) as well as stories with science-related plots. When choosing literature for science concepts, it is important to consider the age of the children, the accuracy of the science content included in the book, and the science background of the author. Many children's books contain inaccurate information or illustrations. Use reputable science resources to compare children's literature to correct science information. Point out to children any inaccuracies or limitations in the book and discuss the correct science concepts with the children.

Including science-related children's literature in your classroom offers the opportunity to integrate

What books might you introduce to extend the science knowledge of these children?

literacy and science as well as extend children's science learning. Following is a list of titles you might choose to include:

- *The Carrot Seed*, by R. Krauss (1945), HarperCollins Publishers
- *From Seed to Plant*, by G. Gibbons (1993), Holiday House
- *The Surprise Garden*, by Z. Hall (1999), Scholastic Trade
- *Redwoods*, by J. Chin (2009), Flash Point
- *What Is Bendy?* by S. Warbrick (1996), Rigby Interactive Library
- *A Log's Life*, by W. Pfeffer (2007), Aladdin Publishers
- *Science Is Everywhere*, by C. Howitt (2010), Ocean Publishing
- *A Seed Is Sleepy*, by D. Hutts (2007), Chronicle Books
- *What Makes a Shadow?* by T. Hoban (1998), Scholastic
- *Urban Roosts: Where Birds Nest in the City*, by B. Bash (1992), Little Brown Books for Young Readers
- *Wiggling Worms at Work*, by W. Pfeffer (2003), Collins

PLAY AND SCIENTIFIC THINKING

As teachers, we need to encourage children's curiosity, and play is an important part of this process. It is through play that children test their theories, challenge their skills, and demonstrate what they know. For example, in Mr. Mahr's class the children have been reading about and observing bees. The children have learned that bees use a waggle dance to communicate to the hive the distance, direction, and desirability of food. One afternoon before snack, Mr. Mahr sees Kenneth and Omar performing a waggle dance of their own. By observing the two boys recreate the waggle dance in their play, Mr. Mahr is able to see that they understand how the bees communicate with one another. As children mature, their play becomes more organized and well thought-out. They begin to plan what they want to accomplish through their play. In play, children do not have to verbally describe their thoughts; they can test their concepts and revise their approaches or ideas at will. Opportunities for large blocks of unstructured play provide children the freedom to explore their ideas. Providing open-ended materials that can be manipulated and used in a variety of ways helps children develop skills in logic and problem solving. Creating a stable block structure or experimenting to determine the best placement of a ramp to use with a toy car are activities that form the basis for many science and higher-order thinking skills and facilitate understanding of cause and effect. If children are encouraged to solve problems through trial and error while they play, they will be comfortable taking risks and sharing their ideas. As teachers, we must remember that children learn through play as they cause things to happen or change. When we outline exactly how to solve a problem for children, we take away their opportunity to solve it on their own.

Curricular Goals—Science

PURPOSE

The aim of the cognitive domain is for children to acquire, apply, adapt, integrate, and evaluate knowledge as they construct new or expanded concepts. Goals for science are drawn from and are consistent with those published by the National Academy of Science (NAS, 2011).

GOALS

As children progress in the area of science, within the cognitive domain, they will:

1. Examine the observable properties of man-made and natural objects, using their multisensory abilities.

2. Learn and apply the scientific process.

3. Explore firsthand a variety of cause-and-effect relationships.

4. Develop and refine their skills to communicate findings.

5. Recognize that knowledge and data come in many forms and can be organized and displayed in diverse ways.

6. Become aware of their thought processes, building more accurate, complete, and complex concepts with time.

7. Explore a variety of scientific equipment such as simple machines, magnets, and measuring instruments.

8. Use scientific equipment appropriately and safely.

9. Acquire scientific knowledge related to the life sciences.

10. Acquire scientific knowledge related to the physical sciences.

11. Acquire scientific knowledge related to the earth sciences.

12. Develop and use an accurate vocabulary related to scientific events, objects, and processes.

13. Participate in recording scientific data.

Sample Science Content

Thinking is different from memorizing. Memorizing a list of facts does not require the individual to understand these facts. It is important that you as a teacher have a basic understanding of the science concepts you are teaching. Well-meaning teachers may unwittingly contribute to children's misconceptions about science. For example, a classic science experience for many young children is creating an "erupting volcano" using baking soda and vinegar. As the baking soda reacts with the vinegar, the teacher explains that this is similar to how a volcano erupts. This is actually incorrect. A volcanic eruption is caused by heat and pressure within the Earth's crust, not by a reaction of acids and bases.

Community experts are good resources for accurate information.

Of course, you cannot be expected to know everything, so it will be important to identify resources to help you expand your background knowledge on many topics. Seeking detailed information on a topic will help you prepare and implement meaningful science experiences for the children in your class. You will want to appropriately research each topic, generating a pool of factual information and identify **primary** and **secondary sources** that children can use to learn about the topic. Doing so increases your knowledge base as well as the accuracy of the information you provide to children. You might use the following to gather information related to your topic:

primary sources First-hand sources of information such as real-life objects, field sites, or topic experts.

secondary sources Indirect sources of information such as books, models, or photographs.

- Reliable Internet sources
- Community or school libraries
- Local experts
- Local museums, businesses, garden centers, and so on.

Effective teachers recognize that children understand and make meaning of science content through well-planned science investigations. Teachers use a combination of on-the-spot teaching strategies and planned activities to address the science goals listed above. In doing so, they also convey important content to their young students. When identifying the terms, facts, and concepts you are going to teach, you must think about what the children already know about the topic and how you can

FIGURE 11.2 Sample science content

General science content

1. Science is part of everyday life.

2. Scientists gather information by observing, examining, comparing, experimenting, and estimating.

3. *Predicting* means to think about what will happen next.

4. Scientists make predictions based on their prior experiences, current knowledge, and ideas about how things work.

5. The tests scientists do based on their predictions are called *experiments*.

6. Sometimes scientists' predictions turn out to be correct; sometimes they are incorrect.

7. Scientists gain valuable information from the test, whether their predictions were right or wrong.

8. Scientists sometimes use tools to help them examine objects and forces. Tools aid in examining things accurately.

9. Some of the tools scientists use include measuring tools (rulers, scales, thermometers, clocks, measuring containers), magnifiers, microscopes, telescopes, light bulbs, cameras, graph paper, prisms, weights, magnets, simple machines (inclined plane, pulley, lever), calculators, and computers.

Content related to insects

1. An insect is a small animal with a hard-shelled body.

2. All insects hatch from eggs.

3. The body of an insect has three parts: head, thorax, and abdomen.

4. The head of an insect has a mouth, antennae, and several eyes.

Content related to leaves

1. Leaves grow on the stems of plants.

2. Leaves vary in many ways (size, shape, color, thickness, texture).

3. Each type of plant has its own special kind of leaves.

4. Differences in leaves help people identify plants.

5. Leaves begin as tiny buds and grow larger as the plant matures.

Content related to rocks

1. Rocks are hard pieces of stone found in nature.

2. Each kind of rock has particular characteristics by which it can be identified and classified.

3. Rocks vary in composition, shape, texture, color, weight, and hardness.

4. Rocks are everywhere (in mountains and hills, under seas, in the soil of forests, the sands of deserts, and in cities).

Source: Kostelnik, Howe, Payne, Rohde, Spalding, Stein, & Whitbeck (1991); Kostelnik, Howe, Payne, Rohde, Spalding, Stein, & Whitbeck (1996).

build on this knowledge. It will be important to verify the accuracy of your content to ensure that you are providing correct information. All content you choose to introduce should be meaningful and worthy of children's time. Examples of appropriate content are presented in Figure 11.2.

Strategies for Teaching Science

THE TEACHER'S ROLE IN CREATING A CURIOUS CLASSROOM

To encourage children's natural inclination to explore and experiment, you must provide an interesting environment full of items to investigate. Effective teachers provide materials, activities, and suggestions that encourage initiative and independent pursuit. You must also model curiosity, questioning, and a sense of wonder. Children will feel comfortable experimenting when they are encouraged to explore and try things on their own. As a teacher of young children, you will aim to support children's emerging understanding of the world around them. The goal is to instill confidence in their sense of themselves as learners. One way you can do this is to help them find the answers to their questions. If you want children to develop skills in science, you cannot do all the thinking for them. Children learn best when they construct knowledge through hands-on, engaging activities. This approach calls for refraining from providing the correct answer, challenging children to think about what the answer might be, and having them follow through by investigating and evaluating their ideas. When extending social-conventional knowledge, good teachers respond to a child's inquiries with correct information; if they are not sure what the answer is, they are honest about not knowing and then work with the child to find the information needed. Science may be evident in many of the ongoing activities in the early childhood classroom, but to further scientific understanding you must also include thoughtfully planned activities. Consider the following guidelines as you implement science learning experiences in your classroom:

- *Establish a classroom atmosphere that encourages exploration and experimentation.* Wonder aloud with the children by stating, "I wonder how we could. . . ." or "What do you think would happen if . . . ?" Provide interesting and engaging environments that provoke children's curiosity and sense of wonder. See the discussion later in the chapter of materials to include in your classroom.

- *Provide sufficient time for exploration and experimentation.* Children need many opportunities for hands-on manipulation. They need repeated experiences to develop understanding. Providing blocks of time to revisit materials and test their ideas will extend children's understanding of concepts. As with any skill, formulating questions and devising ways to find the answer need to be learned and practiced.

- *Use carefully formulated comments and questions to facilitate discovery.* Listen carefully to children and watch to see what they are trying to figure out. Instead of rushing to provide an answer or correct children's thinking, help them focus on aspects of the experience that will allow them to discover the solution. Provide additional materials or experiences to help children further their understanding when they draw incorrect conclusions. See Figure 11.3 for questions you might use to support children's science inquiry.

- *Take advantage of teachable moments as they arise.* Children are curious about their world. Capitalize on events and problems that occur naturally in the classroom, school, or community that capture children's curiosity. As they show interest in the insects they see on the playground or tell you about the new puppy at their house, think about how you can build on these opportunities to help children expand their scientific knowledge. Use projects and themes drawn from the children's interests and to which they have easy access.

- *Begin science investigations with concrete experiences using real objects.* Observe children to see what questions they have and determine activities that would help children answer their questions. Allow children plenty of time to explore a given material before asking them to use it in a prescribed way.

- *Plan science activities that build on one another and correlate with the rest of the curriculum.* Children seldom learn anything from just one exposure. Integrate science into all aspects of the curriculum. For example, children learn about the physical properties of objects in the block area, classroom pets help children understand life sciences, and science-based literature can extend children's knowledge base.

FIGURE 11.3 Questions that support children's science inquiry

1. What did you notice about …?
2. Tell me what questions you have about …
3. How might we find an answer to those questions?
4. What do you think the answer might be?
5. What would happen if you …?
6. Why do you think that happened?
7. What other ideas do you have?
8. How can we find out?
9. I wonder if anyone else has a different idea. Who can we ask?
10. What are some different things you could try?
11. How did you come up with that idea?

- *Extend children's science vocabulary.* Use a wide variety of accurate terms when talking with children about their day-to-day experiences (e.g., relationships among objects; changes in the functioning, position, or characteristics of objects). Convey only accurate scientific terms, facts, and principles to children, checking out any information about which you or the children are unsure.

- *Help children communicate their ideas and observations in a variety of ways.* Use graphic organizers (charts, tables, information webs, Venn diagrams, and flowcharts) to make relationships among concepts concrete and explicit. These organizers also promote children's comprehension and vocabulary development.

- *Encourage children to reach their own conclusions regarding cause-and-effect relationships, and accept the answers they offer.* When children come to incorrect conclusions, plan further experiences or suggest other approaches that might help the children discover the correct answer. Well-constructed follow-up activities can be combined with information books, resource persons, field trips, and provocative questioning to help children further their understanding. Children will better understand particular skills and facts when they are taught in contexts relevant to them.

- *Develop positive science-related learning attitudes and practices in the classroom.* Model an interested, curious, enthusiastic attitude toward science. Encourage children's curiosity by providing them with numerous hands-on scientific experiences and relevant demonstrations. Carry out scientific investigations with groups small enough that all children can become actively involved in the activity. Help children recognize many sources of scientific information, such as books, their experiences, and resource people.

graphic organizers Visual representation used to organize information, thoughts, and ideas.

Venn diagram A diagram using circles to represent sets, with the position and overlap of the circles indicating the relationships between the sets.

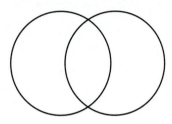

Materials That Support Science and Discovery

Including a variety of items that stimulate children's curiosity is key when selecting science materials for your classroom. Young children are especially intrigued by objects that have various textures, scents, and sounds that they can handle and explore. You may need to demonstrate how to use some tools so children can use them in their investigations and comparisons of objects.

Some items you may choose to include in your classroom are listed below.

- An assortment of familiar and unfamiliar items gathered from nature (pinecones, twigs, rocks, etc.)
- Containers for collecting
  - Bug jars, bug catchers
  - Magnifying glasses
  - Tripod magnifiers
  - Terrarium
  - Plants
  - Measuring tape
  - Rulers
  - Balance scale
  - Prisms
  - Simple machines: levers, ramps, wedges, screws, pulleys, wheels, and axle
  - Animals: worms, hermit crab, gerbil, rabbit, fish
  - Field guides
  - Clipboards

What tools and materials could you provide children to enhance their science learning?

Planned Activities in Science

As you plan activities in science, you will create written plans such as the ones discussed in Chapter 5. Creating successful science plans depends on many factors. You need to think about the particular children in your group and how certain activities should be adapted to fit the needs of individual children. Good science activities allow children to create an action that causes the phenomenon being studied. For example, varying the height of a ramp gives children a chance to test how moving the ramp to differing positions affects the speed of a toy car and the distance it travels. The results of the child's actions are immediate and easily observable.

Initially you will think through each aspect of your science plans in detail as illustrated in the problem-solving activity plan presented in Figure 11.4.

As you gain experience in writing plans you may write abbreviated plans such as those offered for the suggested activities that follow. The goal numbers referred to in each activity correspond to the numbered goals listed earlier in this chapter.

Exploratory Play Activity: Exploring Sand

Ages 3-6

Goal 1: For the children to examine the observable properties of man-made and natural objects, using their multisensory abilities.

Content: Scientists gather information by observing, examining, and comparing items. We can use many senses to explore objects and items.

Materials: Sand

Funnels

Scoops

Sifters

Cups

Sand wheel

Sand molds

Water (for extension)

Procedure: Prepare the activity by placing sand and other materials in a sensory table or large tub. Invite children to explore the sand and the materials provided. Use open-ended questions to support children's exploration, such as "How does the sand feel?" or "What can you do with the sand?" Use behavior and paraphrase reflections to mirror children's statements and actions: "You found a way to use the sand to make that wheel turn." "You think the sand is soft."

To Simplify: Provide fewer items with the sand, such as cups and scoops only.

To Extend: Add water to the sand. Use behavior and paraphrase reflections to echo children's comparisons of the wet and dry sand.

Guided Discovery Activity: Examining a Bird Nest

Ages 3-6

Goal 1: For the children to examine the observable properties of man-made and natural objects, using their multisensory abilities.

Content: Birds build nests of varying complexity, shape, and size. Scientists may examine objects just once—or more often; their examinations may be conducted in a day or two or over an extended period of time.

Materials: Varieties of bird nests of varying complexity, shape, and size

Magnifying glasses

Markers

Paper

Procedure: Invite children to examine the nests. Demonstrate how to examine the nests visually, by scent, and with touch. Provide magnifying glasses to encourage close inspection. Encourage children to compare the nests and describe the differences they see. Allow children to revisit the nest display over time.

FIGURE 11.4 Detailed science plan

Problem-Solving Activity: Using Water Pressure to Move Objects

Age: For all ages

Goal 3: For the children to explore a variety of cause-and-effect relationships.

Content: The physical world is made up of many objects and forces. Moving water is a force used to move objects.

Scientists sometimes change objects and forces to find out how they behave, what will happen next, and how they interact. This is called experimenting.

Scientists think of reasons to explain why something happens.

Materials: Water table or other large tub filled with water

Large basters

Ping pong balls

Tennis ball

Golf ball

Koosh ball

Objectives: Provided materials and teacher guidance, the children will:

1. Explore the basters
2. Use the baster to move the ping pong ball
3. Describe how the force of the water caused the ball to move

Procedures:

Explore Step: Introduce the basters to children, encouraging them to practice filling the baster with water and squirting the water from the baster. You might say, "I've added something interesting to the water table. You can use these to move water from one place to another. Let's try moving the water in the table by squirting water from the baster." Use paraphrase or behavior reflections to direct children's attention to the force of the squirting water.

"Look, Jeremy made ripples in the water when he squirted his baster. Kathryn said she made the water move a lot when she gave a big squirt!"

Action Step: Introduce the ping pong balls and challenge the children to move a ball using the force of the water from the baster. You might say, "I have a challenge for you. Move the ball from this end of the table to that end without touching it with our basters or our hands. Think about how we might use the basters to move the ball." Help children focus on the different effects they cause as they move the balls. You might say, "Where do we have to squirt the ball to make it move a long way?" or "I wonder what would work better, to squirt the ball quickly or slowly?" Use paraphrase reflections such as, "Kathryn said we have to squeeze hard to make the ball move a long way. She noticed we need to use bigger force to move it more."

Description Step: Facilitate discussion of children's conclusions regarding the effect the water had on the movement of the ball. Say, "Tell me what worked the best to move the ball. Tell me why you think that worked."

To Simplify: Have the children use their hands to move the water instead of using the basters. Encourage children to move only the water, not touch the balls with their hands.

To Extend: Add other types of balls (tennis ball, Koosh ball, golf ball) and encourage the children to try to make them move. Discuss the different types of force needed to move the different balls.

Evaluation Questions:

1. If I were to implement this plan again, what would I change and what would I keep the same?
2. How did the children express their understanding of how their actions impacted the movement of the ball(s)? What explanations did the children use to describe the force of the water moving the ball?

To Simplify: Begin with only one type of nest to examine

To Extend: Encourage children to draw a picture of the nests as a way to record what they have observed.

Discussion Activity: Comparing Birds and Insects

Ages 3-6

Goal 5: For the children to recognize that knowledge and data come in many forms and can be organized and displayed in diverse ways.

Materials: Chart paper

Marker for teacher to record children's comments and create diagrams.

Content: Scientists make detailed records of what they have learned. Scientists communicate their ideas to other people and this communication can take many forms.

Procedure: Introduce the discussion by reminding the children that they have learned many things about insects and birds. Explain that you are going to make a list of these things as they tell you what they know. Facilitate the dialog and encourage each child to contribute at least one thought to the conversation. Remind children to listen to one another without interrupting. Create a simple chart with two columns: one for insects and the other for birds. List the facts the children discuss in the appropriate column. If children disagree about something that is said, decide as a group how to record the comment.

To Simplify: Discuss only one topic (either birds or insects). Hold the discussion with a smaller number of children.

To Extend: Create a Venn diagram of insects and birds based on the characteristics discussed by the children.

Demonstration Activity: Planting My Garden

Ages 3-6

Goal 9: For the children to acquire scientific knowledge related to the life sciences.

Content: Outdoor gardening often requires special tools to prepare the ground for planting. Gardens are planted by people using either seeds, seedlings, or both.

Materials: Garden plot

Seeds

Hoes

Trowels

Several seedlings

String

Procedure: Demonstrate how to use the hoe to break up the soil in a garden plot. Describe what you are doing as you demonstrate. "I am making slow, careful movements making sure I am keeping my hoe close to the ground." Encourage children to practice using a hoe. Explain that seeds should be planted at the correct depth in order for them to grow properly. Show children the proper depth to plant seeds and how to cover and water seeds. Have children plant the seeds in the soil.

To Simplify: Provide hand trowels instead of hoes. Use soil that is loose and easily manipulated. Demonstrate how to plant the seeds using a trowel.

To Extend: Demonstrate other techniques such as using a string to make straight rows in the garden or how to transplant seedlings.

Direct Instruction Activity: Recording Your Results

Ages 3-6

Goal 13: For the children to participate in recording scientific data.

Content: Scientists record information they gather to help them remember and let others know what they have observed. In order to study things, scientists collect data, analyze data, communicate results, and formulate conclusions. When scientists record their findings, they call these findings *data*.

Materials: Clipboard with paper containing blank squares to create a simple bar graph
Marker for each child

Bingo chips in assorted (three to five) colors (enough chips that each child can have several of each color to count and graph)

Procedure: Introduce the activity by saying something such as, "There are many different colors of chips here. We are going to make a graph to show us how many of each color we have." Demonstrate how to fill in a square to represent the number of chips of one color. Have the children check your work by counting aloud as a group the number of chips and the number of squares on your graph. Have the children tell you how to graph the next color. As you graph the third color, make a mistake and allow the children to correct you. Following the small group instruction, have each child create his or her own graph with individual sets of chips.

To Simplify: Use only a small number of chips with only two or three colors.

To Extend: Compare the results recorded to those recorded by other children.

Meeting the Needs of Diverse Learners in Your Classroom

Teachers in early childhood classrooms need to meaningfully include all children within planned activities. This may mean providing special equipment or adapting materials or activities to include children with varying abilities. To do this, consider the individual strengths and challenges of the children in your group to determine how best to meet the needs of each child. For example, Ellen Kennick is planning a small-group science lesson focused on observation of natural objects. She has gathered a variety of interesting items including pinecones, rocks, seed pods, edible berries, leaves, flowers, and pine needles for the children to explore. Mrs. Kennick wants to ensure that Veronica, a young child who is legally blind, is included in the activity in a meaningful way. Veronica, like many children with visual impairments, is hesitant to touch textures that are not familiar to her. Realizing this, Mrs. Kennick does not force Veronica to touch the objects but instead describes each object to Veronica and offers her the chance to lightly touch things and decide if she would like to hold them. Mrs. Kennick has thoughtfully chosen objects that have different scents, textures, and even tastes so that Veronica can explore the objects with her other senses. She verbally describes how the other children are investigating the materials by making comments such as, "Marcus is rubbing the smooth rock," or "Andre is smelling the pine needles," and offering Veronica the chance to imitate these behaviors. After the children have had ample opportunity to examine the objects, Mrs. Kennick asks them to record their observations in their journals. She has prepared cards with the names of each item written on them for the children to use as references. She prepares a set for Veronica that includes the word in braille. Knowing that Veronica can perceive only images that have high visual contrast, she provides Veronica with a high-quality, black, felt-tip marker and white paper and a space with good lighting to support Veronica in using the sight she has. By taking such steps, Mrs. Kennick has made sure that Veronica is successfully included in the activity.

Communicating with Families About Science Learning

Regular, informative communication with families can help strengthen the home–school connection. Families appreciate getting information about how we as teachers respond to situations or extend children's learning. Young children ask a multitude of questions, and families may not realize the learning opportunities these questions present for their children. See Figure 11.5 for an example of information you can provide on responding to children's questions.

NEWSLETTER/WEB READY COMMUNICATION

FIGURE 11.5 • How to Respond to Your Child's Questions

As children explore and observe the things they encounter each day, they strive to understand the world around them. Children find countless things to wonder about. *Where are those ants going? Why did that plant die? Why do some things stick to the magnet but others don't?* This questioning is a natural and spontaneous process for children that may seem never ending. But this questioning is exactly what scientists do. Scientists observe and develop questions they want to answer. Then they think about ways to answer their questions. You can support this type of thinking as well. When your child asks a question, don't be too quick to provide the "correct" answer. Instead, challenge your child to think of ways the two of you could find the answer. For example, if you are wondering what types of flowers would grow best in your backyard, you could help your child consult gardening books or websites or visit a local greenhouse together to determine what to plant. Provide opportunities for your child to test ideas and theories. You might plant flowers in different areas of the yard to see which plants grow best under which conditions. Encourage your child to observe closely. Draw attention to details that might be easily overlooked, such as the number of blooms on each plant or the insects observed in the garden. Talk about what you see. You'll find that your child enjoys investigating these questions with you. This sense of investigation will thrive as you work side by side as scientists!

11 Applying What You've Learned

Based on what you now know about teaching science to children, carry out these activities to increase your knowledge and skills.

1. Describe the elements of the cognitive domain related to science.

2. **Key Science Concepts and Skills.** Spend some time observing children in a preschool or kindergarten classroom during free play. Make a list of the questions and comments you overhear the children make. Think about what science concepts the children have shown interest in and how the teacher might support this interest.

3. **Strategies for Teaching Science.** Choose a topic such as insects, trees, or birds and create a list of 20 related facts and vocabulary words appropriate for preschool children. Determine what primary and secondary resources could be used to help children learn about the topic.

4. **Planning Experiences and Activities in Science.** Develop a detailed science plan to teach some of the content you identified above. If possible, carry out your plan with a small group of children.

5. **Meeting the Needs of Diverse Learners.** Consider how you would support a child who has limited English, a child with a hearing impairment, and a child with limited motor skills in learning science. Identify at least three modifications you could make to your science plan to meet the needs of each of these children.

6. **Supporting Science Learning at Home.** Develop suggestions for simple activities that families can implement using a science tool (magnifying glass, balance scale, magnet, etc.). Include instructions and needed items in a "science kit" to be used by families to support science learning at home.

References

Enfield, M., & Rogers, D. (2009). Improving science teaching for young children. In O. A. Barbarin & B. H. Wasik (Eds.). *Handbook of child development and early education: Research to practice.* New York: Guilford Press.

Kostelnik, M. J., Howe, D., Payne, K., Rohde, B., Spalding, G., Stein, L., & Whitbeck, D. (1991). *Teaching young children using themes.* Parsippany, NJ: Good Year Books.

Kostelnik, M. J., Howe, D., Payne, K., Rohde, B., Spalding, G., Stein, L., & Whitbeck, D. (1996). *Themes teachers use.* Parsippany, NJ: Good Year Books.

Lind, K. K. (2005). *Exploring science in early childhood education* (4th ed.). Clifton Park, NY: Thomson Delmar Learning.

National Academy of Science (2011). *National science education standards: Observe, interact, change, learn.* Washington, D.C.: National Academy Press.

Sackes, M., Trundle, K. C., & Flevares, L. M. (2009). Using children's books to teach inquiry skills. *Young Children, 64*(6), 24–26.

Worth, K. (2010). Science in early childhood classrooms: Content and process. SEED papers published Fall 2010.

12 The Cognitive Domain: Fostering Mathematical Thinking

Aidan has discovered an important mathematical tool for a young learner—the fingers on his hands. Today, his teacher asks, "How many children are wearing something blue today?" Aidan balls his hand into a fist and scans his playmates who are sitting in large group with him. Each time he spots someone who fits the teacher's category, he holds out a finger. Finished, he looks down, counts quietly, and shouts, "Four. . . . and me, too. Five!!!!"

All young children demonstrate an early, natural interest in mathematics, which is conceptual in nature and has to do with the systematic relationships using numbers and units of comparison. As such, mathematical knowledge is broader than arithmetic, which centers on the calculation of number.

Children often surprise their teachers with how they make sense of and resolve simple quantitative challenges as they construct their knowledge of quantity, mathematical relationships, and symbols (Copley, 2010). They like thinking about number; enjoy finger plays, songs, poems, and stories that contain number; and respond with enthusiasm to counting tasks involving number. For example, Ms. Kate has her preschoolers help her jump and pick apples from the tree. "How many should we pick this morning?" she asks.

"Nine!" "Eleven!" "One million zillion!" offer the children.

"Let's try eleven," the teacher suggests. "Everyone ready? One . . . two . . . three . . . ."

This chapter is concerned with the development of children's early mathematical thinking.

Including Mathematics in the Early Childhood Classroom

In the past several years, there has been a push for a new understanding of what young children are capable of learning, particularly in the area of math, and the importance of including math instruction in preschool and kindergarten classrooms. Still, typical early childhood classrooms include very little math other than counting and sometimes looking at books with numerals. The result is that children spend little time thinking about math, especially children who are deprived of any games at home that require mathematical application and accelerate the understanding of number (Carey, 2009). Later, children come to think that math is difficult and something they are "not good at."

The purpose of including well-planned mathematics activities each day in early childhood programs is two-fold: (1) to help children become flexible thinkers who are comfortable with all areas of mathematics and able to apply mathematical ideas and skills in a variety of problem-solving situations (Burns, 2007), and (2) to bridge each child's early fundamental knowledge of mathematics to more formal concepts of mathematical knowledge and thinking in the future.

Mathematics can easily become the primary or secondary focus in a variety of activities over the course of the day in art, music, literacy, social studies, science, and physical education. Effective teachers promote children's awareness of mathematical connections by emphasizing them when children are using calendars, looking at clocks, cooking, exploring nature, and playing games that involve mathematical concepts (e.g., "Go three steps forward," "Stop and make three elbows (touch elbows with two other children)!" "Look what happens when I cut this apple in half. Now, how many pieces do we have?" "Oh, oh. We have three chairs and five children.

LEARNING OUTCOMES

After you read this chapter, you will be able to:

- Understand the importance of including a variety of mathematical activities in the early childhood classroom every day.
- Describe key mathematical concepts, processes, and skills that young children should be learning.
- Identify helpful strategies for teaching mathematics to young children.
- Explain ways to meet the learning needs of diverse children.
- Plan engaging mathematical experiences and activities.
- Create opportunities for families to support the young child's mathematical thinking.

How many more chairs do we need?"). They teach measurement by using sand and water in creative ways and by showing children how to use informal ways to measure (e.g., "Let's see how many *large* paper footprints from the bears' home to the classroom door. . . . how many *small* paper footprints. . . .").

Evidence indicates that teachers of young children are less likely to encourage girls to "tinker" than they are to encourage boys—less likely to promote their struggling to figure something out, investigate how something works, or experiment with trial and error. Teachers are more apt to show boys how to work machines such as staplers or technology hardware and software, whereas they tend to quickly take over such tasks for girls. Not surprisingly, men still receive 77 percent of the bachelor's degrees awarded in engineering, whereas girls continue to steer away from math- and science-related fields (Education Week, 2009). You can play a part in turning that trend around by making sure that all the children in your classroom have lots of time to "mess around" with interesting materials, equipment, and developmentally appropriate problem solving that arises during their play.

Just one more shovel of dirt to make it full.

PLAY AND MATHEMATICAL THINKING

Children need a prolonged period of informal exploration through play before they can form basic concepts about shape, one-to-one correspondence, size, weight, texture, and amount. This exploration occurs through such natural activities as building with blocks; pouring water; distributing dishes and silverware in the housekeeping area; working with sand, puzzles, and clay; cooking; and matching, sorting, and counting during their work and play.

Construction play should be prominent in the early childhood classroom. When it is, we see the building of mathematical concepts in children's play with blocks, art work, and the many products they produce to represent something they have seen in their natural world. For example, Patrick and Chloe are discussing the number of legs to put on the spiders they are creating with pipe cleaners. "It's eight," says Chloe. "You need two more."

"Uh, uh," responds Patrick. "My spider only gots six."

"Ask the teacher," Chloe persists. "She'll tell you it's eight. They all got eight."

You can facilitate this kind of learning by making sure your classroom contains plenty of materials that stimulate the emergence of abstract thought and playful application (see Figure 12.1). For example, provide a scale and measuring tape in the pretend play area and suggest that the children might want to weigh and measure their babies to see if the babies are "growing." Provide a notebook to write down numbers for those children who want to record their findings. Place play money and a cash register in an area or have children make their own money. Offer cereal boxes and other props to be sold in a classroom store and encourage children to put prices on the objects. Have children sort blocks by shape and size as they put them away.

Provide lots of games that contain mathematical concepts and plenty of time for children to play them. According to the National Council of Teachers of Mathematics (NCTM, 2011), games increase children's curiosity and motivation, allow for cooperative learning opportunities, inherently differentiate learning, build strategies and reasoning skills, teach life skills, and reinforce mathematical objectives. Take your cues from children's questions to design activities that also do this. For example, in reading a book to children that contained the word *well*, some of the children asked their teacher what a

FIGURE 12.1 Typical math materials for the early childhood classroom

Representation materials such as construction paper, markers, clay, glue, scissors, pipe cleaners, tongue depressors, self-stick dots

Blocks such as unit blocks, pattern blocks, attribute blocks, unifix cubes, snap cubes, Legos®

Geometric shapes in different colors, sizes, and textures; collage materials

Games that teach mathematical concepts, such as Candyland®, Chutes and Ladders®, Cranium®, Cariboo™, and matching games

Playing cards

Puzzles

Collections of natural objects, man-made materials, and manipulative materials such as seashells, rocks, locks and keys, buttons, paper clips, marbles, toothpicks, beads, counters, tiles, geoboards and rubber bands, counters

Sand, water, beans, rice, pasta

Tools such as measuring cups and spoons, coins, clocks, calendars, scales, calculators, rulers, computers, stamps and stamp pads

Equipment such as clipboards, baskets, see-through jars, muffin tins, egg cartons, yarn and string, storage bags, paper cups and plates, spring-type clothespins, paper bags, paper towels, large and small whiteboards, magnetic boards and numerals, flannel boards and cutouts of numerals and objects to match

Books containing mathematical concepts (for more titles, see Owen & McKinney, 2010):

Counting:
- Eric Carle. *Rooster's Off to See the World*. Simon & Schuster, 2002.
- Donald Crews. *Ten Black Dots*. Greenwillow Books, 1986.
- Paul Galdone. *Over in the Meadow*. Prentice Hall, 1986.
- Pat Hutchins. *The Doorbell Rang*. Greenwillow Books, 1994.
- Arlene Mosel. *Tikki, Tikki, Tembo*. Square Fish Books, 2007.

Addition and subtraction:
- Eric Carle. *The Very Busy Spider*. Putnam, 1984.
- Shel Silverstein. "Band-aids." In *Where the Sidewalk Ends*. HarperCollins, 1975.
- Audrey Wood. *The Napping House*. Harcourt Brace, 1984.
- John Becker. *Seven Little Rabbits*. Walker Books, 2007.
- Penny Dale. *Ten in the Bed*. Black Pursuit, 1988.

Measurement:
- Steve Jenkins. *Actual Size*. Houghton Mifflin, 2004.
- Steve Jenkins. *Biggest, Strongest, Fastest*. Sandpiper, 1997.
- Leo Lionni. *Inch by Inch*. Knopf Books, 2010.
- Rolf Myller. *How Big Is a Foot?* Yearling, 1991.
- Shel Silverstein. "One Inch Tall." From *Where the Sidewalk Ends*. Harper Collins, 1974.

Algebra:
- Aliki. *Dinosaurs Are Different*. Crowell, 1985.
- Lois *Ehlert. Planting a Rainbow*. Harcourt Brace & Co., 1988.
- Tana Hoban. *Exactly the Opposite*. Greenwillow Books, 1990.
- Patricia Ruben. *What Is New? What Is Missing? What Is Different?* Lippincott, 1978.
- Esphyr Slobodkina. *Caps for Sale*. Scholastic, 1976.

Patterns:
- Verba Aadema. *Why Mosquitoes Buzz in People's Ears*. Dial Books, 2008.
- Trudy Harris. *Pattern Bugs*. Millbrook Press, 2001.
- Stephen Swinburne. *Lots and Lots of Zebra Stripes: Patterns in Nature*. Boyds Mills Press, 2002.
- Pam Adams. *The House That Jack Built*. Child's Play, 2007.
- Kathy Parkinson. *The Enormous Turnip*. Albert Whitman & Co., 1986.

Geometry:
- Marilyn Burns. *The Greedy Triangle*. Scholastic Paperbacks, 2008.
- Eric Carle. *Draw Me a Star*. Putnam, 1998.
- Tana Hoban. *Cubes, Cones, Cylinders, & Spheres*. Greenwillow Books, 2000.
- Tana Hoban. *So Many Circles, So Many Squares*. Greenwillow Books, 1998.
- Jerry Pallotta. *Icky Bug Shapes*. Scholastic, 2004.

Data analysis/probability:
- Pam Adams. *There Was an Old Lady Who Swallowed a Fly*. Playspaces International, 1973.
- Judy Barrett. *Cloudy with a Chance of Meatballs*. Atheneum, 1978.
- Kathy Stinson. *Red Is Best*. Annick Press, 1998.

If we make the bucket heavier, will it sink below the water in the well?

numeracy The ability to understand and apply basic numerical concepts of addition, subtraction, multiplication, and division.

well was. They had never seen one. Subsequently, this teacher had each child make a bucket from the milk cartons they had been using. He showed them how to attach string to their buckets and lower them into a large container of water (the well). When they found that their cartons only floated on the water, their teacher asked them to think of ways to solve the problem; the children began loading stones into their buckets until they sank successfully under the water. In addition to their understanding of what a well was, they also certainly better understood the concepts of *under*, *over*, and *heavier*.

Encouraging children to explore mathematical concepts during their play is more easily accomplished in classrooms that have an abundance of readily accessible materials such as those found in Figure 12.1. Make suggestions when relevant for children to include particular equipment or supplies and take advantage of times to augment their play with games and books that focus on **numeracy** concepts.

Key Mathematical Concepts, Processes, and Skills That Young Children Should Be Learning

Mathematics in the early childhood classroom calls for a unique set of instructional practices that take active planning by the classroom teacher and require interaction with the children. Children need to understand that mathematics is much more than counting, arithmetic, and learning how to differentiate a square from a circle. To create a mathematics-rich environment that will help children make connections to all areas of the curriculum and learn processes such as problem solving, reasoning, representation, and communication, teachers need to actively plan particular activities and experiences (Copley, 2010). Children's basic concepts of number and their internalization of such skills as grouping and patterning will be critical for future skill building. Ensuring this requires that you provide adequate time, repeated exposure, and continuous opportunities for children's exploration and practice. Figure 12.2 presents a sampling of mathematical terms and facts

---

FIGURE 12.2 **Sample of mathematical terminology and facts for the early childhood classroom**

✔ Ordinal numbers indicate the position in a collection, such as 3rd, 5th, and so on.

✔ Numerals are written symbols used to represent numbers.

✔ Mathematical words that are used for descriptions include:

- positions in space (over, under, above, below, inside, outside)
- amounts (more, less, least, quarter, half, whole)
- size (large, small; smaller than, larger than)
- shapes and parts of shapes (rectangle, square, circle, triangle, line, angle, arc)
- comparative vocabulary (-er, -est)
- speed (fast, slow, quick)
- quantity (more than, less than, the same as).

✔ People count to find out how many things there are.

✔ When counting, each thing is counted only once.

✔ Numbers occur in an order, and that order is always the same.

✔ Matching is when we pair or group objects that are identical.

✔ Things can be grouped or ordered in many different ways.

✔ An object cannot be included in a group if it has nothing in common with the other members of the group.

✔ A pattern is an arrangement of objects, numbers, or events that repeats.

✔ A pattern is predictable.

✔ Some ways that patterns can be represented include appearance, touch, and sound.

> **FIGURE 12.3** A sample of mathematical terminology and facts teachers should know
>
> ✔ *Attributes* are the individual properties of an object (e.g., size, length, height, width, color, shape, scent, tone, use, weight, name, texture).
>
> ✔ *Classification* is the operation of grouping objects according to similarities and differences.
>
> ✔ *Conservation of number* is understanding that the amount does not change when items are spread out or put closer together or when an object changes shape (e.g., moving an amount of water in a tall thin vase to a short, squat vase).
>
> ✔ *Seriation* is putting objects in a group in order from most to least of a particular attribute.
>
> ✔ *Subitizing* is the ability to recognize the number of objects in a group quickly.
>
> ✔ *Cardinal numbers* describe the size of a collection, such as 3, 5, 10, and so on.
>
> ✔ An *empty set* is a set containing no properties.
>
> ✔ *Equivalent sets* have the same numbers of elements.
>
> ✔ *One-to-one correspondence* is the simple matching of one object for another or pairing.
>
> ✔ *Grouping* is a way to organize objects, actions, ideas, events, thoughts, and feelings.
>
> ✔ The same objects and events can be sorted in many different ways by the same person or by different people.
>
> ✔ When grouping or classifying by two or more attributes, it is sometimes helpful to first sort the objects by one attribute or property.
>
> ✔ A group of objects can be broken down into subclasses of objects.

children need to learn. Figure 12.3 presents a sample of the terminology you should be familiar with, even though you won't necessarily use that terminology directly with the children you are teaching.

Basic Mathematics Concepts for 3- to 6-Year-Olds

By the time they are 3 years old, most children recognize and can name the numeric symbols up to 9, have a sense of the verbal sequence of numbers up to 10 and beyond, can often count backwards from 10, and are developing a sense of one-to-one correspondence. These skills are not age-specific; rather, they depend on children's experiences with five different learning paths for number and operations: counting, subitizing, comparing and ordering, early addition and subtraction, and composing number and place value (Clements & Sarama, 2009).

COUNTING AND SUBITIZING

In the beginning, counting emerges in a *rote* manner, and children are not aware that they get some numbers out of order (5, 7, 6, 8, 9, 10) or that they skip numbers (5, 6, 8, 9. . .). Once they have experiences such as clapping each number, practicing verbal counting of small numbers in order, and gain an understanding of one-to-one correspondence by matching one item at a time to something else, **rational counting** appears (Clements & Sarama, 2009).

rational counting Matching each numeral name to an object in a group.

To teach rational counting to a child who has not yet gained this concept, give the child a sheet of colored paper and place one before yourself. Provide counters that are exactly alike. Say, "I am going to count these. Count with me and copy what I do. The number of counters on my paper should be the same as the number of counters on your paper. Right now, both our papers are empty. There are no counters on my paper. That is zero. Are there any counters on your paper? If not, say, 'zero.' Now I am placing one counter on my paper. Zero and one more is one. Now you do it. Good. I have one, and you have one." Continue this process and repeat it until the child is proficient and can demonstrate rapidly. Be sure to note the technique used by the child to count. Did the child glance at the set and state the number or did he or she go back and count them again one by one? Was the child indecisive? Did he or she count without error?

subitize To recognize how many objects are in a small group without having to count each object in the group again.

When children can quickly recognize how many objects are in a small group without counting each object in the group again, they can subitize. You can provide experiences for children who don't yet have this skill by starting them with small groups or sets of two, three, four, and five objects. This skill later on develops into a 6- and 7-year-old's ability to see objects in groups of 10s and 1s, required for understanding place value and two-digit addition and subtraction (Copley, 2010).

Five and three more makes eight.

ADDING AND SUBTRACTING

Although it's true that children even as young as 2 or 3 can add and subtract small numbers ("You get one, and I get one. We need two."), the skill of adding and subtracting does not come naturally. Activities in joining and separating and finding part/whole relationships should become a frequent part of the early childhood classroom and involve direct modeling, counting, and the use of concrete materials. Developing a sense of part/whole relationships is the beginning of learning fractions, which can be demonstrated using simple items such as fruit, crackers, play dough, and other materials. The understandings that children gain from these experiences then become the necessary precursors to build flexible thinking and problem solving children will need as they progress to the early primary grades (Copley, 2010).

SORTING AND CLASSIFYING

In the pretend house, Manny and Lisa were exploring a box of keys of varying shapes and sizes. Manny put aside all the round keys and said, "These are mine. They go to my house. See, I have lots of doors!" Lisa looked at the keys that were left and made two groups, one of gold keys and one of silver keys of varying shapes. She pointed to one pile and said, "These are for my house." Pushing the others into a pile, she said, "These are for grandma's place." Their teacher watched, then took a square copper key from the few keys that neither child had chosen, and said, "Where does this one go? Does it fit into any of your piles?" Manny considered for minute, then put it back in the box announcing, "In the kitchen drawer. It's a lost key."

Consider all the attributes Manny and Lisa may have thought about to create their groupings of keys: size, color, shape, texture, and purpose, to name just a few. In each case, the children sorted the keys based on characteristics they decided made certain keys alike and other keys different. When confronted with a key that didn't fit his thinking, Manny found a way to eliminate it from consideration with an explanation that made sense to him. Deciding which attributes to concentrate on and whether objects fit that property or not represent important reasoning skills. In this activity, there were multiple ways the keys could be sorted—not one "right" way. The children created their own categories and then acted on their judgments to make their piles. To get at the children's reasoning behind their choices, the teacher went on to ask, "Tell me how you decided which keys to put together." Taking advantage of the children's spontaneous explorations, the teacher furthered their mathematical thinking within the context of their pretend play.

Just as Manny and Lisa's teacher did, when you are working with children on the important concept of classification or the grouping of objects according to similarities and differences, it is important to encourage children to choose their own criteria for classification. This prompts children to engage in and develop higher-order thinking processes of reasoning and making their own judgments, rather than simply mimicking the teacher's ideas, which shuts down their thinking. Consequently, in true classification activities, teachers avoid imposing a classification system on children (e.g., "Group all these objects by size."). They encourage children to reason for themselves and to articulate what their reasoning is. Also, it is as important for children to describe why objects are *not* included in a grouping as to explain why certain objects *are* grouped together. To begin the sequence of teaching a young child to classify, follow the steps listed in Figure 12.4.

A sample of classification materials.

FIGURE 12.4 Steps in teaching the process of classification with young children

1. Place a container of objects on the table with the following instructions: "Here is an assortment of objects. Today, we can play some games with them. We can look at them, touch them, handle them, and talk about them so we can learn about them." Then, selecting one of the objects from the table, say, "Show me the _____ that looks just like this one. Tell me one way in which these two things are the same."

2. "Put together all of the things that are like these two things."

3. "Tell me how these things are all alike."

4. "Show me an object that isn't like these things—that doesn't belong in this group."

5. Have children return the objects to the large group of objects. Say, "There are many objects here that are alike in different ways. Show me as many ways to group alike objects as you can."

TECH TIP

Mathematics

Teaching children one-to-one correspondence is one of the most basic and critical mathematic concepts they must learn. A number of excellent, brief videos have been developed by Sesame Street that are readily available on the YouTube website for teaching counting and one-to-one correspondence. For example, children will delight with 20 penguins coming down a water slide one at a time, counting each and pairing only one silly bird with each subsequent number as they count aloud together. You can use a Smart Board to access these.

COMPOSING NUMBER AND PLACE VALUE

It is not until about age 4 or later that most children truly understand number combinations for 4 and 5, then 6 and 7, and on to 10. In order to do this, they must be able to understand the concept of parts of the whole (e.g., $1 + 1 + 1 + 1 = 4$ or $2 + 2 = 4$)—or the whole, given the parts (e.g., $4 = 1 + 1 + 1 + 1$ or $4 = 1 + 2 + 1$). Generally, you will want to begin your challenges to the children in your preschool or kindergarten classroom to understand part/whole relationships with very low whole numbers to begin with and most likely not go beyond 5 or 10.

Later, as these children grow closer to 6 years of age, they will be better able to understand the importance of placement of digits (e.g., 14 is not the same as 41) and the exchange principle (e.g., that 10 ones are the same as 10). Not until then and only after many experiences with two- and three-digit numbers will children be ready to begin their conceptual understanding of place value (Copley, 2010, pp. 55, 65).

TRY IT YOURSELF

Gather together a number of buttons or similar materials with different attributes (e.g., size, color, shape, numbers of holes in buttons). How many different ways can you find to sort the materials into groups?

Curricular Goals—Mathematics

Preschool and kindergarten guidelines developed by the National Council of Teachers of Mathematics (NCTM, 2006) are consistent with those suggested by the National Association for the Education of Young Children (NAEYC) and reflect the common core standards that have been adopted by many states for early mathematics. These include Number and Operations (developing an understanding of whole numbers, including concepts of correspondence, counting, cardinality, and comparison); Geometry (identifying shapes and describing spatial relationships); Measurement (identifying measurable attributes and comparing objects by using these attributes); Algebra (sorting, classifying, and ordering objects; recognizing, describing, and extending patterns); and Data Analysis and Probability (collecting and interpreting information, such as the number of children eating lunch at school versus going home for lunch).

The aim of the cognitive domain is for children to acquire, apply, adapt, integrate, and evaluate knowledge as they construct new or expanded concepts. As children progress in mathematics, they will:

Number and Operations

1. Develop an understanding of the meanings of numbers.
2. Solve quantitative problems such as counting objects in a set.
3. Recognize the number of objects in small groups without counting and by counting.
4. Understand that number words refer to counting.
5. Use one-to-one correspondence to solve problems by matching sets, comparing quantities, and in counting objects to 10 and beyond.
6. Understand that the last word that they state in counting in the correct sequence tells "how many."
7. Count to determine number amounts and compare quantities (using language such as "more than" and "less than") as they order sets by the number of objects in them.
8. Describe sets of objects by the number of objects in each set.

9. Match and recognize sets up to 5 automatically.

10. Count and produce sets of given sizes.

11. Count the number in combined sets.

12. Use numbers to solve problems and respond to practical situations.

13. Use numbers, including written numerals, to represent quantities.

14. Use ordinal numbers (1st, 2nd, 3rd, 4th).

15. Model simple joining and separating situations with objects.

Geometry

16. Develop spatial reasoning; that is, the ability to understand the physical relationship (i.e., direction and position) between oneself and objects or between two or more objects in the environment (e.g., "Miranda, please move over closer to Josh.").

17. Find a variety of shapes in the environment and identify, name, and describe them (squares, triangles, circles, rectangles, hexagons, trapezoids).

18. Build pictures and designs by combining two- and three-dimensional shapes.

19. Discuss the relative positions of objects with vocabulary (e.g., above, below, next to).

20. Interpret the physical world with geometric ideas (e.g., shape, orientation, spatial relationships).

21. Identify three-dimensional shapes such as spheres, cubes, and cylinders.

Engineering with Wikki Stix.

Measurement

22. Identify objects as "the same" or "different," and then "more" or "less," on the basis of attributes they can measure.

23. Identify measurable attributes such as length (shorter, longer) and weight (heavier, lighter) and solve problems by comparing and ordering objects on the basis of those attributes.

Algebra

24. Sort, classify, and order objects by size, number, and other attributes.

25. Recognize and duplicate simple sequential patterns (e.g., square, circle, square, circle, square, circle; ABAB, ABCABC, AABBCC).

26. Identify, duplicate, and extend simple number patterns and sequential growing patterns (e.g., patterns made with shapes) as preparation for creating rules that describe relationships.

Data Analysis and Probability

27. Choose, combine, and apply effective strategies for answering quantitative questions (e.g., simple graphs, tallies, yes-or-no responses).

28. Solve everyday problems by collecting data (information) and using mathematics to answer questions.

29. Learn the foundations of data analysis by using attributes of objects that they have identified in relation to geometry and measurement (e.g., size, quantity, orientation, number of sides or vertices, color) for various purposes, such as describing, sorting, or comparing.

Instructional Strategies

When teaching mathematics to pre-kindergarten and kindergarten children, keep in mind that the children's cognitive capacities are evolving and that if you want to build on their curiosity, you cannot do all the thinking for them. Although you will want to challenge misconceptions they have, you need to find a way to do this by creating experiences and activities that provide adequate time for them to explore, investigate, reflect, and ask questions—rather than cutting their thinking short by giving them the correct answer. Following are ideas that will help you structure a fertile climate for mathematical learning (Kostelnik, Soderman, & Whiren, 2011, pp. 325–327):

1. *Extend children's mathematical vocabulary.* Use a wide variety of accurate terms when talking with children about their day-to-day experiences (e.g., number, size, shape, symbol, position of objects in space, and relationships among objects).

2. *Encourage children to reach their own conclusions.* Allow children to reach their own conclusions, and accept their answers. Pay attention to their interests and build on these to create developmentally appropriate activities that challenge their conceptual thinking when they have arrived at incorrect conclusions. Ask open-ended questions to help you understand why they have arrived at their conclusions and plan subsequent activities (e.g., "Justin, tell me why you think that." "Justin, what would happen if . . . ?").

3. *Use scaffolding to help children develop increasingly accurate mathematical concepts and accurate logic.* You may remember that the strategy of scaffolding was discussed earlier in Chapter 2. The strategy of scaffolding calls for starting where children are having difficulty with a concept or skill but can move forward with the assistance of an adult or more experienced peer. For example, Nina is sure that five counting bears in a line amount to five because she's counted them: 1, 2, 3, 4, 5. Nevertheless, when her teacher puts five more bears underneath, counting as she goes, and then spreads them out, Nina is confused when the teacher asks, "Which row has more bears, the top or bottom row?" When children are having difficulty with a concept or need more practice to become proficient with a particular skill, back up and help them break the task into more manageable parts. Introduce them to the next step in the sequence only when you are sure they fully understand the first step. In this case, Nina's teacher realizes that Nina does not yet understand the concept of number conservation, so she backtracks, involving Nina in supportive experiences with smaller numbers of objects and building toward higher numbers only when Nina answers readily and without hesitation or having to recount the objects.

4. *Place more emphasis on children's understanding of concepts than on rote learning.* Always begin teaching new concepts or skills by using concrete experiences. Allow children ample opportunity to explore given materials before asking them to use it in a prescribed way. Provide a variety of real objects for sorting, classifying, comparing, patterning, measuring, counting, adding, and gaining concepts of number, conservation of number, quantity, and shapes. Present the same mathematical concepts and skills on many occasions and in many ways (e.g., drawing numerals in the air, in sand, in salt, in finger paint, on the whiteboard, and on paper). Involve them in playing a variety of games using cards and dice. When children are involved independently in tasks, circulate among them to observe how they are approaching the task. Structure brief mini-conferences to check their understanding of the targeted concept.

5. *Integrate mathematical concepts and skills throughout all areas of the early childhood curriculum.* Link logical mathematical activities with social studies and language arts as well as with pretend play, affective, aesthetic, physical, construction activities, and classroom games as often as possible. For example, in a game for a small group of young children, Copley (2010) suggests providing each of the children with bags

containing the same number of pennies, nickels, dimes, and quarters. Ask the children to hold their bags of coins behind their backs or put them in their laps. To start the game, the teacher picks one coin from his or her bag and displays it to the children, who then try to find a matching coin in their bags without looking, trying to find the matching coin by touch only. She suggests discussing with children how the size of the coin and the value of the coin are not always correlated (for example, the small dime is worth more than the slightly larger penny or nickel). Copley notes that children quickly notice that the quarter is the easiest coin to find, "since it is biggest and, as the children say, 'more different' than the other coins" (p. 135). This is a game that can be adapted to teach many different attribute skills, including size, shape, and texture.

6. *Use everyday experiences in the classroom to help children connect mathematics in daily living and see math as useful and necessary in their lives.* Capitalize on problems that occur naturally in the classroom that can capture children's curiosity. Incorporate mathematical tools into classroom routines (e.g., calendar, clocks, rulers, nonformal measures, coins, scales, measuring cups and spoons, graphs). Practice simple addition and subtraction in natural settings without symbols, encouraging children to use their own thinking or "headwork" to solve problems. Draw their attention to aspects of daily work and play in the classroom that utilize mathematical concepts (e.g., durations of time: 5 minutes until cleanup, 15 minutes for recess, and 2 weeks off for spring vacation; one-to-one correspondence: a plate for everyone at snack; measuring: half-cup and one-cup measures in the water table).

7. *Use collections to extend and assess children's ability to categorize, classify, and display information.* Give children individual or group opportunities to create collections of natural objects (e.g., rocks, shells, leaves, stones) or man-made objects (e.g., buttons, nuts and bolts, keys and locks, textures of cloth). Offer them guidance on collecting objects and what may be appropriate and inappropriate to collect. Provide opportunities for children to display and tell about their collections.

8. *Observe how children are thinking about mathematical concepts, using materials, making connections, and representing their ideas.* Act on your observations to expand children's mathematical thinking. Interact with children, allowing them to take the lead. Instead of correcting inaccurate concepts on the spot when children's ideas are perceptually immature and when problem-solving strategies are inefficient, provide materials and an environment conducive to a better understanding of mathematical concepts (Copley, 2010). Use open-ended questions and prompts to stimulate further thinking (see Figure 12.5).

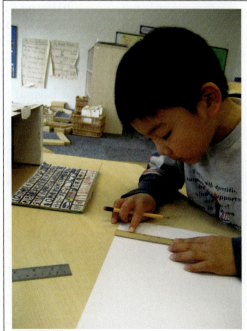

9. *Organize the classroom so that children have easy access to needed materials, tools, and equipment, displaying these on low shelves.* Teach children how to use materials, tools, and equipment skillfully and respectfully, including putting materials away after using them.

10. *Avoid the pitfalls commonly made relative to mathematics in early childhood classrooms.* Some examples:

- Having low expectations of children based on myths about children's lack of reasoning in the early years
- Failing to plan active experiences or design engaging and meaningful classroom activities
- Not giving children time and support for real problem solving
- Isolating math from the rest of the planned curriculum
- Not making needed manipulative and math materials available in the classroom or adequately explaining how to use them

An organized classroom offers easy access to needed materials and tools.

FIGURE 12.5 Sample of open-ended questions and prompts to facilitate mathematical thinking and reasoning

- Why do you think that?
- How did you arrive at that conclusion?
- Tell me about the pattern you see here.
- What do you think will happen if I add this here? If I take this away?
- Is there any other way to show this?
- Show me another way to do this.
- Is there another way to think about this?
- How many different ways can you use these green and yellow blocks to make five of something?
- Tell me why you think this thing is heavier/lighter.
- How is this number different from that number?
- How are these alike? Different?
- How could I measure these two things to see which is longer?

Meeting the Needs of Diverse Learners

When teaching young children, we have to constantly keep in mind that we cannot and should not expect all children to solve problems in identical ways; nor should we expect all the young children in a group to "get it" at the same time. Differences in age, life experiences, brain development, motivation to learn, and language facility will result in each child constructing mathematical understanding in different ways, at different times, and with different materials. Our job is to identify where any young child may need additional help and to create the type of environment in which each can learn mathematics (Copley, 2010, p. 7).

Mathematics is a content area that may be more comfortable for children who are learning to navigate English. The symbols 1, 2, 3, 4, 5, 6, 7, 8, 9, and 10 are displayed commonly throughout the world, and the processes for mathematics are constant in any country. Many of us have learned to count from one to ten or beyond in a number of languages, and Ms. Carol has taken advantage of her knowledge of Spanish to work with two of the children who are entering her room speaking only Spanish. For about 5 minutes a day, she plays a game with them in which she counts objects with them, repeating the number of the objects in both English and Spanish (uno/one, dos/two, tres/three, cuatro/four, cinco/five, seis/six, siete/seven, ocho/eight, nueve/nine, diez/ten, and so on) and the name of the object only in English (uno apple, one apple; dos apples, two apples; tres apples, three apples; cuatro apples, four apples; cinco apples, and so on). She has the two children repeat with her and, at the end, they must tell her the Spanish word for apple (and other objects) and have her repeat after them (uno manzana, one apple; dos manzanas, two apples; and so on). They delight in being able to turn the tables and teach their teacher something while she is, in turn, teaching *them* something. She finds time during the day to use their language when she can, always making sure to include the English words as well.

Planned Activities in Mathematics

In Chapter 5, you learned about creating lesson plans as teaching tools. Let's now apply this to some examples of what can be taught in the cognitive domain when extending children's mathematical skills and concepts. Following are six short-form lesson plans you might implement in your classroom. The goal numbers referred to in each activity correspond to the numbered goals listed earlier in this chapter.

Exploratory Play Activity: Balancing Act

Ages 3–6

Goal 29: For children to identify objects as "the same" or "different," and then "more" or "less," on the basis of attributes they can measure.

Content: An object can weigh more or less than another object.
To *balance* means that items placed on one side of the scale weigh as much or the same amount as items placed on the other side of the scale.

Materials: One or more balance scales

Small items such as coins, plastic counters, small rocks, shells, or small cars

Light items such as cotton balls and feathers

Paper and pencils for extension activity

Procedure:

1. Provide the balance scale and numerous small items for children to work with.

2. Give children many opportunities to explore the balance scales and the items. Be alert for signs that the children are drawing conclusions from their experiments by listening to their conversations and observing their play.

3. Encourage the children to balance some of the items on the scale to find out if they can make the ends even. Ask them such questions as, "What will happen if you put a rock on one side and a car on the other?"

4. Wait for them to experiment. Pose other questions such as, "What do you have to do to balance five coins or two cars?" "What happens when the items are placed side by side or on top of one another?"

5. After some time, introduce new items, such as the cotton balls, and encourage children to explore those.

To Simplify: Use only a few items at a time as children may become confused with a large amount of material to consider.

To Extend: Suggest to children that they make drawings of the objects presented in an equation form.

Guided Discovery Activity: Animals on Parade

Ages 3–6

Goal 30: For children to identify measurable attributes such as length (shorter, longer) and weight (heavier, lighter) and solve problems by comparing and ordering objects based on those attributes.

Content: Things can often be seriated or ordered in many different ways, including by size, length, height, width, color, shape, scent, tone, use, weight, and texture.

Materials: Assortment of six to eight animal figures

Procedure:

1. Present an assortment of six to eight familiar animal figures to a small group of children. The animals may vary on size, dark to light color, thin to fat.

2. Encourage the children to explore the materials before conducting the activity so that they are able to attend to the seriation task. Make sure the children also know the animal names.

3. Tell the children that the animals have decided to have a parade but cannot decide on the marching

"Can you think of a way to line up the animals?"

order and would like some suggestions from them. Tell them, also, that the animals have decided that the animal with the most of some characteristic (e.g., size) is to go first, with the others in order behind the leader. The animal with the least of that attribute will be at the end of the parade.

4. Invite the children to experiment with creating the parade. As they work, continue to remind the children of the agreed-upon criteria. Encourage them to verbally describe how they are placing the animals and why.

5. When they are satisfied that they have the correct order, have them evaluate whether or not all the animals have "observed the rule," based on the attribute selected.

6. Ask them to draw the parade of animals to make a record of the way they seriated the figures.

To Simplify: Use only three or four animals initially. Add others, one at a time, after the children have ordered the first group.

To Extend: After the initial group of animals is arranged, introduce a different animal and ask the children to show you where it will belong in the order. Ask them to explain the placement. Continue adding new animals.

Problem-Solving Activity: What's My Rule?

Ages 3-6

Goal 23: For children to sort, classify, and order objects by size, number, and other attributes.

Content: Things can often be grouped or ordered in many different ways (e.g., size, length, height, width, color, shape, scent, tone, use, weight, and texture). People use grouping as a way to figure out similarities and differences.

Materials: Sets of colorful food picture cards that can be sorted on the basis of color, kind (fruit, vegetable, meat, bread, milk), or size

Trays, baskets, or boxes in which to sort the cards.

Procedure:
1. Give children some time to explore the colorful food cards by looking through and handling them.

2. Tell children you have a problem. You need their help in sorting or classifying the cards into some kind of groups based on an attribute they decide on.

3. Divide them into groups of three or four and provide each small group with a set of food cards and trays or baskets for sorting.

4. Tell them to decide on a rule for sorting and to go ahead with the task.

5. When they have had adequate time to create a rule and complete the work, bring them together as a large group and have each group describe what their rule for sorting the cards will be. Highlight differences in the rules they constructed, reminding them that there can be different ways to sort and classify objects.

To Simplify: Work with the children in a large group. Have one child select a card and ask, "Who can find another food that belongs with this one?" Ask why the child made that choice. Ask, "Who else can find a card that goes with these two?" and continue the process, asking the children to guess what the rule is.

To Extend: Have each group meet again to decide on a new rule and re-sort their cards.

Discussion Activity: How Many in the Housekeeping Area?

Ages 4-5

Goal 17: For children to solve everyday problems by collecting data (information) and using mathematics to answer questions.

Content: People use mathematics to solve everyday problems.
"How many" can be quantified by a certain numeral.

Materials: None needed

Procedure:
1. To solve the problem of too many children at one time playing in the housekeeping area, meet with children in a large group.

2. Share the problem and ask for their ideas about how many children should be in the housekeeping area at any one time and how that number should be communicated to others.

To Simplify: Provide a few strategies for communicating the number to others and have children vote after discussing each of them.

To Extend: Have children construct a sign for the housekeeping area to post the number allowed in at any one time.

Demonstration Activity: Over, Under, In Between

Ages 3-4

Goal 22: For children to discuss the relative positions of objects with vocabulary such as *above*, *below*, and *next to*.

Content:
1. *Above* means over or on top of.
2. *Next to* means close to.
3. *Beside* means at the side of.
4. *Between* means in the middle of two things.
5. *Under* means below something.
6. Location words are used to give directions.

Materials: One small red and one small blue block for each child

A small animal or person figure for each child

Procedure:
1. Give children a few moments of exploration time.
2. Direct the children to watch you and do just as you do with your materials.
3. Perform the following actions and accompany your movements with verbal description as you work:
   a. Place the red block *above* the blue block.
   b. Place the figure *next to* the blue block.
   c. Place the figure *in front of* the blue block.
   d. Place the red block *beside* the figure.
   e. Place the figure *behind* the red block.
   f. Hold the red block *over* the figure.
   g. Hold the figure *under* the blue block.
   h. Hold the red block *up*.
   i. Hold the blue block *down*.
   j. Place the figure *between* the blocks.
   k. Place your figure anywhere you want, and when it's your turn, use the correct location word to tell others where you put it.

To Simplify: Introduce only a few directions at a time. Review previously introduced location words before teaching new words.

To Extend: Once these location words are mastered, add additional blocks so that children can construct a simple walled enclosure and practice the words *inside*, *outside*, *near*, and *far*.

Direct Instruction Activity: Concentration

Ages 4-6

Goal 1: For children to develop an understanding of the meanings of numbers.

Content: A set may contain any quantity of objects.

People count to find out how many objects are in a set.

A numeral is a symbol that represents a number or quantity.

Materials: Set of small, laminated cards containing numerals 1 through 5

Set of small, laminated cards containing sets of dots, 1 through 5

Procedure:

1. Show children the laminated cards and how they can either pair numerals together, pair sets together, or pair a numeral with a set that contains the same number represented by the numeral.
2. Place the cards in random order face down on a table.
3. Choose two cards and show them to the children.
4. Ask a child if they are a pair or not. Ask why or why not.
5. If the cards are a pair, give them to the child. If not, place the cards face down again on the table.
6. Have children take turns to select two cards to pair until all the cards have been taken.
7. Have the children return the cards and play the game independently.

To Simplify: Limit the numerals and sets on the cards to 1 through 3; use only numerals or only sets to match to begin with.

To Extend: Extend the numerals and sets on the cards to 1 through 10.

Communicating with Families About Early Mathematics

The more knowledgeable families become about your program, the more likely you can draw them in as partners in their child's learning. To ensure that they understand and have appreciation for the broad content included in early mathematics, plan to have a "math fun night" with just adults—no children allowed! Start the evening by introducing them to Mrs. Fibonnaci, the teacher in Jon Scieszka's delightful *Math Curse* (1995), who tells us that almost anything can be thought of as a math problem. Instead of lecturing, get family members participating right away in a round robin of enjoyable, non-threatening activities such as playing Uno, measuring ingredients to make their own no-cook snack, classifying objects from their purses and pockets in a number of ways, and building structures together with unit blocks. Near the end of the evening, involve the families in a brief "what did you learn?" discussion. Reinforce that play is the medium through which young children learn—and that what their children are learning is building a rock-solid foundation for later mathematical skills and concepts their children will need. Invite them to repeat some of the same activities at home with their children and to watch for a newsletter (see Figure 12.6) that will be coming soon to suggest other activities to teach mathematical thinking.

NEWSLETTER/WEB READY COMMUNICATION

FIGURE 12.6 • Mathematics Activities You Can Do at Home

Here are some ideas for mathematics activities that can be done at home to reinforce what we're focusing on at school for the rest of the month. We're measuring and counting everything around here! You can join in by working with your child to discover the following:

- Use a tape measure to see how tall each member of the family is.
- Weigh yourselves. Who is the heaviest? Who is the lightest? Include your cat or dog if you have one.
- What is the largest window in your house?
- How many steps does it take to go from the back of your kitchen to the front door? Count them.
- If you have stairs, how many steps to get from the bottom to the top?
- How many lamps do you have? How many have burned-out bulbs?
- How many children's books does the family own?
- Empty out a sock drawer. In how many ways can you sort the socks?

Try to think of other activities that involve mathematics and have your own math fun at your house. Your child's brain will thank you for it. Watch for our next newsletter. We'll have some ideas for having fun with shapes. Let us know if you come up with some math activities at home that your child can teach us about.

12 Applying What You've Learned

Based on what you now know about teaching mathematics in the early years, carry out these activities to increase your knowledge and skills:

1. **Importance of Math in Early Years.** What would you say if someone said, "We need to focus on socialization and literacy prior to grade 1. Math can be left until then because you don't have time to do everything!" Provide a strong rationale for including mathematics and a strategy for finding the time to do so.

2. **Integrating Literacy and Mathematics.** Visit a bookstore or library and survey the children's book section to find at least three books children would enjoy hearing you read. What are the math concepts taught in each of the books? For what ages do you think the books are appropriate? Why?

3. **The Pits.** Review instructional strategy #10 in this chapter where pitfalls are listed (p. 233). Reflect on the classroom in which you are volunteering or responsible for the planning. Do you see any of the pitfalls operating? If so, describe what you believe needs to be put in place to turn the situation around.

4. **Going from Short to Long.** Select one of the short-form mathematics lesson plans in this chapter. Compare it with the long-form plan in the appendix. What would have to be added to the short-form plan in order to qualify it as a long-form plan? How would it benefit an inexperienced teacher to write a long-form plan?

5. **Getting the Mathematics Low-Down.** Interview a teacher of 3-year-old children. What kinds of mathematical content has been included in his or her instructional plans for this week? For last week? Ask questions to evaluate whether or not this teacher appears to have developmentally appropriate expectations of children's abilities and one situation where he or she had to either simplify or extend an activity to meet a child's learning needs.

6. **Game Night.** Think about working with a colleague to set up an hour-long early-evening program for family members to experience some of the activities you use to promote conceptual learning in mathematics. How would you introduce the evening? What are five activities you would include? How would you help family members identify what they are learning in each of the activities?

References

Burns, M. (2007). *About teaching mathematics.* Sausalito, CA: Math Solutions Publications.

Carey, B. (December 22, 2009). Understanding the capabilities of young minds. *International Herald Tribune,* p. 5.

Clements, D. H., & Sarama, J. (2009). *Learning and teaching early math: The learning trajectories approach.* New York: Routledge.

Copley, J. V. (2010). *The young child and mathematics* (2nd ed.). Washington, D.C.: National Association for the Education of Young Children and Reston, VA: National Council of Teachers of Mathematics.

Education Week. (November 11, 2009). *Teaching girls to tinker.* In ExchangeEveryDay (exchangeeveryday@ccie.com).

Kostelnik, M. J., Soderman, A. K., & Whiren, A. P. (2011). *Developmentally appropriate curriculum: Best practices in early childhood education* (5th ed.). Upper Saddle River: Pearson.

National Council of Teachers of Mathematics. (2006). *Curriculum focal points for prekindergarten through grade 8 mathematics: A quest for coherence.* Reston, VA: The National Council of Teachers of Mathematics.

National Council of Teachers of Mathematics (2011). *Illuminations summer institute.* Retrieved from http://illuminations@nctm.org.

Owen, A., & McKinney, S. (November, 2010). *Math is more than 1, 2, 3.* Anaheim, CA: NAEYC Annual Conference.

Scieszka, J., & Smith, L. (1995). *The math curse.* New York: Viking Juvenile.

13 The Language Domain: Enhancing Communication and Early Literacy

In Janet Vineberg's classroom, the three bears have taken over. Children can't wait to experience the engaging activities planned for them each day. Today, Janet is taking them on a bear hunt. Gathering them together in the large-group area, she shows them captioned "secret" pictures of what they will see. The first is of a heavy metal gate, and she tells them how they will have to *unlatch* it. She shows them a picture of the tall mountain they must *scale* or climb, a tree they will have to *shinny up* and what that means, a *swift* river they will have to cross, and a *shadowy* and *murky* cave they'll have to explore. Let's go on the hunt with them!

Teacher: We're going on a bear hunt!

Children: We're going on a bear hunt!

Teacher: We're gonna catch a big one!

Children: We're gonna catch a big one!

Teacher: I'm not afraid! Are you? Are you?

Children: I'm not afraid! Are you? Are you?

Teacher: Not me!

Children: Not me!

Teacher: Here comes the heavy metal gate!

Children: (continue to echo what the teacher says)

Using this favorite chant that can be accessed readily in picture books, on the internet, on DVD, or on musical CDs, Ms. Vineberg is expanding the children's receptive and expressive vocabularies, modeling the rhythm and expressiveness of a good story, and helping the children understand the connection between print and speech via the captioned pictures. She is also completely holding their interest.

T his chapter is concerned with the development of children's early language and literacy skills: listening and viewing, speaking, writing, and reading.

Language and Literacy Development in the Early Years

By 3 years of age, most children will have developed a basic receptive vocabulary of thousands of words in their primary language. They will display a fundamental knowledge of correct grammatical structures and demonstrate that they can use language for the following functions (Halliday & Webster, 2006):

- Instrumental—to satisfy their needs and wants: "I want more milk."
- Regulatory—to control others: "You can't get ahead of me in line."
- Interactional—to create interactions with others: "Do you wanna play with me?"
- Personal—to express personal thoughts and opinions: "I don't want to go to bed. I'm not tired yet."
- Imaginative—to create imaginary worlds: "Let's pretend that we're dogs and go under the table. That's our dog house, okay?"
- Heuristic—to seek information: "Do I go to school today?"
- Informative—to communicate information: "My mom says we're going to move to a new house."

FIGURE 13.1 Sample language and literacy terms for teachers of young children

Alliteration A string of words beginning with the same sound (Susy sells sea shells . . .)

Alphabetic awareness Understanding that there are 26 letters in the English alphabet and that individual letters and letter combinations have names and match specific sounds in oral language

Alphabetic stage of writing Vowels appear in child's writing (e.g., Kak for cake)

Concepts about print Understanding how print works (e.g., leaving spaces between words, capitalization, punctuation, reading from top to bottom and left to right)

Consonant stage of writing Using mostly consonants in writing, beginning with first and last sounds and then insertion of middle sounds (e.g., Dg for dog, rng for running)

Conventional spelling "Book spelling," spelling words correctly

Dyslexia Impaired ability to understand written language

Fluency Functional literacy, ability to read smoothly, expressively, and with greater automaticity (automatic recognition of words)

Genres Types of literature (e.g., poetry, narrative, fiction, short story)

Graphemes The written letter symbols in an alphabet

KWHLH Activity to identify what children know about a phenomenon (K), what they want to know (W), how they might find that information (H), what they learned (L), and how they learned it (H)

Onsets and rimes Onsets are the beginning sound of any word before the first vowel. Rimes (not to be confused with rhymes) begin with the vowel and share the same spelling endings. For example, in the word *fat*, the onset is *f*, and the rime is *at*. Words such as fat, rat, bat, sat, mat, cat are said to be "word families."

Oral language development Includes receptive vocabulary (words we understand) and expressive vocabulary (words we use to express our thoughts and needs)

Phonemes Discrete sounds in a language

Phonemic awareness Understanding that the speech stream consists of a sequence of sounds or phonemes

Phonics A tool to help make concrete connections between individual graphemes and their associated sounds and to understand vowel and consonant patterns

Phonological awareness The ability to hear differences and similarities in the sounds of words or parts of words, the ability to separate and blend sounds in words, the ability to manipulate sounds to make new words

Prosody The "music" and rhythmic sounds of one's own primary language

Retellings Telling the important events of a story that has been read in the order they happened

Syntax Grammatical structure of a sentence

Semantics Meaning that is conveyed in written or spoken language

Temporary spelling Approximations that children use in the emergent stage of literacy

Word awareness Discovering that the words in print are the words we say

Pointing out something interesting.

Still, children have a great deal to learn in the early years as they continue to expand their listening skills, develop phonological, phonemic, and alphabetic awareness (see definitions in Figure 13.1), understand more formal conventions of language, and build their speaking abilities. They will later transport these foundational language abilities into the realm of literacy as they become readers and writers—and the academic success they have later on will depend greatly on what happens in the years between the ages of 3 and 6 (NELP, 2009).

Key Language and Literacy Content in the Early Childhood Classroom

Although emergent literacy begins in infancy and continues until children are conventionally literate and can read and write independently

(Bennett-Armistead, Duke, & Moses, 2005), **oral language development** in preschool and kindergarten is a critical precursor. Thus, early childhood educators must be aware of and target their instruction toward developing key language concepts and skills. In this section, we'll take a closer look at what these concepts and skills are.

ORAL LANGUAGE DEVELOPMENT: THE BIG IDEAS

James and Billy have become great friends because of their mutual interest in airplanes. Today, they are underneath the science table, which has become their shared cockpit and jet. They talk together about where they are flying to this morning, what they need to check out before they go, and how long it will take them to reach their destination. Although they are only 4 years old, both boys have experience in flying internationally, and both have had an opportunity to visit a cockpit in a real airplane, fueling their abilities and motivation to communicate with one another in their imaginary play. Most important, they have a shared language: English. Nearby, a classmate who does not speak English watches closely but does not attempt to join them. "Maybe you could take on a passenger for this flight," suggests the teacher. "Maybe Hao Hao could come on board. What do you think?" The co-pilots look at one another and then signal for Hao Hao to come on board.

Language is essential to society, forming the foundation for our perceptions, communications, and daily interactions with others. To function successfully in a society and its culture, children need to develop a wide range of oral language competencies (Otto, 2009). Between the ages of 3 and 6, oral language tasks will include:

- Building a strong receptive vocabulary
- Developing the confidence and motivation to use language expressively with others
- Developing phonological awareness

Without formal instruction, children in preschool and kindergarten become quite expert at learning the rules of universal grammar and expanding their vocabulary if they have good models and are in a communication-rich environment. Learning to express their thoughts to others is expanded when adults in the setting have built good rapport with a child and use questioning, expansion (or recasting), and repetition, interacting often and in a friendly way:

Child: We gots a new dog.
Teacher: Oh, you have a new pet at your house (expansion). When did that happen? (questioning)
Child: My dad brought him home yesterday.
Teacher: Ah, your dad brought him home (repetition).
Child: Yeah, and he peed on the floor.
Teacher: Oh, oh. Wetting on the floor. A problem to be solved, huh? (expansion, questioning)

Because the capacity to develop oral language and speech is built into children naturally, most do so without a problem. When breakdowns in the process happen,

concepts about print
Understanding how print works (e.g., leaving spaces between words, capitalization, punctuation, reading from top to bottom and left to right).

alphabetic awareness Understanding that there are 26 letters in the English alphabet and that individual letters and letter combinations have names and match specific sounds in oral language.

oral language development Includes receptive vocabulary (words we understand) and expressive vocabulary (words we use to express our thoughts and needs).

they may result in one or more of the following difficulties during the preschool and kindergarten years (Wingert & Kantrowitz, 1997):

- Starts talking later than other children
- Has pronunciation problems
- Has slow vocabulary growth
- Is often unable to find the right word
- Has trouble learning numbers, the alphabet, days of the week
- Has difficulty rhyming words
- Is extremely restless and distractible
- Has trouble interacting with peers
- Displays a poor ability to follow directions or routines
- Avoids puzzles, drawing, and cutting

genres Types of literature (e.g., poetry, narrative, fiction, short story).

Oral language development in the early childhood setting is fostered through daily use of interactive conversation between peers and between children and adults. Songs, finger plays, the daily reading of different genres of literature, pretend play, nursery rhymes, questioning and answering, adult explanations during demonstrations, and activities to purposefully expand receptive vocabulary are essential for children's optimal growth in language. Children with rich vocabularies understand a great deal of what they hear, see, and later read because they know a lot of words. That helps them construct new knowledge and continue to develop a deeper, more flexible understanding of the core meaning of words (Paynter, Bodrova, & Doty, 2005, p. 4). Some basic understandings children need to have relative to language development are listed in Figure 13.2.

Purposely building enjoyable listening activities into the day to enhance children's auditory skills through listening and response interactions will be essential. Some of these activities can be seen in Figure 13.3.

phonological awareness The ability to hear differences and similarities in the sounds of words or parts of words; the ability to separate and blend sounds in words; the ability to manipulate sounds to make new words.

Phonological awareness includes skills children usually master by 4 or 5 years of age and will be critical to later reading and writing abilities. Although there isn't a particular order in which the skills develop, they include a child's ability to:

- Separate words into syllables or beats
- Recognize rhyming words
- Generate rhyming words
- Recognize words that start or end with the same sound
- Generate words that start or end with the same sound

FIGURE 13.2 What children need to understand about their language

When someone is speaking to us, we should stop and listen.	Body language is how people use their bodies to communicate messages beyond the words they are saying.
Words are powerful and carry a message and meaning.	Words can be separated into syllables, or beats.
Rhymes are words that sound the same.	There are rhyming words that end in the same sound.
When speaking with others, it is helpful to look at them and to speak clearly.	We can move sounds around to create new words (e.g., fan, man, ran, tan).
When someone else is speaking, it helps to listen to the tone of his or her voice and to watch the expression on his or her face.	Having a conversation means that we take turns talking.
	What we say can be written down.

FIGURE 13.3 **Activities to enhance auditory skills**

- Oral or musical signals given to children to alert them to a change in activities (e.g., Hang a wind chime in your room that is sounded at the end of center play)
- Auditory memory games
- Sound cans from which children match similar sounds
- Activities to determine whether children can follow one-, two-, and three-step directions or oral commands
- Helping children to hear sounds in words by stretching them out and purposefully slowing down pronunciation
- Games that challenge children to imitate sounds (such as loud-soft, speed, high and low pitch, holding their noses)
- Times when children listen to the sounds of crunchy foods that are chewed or broken in half
- Songs, such as "Pop Goes the Weasel" or games such as Simon Says in which children must listen to and respond to a signal
- Matching games in which pictures of animals must be matched to the sounds they make
- Hidden-sound activities in which children must identify and discriminate certain sounds (e.g., baby rattle, tambourine, toilet flushing, stapler, scissors cutting) that are made behind a screen or on a recorded message
- Play-telephone activities
- Sound stories during which children make a related sound every time a particular word is mentioned in the story (e.g., making the sound "yum-yum" whenever the word *spinach* is heard or appears)
- Games that provide clues that children must listen to so they can identify a particular object in the room or in a secret box
- Stories on tape with interactive headphones so that children can listen together to a story

---

- Blend sounds into words
- Segment words into sounds
- Move sounds around to create new words (Bennett-Armistead, Duke, & Moses, 2005, p. 92).

Children will not automatically pick up these skills without being given targeted experiences, and not all entering kindergarten children have them; these are children who will lack the ability to become solid readers and spellers later on (Soderman & Farrell, 2008; NELP, 2009). As you can imagine, children who are lucky enough to have lots of experience with nursery rhymes will have more highly developed phonological awareness. Also, those who have had fun with words—silly words (goopy, soupy, boopy), nonsense words (anana, tabana, fanana), poems, chants, music, and onsets and rimes (word families) will have the strong underpinnings they need to connect language to literacy.

The daily schedule should be structured loosely enough that there is plenty of opportunity for casual conversation, and adults should be sure to allow plenty of input from and exchanges with the children. The daily schedule should never be so tightly structured that only limited opportunities are offered to engage in plenty of casual conversation; nor should adults do most of the talking without much input from and exchanges with children. In classrooms where children are read to only one day a week, the more sophisticated vocabulary that is nurtured when listening to well-written children's books and engaging in discussion afterwards is essentially lost. Conversely, in classrooms where children are transported each day to imaginary worlds and situations and become familiar with higher-level language through text, strong foundations are set for the next stage to come—reading and writing.

EMERGENT LITERACY DEVELOPMENT: THE BIG IDEAS

The oral language skills that children have developed will set the stage for the emergent literacy that is to take place in the next phase of language development. During this period, major developmental tasks in literacy will include the development of:

- Phonemic awareness
- Alphabetic awareness
- Concept of print
- Reading conventions
- Writing conventions

As children move toward kindergarten and into the early primary grades, they will increase their conscious connection between language and print. Although they differ dramatically in terms of motivation to learn to read and write, most 4-year-olds are interested in being able to identify and differentiate between letters and write their names and some other familiar words (mom, dad, love, like, dog, cat, house, names of friends). They begin to understand how books work (concepts of print) and how much fun it is to be able to write a message to a friend. When they discover the general mystery of decoding (the understanding that alphabet letters all have unique sounds attached to them and that you can sound out a word if you know that), they are off and running! Being able to demonstrate to someone that he or she knows what reading is all about is one of the memorable accomplishments in early childhood (and in early parenting).

Unlike the development of speech and language, reading and writing are not "normal" or built into the species; in order to read and write, children have to have a lot of experience and directed instruction with print. There are all kinds of things to learn: Letters have shapes that are made out of straight lines, curved lines, and a combination of curved and straight lines; letters have names; letters have sounds; letters can be written in what is called "lower case" and also at other times in what is called "upper case," and you have to learn the difference. Letters can be put together in certain ways to spell words you say, such as your name or your friends' name. There are "consonant" letters and "vowel" letters to put together to spell words, and every single word needs a vowel. Such is the world of the emergent writer.

Because we do not want to interfere with children's determination to put their approximations and first attempts on paper, early childhood teachers need to be aware of several "rules" that just make sense to us:

1. Preschoolers, kindergarteners, and first-graders should be allowed to use temporary spelling rather than have their work corrected by the teacher, which tends to shut down their effort.
2. Preschoolers and kindergarteners should not be required to use lined paper so that they can concentrate instead on which letter to choose, how to shape it, and how to put letters together to make words—not on how to get their words on the line.

---

phonemic awareness Understanding that the speech stream consists of a sequence of distinct sounds—or phonemes—in a language.

temporary spelling Approximations of spelling of words that children use in the emergent stage of literacy.

3. Children in early childhood should be encouraged to draw about their ideas prior to writing about those ideas.

4. Children should be encouraged to read back their writing (sharing what we write with others is the purpose of writing) and to talk about their pictures.

5. Writing centers should be placed near a word wall on which the teacher has posted all of the children's names and other familiar words they use frequently in their writing.

Emerging reading, like writing, requires that children develop the ability to sound out or decode the beginning, middle, and end sounds that are inside of words (phonemic awareness). Children must learn to rapidly and automatically recognize letters and frequently-seen (sight) words (I, a, am, and, do) (NELP, 2009). Big Books are a marvelous tool for the early years. Because children can readily see the print, teachers can stop in places where the power words appear and ask children to read them, reminding them when they do, "You're readers! You can read!" The children can read the word wall regularly, and they can have fun with this by snapping fingers, clapping, or stamping as they recite the letters in each word.

Although comprehension in the earliest years is not as much a focus as is developing decoding skills, it is still important. Children need to recognize that stories contain certain elements to pay attention to, such as the idea of the story, the characters that make up a story, the setting, the problem, events, and the solution. Literacy terms and facts that are important to teach young children can be seen in Figure 13.4.

As an early childhood teacher, you will spend a major part of your instructional time on language and literacy. Although it is serious business, we hope that you will also have fun with it. Here's where your ability to be creative will really pay off as you think of engaging, meaningful, and useful activities to grow this important area of human development. Following are more specific goals in the language arts domain.

FIGURE 13.4 Sample literacy terms and facts for children

There are 26 letters in the English alphabet.

Letters have sounds and names.

Words are made up of letters.

Letters must be in a certain order to spell a word.

Sentences are made up of words.

Anything that is said can be written down.

People write for many purposes.

Words have beginning, middle, and end sounds.

When we read, we read words, not pictures; words can tell a story but pictures can tell a story, too.

Print says the same thing today as it will tomorrow.

Letters can be written in upper or lower case.

Capitalize means to use the upper case of a letter.

The first letters of names are always written in upper case or capitalized.

When we write, we leave spaces between words.

We read in English from top to bottom and from left to right.

A *period* is a dot or punctuation used to mark the end of a sentence.

When we write a question, we put a question mark at the end.

Curricular Goals—Language Domain

The following purpose and goals are consistent with the standards of the International Reading Association and the National Council of Teachers of English.

PURPOSE

The purpose of the language domain is for children to communicate their ideas and feelings and to accurately interpret the communications they receive. As children progress in language, they will:

Listening and Viewing

1. Interpret unspoken messages, including tone of voice, facial expression, and body language
2. Identify sounds in their environment
3. Listen and view for pleasure
4. Demonstrate courteous listening behaviors
5. Increase their receptive vocabulary
6. Demonstrate auditory memory, comprehension, and critical listening by repeating in correct detail and sequence the messages they hear

Speaking

7. Articulate their ideas, intents, emotions, and desires
8. Ask and answer questions
9. Create and describe imaginative situations
10. Use correct pronunciation, grammar, and appropriate body language (eye contact, body position, and gestures) to alert a listener to their intent and to convey meaning
11. Increase their expressive vocabulary over time
12. Use increasingly complex sentence structure
13. Adapt their language to the audience and situation
14. Develop self confidence and poise during group speaking and creative dramatics activities

Writing

15. Recognize that messages are conveyed to others through written symbols (drawing and writing)
16. Understand that speech can be preserved through writing
17. Observe and imitate writing
18. Connect letter sounds to graphemes
19. Generate graphemes
20. Put their thoughts on paper, first through simple pictures and then incorporating simple print into their drawings

graphemes The written letter symbols in an alphabet.

Reading

21. Recognize graphemes—the letters of the alphabet
22. Recognize that people get meaning from print
23. Enjoy shared reading experiences with varied genres of literature
24. Practice reading-like behavior

25. Increase their receptive and expressive reading vocabularies

26. Respond to written symbols in the environment (e.g., their name and others' names, signs, advertisements, labels)

27. Predict, on the basis of the information in the text and their personal life experiences, what will come next in stories that are being read

28. Develop general concepts of print (e.g., that books are read from front to back; that we read words, not pictures; that spaces are used between words)

29. Develop an understanding of story elements and structure (e.g., story sequence, main ideas, characters, setting, and plot development)

30. Show comprehension of what has been read to them by retelling and dramatizing

31. Become familiar with libraries as interesting places to find books and other materials for entertainment and information.

Teaching Strategies

To optimize the language and literacy acquisition of the children in your classroom, use the following 6 strategies:

1. *Regularly evaluate whether your classroom environment can truly be called "communication-rich."* The most important thing in creating a true communication-rich context for young children is to have a teacher who models appropriate, rich language usage. A healthy buzz should be audible in the classroom, where adult voices are not dominant over the children's and where children observe the expectation for using "indoor" voices.

Not all of the children can be expected to use standard English, but you need to have good command of it yourself. Your diction needs to be clear and understandable, with interesting vocabulary that stretches the children's understanding of and interest in the way you use language. Be careful not to neglect children who do not expect or demand attention, and make a personal conversation with every child a daily habit.

Some of the richest teaching moments you will experience will be those you didn't plan. Take advantage of spontaneous events to promote children's language development through conversations and discussion. For example, you notice that Melanie and Kevin are talking about taking a trip on a train they have set up using a row of chairs. Even though your school day is busy from beginning to end, stop and take a moment to start a conversation with them about where they might go, how they plan to get there, and what kinds of things they think they should take on the trip. Then, bow out of their play and move on to other children. Having a schedule that allows for plenty of free time for children to interact with one another and with you will be more effective than having one that is tightly targeted toward scripted teaching plans and mostly teacher-directed activity.

When a child states something, take advantage of the chance to enhance language by repeating it and using a new term or adding an appropriate clause. Use an interesting synonym for a word or two, add a related idea, or challenge the child to think of one. Use open-ended questions and paraphrases as stated in Chapter 12 to accomplish this.

Genuinely listen to what children are saying, taking time to respond and expand on what they are saying. Frequently talk out loud about what you are doing, using explanatory talk, as you demonstrate activities, explain how things work, and share with children why you've made a particular decision. Encourage lots of interactive communication in your classroom by modeling open-ended questions, actively supporting peer-to-peer conversation, and connecting unfamiliar words to those that children already know. Notice whether or not there is a healthy buzz going on during center activity and enjoyable, extended conversation during snack and lunch. Ask yourself, "Are all the children in my room benefiting each day, including shy children and those who speak little English, or am I speaking mostly to those children who first speak to me?" (Bennett-Armistead, Duke, & Moses, 2005).

Matthew prepares today's menu for his restaurant.

Isla says to her friend, "Pretend I'm the teacher and I'm reading to the class."

2. *Create a print-rich visual environment.* When you consciously create a learning environment that highlights print, it should be one where print is visually observable and modeled in lots of engaging ways. It should be one where print is celebrated by actively drawing attention to it, talking about it, and using it for real purposes. Mrs. Gatrell's room is just such a room. Matthew is printing out the menu for the day in the pretend restaurant. His shelves are stocked with labeled boxes and cans of food. The front covers of books are displayed attractively on the tops of bookcases and in front of baskets of books. Small *stop*, *exit*, and *yield* signs are visible in the block corner where a group of children is creating a small town with stores and buildings on which they have written names with the help of Mrs. Gatrell (gas station, library, grocery store, school). Two girls are writing messages to one another, which they will put into the mailbox for delivery on Friday. Isla is in the reading corner pretending to be the teacher and reading to a small group of friends.

The children in Mrs. Gatrell's room are learning a lot about how print works because she highlights certain aspects of it daily, always letting them in on the small mysteries of what letters are called, what they sound like, and how they are put together to say something. She is alert for spontaneous opportunities to encourage children to use it in their play and never fails to express her delight when they do. "Let me see what is on your menu today," she says to Matthew. "Ohhh, look," she says excitedly to a couple of children nearby, "Matthew is featuring fish ("fs") today in his restaurant. It's on his menu. Anyone hungry?" Immediately, Matthew's restaurant attracts three more customers, and he hurries over to provide his new menu to them.

As you think about ways to share and promote the importance of print, you will want to equip your classroom with the tools, props, materials, and equipment that should be found in a literacy-supportive environment (see Figure 13.5) (Soderman, Gregory, & McCarty, 2005). In Figure 13.6, we've listed some of our favorite books for expanding young children's literacy understandings. Although many items should be continuously available in the classroom throughout the year, you will want to introduce new ones periodically related to current themes or projects and draw children's attention to them.

You will want to integrate language development activities and quality literature throughout all areas of instruction. Highlight print in every area of the classroom. Some examples are word walls, song charts, captioned pictures, predictable charts, directions, menus, interesting materials in the writing center, children's pictures and writing at their eye level, and writing materials in every center. Frequently draw children's attention to concepts of print (e.g., shapes of letters, how letters make up words, spaces between words, rhyming words, how books work and are read, types of punctuation).

FIGURE 13.5 **Classroom props and tools: must-haves for the literacy-supportive environment**

Pretend play Paper, pencils, phones, books, telephone book, cookbooks, newspapers and magazines, catalogs, menus, telephones, other props and pictures suited to your theme

Blocks Small paper and cardboard for making signs, digital camera, writing utensils, craft stick, tape, blueprints, posters of buildings and construction sites, animals, small human figures, cars and trucks

Art Paper of different shapes, sizes, textures; easel, paint, and brushes; captioned pictures of artists' work; writing materials; various media

Computer Sign-up sheet and pencil for those waiting for a turn in line, books to look at while waiting, menu of games, rebus directions for turning computer on and off

Snack Signs for washing hands, picture and number of snack items to take, label of the snack of the day, name cards to place on table for snack

Story center Books, story props, flannel board and figures, earphones for electronic books, puppets and small puppet stage, paper and markers, small couch or bean bags

Writing center Markers, stamps, books, blank books or personal journals, envelopes, computer, paper, pens, colored and black pencils, stapler, tape, highlighters, magnetic letters and board, paper punch, paper clips, glue sticks, stamps and stencils, letters to trace, alphabet cards, pocket chart and word cards to organize, big-print dictionary, large and small whiteboards, clipboards, pipe cleaners, year, tissue paper

Around the room Baskets of information and narrative books; signs of the areas; labels on objects, areas, personal property; board displaying environmental print to read (names of popular stores and restaurants); classroom rules and directions; signs related to theme; lists; song charts; predictable charts written by children; morning-message flip easel; children's work; interesting pictures of completed projects/themes, labeled with one-word or brief narratives and children's names; word wall; lists of songs we know; job charts; daily schedule; big books; poetry charts and books; newspapers; magazines; construction paper and tag board; fabric; tape recorder or CD player and headphones; left- and right-handed scissors; sign-in sheet; cards with student names on them for use with name games; pictures of students to be used with personal messages

---

FIGURE 13.6 **Books to develop literacy understanding in young children**

Archambault, J., & Martin, B., Jr. (2000). *Chicka Chicka Boom Boom*, Aladdin.

Bartow, B. (1993). *The Little Red Hen*. HarperFestival.

Carle, E. (1994). *The Very Hungry Caterpillar*. Philomel Books.

Cowley, J. (1999). *Mrs. Wishy-Washy*. Philomel Books.

Dr. Seuss (1963). *Hop on Pop*. Random House.

Galdone, P. (1981). *Three Billy Goats Gruff*. Clarion Books.

Keats, E. J. (1962). *The Snowy Day*. Penguin Putnam.

Lionni, L. (1963). *Swimmy*. Scholastic.

Martin, B., Jr., & Carle, E. (1996). *Brown Bear, Brown Bear, What Do You See?* Henry Holt & Co.

Numeroff, J. J. (1985). *If You Give a Mouse a Cookie*. Harper & Row.

Pallotta, J. (1991). *The Underwater Alphabet Book*. Charlesbridge.

Rosen, M. (1989). *We're Going on a Bear Hunt*. Margaret K. McElderry Books.

Taback, S. (1997). *I Know an Old Lady Who Swallowed a Fly*. Viking Juvenile.

Wood, A. (1984). *The Napping House*. Harcourt Brace.

Wood, A. (1992). *Silly Sally*. Harcourt.

3. *Model and teach the importance of developing and using good listening and viewing skills* as follows:

a. Stop to look at each child when he or she speaks, asking relevant questions, and asking other children to respond as well.

b. Give appropriate cues to help them listen better. Say, "Look up here," or "Watch me"; use voice inflections; change your volume appropriately for the small- or large-group setting. Prepare children for viewing experiences prior to having them watch a video or take a field trip by providing information about what they will be seeing and what you want them to look for.

c. Alert children to sounds in their environment that are easily overlooked and to sound-symbol relations in written language (e.g., "Look. Your name, Bethany, starts with the same sound and letter as bear: B, buh.").

d. Provide visual props such as pictures or real objects when introducing concepts or vocabulary that may be difficult to understand.

4. *Involve children every day in enjoyable writing experiences.*

a. Write in front of children every day. In large group, have children take turns dictating a message centered on their own experiences. This allows them to hear and see their words in print, written in "book" language. By watching you write, they learn the names of letters, that spoken words can be written down, that words are made up of combinations of letters, that writing goes from left to right, that words are separated from each other by a wider space than the space between letters, that the first letters in words that begin sentences and words that are someone's name should be capitalized, that sentences are made up of words, and the ways in which punctuation is useful (Seefeldt, 2005).

b. Provide daily opportunities for children to draw and write (using invented spelling) and then share their pictorial and written representations with their peers, reinforcing the idea that writing is for a purpose. Include ample writing activities, suggestions, and materials in daily play-based experiences. Place writing materials in all centers of the room: order blanks for the pretend restaurant, sticks for making words in the sandbox, and so forth.

5. *Plan literacy games, songs, and other play-oriented activities to enhance children's phonological and print awareness.* Help children to develop the letter-sound associations and the phoneme-grapheme knowledge they need to have by carefully embedding these activities in meaningful experiences. Call attention to letters individually in their names and in words when you are reading. Highlight the configuration of letters by drawing around them, pointing out directional and other unique features of particular letters. Also, for older children, point out examples of upper- and lower-case letters when they appear in print that is interesting to them.

6. *Involve children every day in engaging reading experiences.* Read to them at least once or more each day, modeling expression, phrasing, and **fluency**. Have them read interactively with you, using Big Books or song charts and having them echo back sentences you have just read as you run your hand underneath the print. When reading:

a. Make sure you hold the book so that everyone can see it without having to switch their positions.

b. Draw children's attention to the book by saying, "Watch me. I have a book called _____ that was written by_____. _____ is the illustrator and drew the pictures."

c. Turn the pages from the bottom so they are turned without interrupting the children's observation of the pictures.

fluency Functional literacy, ability to read smoothly, expressively, and with greater automaticity (automatic recognition of words).

d. Vary the pace, pitch, volume, and rhythm of your voice to enhance the meaning of the story, articulate individual sounds, and refocus the children's attention.

e. Bring children's attention to unfamiliar words, explaining what they mean before going on.

f. Talk with children about the story afterwards, paying attention to the pictures and talking about story elements (e.g., main idea, characters, problem and solution, events).

g. Make the book available afterwards for independent examination by children.

TRY IT YOURSELF

Choose a narrative picture book that you especially enjoyed as a child and, after finding it, read it aloud to yourself. Practice making the story come alive, thinking about all the steps outlined above. Then, read it to a small group of young children. Were any of the steps difficult to implement? How could you improve your reading-aloud skills?

Planned Activities in the Language Domain

Exploratory Activity: So Many Books!

Ages 3–6

Goal 23: For children to enjoy shared reading experiences with varied genres of literature.

Content (terms and facts):

1. Pictures in books help tell the story.
2. Books are read from front to back.
3. We can learn new things from looking at and reading books.

Materials: A number of children's narrative picture books

Procedure:

1. Collect an age-appropriate variety of narrative picture books.
2. Place the books in a large basket or on the carpet in front of you.
3. Tell children, "I have some interesting picture books for you to look at. You can choose one of them and see what you can learn about the story by looking through the pictures from the front of the book where the story begins (demonstrate) to the back of it where the story ends."
4. Invite the children to select a book and explore it.
5. Respond to and expand on children's verbal remarks about what they're finding.

To Simplify: Use only narrative picture books that are familiar to the children or books previously read to the children.

To Extend: Add a selection of factual, information (expository) books with plenty of illustrations and invite children to find something new and interesting to share with a partner.

Guided Discovery Activity: Letter/Object Boxes

Ages 4–6

Goal 18: For children to connect letter sounds to graphemes.

Content:

1. Letters have both a name and a sound (e.g., B, buh).
2. Words we say are made up of a sequence of sounds (e.g., cat = kuh, aah, tuh).

3. We spell words by writing down the letters that match sounds in the word (e.g., dog = duh, d; ow, o, guh, g).

4. All objects have names, and names have beginning sounds.

Materials: 26 boxes, each labeled with an upper-case and lower-case letter of the alphabet, A through Z

52 small objects children have seen or handled before

Procedure:

1. Tell children that all objects have names, and all names are made up of sounds.

2. Hold up several of the object and ask children to name each of them.

3. Ask what sound each of several objects begin with.

4. Tell children that you need to place the objects in the correct box—the one that is labeled with the first sound the object makes.

5. Demonstrate placing some of the objects in the correct boxes.

6. Encourage individual children to come up, select an object, and place it in the correct box.

To Simplify: Begin with only a few boxes and objects starting with most familiar graphemes (e.g., Bb, Mm, Cc, Pp).

To Extend: Have children begin to bring small objects from home to add to the collections; empty a box and have children say the name of each object, emphasizing the beginning sound; write the name of the objects in that box.

Problem-Solving Activity: Guess Who's Speaking?

Ages 4-6

Goal 2: For children to identify sounds in their environment.

Content:

1. In order to listen carefully, we need to pay attention.

2. One of the most important senses we have is our sense of hearing.

3. We can identify familiar persons who are speaking to us just by listening to their voices.

Materials: Chair for child

blindfold (optional)

Procedure:

1. After a time in the classroom when you have become familiar with each child's voice, demonstrate that you can tell who they are just by listening to their voices and not seeing them.

2. Turn your chair around; cover your eyes and have each one of the children say good morning to you. Return each greeting, saying, "Good morning, ____" (using his or her name).

3. Invite several children to take your place and repeat the activity.

To Simplify: Demonstrate the activity several days in a row before inviting children to be listeners; encourage children to pay special attention to the sound of each classmate's voice.

To Extend: Have children dismiss their classmates from large group by listening to someone say, "I am sitting quietly and waiting to leave."

Discussion Activity: Storytelling

Ages 3-6

Goal 29: For children to develop an understanding of story elements and structure (e.g., story sequence, main ideas, characters, setting, and plot development).

Content:

1. Every story has a title and an author.

2. Every story has one or more characters.

3. Every story takes place in one or more settings.

4. A story plot is what happens in the story—the events that happen that lead to a problem and a solution.

FIGURE 13.7 Sample of story element cards

Materials: Story element cards (see Figure 13.7) to be handed out to individual children in a group

Picture book to read.

Procedure:

1. Make up the following individual 3" x 3" story element cards: Title, author, characters, setting, problem, solution, event. Draw simple figures to illustrate each card. Laminate them.

2. Tell children that you want to see if they can retell the story after you have read it, and you are going to pass cards out to certain people to help with the retelling. Remind them that everyone will get a chance to retell part of a story sometime that week.

3. Hold up each card and explain what the rebus drawing is and what the words say. Hand the card to one of the children to hold.

4. Begin with the title and name of author; read the story.

5. Ask each child who holds a card to help retell the story (first, the title of the book and the author; description of the most important character; where the story takes place; an event leading to the problem; the solution). Collect the cards from the children as they participate in the retelling.

To Simplify: Use cards only for title and character to begin with, adding cards as children are better able to remember elements.

To Extend: Add cards such as *main idea*, *vocabulary word*, and *illustrator* for older children.

Demonstration Activity: Look! I Can Write My Name

Ages 3-6

Goal 17: For children to observe and imitate writing.

Content:

1. Letters are used to make words.

2. Letters have names.

3. Names are made up of letters.

4. We place letters in a certain way to spell a word.

Materials: A name card for each child

Baggie of letters matching the letters on the name card.

Procedure:

1. Tell children that you have a "gift" of letters for each one of them and their name cards. The letters are special and make up only their name.

2. Show the children your bag of letters and how you can place them over your name card to spell your name.

3. Hand out the name cards and letters.

4. Invite the children to match the letters in their gift bag to the letters on their name card. Tell them to let you know when they're finished by saying, "Look, I can write my name."

5. Check the letters with the child to see that they match.

6. Have the children take the letters and name cards home to show their families how they can write their names.

To Simplify: Place the first and last letters on each child's name card and then have them complete the name, then mix the letters up to have the child match all of them independently.

To Extend: After children have practiced, have them trade their bags with a partner and spell out a friend's name; have children see if they can spell any other word using the letters in their names.

Direct Instruction Activity: Readers' Theater: "The Three Pigs"

Ages 3-6

Goal 14: For children to develop self confidence and poise during group speaking and creative dramatics activities.

Content:

1. Stories can be read, told, and acted out.

2. Acted-out stories are called *plays* or *Reader's Theater.*

3. Persons who act out stories in plays are called *actors.*

4. A person who reads a story as it is acted out is called a *narrator.*

5. Plays have an *audience*; that is, people who watch and listen.

Materials: Familiar book (e.g., *The Three Pigs*)

Props such as a character faces on sticks (Wolf, Pig 1, Pig 2, Pig 3)

Small cardboard "houses" (straw, wood, brick)

Procedure:

1. Read *The Three Pigs* story to children several times and have the children participate whenever possible in repeating what the characters say.

2. Explain to the children that you are going to participate in what is called "Readers' Theater" and that you are going to have them act out the story of *The Three Pigs.* Tell them everyone will get a chance to be an actor and also part of an audience.

3. Ask for volunteers to play the part of the Wolf, Pig 1, Pig 2, and Pig 3. Show them the small houses to incorporate into the story as it is read.

4. Read through the story the first time, providing guidance to the actors about what to say and what to do.

5. Repeat the activity, using new players each time so that all children have a chance to be part of the audience as well as to act.

To Simplify: Prior to having the children take individual roles to act out the story, tell the story and encourage the children to act out the story as an entire group.

To Extend: Have children practice and present other Readers' Theater plays.

Acting out the story, "The Three Pigs."

Meeting the Needs of Diverse Learners

Chris began life with abnormally small ear canals because of a condition known as Treacher-Collins Syndrome. Until the age of 4, his hearing loss was significant because of conductive defects in his middle and inner ear; a cleft palate (the roof of his mouth had failed to close during embryological development) also hampered speech. The resulting language deficits made communication difficult. Following corrective surgery and the insertion of tubes in the canals, his teacher reported that he seemed to be "making up for lost time" but that he would continue to need focused attention.

Estimates are that approximately 1 in 1,000 infants is born with a severe to profound hearing loss and that this incidence doubles during infancy and childhood. Hearing losses in young children affect both receptive and expressive development of spoken language, particularly when hearing loss occurs prior to 2 years of age, when the most rapid language acquisition is taking place (Batshaw, Pellegrino, & Roizen, 2007).

When children have weak foundations in early language and literacy development, they can easily fall behind other children across the curriculum and in general academic performance. We also know that boys are more inclined than are girls to fall into categories of learning disabilities and literacy deficits. They read and write, on average, 12 to 24 months later than girls do and are at a disadvantage later on when early deficits accumulate and lead to greater and greater difficulties (Sadowski, 2010).

Children who are learning English as a second language (ESL) can be especially vulnerable if not provided additional support by the classroom teacher and English-speaking peers. Vocabulary can be enhanced by talking about a picture that the child has drawn or an engaging photograph and labeling the details in English (and the child's home language, if possible). Singing songs, reciting and acting out nursery rhymes, and reading books in English that also appear in print in the child's home language (e.g., *Rainbow Fish*, by Marcus Pfister) are also helpful. Simple scripts can be given to children initially to communicate their wishes to peers and teachers (e.g., "Stop. I don't like that." "May I play, too?" "I'd like more snack." "I have to use the toilet."). The creative teacher will use any number of imaginative ways to build the ESL child's receptive vocabulary and encourage expression.

All children benefit by building a strong vocabulary in the early years, and this is something that teachers can promote in their many back-and-forth and one-on-one conversations they have with children. Teachers can also purposefully teach new vocabulary without overwhelming children by connecting new words with already familiar concepts. Let's listen in on a child whose skillful teacher is introducing the term *absorb*:

Teacher: What's happening with the water? What do you see?

Child: It's going into the paper.

Teacher: How is the water going into the paper?

Child: It's soaking it up.

Teacher: It is soaking it up! Another word we use to say this is absorb. The paper is absorbing the water and holding it the same way a sponge does. How much water do you think I could pour onto the paper and it would still be absorbed?

Child: Well, some of the water is already leaking out. So maybe not any more.

Teacher: Let's see what happens when we pour water on the plastic. Does it absorb it?

Child: No! It's sliding off.

Teacher: That's right. The plastic repels the water. It slides off just like you said. It can't be absorbed (Goodson and Layzer, 2009, p. 6).

Communicating with Families in the Language Domain

syntax Grammatical structure of a sentence.

Children begin the very first stages of language and literacy development inside the family. This is where they informally develop a rudimentary vocabulary and **syntax** (not always English, by the way), see how people use print, learn how to interpret or "read" others' non-verbal behavior, and develop a basic understanding of the give-and-take rules of conversation.

Remind parents and caregivers how important everyday conversation with their children is in expanding oral language skills. Parents who do not speak English should be encouraged to talk with and read to their children in their home language. These conversational exchanges provide the adult with opportunities to model active listening skills, vocabulary, and syntax, and they encourage children to express their thoughts and feelings verbally.

Simply "talking out loud" about what they are doing—a sort of private speech, which we all learn to keep internal—is valuable in adding to a child's verbal skills. For example, in getting dinner ready, Michael's mother says, "Hmmmm. We need to set the table for two more people tonight because Grandma and Grandpa are coming. That means two more plates, two more spoons, and two additional forks at each place. Also two more place mats, right? We'll need two more chairs, too. Let's go get them."

As children expand their literacy concepts and skills in your classroom and move toward a better understanding of what reading and writing are all about, family members can continue to be excellent partners in the ongoing process. Invite families to participate actively by labeling objects at home, visiting the local library and reading to children each evening, limiting television and video play in order to play games and expand conversation, and providing plenty of art and writing materials. A fun game is "Treasure Hunt": hiding simply written notes that lead to finding other notes and finally a book, a treat, or some other surprise. Another is one you probably played as a child: "I Spy." A parent or caregiver can tell a child, "I spy something that . . . ," providing clues that become more and more apparent until the child guesses the object.

Parents can be invited to participate in the classroom as guest readers, which is particularly effective for young dual language learners if books can be introduced in their home language before reading it in English (Gillanders & Castro, 2011). Families enjoy opportunities to come to school for special occasions where children can demonstrate literacy activities in which they're involved, such as Reader's Theater. Asking families to provide learning materials, as in the following newsletter, is also a good way to share educational objectives and information (Soderman, Gregory, & McCarty, 2005). See Figure 13.8. Remember that parents of children who are English language learners may not be able to understand spoken or written communications in English, but that translation is easily accessible on line.

NEWSLETTER/WEB READY COMMUNICATION

FIGURE 13.8 • Can You Help Us with Some Print Samples?

Environmental print is the print we see around us every day—the print on signs, labels, advertisements, and product packaging such as cereal boxes. It is usually the first print your child recognizes as literacy skills begin to emerge. Beginning readers find environmental print easy to "read" because of the shapes, colors, and pictures that surround the words. As you are out in your community, point out signs you frequently see (e.g., Toys R Us, Burger King, STOP) to your child and say, "I can read that. It says. . . .)" Later, say, "There's that sign again. What do you think it says?"

Have your child bring environmental print samples to school. Coupons, newspapers, and magazines are excellent sources. We will use the samples in a variety of ways. I will post them on a bulletin board for everyone to read and in our pretend play centers. We will use them for buddy reading, whole-group reading, and when we are writing. Please spend about a week doing this activity at home with your child. If you find more words during the year that we can add to our "I CAN READ" board, then please send them in at any time.

 # 13 Applying What You've Learned

Based on what you have learned about language development, try the following activities to broaden your skills.

1. **Observing Child Speak.** Visit an early childhood classroom. Observe and record at least 20 utterances by different children. Review the seven functions of language listed early in this chapter. How do the observed utterances of the children fit into these categories? Can you observe any differences in younger versus older children?

2. **How Rich Is It?** Visit an early childhood classroom. Given what you read about the importance of a communication-rich and print-rich classroom, how would you rank this classroom (1 = low, 10 = high)? Provide the rationale for your answer.

3. **Ask Your Colleagues.** Interview three classmates who intend to teach young children. Ask each one, "In what way would you address early writing with 4- and 5-year-olds? What would be one way you would begin to address early reading with this same age group?" How do their answers differ from one another or from your own ideas about how to do this? Would you evaluate each of their answers as developmentally inappropriate or appropriate?

4. **Scan the Bookstore.** Most early childhood classrooms have children who enter with limited English. Visit a bookstore that carries professional literature. What books can you find that contain useful strategies for supporting English language learners? What are two strategies you feel would be helpful in working with very young children?

5. **Literacy Partners.** You have three parents who approach you with questions about ways to get their 4-year-olds reading. How would you respond? What kinds of tips could you suggest for families to help them become effective partners in their children's literacy development?

References

Batshaw, M. L., Pellegrino, L., & Roizen, N. J. (2007). *Children with disabilities* (6th ed.). Baltimore: Paul H. Brookes Publishing Co.

Bennett-Armistead, V. S., Duke, N. K., & Moses, A. M. (2005). *Literacy and the youngest learner.* New York: Scholastic.

Gillanders, C., & Castro, D. C. (January 2011). Storybook reading for young dual language learners, *Young Children, 66*(1), pp. 91–94.

Goodson, B., & Layzer, C. (2009). *How to talk and listen: An oral language resource for early childhood caregivers.* National Institute for Literacy. Retrieved from EBSCOhost. (Booklet)

Halliday, M. A. K., & Webster, J. (2006). *Language of early childhood.* New York: Continuum.

Mulligan, S. A. (November, 2003). Assistive technology: Supporting the participation of children with disabilities. *Beyond the Journal,* 59, 1–2.

National Early Literacy Panel (NELP). (2009). Report of the National Early Literacy Panel. Jessup, MD: National Institute for Literacy and National Center for Family Literacy (NCFL).

Otto, B. (2009). *Language development in early childhood.* Upper Saddle River, NJ: Pearson.

Paynter, D. E., Bodrova, E., & Doty, J. K. (2005). For the love of words: Vocabulary instruction that works. San Francisco, CA: Jossey-Bass.

Sadowski, M. (July/August, 2010). Putting the "boy crisis" in context. Harvard Education Letter, *26*(4).

Seefeldt, C. (2005). *How to work with standards in the early childhood classroom.* New York: Teachers College Press.

Soderman, A. K., & Farrell, P. (2008). *Creating literacy-rich preschools and kindergartens.* Upper Saddle River: Pearson.

Soderman, A. K., Gregory, K. M., & McCarty, L. T. (2005). *Scaffolding emergent literacy: A child-centered approach for preschool through grade 5* (2nd ed.). Upper Saddle River: Pearson.

Wingert, P., & Kantrowitz, B. (1997, October 27). Why Andy couldn't read. Newsweek, *103*(17), 56–64.

14 The Physical Domain: Learning to Be Fit, Healthy, and Safe

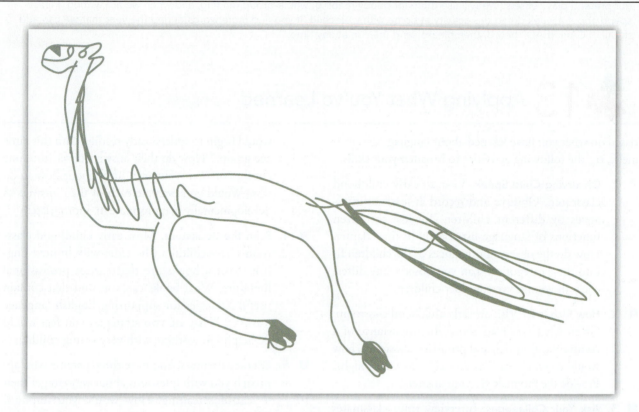

Patrick entered the "creation station" where art supplies were readily accessible to him. He selected a pencil and manila paper and began to draw with relaxed, firm strokes, gripping the pencil an inch above the point as he finished the face of his horse. His forearm swept easily across the page as he drew the body and tail; his fingers and wrist were relaxed as he added details and the mane.

At 4½ years old, Patrick's drawing is the result of maturity and much practice in the control of his arms and hands. Supporting children's success in motor control is part of the physical domain, as are all of the following behaviors:

- Hopping
- Catching a ball
- Printing a capital letter *A*
- Tying a bow
- Washing hands before eating
- Eating fruits and vegetables each day

The physical domain has two major components, both related to optimal health and well-being: (1) motor development, and (2) health, safety, and nutrition. Motor development includes all knowledge and skills related to body movement, control of the hands and feet, and the coordination of perception with action as well as active play. The health, safety, and nutrition component includes the information children need for long-term good health as well as the skills needed to use good health practices at home or at school.

Motor Skills and Motor Development

"Look at me, look at me!" Naomi, almost 4, calls out to everyone as she climbs to the top of the climber for the first time. Mrs. Shin watches and smiles as she tests herself against previous performance.

Trey, who just turned 3, falls as he runs as fast as he can across the grass. His teacher is not alarmed. She knows that such little falls are common at this age because children are growing so fast that their balance is not yet well developed.

Five-year-old Ruth holds the small ball that is suspended on a string from above in one hand and a Styrofoam mallet or ping-pong paddle with the other hand. Once the ball is still, she chops downward and hits the edge of the ball. Mrs. Shin moves over to show her again how to hold the mallet (or paddle) and swing across her body in order to strike the ball more squarely in the middle.

Naomi, Trey, and Ruth are each happily engaged in one of the fundamental motor skills—climbing, running, and striking. These children will progress sequentially through recognizable levels of skill development, becoming increasingly capable as they mature and learn through observation, instruction, and practice. As is true in other areas of development, physical proficiency varies from child to child as well as within the same child for different skills such as running and catching. For instance, a child who may run smoothly and fast may not yet be proficient in other fundamental motor skills such as catching a ball. These individual differences are influenced by gender, physical maturation, and opportunities for learning and practice. For example, in a study of Head Start children, about 43% were developing typically, 41% exhibited some physical delays, and 16% displayed substantial deficiencies in their motor skills (Woodard & Yun, 2001). Motor skill development also is time sensitive. If children do not acquire the basics by age 6 or 7, they might never do so during elementary school (Gallahue, 1993, Sanders, 2006). In addition, children who engage in vigorous motor activity between periods of focused learning appear to learn more than those who do

LEARNING OUTCOMES

After you read this chapter, you will be able to:

- Describe the elements of the physical domain.
- Describe key concepts, processes, and skills for children to learn in the physical domain.
- Identify strategies for teaching in the physical domain.
- Plan engaging experiences and activities in the physical domain.
- Explain ways to address the needs of the diverse learners in your classroom.
- Create opportunities for families to support learning in the physical domain.

Climbing is fun, scary, and brings feelings of competence.

Children practice skills such as striking at a ball over and over until they meet with success.

perception The integration of sensory input, cognitive processing, and muscular response, if it is called for. All perception is both sensory and cognitive, never just one or the other.

fundamental motor skills The basic movement from which more complex movements are made in sports, dance, and games (e.g., throwing, running).

locomotor movement Moving from one place to another (e.g., rolling, jumping, galloping).

not (Sattelmair & Ratey, 2009). Thus, early childhood programs have a critical role to play in helping children develop the physical skills they need to lead happy, healthy lives.

MOTOR SKILL BASICS

Children use locomotor movements when they go from one place to another, nonlocomotor movements when they stay in place and move parts of their bodies, and manipulative movements when they control objects with their hands or feet. You will be instrumental in enabling children to display increasingly mature motor skills such as the ones listed in Figure 14.1. These competencies enable children to stay fit, maintain an appropriate weight, engage in games and big body play, reduce the side effects of stress, and enhance their mental and physical health. As you read through the list of actions, think about when and where children might engage in these behaviors and consider some potential activities that you could introduce that would facilitate learning and practice.

PERCEPTUAL MOTOR SKILLS

Rafael lifted his arms up to catch the ball moments after the ball flew past him.

Sally bumped into the table as she moved through a narrow pathway on her way to the blocks.

Neither Jose nor Sam could find the small ball in the large crate filled with a variety of toys and materials.

Yoga poses require control and static balance.

FIGURE 14.1 Selected gross motor skills usually learned between 3 and 6 years of age

Locomotor Skills

Walk	Run	Leap*	Jump	Hop*
Roll	Start	Skip*	Slide	Creep
Climb	Stop	Dodge*	Gallop*	

Nonlocomotor Skills

Bend	Stretch	Twist	Bend	Curl
Whirl	Spin	Rock	Swing	Pull
Lift	Sway	Turn	Hang*	Push

Manipulative Skills (Projecting and Receiving Objects)

Throw	Catch*	Strike*	Bounce	Roll
Dribble*	Trap	Hug	Volley*	Kick

*These skills generally appear later in the early childhood period.

During the early childhood years, children are improving their coordination of perceptual processes (sight, hearing, scent, taste, and touch) with movement. They use all of their capacities as they explore, handle objects, and engage in ordinary tasks. As you can see, Rafael has not yet learned to estimate the speed of the ball or how to move into the right position to catch it. Sally still makes errors in figuring out where she is in relation to the furniture when she is in a hurry. Jose and Sam have difficulty in finding one specific object in a jumble of many different objects. These challenges are typical of children ages 3 through 6. With time and practice, perceptual motor skills—movements that lead to academic or cognitive outcomes (Payne & Isaacs, 2011)—improve gradually throughout childhood and adolescence. Six aspects of perceptual motor development are of particular importance during early childhood: balance, spatial awareness, figure-ground perception, temporal awareness, and body and directional awareness. These are described in Figure 14.2.

This pose strengthens the core as well as stretches.

FIGURE 14.2 Perceptual motor skills in practice

Skill: Definition	Younger Children	Older Children
Balance. Static balance is the ability to maintain a posture while holding still.	Tree pose (yoga) or stand on one foot.	Warrior pose (yoga) or stand with right arm and left leg extended far forward, knees bent, holding still.
Dynamic balance is the ability to remain in a posture while moving.	Stand on one foot while moving the other foot backward and forward.	Walking forward, backward, sideways, and so on, on a balance beam.
Spatial awareness. The understanding of body location in relation to other body parts and objects.	Completion of a simple obstacle course without touching other people or bumping into equipment.	Location of personal space with adult guidance (space where arms and legs extend away from body without touching others). Stopping to avoid collision.
	Basic vocabulary about space, such as *near*, *there*, and *close*.	Extended spatial vocabulary such as *through*, *between*, and *behind*.
Figure-ground perception. Determination of what is in the foreground and background.	Noticing objects that are on a placemat or surrounded by space.	Locating hidden objects in a picture.
	Recognition of name spoken in a moderately noisy place.	Selective listening, and ignoring distractions, such as identifying an instrument in a recording.
Temporal awareness. The estimation of speed, timing, and development of rhythm.	Clapping, marching, tapping to a rhythm.	More complex rhythm patterns and the beginning of intercepting a ball.
	Limited vocabulary about time, such as *5 minutes*, *now*, and *after snack*.	More, but limited, vocabulary such as *yesterday*, *tomorrow*, and *week*.
Body awareness. Names and functions of body parts.	Basic vocabulary such as *hands*, *feet*, *knee*, and *belly*.	Expanded vocabulary such as *hips*, *pelvis*, *shin*, and *shoulder*.
Roles or movements that can be created with the body.	*Copy*, *lead/follow*, and *meet*.	Following verbal directions with demonstrations for a variety of movements. Emerging understanding of *left* and *right*.
Directional awareness. Combination of concepts denoting direction and where the body is now or where it will be.	Movement of own body to be *side-by-side*, *on/off*, or *up/down*.	Emerging understanding of the letters and figures of 3, m, E, and w, where meaning is altered by direction.

nonlocomotor movement
Staying in place while moving the body core or extremities (e.g., twisting, bending).

manipulative movement
Controlled moving of an object with hands or feet (e.g., throwing or kicking a ball or threading a bead).

perceptual motor skills Movements that lead to academic or cognitive outcomes (eye-hand coordination, figure-ground discrimination).

fine motor skills Use of the hands to move objects precisely.

targeting Putting one object in another or precisely on another (e.g., to hit a target).

Practice in perceptual motor learning comes about through the hands-on activities children experience in everyday life—eating with a spoon, putting on their shoes, moving around the room, putting together a puzzle. As a teacher, you enhance children's skills by providing equipment and materials that require these various skills and by bringing perceptual motor concepts to children's attention, such as when you point out the colors or contours of a puzzle piece. ("See, this piece has a little bit of pink on it." Or, "Look for a piece with a curved side.")

FINE MOTOR SKILLS

Tien Yien, who just turned 3, rotates the doorknob to enter the classroom, unzips his coat before hanging it on the hook, and eats independently with a spoon. However, he approaches an adult and asks for help to unfasten his jeans, does not zip up his coat, and is inconsistent in using a three-point grasp when he draws or writes.

Maddie, in kindergarten, manages her own clothing, including tying her shoes. She shows good control of her marker and makes correctly spaced upper- and lower-case letters. She enjoys copying numerals that she finds on signs around the room and demonstrates control when cutting and pasting. Overall she is showing increasing precision and control of her hands. See Figure 14.3.

Fine motor skills require maturation, instruction, and practice to achieve competence. Children practice in everyday situations and also within planned activities to do the following:

FIGURE 14.3 Maddie is learning to write the numerals she sees around her

- *General.* Open doors, pick up small objects, build with small blocks
- Targeting. Complete puzzles, string beads, lace, place small objects precisely, sew, pick out letters on a keyboard
- *Cut and paste.* Grasp paper and scissors correctly, increasing control of pasting, gluing, and cutting
- *Self-help.* Fasten and unfasten clothing, eat and drink independently, take care of materials, spill infrequently
- *Graphic tools.* Use writing implements with increasing control, draw recognizable letters and numerals, draw geometric and realistic shapes
- *Using tools.* Use tools while engaging in a variety of activities (scissors, tweezers, fork, spoon, knife, keyboard)

All of these skills begin as unrefined global movements that gradually become more precise. Take a moment to consider how Tien Yien will eventually perfect his writing skills, moving from a fisted grip to one in which he will be able to hold a marker or pencil with more specific finger placement. This is illustrated in Figure 14.4.

Children use all of their motor competencies together to produce more complex and varied movements over time. Their mastery of these movements will vary from one to another and within the same skill set. For example, Tien Yien is likely to use a strong or firm grip on a pencil as he makes curved and straight lines as part of a drawing.

He might wobble and is likely to move his marker slowly with several stops and starts as he copies a letter shape. On the other hand, Tien Yien can stamp his feet fast rhythmically to music, accelerate or decelerate, and hold himself in place as requested. Such unevenness in skill development is to be expected.

MOVEMENT CONCEPTS

As children strive to perfect their motor skills, they build meanings and learn the vocabulary of movement from adults and other children. For example, Howie, age 4, calls out, "Look how far I can jump!" as he jumps, swinging his arms high overhead. Miranda, about the same age, listens intently and follows directions when her teacher says, "Place

Children learn movement concepts as adults provide demonstration and instruction individually or in groups.

FIGURE 14.4 Fine motor progression for writing skills

Tien Yien, age 3, grasps the marker in a pincer grip and moves it with his wrist, elbow, and shoulder.

Writing one's own name is a milestone celebrated by children and adults alike. Preschoolers and kindergarten-aged children want to write their names even though printing letters can be challenging and fatiguing for them. With practice, by age 7, most young children write more fluently and easily. In general, children's writing progresses in the following ways:

- Fist grip, thumb away from point
- Fist grip, thumb toward point
- Hand moves closer to point; movement shifts from shoulder to elbow, to fingers
- Tripod grip with noticeable wrist movement; little finger movement
- Mature tripod grip with implement resting on middle finger; rapid finger movement
- Refinement of movement; less stress and fatigue

Tien Yien's teacher provides many opportunities for him to handle writing implements of many kinds. She also offers coaching (showing him how to grip the marker or showing him how to relax his grip and shake his hands to relax his fingers if his grip is too tight) and encouragement.

FIGURE 14.5 Selected movement concepts

Effort	Pathways	Time	Percussive/vibrate	Space
Strong	Straight	Accelerate	Stamp	High (between shoulders and head)
Firm	Curved	Fast	Pound	Medium (waist)
Light	Zigzag	Decelerate	Punch	Low (below the knees)
Fine	Twisted	Slow	Shiver	
		Sudden	Wobble	
		Sustained	Shake	
			Flutter	
			Swing	
			Shudder	
			Tremble	

Stops	Direction	Spatial Relations	Flow	
Freeze	Forward/backward	Over/under	Free (outward from the body)	
Pause	Diagonal/sideways	In/out	Bound (close to the body)	
Hold	Up/down	Between/among	Smooth (continuous)	
Grip	Lift/lower	In front/behind	Jerky (starts and stops)	
Brake	Rise/fall	Above/below		
Pull up	Reach/collapse	Through/around		
Rest		Near/far		
		Meet/part		
		Expand/contract		

the red cube behind the cup." David watches Howie and Miranda, listens, and learns. A selected listing of movement concepts related to motor development is offered in Figure 14.5.

TRY IT YOURSELF

Develop an exercise in which you step in place in a variety of ways. Use Figure 14.5 as a resource for developing your ideas. Consider effort, time, space, direction, flow, pathways, percussive, stops, and spatial relations to guide your movements. These examples will help you get started.

Effort (light)	Tap toe straight down
Percussive	Stamp feet
Spatial relations	Feet together then feet apart (in and out)

For each stepping action, repeat the motion two to four times. Add music to maintain rhythm. Try this again, thinking of actions that can be done with the arms. How many ideas did you have for moving your body? Was this fun to do? Might children enjoy such an activity?

BIG BODY PLAY

Mrs. Rice scans the playground. Heidi is doing a step/hop, leading with her right foot most of the time (attempt at skipping), swinging her arms high above her head as her feet leave the ground and singing to herself. Sanjay and Nick are laughing as they roll over one another down a low hill, hurry back up the hill, wrestle to the ground, and roll down again. Rahul, Michael, and Douglas appear to be chasing Mark but before they catch him, he raises his hand and they all turn around and run in the opposite direction. The rest of the group are playing with wheeled vehicles or in the sandbox, so Mrs. Rice moves physically closer to Sanjay and Nick without turning her back on the runners, providing the close supervision needed by children engaged in vigorous physical activity.

The children have relaxed, happy faces; are willing to participate; and are even willing to return to the same play style or modify their behavior so that they can extend this boisterous play. For these reasons, Mrs. Rice remains comfortable with their play and provides the close supervision necessary for their continued success and safety. Mrs. Rice will quickly intervene if she sees aggression (biting, hitting with fists, angry facial expressions). She understands that, in the long run, vigorous play is more likely to lead to negotiation and cooperation than to fighting. Other benefits of active play are:

Children enjoy vigorous running and may simply run in a group or chase one another.

- Self-empowerment as children learn to control their bodies
- Fitness and physical health
- Negotiating skills and cooperation
- Understanding of fairness and reciprocity
- Standing up for oneself
- Strong relationship to cognitive development and attention in other parts of the program (Carlson, 2011).

All of the motor skills contribute to the physical and mental health of children. Much of the practice needed is acquired during active play, though children also need deliberate instruction in specific skills. In addition, children have much to learn to make healthy choices. A comprehensive health curriculum provides information that enables children to make good decisions and to better understand their roles in the family and community.

Health, Safety, and Nutrition

Children learn about health, safety, and nutrition through daily events and routines as well as through formal instruction. To begin, consider how Mrs. Huff teaches Brian, aged 3½, during his first week in the childcare center. She does the following regularly for all new children:

- Demonstrates hand washing and reminds him to do so at the beginning and end of the day, before and after meals, after outdoor play and using the bathroom
- Guides him in brushing his teeth
- Demonstrates or assists as needed in putting on or removing outdoor clothing

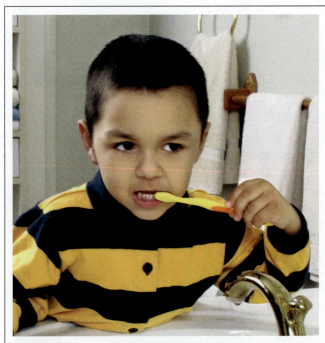

Brushing teeth after every meal is a good health practice and part of programs that serve meals.

- Tells him when and where it is safe to run or engage in vigorous activity
- Cues him to have at least three limbs on the climber when he climbs
- Provides drinking water outdoors and reminds him to drink
- Shows him how to use a helmet when riding a tricycle
- Encourages him to try new foods, chew slowly, and stop eating when he is full
- Provides for relaxation and rest during the schedule
- Monitors toileting and provides instruction if needed (wiping, flushing, washing)
- Incorporates fitness exercises and stretching during the day

Mrs. Huff also plans intentional activities on health and safety topics and thematic units to expand children's understandings. Children are very interested in their bodies, how they grow, keeping safe, and relating to other members of the community. The following list shows eight areas of a comprehensive health curriculum, with sample topics:

- *Safety and first aid.* Fire and water safety, school rules, transportation safety, injury prevention, personal safety, strategies to use when lost
- *Nutrition.* Identification of foods and nonfoods, food sources, body using food, culture and food, healthy food choices, healthy snacks
- *Consumer health and safety.* Health helpers, health products and their functions, aids for visual or hearing impairment, when to tell an adult, vehicle safety, playground safety
- *Community health.* Emergencies, fire and police, immunizations, recycling and conservation, pollution
- *Growth and development.* Senses, body parts, body functions, living and nonliving, abilities of people who are differently abled, functions of eyes and ears
- *Substance use and abuse.* Definition of drugs, contrast with medicine, identifying alcohol and cigarettes as drugs
- *Personal health practices.* Protective equipment; care of teeth, skin, and hair; care in handling body waste; sleep and rest; seat belt use; eye and ear protection; exercise
- *Disease prevention and control.* Prevention of the spread of germs, how and when to get adult help when an adult family member is really sick (911), food choices and good health

Curricular Goals—Physical Domain

STANDARDS FOR MOTOR DEVELOPMENT AND FITNESS

The following goals are consistent with the health education content standard (National Health Education Standards, 2009). The National Association for Sport and Physical Education (NASPE, 2013) has recommended the following minimum standards to maintain fitness in young children:

- Have children participate in 60 minutes of structured, health-related fitness and movement skills daily
- Have children engage in 60 minutes of unstructured physical activity
- Focus on fundamental motor skills and movements listed in Figure 14.1
- Have children use equipment indoors and out that meets safety standards
- Hire persons who are trained to supervise and facilitate children's movement skills

The standards related to mental health and social relationships are addressed in the affective and social domains.

PURPOSE

The purpose of the physical domain is for children to develop confidence and competence in the control and movement of their bodies and to develop the attitudes, knowledge, skills, and practices that lead to maintaining, respecting, and protecting their bodies.

GOALS

Movement

As children progress they will:

1. Gain confidence in using their bodies
2. Identify body parts by name and location
3. Develop spatial awareness (understanding of personal and general space, direction, and spatial relations)
4. Develop temporal awareness (awareness of speed, timing, duration, and rhythm)
5. Distinguish the foreground from the background visually and auditorily
6. Engage in a variety of activities that require static and dynamic balance
7. Engage in a variety of activities that require coordinated movements with large- and small-muscle systems
8. Sustain vigorous motor activity with time to develop endurance
9. Engage in activities to develop muscular strength in all parts of the body (climbing, hanging, etc.)
10. Engage in a variety of activities that require flexibility, agility, and stretching
11. Move the major joints of the arms, legs, and trunk through a full range of motion
12. Use their whole bodies in appropriate activities to strengthen muscles and muscle groups
13. Demonstrate appropriate form in the fundamental motor skills (jumping, hopping, running, skipping, leaping, galloping, sliding, and climbing)
14. Demonstrate appropriate form in the control of objects (throwing, catching, kicking, and striking)
15. Demonstrate competence in nonlocomotor skills (bending, twisting, pushing, pulling, swinging, etc.)
16. Demonstrate good posture while walking, sitting, or standing
17. Demonstrate, imitate, or create movement in response to selected rhythms
18. Demonstrate locomotor skills in time to rhythmic patterns using a variety of movement concepts

19. Demonstrate control of speed, direction, and force of movement through space
20. Coordinate wrist, hand, finger, finger–thumb, and eye–hand movements
21. Control the movement of their bodies in relation to objects
22. Use tools skillfully, including implements for eating, writing, dressing, and playing
23. Display a positive attitude toward their bodies; appreciate their competence and that of others

Health and Safety

As children progress they will:

24. Use practices that keep their bodies and their environments clean and sanitary
25. Acquire attitudes, knowledge, and skills about physical activity that predispose them to maintaining physically fit lifestyles
26. Acquire and practice sound nutritional habits and healthy eating behaviors
27. Demonstrate self-help skills such as nose blowing, hand washing, using the toilet independently, tooth brushing, grooming, and other behaviors that reduce health risks to themselves or others
28. Identify and practice appropriate safety procedures for school, playgrounds, home, and the neighborhood
29. Apply health, nutritional, and safety knowledge when making choices in daily life
30. Identify trusted adults and professionals who help promote health and safety (community health helpers)
31. Differentiate between situations when a health-related decision can be made individually or when assistance is needed
32. Demonstrate how to tell a trusted adult if threatened or harmed and how to ask for help (call 911)

SAMPLE CONTENT IN THE PHYSICAL DOMAIN

Teachers use a combination of on-the-spot teaching strategies and planned activities to address the goals listed in the previous section. Such lessons also incorporate relevant content associated with the physical domain. Some examples are presented in Figure 14.6.

Teaching Strategies for the Physical Domain

Here are some basic teaching strategies to use as you teach in the physical domain. Some of them help fit concepts into routines and daily activity; others are effective in direct instruction.

    1. *Keep children safe.* Incorporate health and safety information in regular activities involving movement such as how, when, and where to climb, run, or chase. Check for hazards (which can cause injury and must be avoided) indoors and out daily. Anticipate potential risks (which involve the possibility of suffering harm or loss and can be managed through planning and supervision) when using tools (knives or scissors) or materials (building with blocks over the head) and plan supervision accordingly. Make modifications for children with special needs.

hazard Something that can cause injury and thus must be avoided.

risk Something that has the potential for causing harm but can be managed by supervision or planning.

FIGURE 14.6 Sample content for the physical domain

Task/Area of Competence	Sample Content for Children to Learn
Fundamental motor skills	1. A hop is a jump on one foot. (Define also by demonstration.) 2. A skip is a fast combination of a hop and a step. (Define also by demonstration.)
Perceptual motor skills	1. Looking forward helps to maintain balance when moving. 2. Pathways may be forward/backward, curved, straight, and zigzagged. 3. The placement of lines and circles in letters makes a difference in the letter name (e.g., *p, d, q, b*).
Fine motor skills	1. To cut, push a little with the thumb and pull a little with the fingers on the scissors. 2. To string a bead, hold the bead in one hand, the string in the other, and push the string through the hole in the center. 3. To pour, hold a cup in one hand and the pitcher in the other, bring them together, and tip the pitcher up.
Movement concepts	1. A *freeze* is when all movement stops immediately. 2. *Personal space* is as far as a person can reach in any direction without touching someone else. 3. People and objects move in many different directions.
Safety	1. Children are safer when only one is at the top of the slide at a time. 2. It is safest to cross the street at a corner. 3. It is safest to stay on the sidewalk, away from moving cars.
Nutrition	1. Children who eat foods of many colors are usually eating a healthy diet. 2. People learn to like new foods by tasting them several times. 3. Family members have a variety of ways to fix healthy food.
Consumer health	1. A doctor specializes in healing bodies that are sick or injured. 2. A nurse monitors sick people, gives medicine, and sometimes draws blood. 3. Glasses are tools people wear to help them see; hearing aids help them hear.
Community health	1. It is not safe for anyone to play with fire; fire can hurt people, animals, and property. 2. A firefighter puts out fires with water and special equipment. 3. Fire gives off light, is very hot, and burns things.
Growth and development	1. Every person has a body that belongs only to him or her. 2. Each body part has a name. 3. The skin is a waterproof covering that protects the body; skin holds the other body parts together and inside the body.
Substance use and abuse	1. Cigarettes and other tobacco products are drugs. 2. Smoking cigarettes makes the lungs dark and may cause illnesses. 3. Medicines are given to sick children by parents, nurses, or others with special permission of parents.
Personal health practices	1. Bicycle riders are safest when they wear bike helmets. 2. Riding in a child restraint seat, safety harness, or booster seat keeps children safer while in vehicles. 3. Brushing teeth after eating helps prevent cavities.
Disease prevention and control	1. Colds are less likely to spread if you turn your head into your elbow when you sneeze. 2. Germs are removed from hands when hands are washed for 20 seconds or sanitized. 3. People are less likely to catch colds or the flu when they have lots of fresh air.

2. *Demonstrate all movement skills.* Young children learn best by imitating the motions of someone else (an adult or another child). Keep in mind that 3- to 6-year-olds are just in the process of acquiring skills and their imitations will not be exact. For example, running with arms and legs moving in opposition and the arms close to the body usually occurs between the ages of 4 and 5. The process should be as follows:

1. Show the child the action
2. Encourage the child to approximate your movement
3. Demonstrate first in silence, then add verbal descriptions, then put them together
4. Provide many opportunities for practice
5. Repeat this sequence over and over

Demonstrate good health habits yourself (e.g., brush your teeth after meals, make wise food choices while eating with children, and participate in physical exercise). Children notice and follow your example. Enjoy yourself; show enthusiasm.

3. *Provide suggestions and strategies to support the child's learning.* Observe what children do or fail to do in a particular task; then think of ways to make it easier for them to succeed (Sanders, 2002). For example, suggest that a child hold the paper horizontally when cutting with scissors; put masking tape on a marker or a paintbrush where the child should grip it; place a silhouette of feet on the floor where a child should stand when striking at a ball hung from the ceiling.

4. *Give oral cues, presented one at a time, to help the child attain greater control or efficiency* (Sanders, 2002, 2006). Break down the movement into its component parts to help develop the oral cues. Combine oral cues with pointing or demonstration. Some examples are shown in Figure 14.7.

5. *Provide encouragement and feedback.* Compare new performance with previous level of performance. *"Look how far you jumped today. This is your biggest jump!"* or *"You cut the curved lines so smoothly,"* or *"You found the Princess Memory game on a very crowded shelf in that cupboard."* Celebrate success. Avoid comparison and competition among the children.

6. *Emphasize qualitative movement over quantitative outcomes.* Form is important. Good posture, the position of the paper, and the grip on the writing implement

---

FIGURE 14.7 **Examples of oral cues**

Locomotor	Galloping	Keep the same foot in front when you run.
		Swing your arms up high and hard.
Manipulative	Catching	Watch the object.
		Get your hands in position to catch.
		Reach for the object.
Figure-ground	Placing puzzle pieces	Look at the picture of the puzzle before taking it apart.
		Slide your finger along the edge of the piece.
		Find a similar edge.
Spatial relations	Printing letters	Start at the top (left) corner.
		Place each letter in order (of the model name card).

are critical for good penmanship. Similarly, the orientation of the body, the step on the foot opposite the throwing arm, the rotation of the body, and follow-through are extremely important for long-term success in throwing. Skills established in early childhood tend to last, and speed, strength, and endurance improve as children mature. Using good form also prevents injury.

7. *Use accurate vocabulary in context.* Teach definitions of movement concepts such as *stamp* or *freeze* as well as directional vocabulary such as *diagonally* or *up/down* by demonstration. Incorporate vocabulary related to spatial and time awareness into other domain activities as opportunities arise. Point to body parts such as *hip, shoulder,* or *pelvis* as you say the word in the context of an activity. Label genitals with correct terminology: *penis* and *testicles* for males, *labia* and *vulva* for females. Mrs. Sola paraphrased George's comment about Billy's "balls" with "You noticed that Billy has testicles just like you. All boys do."

Be aware of word choice in health education, such as when discussing healthier choices, and avoid using terms like "bad" food when the food is safe but not necessarily the best choice. Use accurate, precise vocabulary in discussing all health topics informally as well as in preplanned activities.

Teach the meaning of the word *freeze* in the first week of school and practice it. Use "*Freeze!*" in situations where children should stop suddenly for safety or for gaining self-control. Combine the word with a nonverbal signal so that children know what to do when they cannot hear you.

8. *Provide sufficient time, space, and supervision for big body play* (Carlson, 2011).

- Schedule longer outdoor play and physical activity periods (30 minutes or more) and encourage children to reach moderate-to-vigorous levels: *Miss Neuder called out to her group of unengaged children, "Run, run as fast as you can. You can't catch me, I'm the Gingerbread Man," as she ran across an open grassy space. Later she asked, "Now who wants to be the Gingerbread Man?" The play continued with children taking the lead.*

- Supervise rough-and-tumble play constantly and other vigorous play nearly constantly. Avoid distractions and chatting with adults on playgrounds. Insufficient supervision is the major factor in a range of childhood injuries (Morrongiello, 2005).

- Help children create rules for rough-and-tumble play. These rules might include when and where the play can occur; how to communicate about stopping rough-and-tumble play; and identifying any kinds of play that are prohibited.

- Scan the environment and remove hazards. Clear pathways to avoid tripping. Eliminate sharp or pointed objects or corners. Eliminate loose or rusty parts, protruding nails, or flaking paint.

- Check fall zones and provide pads, sand, or pea gravel when surfaces are elevated.

- Set up the indoor and outdoor environments with age-appropriate equipment and furnishings that are in good condition and that meet safety standards.

- Support children's turn-taking skills and communication skills. Children who are rejected by others often have difficulties with these.
  - Help a less-skilled child to read a nonverbal cue: "*John is laughing and trying to tag you to join the play. That is not hitting.*"
  - Coach children on movement effort or strength: "*Ashir, try tagging gently when it is your turn, like this—see how gentle that feels. Tagging too hard can hurt.*"
  - Help a child to reflect on the meaning of what she sees: "*Elizabeth, see Maggie's face is really red and she is breathing hard. I think she needs a moment to rest.*"

TECH TIP

Physical Domain

Using a digital camera, camcorder, or other device, video a child performing a skill (running, catching a ball, using a writing implement, or brushing teeth). These should be short, 1 to 3 minutes. Review the video with the child, pointing out what the child did correctly. Make suggestions for improvement. After opportunities for coaching and practice, repeat this sequence. Compare the less-skilled and more-skilled clips with the child.

rough-and-tumble play
Movement play where children run, hop, fall, chase, wrestle, or kick while laughing or showing pleasant expression. May include play fighting.

- Explain and model sharing: "*All of you want to jump over this board. Harry, you will jump just after Melissa.*"

9. *Incorporate periods of physical activity throughout the day as a part of the routine.* **Exercise** is planned, structured, and involves repetitive movement. It comes in three types: flexibility (stretching to reach or bend), aerobic (moving arms and legs repetitively), and strength (developing the power to lift or move objects) (Campos, 2011). Activities will vary by intensity: light, moderate, and vigorous. Use light-to-moderate exercise in classrooms and more vigorous forms in gyms or outdoors. Here are some suggestions:

> **exercise** Planned, structured, repetitive movement.

- Engage in light exercises of the arms, shoulders, and hands before engaging in a fine motor activity such as coloring or writing.
- Act out a familiar story.
- Develop routines to music that you use as a part of group time. Use slower, sustained music and flexibility exercises or moderately paced music and aerobic exercises at different times of the day. The music should cue the type of exercise.
- Plan many centers where children engage in large-motor activity such as building with big blocks, pushing trucks, and climbing on an indoor climber.
- Do basic stretches before going outdoors.

10. *Use mealtimes and snack times to teach nutrition and proper eating habits.* Encourage children to eat slowly and chew thoroughly. Ask children to try a "no-thank-you helping" (about a teaspoon full) of unfamiliar foods. Expose children to familiar foods prepared by different ethnic groups (e.g., vegetable soup). Help children to understand that families may make different but healthy food choices. For example, children of Japanese heritage may have soup for breakfast instead of cereal or tortillas and beans. Incorporate nutritional information into conversation at mealtimes.

11. *Use straightforward "do it" signals to deliver health and safety reminders.* A few examples:

- Get a drink of water as you go indoors. Your body needs water after active play.
- Throw your tissue in the trash. No one else will be exposed to your germs.
- Wash your hands before you leave the bathroom. Clean hands don't spread illnesses.
- Cover your mouth with your elbow when you cough. Coughs spray germs in the air.

After the "do it" signal is given, pause and provide reasons and explanations.

Remember to wash your hands.

12. *Demonstrate respect for the family circumstances and cultures of the children.* Food choices are related to the culture of origin. For example, if you discuss breakfast, be very accepting of parental choices that are nutritious but dissimilar to your own, such as fish flakes and rice, dark bread with cream cheese and smoked fish, oatmeal, or scrambled eggs and toast. Work with adult family members on topics related to health, growth and development, and personal health habits to avoid undermining parental teaching and still support children's ideas of health and safety.

13. *Keep in mind some of the following tips that minimize risk and discomfort in vigorous activity.* Help children to attain fitness and enjoy exercise. Some specific suggestions are shown in Figure 14.8.

FIGURE 14.8 Tips for adult-directed exercises

- Warm up and cool down with stretching exercises.
- Remind children to tighten their abs (belly muscles) or their glutes (butt cheeks) when leaning.
- Use low-impact exercises (e.g., doing a jumping jack by stepping out and in instead of jumping feet apart and together) in adult-directed activities. Children rarely over-exert when playing independently, but will try to do what you ask.
- Modify exercises as needed for obese, health-impaired, or less-able children; keep everyone moving.
- Remind children to soften their knees (bend slightly) or the elbows during activities. Avoid locking joints.
- Avoid over-flexing of joints. Children are very flexible and sometimes allow joints to go too far. "Bend your knee (or thumb or elbow) the other way."
- Keep children hydrated. Remind younger children who are unreliable in reporting thirst to drink before, during, and after vigorous activity.
- Build in "resting" segments. For example, if you are moving one leg several times, shift to the other. Also shift between body segments such as the core of the body, arms, and legs. Achieve the total desired repetitions by returning after the movement of other body parts and doing the routine again.
- Limit the number of repetitions of an exercise to avoid stress on knees and elbows.

FIGURE 14.9 Peter's story

Five-year-old Peter displays symptoms of asthma: lack of appetite, fatigue, dark circles under his eyes, and low level of activity. His parents sought medical care several times when his wheezing became severe; he had shortness of breath and difficulty in talking. These frightening asthma attacks appear to be triggered by vigorous exercise and sometimes cold air. Mr. Aroche reviewed the Action Plan for Peter with his parents when he entered the program, and together they discussed how Peter's needs would be met.

- All adults, including substitute teachers, will be alerted to Peter's needs, read the Action Plan, and know where the emergency inhaler is stored. (An Action Plan documents the conditions when parents are to be notified, emergency inhaler administered, and when 911 should be called.)
- Mr. Aroche will monitor Peter carefully during physical activity, listening for wheezing or other breathing difficulties, though Peter will go outside with other children in his group.

- Peter will return indoors if symptoms appear. He will also be offered a place to rest and/or calm down as needed.
- Peter will receive the same instruction as other children, but the speed, repetition, and difficulty of exercises will be reduced for him as needed. For example, just moving the legs instead of both arms and legs in a dance activity would be appropriate. Increasing the frequency of short rest periods is also appropriate.
- Mr. Aroche will explain to other children, "Peter sometimes has difficulty breathing," if an asthma attack does occur.
- Mr. Aroche will close windows when pollen counts are high or when air pollution is a particular problem in the area, as these also might trigger an asthma attack.
- Peter's parents will keep him on maintenance medication and notify Mr. Aroche of any changes in the Action Plan.
- Peter has agreed to tell Mr. Aroche, or any other teacher, if he feels that an attack is coming on. (People often feel a tightening in the chest and other internal symptoms before external ones are noticed.)

Meeting the Needs of Diverse Learners

The teaching strategies just described apply to all children. However, sometimes adjustments must be made in the level of performance expected if children have disabling or health conditions that might be affected by an activity. The particular strategies used will vary based on specific circumstances, but planning in advance is always advantageous. See Figure 14.9 to see how Mr. Aroche planned to adjust activities to suit the needs of Peter, who has asthma.

You probably noticed in Figure 14.9 that Peter, his family, and his teacher contribute to the planning for Peter's success during his kindergarten year. What strategies from this or other domains might be useful in helping Peter to increase his physical competence and confidence?

Typical Materials to Support Learning in the Physical Domain

You have seen playgrounds for young children with climbers, swings, and a variety of surfaces. The materials suggested here are more varied and movable. Many materials are available for health education, depending on the topic. A sample is available in Figure 14.10.

FIGURE 14.10 Materials in the physical domain

Movement Curriculum (Large Motor)

Balance beams	Balance boards	Balls
Beanbags	Carpet squares	Traffic cones
Plastic bats	Foam bowling pins	Foam hockey sticks
Jump ropes	Mats	Records, CDs, or iPod
Scarves	Scoops (to help with catching)	Target board

Movement Curriculum (Fine Motor)

Pegs and peg boards	Small and large beads with strings	Small blocks or Legos®
Puzzles	Markers, chalk, crayons	Scissors
Computer keyboard	Paint and glue brushes	Games with small pieces

Health Curriculum

Posters of health workers	Cars, traffic signs	Fresh fruits and vegetables (cooking activities)
Doctor kit	Big blocks & unit blocks	Picture books on health & safety topics
Toothbrush and toothpaste	Model of mouth/teeth	Pictures of differently-abled
Hats/costumes of police and firefighters; emergency vehicles	Pretend play set up: Dolls, dishes, housekeeping furniture, dress-up clothes	Pretend play (Dental office) mirror, flashlight, chair, bib, cups for water, an x-ray of a mouth, plastic gloves, and popsicle sticks for tools.

Books

Rathmann, P. (2005). *Officer Buckle and Gloria*. New York: G. P. Putnam's Sons. (Safety)

Swanson, S. M. (2008). *The house in the night*. Boston: Houghton Mifflin. (Relaxation, sleep)

Lin, G. (1999). *The ugly vegetables*. Watertown, MA: Charlesbridge Publishing. (Food)

Cuyler, M. (2001). *Stop, drop, roll*. New York: Simon & Schuster Books for Young Readers. (Fire safety)

Jacobs, P. D., & Swender, J. (2010). *Firedrill*. New York: Henry Holt. (Fire safety)

Verdick, E. (2006). *Germs are not for sharing (Ages 4–7)*. Minneapolis: Free Spirit Publishing. (Disease control)

Garabedian, H. (2008). *Itsy bitsy yoga for toddlers and preschoolers*. Philadelphia: DaCapo Press (Perseus Group). (Yoga illustrations for adults and children)

Websites

The following is a list of websites you may use as a resource when planning activities in the physical domain.

- win.niddk.nih.gov
- presidentschallenge.org
- kidshealth.org
- kidshealth.org
- www.healthykidshealthyfuture.org

Planned Activities in the Physical Domain

In addition to using the teaching strategies and the materials suggested in this chapter, you will create planned activities to support the physical domain. Here are some activity ideas to get you started. Some are examples of how to teach children motor skills and some focus on content related to health or safety. The goal numbers referred to in each activity correspond to the numbered goals listed earlier in this chapter.

Exploratory Play Activity: Exploring Pounding

Ages 3–6

Goal 8: Engage in a variety of activities that require coordinated movements with large- and small-muscle systems.

Content: A hammer is a hand tool used for pounding or striking another object.
Strike: to deliver a blow.
Greater force is achieved by holding the handle of the hammer farther from the head.
Greater control is achieved by holding the handle of the hammer near the head.

Materials:
All children:

Two pairs of safety goggles

Work bench or tree stump

At least two clamps to hold a piece of wood in place

Soft wood such as pine in planks that can be held in place

Less Experienced Children:

Rubber mallet

Empty egg cartons

Golf tees

Tacks

Large head short nails

Container to hold materials

More Experienced Children:

Lightweight carpenter's hammer (real one)

Soft wood scraps

Big head short nails, big head medium nails, small head nails

Bottle caps or small pieces of cardboard

Container to hold materials

Procedure:
1. Put on your own safety goggles and give a pair to each child. Ask onlookers to wear goggles too.
2. Lay the materials out. Invite a child who shows interest to pound on the stump or piece of wood and see the result.
3. Add items to strike, such as a tack or nail, after children can hit the wood (or egg cartons, etc.) several times in a row.
4. Supervise closely. Name materials. Use behavior reflections to reinforce content (e.g., "You held the hammer near the head and could hit the [nail, golf tee, tack]"). Incorporate terms in conversation as child plays.

Safety Tips: Keep track of golf tees, nails, and so on. Avoid clutter on the table. Limit the number of children to one or two pounding at once.

To Simplify: Demonstrate holding a golf tee and pounding with a toy hammer or hold the child's hand that is grasping the hammer and hit it with him or her.

To Extend: Provide bottle caps, cardboard, or thin wood scraps for a child to nail to a piece of wood.

Guided Discovery Activity: Dental Office Pretend Play

Ages 3–6

Goal 25: Learn practices that keep their bodies and their environments clean and sanitary.

Content: Teeth are the hard, white, bonelike protrusions through the gums.
A dentist is trained to help people maintain, repair, or clean teeth.
A dentist uses many instruments and tools to examine, clean, and repair teeth, such as lights, mouth mirror, probe, chisels, excavators, x-ray machines, and so on. Dental hygienists clean teeth.

Materials:
Dental mirrors
Flashlight*
Chair*
Bib*
Cups for water*
An x-ray of a mouth
Plastic gloves*
Popsicle sticks for tools*
Sterilizing solution for cleaning mirrors and container
Sanitizing wipes
Waste basket*
Phone
Appointment book
Small pad of paper for bills
Pencil or marker
Posters of dentists at work and related picture books
For teacher: digital camera, notepad, and pen.

Procedure:
1. Set up a dentist's office. Start with the * materials. Add remaining materials over time. Maintain the setup for several days.

2. Encourage exploration of the materials; explain uses. Provide content as it fits into conversation or in short statements. "The dental mirrors allow the dentist to see the top teeth" or "The popsicle stick can be used like a dentist uses a probe to poke a tooth to see if there is a cavity."

3. If needed, ask who has been to the dentist or had his or her teeth cleaned and invite that child to be the (dentist or hygienist) first. Take a role if needed.

4. Suggest that the pretend dentist tell the patient what will happen.

5. Explain that things put in the mouth (mirrors or popsicle sticks) must be discarded or cleaned and not used for another child. Maintain high standards of sanitation throughout.

6. Once play is underway, step away. Photograph action. (Children incorporate knowledge into pretend play, but also use imagination.) Later, take dictation in the language center as children tell what they were doing/feeling/thinking in the photographs.

7. Note misinformation to be corrected in other centers or during group time. Facilitate play as needed.

To Simplify: Suggest that children who have never been to a dental office and have no idea of what occurs there play the office person in the beginning. Explore the materials. Later, as basic information is learned, they can take on the role of dentist or patient. Note: Exploration of teeth with dental mirrors and x-rays will have high interest.

To Extend: For skilled, well-informed players, set up the environment and stand back, except for #5 above. During conversation, ask what else dentists do and what they need to do it. Inquire why specific tools are needed.

Problem Solving Activity: Creative Movement

Ages 3–6

Goal 13: Use their whole bodies in appropriate activities to strengthen muscles and muscle groups.

Content: A *freeze* is when all movement stops immediately.

Personal space is as far as a person can reach in any direction without touching someone else.

People and objects move in many different directions.

Materials: iPod, computer, or CD with music at a moderate tempo

Procedure:

1. Carry out the activity in a large open space.

2. Ask children to move away from each other so that no one can touch anyone else. Tell them this is their personal space and that they should stay in it. Demonstrate and assist if necessary. Ask them to sit.

3. Discuss what it means to freeze. Demonstrate as needed. Briefly ask them to wave at you until you say "Freeze!" and then stop right away.

4. Review parts of the body by name, including shoulder, neck, elbow, and so on.

5. Explain that they will move to the music, but they cannot get any higher than the top of where their heads are now. They must remain low. Ask them to listen to the music and you will give a few suggestions as to what body part to move. Then they can figure out new ways to move themselves.

6. Begin music. Ask children to move their necks, elbows, or bellies while sitting. Then call "Freeze!" and stop the music. Point out interesting postures or movements. Tell them that they can find another way to move and start the music. Repeat.

Suggested challenges for children to try: Find a way to move with your back on the floor; head lower than your shoulder; looking up with hands and feet on the floor, and so on. Throughout, use behavior reflections to describe children moving rhythmically, interesting positions, and care in avoiding others.

To Simplify: Focus on simple movements such as tapping, clapping, nodding, and flapping arms.

To Extend: Use variations of effort, spatial relations, flow, direction, and time to vary children's movements.

Use music with various tempos.

Ask children to think up additional ways to move and to lead the group briefly.

Discussion Activity: Identifying Writing Implements

Ages 3–6

Goal 23: Use tools skillfully, including implements for eating, writing, dressing, and playing.

Content: Any object that can make a mark on a surface is a potential writing implement.

Some writing implements require more effort and skill to use than do others.

Choosing the best implement for writing on a specific surface is necessary for skill or success.

Mark: a noticeable impression or symbol, or writing.

Materials: Large paper, marker, and easel

A covered basket with writing implements, a stick, a soft stone, and a paintbrush in it, as well as some objects that are not writing implements

Paper, sand surface, sidewalk, and/or chalkboard for drawing on

Procedure:

1. Gather a group near the easel and pose the problem. Record every answer, repeating the suggestions. Use paraphrase reflections. Sample questions:

   • If you were outdoors and wanted to leave a message on paper for a friend and did not have a pencil, what could you use? On the sidewalk? In sand?

- What tools could you use to make marks on paper?
- Which tools are easiest to use? Work better? Why do you think so?

2. Review the whole list; incorporating content. Follow up by suggesting that children choose a writing implement to use to draw or write on an appropriate surface for that implement.

Note: Children may identify electronic devices. That is OK.

To Simplify: Let children open the basket and pick out a writing implement. If a child pulls out a toy cup, ask how that would work. Use paraphrase reflections.

To Extend: Discuss which implements are easier to use, and which leave more enduring impressions (marks). For example, a mark in the sand, a mark made using water and a stick, and a mark made with chalk have varying endurances.

Demonstration Activity: Skipping

Ages 3–6

Goal 14: Demonstrate appropriate form in the fundamental motor skills such as jumping, hopping, running, skipping, leaping, galloping, sliding, and climbing.

Content: A skip is a hop-stride-hop pattern.
Swinging the arms upward while moving into the hop propels you up and forward.

Materials: None

Procedure: Demonstrate skipping at normal speed. Then demonstrate the hop-step pattern slowly. Repeat with verbal cues. Ask children to join in as they can. Coach children as needed: "First you do it on one leg, then the other"; "Swing your arms up when you hop"; "Step, hop, step, hop." Celebrate successes and approximations.

To Simplify: Hop in place first on one foot, then the other.

To Extend: Encourage children to skip a longer distance or faster.
Suggest that skilled skippers demonstrate for beginners.

Direct Instruction Activity: Hopscotch

Ages 3–6

What skills do younger children need to have to play hopscotch, too?

Goal 3: Develop spatial awareness.

Content: Games have rules.
Rules allow everyone to know how to play fairly.
Hop: to jump on one foot (demonstration).
Jump: leap, both feet off the ground (demonstration).
Forward: toward what is ahead or in front (demonstration).
Space: a limited extent where objects and events occur.

Materials: Chalk

Round flat stones no bigger than a fifty-cent piece

Procedure:

1. Draw the simplest hopscotch pattern on a hard surface and invite children to play. Explain that hopscotch has rules:

   a. One player jumps at a time to the space where the stone lands, then picks up the stone. Encourage another child to help the player who has to pick up the stone while standing on one foot.

   b. Hop where there is one space and jump where there are two spaces side by side. Avoid landing on the lines.

   c. Go forward to where the stone lands.

   d. End turn after picking up the stone.

2. Demonstrate the throwing, hopping, and jumping pattern, and picking up the stone.

3. Invite each child in turn to try to throw the stone and move through the pattern. Clap when children are successful. Remind children as necessary when to jump or hop. Remind children about turn taking. Coach as needed: "Bend your knees when you land."

4. Provide materials on successive days, monitoring performance, and provide repeat instructions as needed. Children move to independent practice quickly.

To Simplify: Focus on the skills of jumping, hopping, and throwing. Show children how to bend their knees for a better takeoff in jumping and to swing their arms forward and upward to maximize momentum.

To Extend: Extend the length of the hopscotch pattern (requires more endurance). Introduce the rule that your turn ends if you land on a line or throw the stone so it does not land in the pattern (requires greater motor control).

Communicating with Families

Learning motor skills, developing healthy habits, and incorporating safe practices are shared responsibilities of families and programs. Many topics of mutual concern come up that are related to this domain. Information you might provide families about outdoor play is in Figure 14.11.

NEWSLETTER/WEB READY COMMUNICATION

FIGURE 14.11 • Ready to Play Outdoors

Young children love to engage in energetic, vigorous play outdoors. When encouraged to do so, they run, jump, climb, throw, catch, and kick balls. For good health and fitness, children should have at least 60 minutes of vigorous play every day. Children need opportunities to play physically on weekends and after school. In addition, other important parts of the curriculum are taught outdoors, including science and nature study, safety, and social skills.

Teachers take children outdoors every day that it is safe to do so. This means that children stay inside only when the weather is severe with wind, sleet, snow, or rain or when they might be at risk for frostbite. However, children play outdoors during seasonally cold or damp conditions and need to come to school dressed accordingly with the appropriate boots, mittens, coats, hats and scarves. If you think that your child is not well enough to play outside, then perhaps he or she is not well enough to be in a group of children. Your child is more likely to catch cold by being indoors with others who have colds than by playing outdoors.

Children are also kept indoors under extremely hot conditions. Teachers adjust schedules to take children out when the sun is less intense, to avoid the hottest part of the day. You can help by dressing your child in loosely fitted, light-colored clothing and by applying sunscreen to all areas of the skin that would be exposed to the sun. Don't forget the feet, hands, ears, and nose, as these often get burned if not protected. [Sunscreen is available at the entrance of the classroom if you have forgotten to do this at home. (optional inclusion)] Thank you so much for preparing your child to participate in the full range of activities at school during outdoor play.

14 Applying What You've Learned

Based on what you have learned about the physical domain, try the following activities to broaden your skills.

■ 1. **Knowing the Physical Domain.** Describe the elements of the physical domain and why this domain is important.

■ 2. **Physical Domain Concepts and Skills.** Identify three key skills and/or three key concepts that are important for young children to learn in each of the following areas of the physical domain: large motor, fine motor, perceptual motor, health, safety, nutrition, and fitness.

■ 3. **Locating Risks and Hazards.** Visit an early childhood classroom and observe children in session. A hazard involves danger and can cause injury, and therefore must be avoided. List any hazards that you see occurring during activities (electric cords to trip over or hanging down in a cooking activity; children mouthing small manipulatives; tripping hazards in pathways). A risk involves the possibility of suffering harm or loss and can be managed through planning and supervision. List the potential risks you see in the room or playground and note how teachers are managing the risk (teachers enforce that there be no running indoors; mats are under climbers and other elevated spaces). What steps would you take to minimize risk in this environment? What skills or concepts would you teach children to participate in their own safe-keeping in this environment?

■ 4. **Adapting an Exercise Routine for Children.** Observe or participate in a session of *low-impact* exercises. Record the actions involved. Develop a simple routine of movements for a group of children, based on your experience. (Young children rarely repeat exercises to the point of stressing their bodies unless they have others urging them

to do so. Low-impact exercises have lower risk of injury to those who participate.)

■ 5. **Write a Plan.** Write a short-form activity plan for stepping in place to use with children as a routine before starting group time. Select music that is moderate in tempo. Include the list of moves you developed in the Try It Yourself feature of this chapter.

■ 6. **Adapting to Meet Diverse Needs.** You have just learned that a new child will be entering your classroom next week who is hearing impaired.

• What information do you need to ensure safety on the playground?

• Identify at least three sources of information regarding the needs of a child with hearing impairment as applied to the physical domain.

• With a classmate, brainstorm a list of strategies that you might find useful in adapting your supervision of outdoor play.

■ 7. **Notifying Parents of Exposure to Lice.** Family members and teachers work together to maintain sanitary and healthy conditions where children are gathered in groups. One parent has reported that lice were discovered in her child's hair. Discuss the following:

• What is your responsibility?

• Where can you locate information about lice and how lice are transmitted from one person to another?

• Talk with the head teacher in your practicum or volunteer placement about how parents are notified of these kinds of health issues. Find an example of a notice used by a program and identify three things to include in a notice you might write yourself.

References

American Association for Health Education. (2009). *Health education standards.* Retrieved from www.aahperd.org/aahe/publications/HE-Standtard.cfm

Campos, D. (2011). *Jump start health! Practical ideas to promote wellness in kids of all ages.* New York: Teachers College Press.

Carlson, F. M. (2011). *Big body play.* Washington, D.C.: National Association for the Education of Young Children.

Gallahue, D. (1993). Motor development and movement skill acquisition in early childhood education. In B. Spodek (Ed.), *Handbook of research on the education of young children* (pp. 24–41). New York: Macmillan.

Morrongiello, B. A. (2005). Caregiver supervision and child-injury risk: I. Issues in defining and measuring supervision; II. Findings and direction for future research. *Journal of Pediatric Psychology, 30*(7), 536–552.

National Association for Sport and Physical Education. (2013). *Active start: A statement of physical activity guidelines for children from birth to age 5* (2nd ed.). Retrieved from www.aahperd.org/naspe/standards/national-Guidelines/ActiveStart.cfm

National Health Education Standards. Retrieved March 18, 2009, from http://www.aahperd.org/aahe/pdf_files/standards.pdf

Payne, V. G., & Isaacs, L. D. (2011). *Human motor development: A lifespan approach* (8th ed.). New York: McGraw-Hill.

Sanders, S. W. (2002). *Active for life: Developmentally appropriate movement programs for young children.* Washington, D.C.: National Association for the Education of Young Children.

Sanders, S. W. (2006). Physical education in kindergarten. In D. F. Gullo (Ed.), *Teaching and learning in the kindergarten year.* Washington, D.C.: National Association for the Education of Young Children.

Sattelmair, J., & Ratey, J. J. (2009). Physically active play and cognition: An academic matter. *American Journal of Play, 1*(3), 365–374.

Woodard, R. J., & Yun, J. (2001). The performance of fundamental gross motor skills by children enrolled in Head Start. *Early Child Development and Care, 169*, 57–67.

15 The Social Domain: Reaching Out to Others

"I Spy" sculpture created by Nora, Kashi, Madelyn, and Terry.

Ms. Iversen observed that 4-year-old Nora seemed unsure of how to interact with other children and spent a lot of time on her own in the classroom. One of Nora's favorite solo activities was looking at the *I Spy* books in the Library Corner.

Building on Nora's interest in *I Spy*, her teacher planned a small-group activity to get Nora more involved with her peers. She invited Nora, Kashi, Madelyn, and Terry to work together to create a three-dimensional "I Spy" sculpture out of small objects from the scrap box. All week, Ms. Iversen encouraged the children to work on the project and coached them in the give-and-take of building something together. By Friday, their "I Spy"

sculpture included more than 50 small objects tucked among cardboard and wood scrap shapes. Signs created by the children directed observers to "spy" certain objects hidden within the sculpture, such as a picture of Nora, a fish, and an elephant. As the teacher took a photo to record the children's work, Nora announced excitedly, "I helped! Terry and Kashi and Madelyn did too. It was a big job!"

ora discovered it was fun working with others. It felt good to be part of a group and to accomplish a big job she could not have managed by herself. Besides increasing Nora's confidence in interacting with peers, making the "I Spy" sculpture gave all four children chances to practice important skills: sharing materials, helping one another, suggesting ideas, compromising, and reaching agreements. All of these fall within the social domain.

Whereas the affective domain focuses on "me," the social domain focuses on "we." Being social implies interaction—interaction with peers and adults, interaction with friends and strangers, and interaction with community and culture. That is what this chapter is about.

Let's begin by examining where the social domain fits in the overall scheme of things.

LEARNING OUTCOMES

After you read this chapter, you will be able to:

- Describe the importance of the social domain.
- Describe key social concepts, processes, and skills for children to learn.
- Identify strategies for teaching in the social domain.
- Plan engaging experiences and activities in the social domain.
- Explain ways to address the needs of diverse learners in your classroom.
- Create opportunities for families to support social learning.

The Importance of the Social Domain

Developing personal relationships, participating effectively as a member of a group, and appreciating similarities and differences among people are typical social lessons children must learn. The more adept children are in learning such things, the better off they become (Ladd, 2008). For instance, children who have well-developed social skills tend to be accepted rather than rejected or neglected by other children and adults. Peers invite them to be friends or ask them to join them in their play. Socially skilled children are viewed as friendly, cooperative, and responsible, making them congenial companions and more popular than their less-skilled peers.

Research tells us that when children are socially accomplished, they gain a sense of well-being that translates into greater happiness and confidence at home and at school. Social success is also associated with academic achievement. It is easier for children to learn to read, explore scientific phenomena, or carry out music or art activities when they are not preoccupied with how to control their impulses or unsure about how to get along with others. This is why socially skilled children have more positive attitudes toward school, fewer absences,

Socially skilled children have an easier time making friends.

FIGURE 15.1 The benefits of being socially skilled

Socially skilled children describe themselves as mostly:

- Happy
- Confident
- Satisfied
- Successful

Other people see socially skilled children as:

- Friendly
- Cooperative

- Responsible
- Fun to be with
- Helpful

In school, socially skilled children:

- Have fewer absences
- Develop positive attitudes toward school
- Exhibit greater classroom participation
- Tend to have higher grades than do children lacking social skills

---

more classroom participation, and higher grades than do children whose social skills are poor (Hyson, 2008; Epstein, 2009). These benefits are summarized in Figure 15.1.

Obviously, every way you look at it—from a personal, interpersonal, or academic perspective—social development makes a great deal of difference in young children's lives. Luckily, children's play provides the perfect context for social learning.

PLAY AND SOCIAL LEARNING

The most natural way young children explore the social domain is through play. Play gives children opportunities to interact, to make friends, and to try out behaviors associated with social skills, socialization, social responsibility, and social studies (Smith & Pellegrini, 2008). For instance, within play children try out invitations ("Let's play in the blocks."), decide what they will play ("Let's build an airport."), determine how to play ("You make the tower, okay? I'll make the runway."), negotiate play rules ("This runway is only for big planes. Little planes go over there."), and take on new roles ("We're the pilots, right? Sam, do you wanna be up in the tower?"). To make the most of these opportunities requires adult support.

The teacher has provided opportunity, time, and materials to enable these boys to become deeply absorbed in their block play.

ADULT SUPPORT

Effective early childhood educators consciously facilitate play as an integral part of classroom life. They do this by creating *opportunities* for children to play each day, by making sure children have *enough time* to become absorbed in play, and by providing a wide array of *safe, hands-on materials* for children to use. As children play, *teachers observe* them carefully, looking to see who plays with whom, what play themes emerge, what kinds of play children pursue, and the level of skillfulness individual children exhibit. Finally, *teachers actively guide* children's skill development as needed. These crucial supports are summarized in Figure 15.2.

Now, let's see how the social domain is organized.

FIGURE 15.2 Play basics

What Children Need to Play

- Opportunity
- Time
- Materials
- Adult awareness and support

Key Dimensions of the Social Domain

The ultimate focus of the social domain is for children to become more socially competent. Social competence involves everything children need to know to navigate the social environment effectively and appropriately. This includes:

1. *Social skills:* Interacting with others.
2. *Socialization:* Adopting the values, beliefs, customs, and rules of society.
3. *Social responsibility:* Caring for one another and for the world in which we live.
4. *Social studies:* Developing the ability to contribute to the public good in a diverse and democratic society.

These four dimensions are depicted in Figure 15.3 and are characterized by distinctive, interrelated content.

As you can see, the social domain encompasses everything from getting along with others to learning to live within the whole of society. The best way to get started on such a big agenda is with social skills.

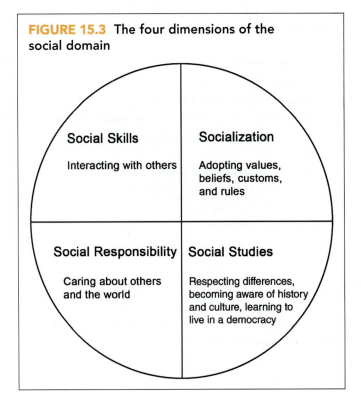

FIGURE 15.3 The four dimensions of the social domain

Social Skills
Interacting with others

Socialization
Adopting values, beliefs, customs, and rules

Social Responsibility
Caring about others and the world

Social Studies
Respecting differences, becoming aware of history and culture, learning to live in a democracy

social competence The ability to recognize, interpret, and behave effectively and appropriately in social situations.

SOCIAL SKILLS

Janet Fischer reads a book at group time about dinosaurs behaving badly when friends come to play. The children laugh out loud as the dinosaurs mope and pout when they don't get their way, when they hide all their toys and refuse to share, and when they actually throw all their toys in the air! The teacher asks, "Is that what you do when you play with your friends?" The answer from the children is a resounding, "NO!"

Most preschoolers recognize that moping and pouting, refusing to share toys, and throwing them in the air are not actions that make you a desirable playmate. That's the humor of the story. Yet learning what to do instead does not come automatically to young children. They are novices at interacting with others and have an incomplete understanding of how to satisfy personal goals while also paying attention to other people's needs. Social competence takes a long time to achieve. It involves trial and error, practice, and paying attention to feedback from many different people in many situations. Sometimes the lessons are obvious and sometimes they require adult explanation. Sometimes children are successful in carrying out effective social behaviors and sometimes they

Children need many playful, pleasant opportunities to practice social skills.

> **FIGURE 15.4** Key social skills
>
> - Starting conversations
> - Inviting others to play
> - Responding to play invitations
> - Using a not-too-loud nor too-quiet speaking voice
> - Matching facial expressions, body movements, and words
> - Keeping a conversation going
> - Answering another child's questions
> - Expressing appreciation
> - Expressing affection
> - Recognizing other people's feelings and needs
>
> - Waiting and taking turns
> - Following game rules
> - Sharing materials
> - Offering to help or comfort
> - Listening to other people's ideas
> - Suggesting ideas
> - Making plans
> - Resolving conflicts without hitting, hurting, or retreating
> - Controlling angry outbursts
> - Acknowledging mistakes
> - Excusing others' mistakes

social skills Interacting with others.

miss the mark (Hyson, 2004). Consequently, children spend a lot of time developing basic social skills.

Typical examples are presented in Figure 15.4. What abilities might you add to this list?

HOW ADULTS ENHANCE CHILDREN'S SOCIAL SKILLS

Aubrey lines child-sized chairs up in two rows, three chairs on each side, with an aisle down the middle. A seventh chair is centered up front. She is so absorbed in getting the chairs just right that she does not notice Emma watching from the side. After a few minutes Aubrey says aloud, "The bus is ready to pull out."

She notices Emma and invites her to play. "Emma, let's go! The bus's ready. Here's your ticket, okay?"

Emma smiles, and moves over to the chairs. She asks, "Is this bus going to Lincoln or Montana? I think it's going to Montana."

"No, it's going to Lincoln," Aubrey says. "Now I'll be the driver. Hurry, we'll be late!"

"It's going to Montana," Emma insists.

At this point Aubrey says in her best driver voice (deep and low), "Now, take your seat! Click it or ticket!"

"Okay," Emma says, "but it's going to Montana."

"Yeah, but let's say it's going to Lincoln *and* Montana, all right?" suggests Aubrey. This seems to satisfy Emma, who sits down on a chair and begins to make motor sounds.

Review the social skills identified in Figure 15.4. Which of these do you see in Aubrey and Emma's play?

Perhaps you said:

- Inviting others to play
- Keeping a conversation going
- Sharing materials
- Listening to other people's ideas

- Suggesting ideas
- Resolving conflicts without hitting, hurting, or retreating

Based on this episode, we can see that Aubrey and Emma are highly skilled players taking advantage of the opportunity, time, and materials provided by their teacher to practice valuable social skills. If you were their teacher, you might use a behavior or paraphrase reflection to acknowledge their enjoyment of the interaction: "You're riding on your bus together." Or, "It's fun to ride with a friend." On the other hand, seeing that Aubrey and Emma are playing together cooperatively, you might write a short observational note but stay silent so as not to interrupt their play. Your strategies would change, however, if either child exhibited some problem relative to their play. Sample play problems include children being unsure of how to enter a group at play, children not knowing how to keep the play going, children squabbling over objects, or children using hurtful behaviors to assert their will. Social challenges like these provide teachable moments during which adults can intervene to help children learn more productive ways of interacting. Common play interventions involve modeling, expanding, coaching, and mediating children's play.

MODELING

Abigail stands at the edge of the pretend restaurant, unsure of how to enter the area in which three other children are playing. Her teacher takes her by the hand and together they sit down in the restaurant. The teacher says, "We're hungry. What is good to eat at this restaurant?" Jason says, "We have soup." The teacher says, "My friend and I would like some soup—okay with you, friend?" She looks and nods at Abigail. Abigail tells Jason, "I want soup." The teacher pretends to eat the "soup" she is served and encourages Abigail to do the same.

In this situation, Abigail's teacher used modeling to help Abigail become involved with the other children. The teacher's words and actions gave Abigail an example to imitate and facilitated her incorporation into the restaurant play.

Adults model many things for young players—how to *carry out a role* (eating soup), sample *verbal scripts* ("We're hungry"), *ways to enter and exit* the play (sitting at the table), as well as *how to use certain materials*—blocks, paint, puzzles, and so forth. In circumstances such as these, teachers avoid taking over the play or staying too long. Instead, they model one or two skills and then gracefully exit so the children can carry on independently.

EXPANDING PLAY

Sometimes players have difficulty keeping things going. When this happens, teachers may intervene briefly to help children expand their play in new directions. Typical expansion strategies include adding new props, introducing additional roles for children to consider, and asking open-ended questions or providing information to prompt fresh ideas (Dombro, Jablon, & Stetson, 2011). Michael O'Shea, a teacher in a mixed-age class, uses all of these techniques when the children's airport play in the block area is not holding their interest. He observes that besides making their planes take off and land, the children don't know what else to do. Michael enters the area and asks, "Hello. Where is the baggage claim at this airport? I just got off my plane and I need my suitcase to take home. Is there someone in charge of luggage?" Two children say, "Over here," and begin constructing a platform to hold suitcases. Michael suggests that children look around the classroom to see if there are materials they might add to their airport to make other things—one child announces they need

"Jeremy didn't like it when you took the red paint. He was still using it. Say, 'I want it next,' so he will know you want a turn."

tickets, and goes off to get materials to make some. The teacher's intervention reinvigorated the children's play by providing new information and helped them expand the scenario as well as their interactions with one another.

COACHING

Teachers employ several strategies to coach children through social situations. Two useful techniques are giving children information about how their actions affect others ("When you pushed Selena, she got upset.") as well as information about how others might perceive their behavior ("When you don't say hi, people think you don't want to play.").

Adults also demonstrate skills, encourage children to imitate their actions, and provide sample scripts for children to try. See how Mr. Todd uses coaching in this example to help James practice more effective social strategies with a classmate.

James, a 4-year-old in Mr. Todd's class, has developed a habit of being loud and demanding. The teacher notices that other children tend to avoid James or ignore him.

James and Robert are working at opposite ends of the play dough table.

James builds an animal using the dough and some plastic squiggles. In a loud insistent voice he demands, "Look at what I did."

No one responds.

James almost shouts, "Robert!! Look over here."

Robert glances up, but says nothing.

Mr. Todd moves over to James. He says quietly, "You want Robert to see. When you shout, you sound angry or mean. Kids don't want to play with someone who sounds mean. Talk to him in a softer voice like this (models quiet tone).

James tries again more quietly. "Robert, look."

Robert looks up briefly and says, "Uh-huh."

Mr. Todd says to James, "Tell him more. Say, 'I made this animal.' Robert might listen if you keep talking in a friendly way."

James says more quietly, "Look, Robert. This is a horse. See?"

Robert looks at James and then says, "Yeah. Here, I could turn this into a horse (holds up some play dough). I can add legs." He adds two pipe cleaners to the dough.

The two boys begin talking about their horses and what else they could make. Mr. Todd observes a moment then moves on. He checks back periodically to see if further support is needed.

Here the teacher coached James by giving him information about how people might react to his loud voice and harsh tone, demonstrating how to talk more quietly and offering sample scripts to help him practice better verbal skills. Although this one coaching episode will not necessarily turn things around for James, it has given him a chance to experience a more rewarding interaction with a peer using friendly language. It has also helped Robert see James in a new light. With practice and continued coaching, James is likely to improve his social skills and his standing with his peers.

MEDIATING

Because children are newcomers to the social scene, they sometimes get into conflicts over objects (children argue over who gets to use the steering wheel), rights (children argue over who gets to be first outside), and territory (the girls want the block area all to themselves) (Wheeler, 2004). Such conflicts are a normal part of learning to get along and provide opportunities for children to practice reasonable ways to resolve differences. Although it may seem easier just to tell children, "Stop fighting," or for you to take a disputed object away, such tactics deprive children of valuable learning opportunities. A more productive approach is to mediate the conflict.

Use children's disputes to teach them the basics of conflict resolution.

Becoming a Mediator   When teachers mediate children's disputes, they take on the non-evaluative role of tutor, not judge. In other words, adults remain neutral, guiding children toward mutually satisfying solutions. They avoid taking sides or trying to establish who is right and who is wrong. Their goal is for each child to come away with new skills and the satisfaction of working toward resolution. The mediation model presented in Figure 15.5 helps children move in this direction. When children progress through the mediation process, they have opportunities to observe problem solving firsthand.

FIGURE 15.5 Conflict mediation

Step in the Process	Your Role
1. Start mediation	Assume mediator role.
	Stop children's hurtful actions.
	Neutralize object or territory (hold the object or occupy the space yourself until a solution is reached).
2. Clarify each child's point of view	Ask each child in turn what he or she wants.
	Paraphrase.
	Remain neutral (don't agree with one child or the other).
3. Sum it up	Define the problem in mutual terms (*You both . . .*).
4. Generate alternatives	Solicit ideas from the children about what to do.
	Suggest some possibilities if children are stymied ("Sometimes when two people want the same thing they decide to share or take turns. What do you think?").
	Ask children to evaluate each alternative.
5. Agree on a solution	Summarize points of agreement.
	Identify the resolution when it happens.
6. Reinforce the problem-solving process	Praise children for working together.
7. Follow through	Help children carry out the agreement.

Here is an example of mediation in action.

The teacher looks up to see Lyle and Hank arguing. She approaches them.

Step 1 Start Mediation

Teacher: (Kneeling between two boys with an arm around each.) You look angry, Lyle, and Hank, you seem really upset. (The boys nod yes.) What's the problem?

Step 2 Clarify

Lyle: I want to be the dad. I said so first.

Hank: You're always the dad. I want to be big.

Lyle: I'm the biggest, so huh! You can't be the dad. You're too little.

Step 3 Sum Up

Teacher: So the problem is, Lyle, you want to be the dad, and Hank, you want to be the dad too. (Both boys shake their head yes.) What can you do to solve this problem?

Step 4 Generate Alternatives

Lyle: I could be the dad today, and then you can be the dad the next day.

Hank: Well, I could be the dad today.

Teacher: It sounds like you both want to be the dad today.

Lyle: We don't need two dads. Hank, you could be the ladder guy and wear the tool belt!

Hank: And the gloves?

Lyle: Ok, the gloves (both boys smile).

Step 5 Come to Agreement

Teacher: So, Lyle, you're going to be the dad, and Hank, you're going to be the ladder guy who wears the tool belt and the gloves.

Step 6 Reinforce

Teacher: You figured out how to solve your problem. That was hard work, but you did it!

Both boys nod yes and go off to the pretend play area.

Step 7 Follow Through

When the teacher checks on them later, the dad and the ladder guy have built a swamp boat and are giving rides to the other children (based on Epstein, 2009, p. 19).

In addition to mediating angry encounters, teachers plan social problem-solving activities that give children practice compromising, bargaining, and sharing. Gradually, children increase their conflict resolution strategies, conflicts become less frequent, and solutions are reached more quickly (Gartrell, 2006). All of these outcomes contribute to more peaceful classrooms.

SOCIALIZATION

Walk with the scissors. Don't run.

Put the blocks away at cleanup time.

Share the play dough.

These are typical rules you might have in your classroom. They are designed to keep children safe, protect property, and help children respect the rights of all. Although children begin following rules like these at home, they arrive at your program still with much to learn. Socialization involves teaching children how to adapt their behavior to

socialization Adopting the values, beliefs, customs, and rules of society.

the rules and customs of society. Understanding rules and being able to follow them takes time and practice. Also, children vary in the rates at which they acquire rule-related knowledge and skills. Regardless of the timetable, socialization focuses on children learning to act appropriately even when adults are not present—in other words, achieving self-regulation. Mostly teachers help children learn the rules of human interaction through ordinary encounters with peers and adults. Adults remind children of rules, give them reasons to follow the rules, redirect mistaken behavior, and reward appropriate actions. However, planned activities are useful too. Inviting children to help create rules, giving children practice following rules within games and routines, and helping children communicate their rules to others are further means for addressing socialization.

These children are practicing following rules—and having fun, too!

SOCIAL RESPONSIBILITY

Zachary and Scott work together putting the science materials away.

Lamont is upset when someone accidently steps on his sand town. Chloe rushes over to help him rebuild.

The kindergartners pick up litter on the playground.

These simple prosocial acts represent the very best of human behavior—cooperating, helping, comforting, taking care of one another, and taking care of the world in which we live. The opposite of aggression, kind and responsible actions like these constitute the social responsibility dimension of the social domain. As children become more socially responsible, they also develop a key social skill: empathy. Empathy is the ability to understand another person's feelings and experiencing a bit of that emotion oneself (Epstein, 2009). Children become more empathic as they learn to recognize the needs and feelings of others and then act in accordance with those needs.

prosocial Positive behaviors that are the opposite of aggression—acts of kindness such as helping, cooperating, encouraging, and comforting.

social responsibility Caring for one another and for the world in which we live.

DEVELOPING SOCIAL RESPONSIBILITY

The ultimate expression of social responsibility is taking some action with the intent of doing good for others. In such instances, people act without expecting any reward beyond personal satisfaction. For instance, Troy is exhibiting social responsibility when he helps Chris clean up the blocks not to get a sticker or praise from his teacher, but because it feels like the right thing to do. It takes more than simply reminding children to be kind to help them progress along the developmental path to social responsibility. For people to act in socially responsible ways, they must first recognize that help or cooperation is needed, then they must decide what to do, and finally, they must do it. Thus, there are three steps to demonstrating socially responsible behavior:

- Awareness
- Deciding
- Doing

Because of their immature thinking and lack of experience, children often need help in navigating these steps. They may get stuck at any phase. When this happens, children benefit when adults model prosocial behavior and provide explanations that fill the gap between what children know and can do on their own and what might best fit the situation. Consider the examples presented in Figure 15.6.

FIGURE 15.6 Phases of social responsibility and teacher support

Social Responsibility Phase	Necessary Developmental Abilities	Potential Challenges	Example	Translation	Possible Support Strategy
Awareness	Child must tune in to the other person. Child must accurately interpret the body language, actions, and words he sees and hears.	Child may be too focused on his or her own needs to recognize the needs of others. Child may not notice cues or may not interpret cues accurately.	Harry is struggling to carry an overflowing box of playground balls outside. He keeps readjusting the box on his thighs so he doesn't drop it. He approaches the classroom door to the playground, but his hands are too full to open it. Clare is standing nearby watching.	Clare is unaware that Harry's nonverbal behaviors are signals that he needs help.	Teacher points out Harry's need for help. "Clare, look at Harry. He is having a hard time carrying that big box. He needs our help."
Deciding	Child must figure out what the other person needs.	Child may not know what is needed. Child may misinterpret what is needed.	Edda is an active 3-year-old whose left leg is much shorter than her right leg. She is capable of moving around the classroom on her own, but Courtney often picks Edda up and bodily moves her from one spot to another. When the teacher asks Courtney what she is doing, she proudly says, "I'm helping!"	Courtney has decided to help, but does not understand what Edda needs.	Teacher says, "You want to help. Let's ask Edda if she needs you to pick her up." Or, "You want to help Edda. Edda likes to walk on her own. Let her do that. She does want a friend though. You could help by asking her to play in the sand with you."
Doing	Child must be able to do what is needed.	Child may not have the necessary skills.	Dalili is trying to build a tower out of cardboard boxes. She becomes upset when it falls down because the boxes at the base are unsteady. Anthony offers to tape the boxes together, but the tape is too flimsy and his fingers get stuck in it.	Anthony sees that Dalili needs help, he decides to help, and he has an idea of what to do. However, he needs coaching in how to carry out the task more effectively.	The teacher points out that Anthony has a good idea, but the tape is too thin. She offers some thicker tape as an alternative.

ENVIRONMENTAL AWARENESS

Just as children can learn to be kind and helpful toward people, they can also learn to help the planet on which we live. Thus, environmental awareness is another form of social responsibility. Environmental awareness begins with learning more about the natural world and then assuming some responsibility for taking care of it. Tending a classroom pet or watering plants are meaningful ways for children to begin. The three Rs of environmental responsibility—recycle, reduce, and reuse—can be incorporated into daily lessons and routines. Children could *recycle* greetings cards as collage materials, *reduce* waste by using paper on both sides for writing, and *reuse* food scraps by putting them into a compost pile. Something as simple as starting a classroom-recycling center for plastic and paper or planting and harvesting a salad garden can highlight environmental concepts as well. It is never too early to begin such lessons, especially when they are based on children's everyday experiences. It is from many small acts of social responsibility that children develop a connection to the world and feelings of responsibility and self-efficacy in taking care of our limited natural resources.

SOCIAL STUDIES

In what ways are people the same?

In what ways are people different?

What is in my community and how does a community work?

These questions capture the essence of social studies in early childhood education. Children explore them every day through personal experiences in their families, classrooms, and neighborhoods. Social studies concepts revolve around individual people and groups of people, time past and present, places and environments, civic practices, and human connections worldwide (National Council for the Social Studies [NCSS], 2012). We see these concepts in action when we observe the children in a Head Start classroom try foods representing different families and when they play two versions of a similar singing game, each with a different ethnic origin. Social studies concepts are addressed when children bring in pictures of themselves as babies and dictate stories about what they were like then and what they are like now. The same is true when the class takes a walk in the neighborhood, and afterwards some children use blocks to recreate the experience while others make a picture map that represents the buildings and other landmarks they observed near their school. Because young children's social understandings are rooted in human relationships and the environments in which people live, everything we have discussed in this chapter feeds into social studies knowledge. Two additional social studies themes to explore are human diversity and enacting democracy in the classroom.

HUMAN DIVERSITY

The United States is one of the most diverse countries in the world, and its population is becoming more varied each year (Shrestha & Heisler, 2011). To function effectively in society, children must learn to live harmoniously with people of different races, ages, genders, languages, appearances, cultures, socioeconomic backgrounds, family compositions, spiritual beliefs, and abilities. Children observe similarities and differences among people early. Before they are 3 years old, children notice people's physical features and begin to compare these with their own (Willis, 2009). Initially, they focus on visible traits such as those related to gender, race, language, and dress. Awareness of physical disabilities appears by ages 4 or 5 (Anti-Defamation League, 2011). By middle childhood, children become aware of more subtle attributes such

social studies Developing the ability to contribute to the public good in a diverse and democratic society.

as cultural customs, ideas, and beliefs. As is true for all facets of development, when it comes to diversity, children gradually progress from:

- *Simplistic thinking to more complex thinking.* For instance, children see attributes similar to their own as familiar and good and may feel fearful or suspicious of differences; with exposure and experience, children can enlarge their thinking to see similarities as well as differences as positive features of the human experience.
- *Egocentric thinking to other-oriented thinking.* For instance, a child may think "my mother has a job, so all mothers work"; eventually children recognize that there is more than one possibility: "My mother has a job, Sam's does not."
- *Mistaken thinking to more accurate thinking.* For instance, initially, children do not realize that gender is a stable attribute. Younger children may believe a child is a boy because she is wearing pants or has short hair; later, children recognize that gender is a permanent biological trait unaffected by clothing or hair style.

In concert with these developmental progressions, children also absorb messages about diversity from external sources, including adults, peers, objects in the environment, and the media. These messages influence their notions of whether certain attributes are desirable or not. Depending on what they see and hear, some children conclude that people unlike themselves are inferior and that differences are negative. Such beliefs lead to prejudice and intolerance. Other children come to see differences as positive factors that contribute to each person's uniqueness. These children form favorable feelings about people who are different from themselves. Such conclusions lead to acceptance and respect for others. Which mindset prevails is influenced by the messages you convey about similarities and differences in your classroom, by the teaching materials you use, and by the manner in which you respond to children's curiosity about people.

Valuing and Respecting Diversity *Teachers who value diversity* see differences among individuals and groups as normal and positive. They believe there is no one right way to be, to think, or to believe. *Teachers who respect diversity* treat all people as individuals and are not influenced by stereotypes. They recognize that individuals and groups share some characteristics (e.g., speak the same language or share the same ethnic heritage) but differ on others (e.g., have different abilities or like different things) (Epstein, 2009). In developmentally appropriate classrooms, valuing and respecting diversity is infused into all aspects of the program—in the materials the children use, the activities they experience, the words they hear, the people with whom they interact, and in how they are treated. This makes attention to diversity routine, not something reserved for isolated times of the year. When you enact this philosophy, you convey these messages to children:

- You are a valuable member of our classroom and our society.
- People have much in common.
- People are not alike in every way. Our differences make us unique and enrich our lives.
- We have much to learn from one another.

Creating Mirrors and Windows on Diversity Programs that celebrate diversity create inclusive physical environments that incorporate equipment and materials representing a wide range of human differences. The surroundings reflect the children, families, and communities in which children live. In other words, pictures on display, books, props, music, and other supplies and experiences serve as "mirrors" through which children see themselves and their families represented. These items affirm children's self-identities and give children chances to depict and explore relevant personal experiences throughout the day, both indoors and outside. Additional materials serve as "windows" into the community at large. They provide children with authentic opportunities to learn more about the society in which they live and to become acquainted with people, customs, and beliefs that are different from what is immediately familiar and accessible. See Figure 15.7 to consider this idea in relation to three young children who might be in your class.

Talking with Children about Diversity Children want to know why people are different from themselves, what it means to be different, and how the differences they observe relate to them (Gonzalez-Mena, 2010). In the process of exploring these

FIGURE 15.7 Creating mirrors and windows. What could you do to help these children see themselves in your classroom?

ideas, children sometimes make erroneous assumptions ("Brown skin is dirty") or express themselves through stereotypic or hurtful remarks and actions (a child laughs at another person's accent). Although such words and behaviors may make teachers uncomfortable, it is important to respond and to respond in a matter-of-fact way. Not responding tells children it is not acceptable to talk about differences or that their erroneous conclusions are correct. Responding harshly or simply telling children to hush conveys that noticing differences is wrong. None of these messages help children develop more factual concepts or empathic behaviors. What children need is accurate information delivered in a way that makes sense to them without instilling fear or shame. Here are some examples:

- Child points to a man in a wheel chair: "Is he sick? Is it catching?"
  Reply: "Sometimes people get hurt or have a disease so they can no longer stand or walk on their own. Whatever happened, it isn't something that you will catch from him."
- Child laughs at another child's accent: "She talks funny!"
  Reply: "People have different ways of talking. We talk the way our families talk. You sound like your family. Tereza sounds like hers."
- Child asks, "Why is she fat?"
  Reply: "People come in different sizes. It's okay to be different sizes."

In situations like these, teachers listen carefully to what children are saying and sometimes ask questions before answering, such as, "Tell me why you think. . . ." This gives them a chance to gauge what the child is really asking or what the child already knows. If adults get stumped, a good response is, "That's a good question! I'm going to think about that and get back to you," and then they do (Derman-Sparks, 2011). Most important, early childhood professionals do not let prejudicial remarks go by without intervening. They make clear to children that name-calling of any kind, whether it's about someone's ethnic background, skin color, gender, or physical appearance, is hurtful and wrong.

PRACTICING DEMOCRACY

Citizens in a democratic society need to develop certain skills if democracy is to continue (Seefeldt, Castle, & Falconer, 2014). Some of these are:

Participating in group discussions and decision making
Respecting people's right to speak
Helping to develop rules and following them
Identifying and resolving group problems
Paying attention to the needs of individuals and of the group

These abilities are fostered in early childhood programs through daily small- and whole-group discussions. Topics might range from introducing a new member to the group, to creating rules for the block area, to developing a group plan to make cleanup go more smoothly. Through such experiences, children gain practice in deliberating with others, offering suggestions, hearing other people's ideas, making group decisions, and following through on decisions made. Similarly, children might vote on their favorite snack, what to name the guinea pig, or what game to play outside. They may find themselves in the majority one day and in the minority on another. In every case, there are lessons to be learned about respect, consideration, and living with group decision making that might or might not mirror one's own favorite choice. This is democracy in action!

Curricular Goals—Social Domain

PURPOSE

The purpose of the social domain is for children to develop successful ways of interacting with others, internal behavior controls, and prosocial values.

GOALS

The following goals are based on content standards developed by the National Council for the Social Studies (2012) and state standards related to social development.

Social Skills

As children progress within the social domain, they will:

1. Develop social skills such as:
   - Initiating play
   - Joining a group at play
   - Making suggestions
   - Taking suggestions
   - Finding ways to deal with unpleasant social situations and the emotions associated with them
2. Show awareness of other people's viewpoints
3. Recognize others' emotions
4. Negotiate conflicts in peaceful ways by compromising, bargaining, and standing up for their own rights

Socialization

5. Conform to reasonable limits on behavior
6. Identify reasons for rules
7. Distinguish acceptable from unacceptable behavior in various social settings
8. Develop skills related to self-regulation (impulse control, resisting temptation, delaying gratification, carrying out positive actions)

Social Responsibility

9. Show awareness of and concern for the rights and well-being of others
10. Demonstrate skills associated with cooperation (working with others toward a common goal)
11. Demonstrate skills associated with helping (sharing information or materials, giving physical assistance, offering emotional support)
12. Care for the environments in which they live (including cleaning and taking care of their own things in the classroom)

Social Studies

13. For children to explore their own and others' human attributes and cultural practices
14. Demonstrate understanding and respect for people's similarities and differences
15. Learn how people live together in families, neighborhoods, and communities
16. Carry out democratic principles and practices (e.g., identify problems/issues within the group, deliberate openly, make group decisions, follow through on group decisions)

FIGURE 15.8 Sample social content

Developmental Task	Sample Content for Children to Learn
Social Skills	• Friends know each other's names. • People feel friendly toward people who take turns, share, listen to their ideas, like to do some of the same things, and let them do some things their way.
Socialization	• People make rules to keep things safe, to protect people's rights, and to safeguard property. • Groups of people agree on rules so they can live together safely and happily.
Social Responsibility	• Some ways to help include offering physical assistance, information, or materials. • Sometimes the best way to help is to let people do things on their own.
Social Studies	• Families sometimes do things the same way other families do; sometimes they do similar things their own way. • People live in communities with people who are like them in some ways and different in other ways.

Sample Social Content

As teachers interact with children within the social domain, they are constantly communicating social content. Some examples are presented in Figure 15.8.

Teaching Strategies for the Social Domain

1. *Help children learn one another's names.* Children feel most comfortable approaching and playing with children whose names they know. Use children's names frequently, especially in positive situations. Identify children who are playing near one another: "Martin, you and Becca are both playing with the magnets." Sing name songs and play name games all year long.

2. *Intervene if children experience play-problems they cannot resolve on their own.* Move closer to children experiencing problems but give them chances to work things out if possible. If play stagnates, if children's quarrels become overwhelming or potentially dangerous, or if a child needs help getting in or out of the play, step in briefly. Use modeling, elaborating, coaching, or mediating as necessary. Once things have improved, step out so children can resume their interactions independently.

3. *Enhance children's understanding of other people's emotions.*
   - *Label emotions children have in common* ("Saul, you're pleased we are having macaroni. Steve, you're pleased too").
   - *Describe children's differing reactions to similar situations* ("Saul, you're glad we're having tomatoes. Steve, you don't like tomatoes").
   - *Draw children's attention to the physical and contextual cues associated with people's emotions.* Begin by pointing out emotion-related behaviors ("Look at Ramone. He's got a big smile on his face. That means he liked it when

you shared the paint.'). Eventually, ask children to self-identify what another person might be feeling based on actions and words ("See Sandy. Look at her face. How do you think she's feeling?").

4. *Help children recognize how their behavior affects others.*

- *Point out the impact of one child's behavior on another* ("Sarah laughed when you told that funny story.").

- *Ask children how they feel about another child's actions* ("Did you like it when she took the brush?").

- *Invite children to talk about their emotions to one another* ("You can tell Lela you liked it when she shared her blocks with you.").

- *Ask children to assess how their actions might affect someone else* ("How do you think Gervaise feels right now? How can you tell?").

5. *Structure activities to promote social skills practice.* Provide group supplies rather than individual sets of materials to promote cooperation and sharing. Deliberately set out materials so that children must ask for, bargain, or trade to get what they want. Challenge children to carry out activities with a partner or in a small group that traditionally they do alone, such as paint a picture, finish a puzzle, build a bridge, or read a story.

6. *Point out socially responsible behavior as it happens.* Draw children's attention to their kind acts of helping, cooperating, encouraging, or comforting. When Theresa pats a sad Nathan on the back, point out that she is *comforting* him. When children remain quiet while a peer does her show-and-tell, say aloud that they are *helping* her to concentrate. When children take turns, mention that this is a way of *cooperating* with one another.

7. *Give children genuine opportunities to help, cooperate, and take care of the environment every day.* Encourage children to help you and to help each other by carrying materials, finding something lost, or offering information about how something works. Identify tasks that teams of children could do, such as getting out the trikes or setting up the lunch tables. Develop jobs for children to do to take care of their indoor and outdoor environments, such as tending plants, recycling scraps, and making sure the bird feeders are full.

When Eric helps Kyle with his project, the teacher says, "You found a way to help Kyle finish his design. That was a friendly thing to do."

8. *Walk children through the steps involved in socially responsible behavior.*

- Make children *aware* when someone needs assistance ("Janice is cleaning up the art area alone. That's a big job for one person. She needs help.").

- Point out situations in which people *decide* to be socially responsible ("Janice needs help cleaning up. I think we should help her.").

- Assist children in determining what *action* is most suitable ("We could pick up the extra paint brushes or hang up the smocks.").

- Encourage children to *evaluate results* ("Were there enough of you, or did you need more people to help?").

9. *Create classroom environments in which a wide range of human diversity is evident.* Integrate diversity-related materials and experiences into your daily routines.

Post artwork and photographs that represent the everyday lives of boys, girls, men, and women of all ages, abilities, and ethnic backgrounds. Begin with images that represent attributes found among people in the class; gradually expand to include others from the community. Make a special effort to find pictures that depict nonstereotypical jobs; families of varying compositions; and people of different ages, cultures, and abilities interacting with one another. Make available art supplies, block accessories, pretend-play clothing and props, music, games, computer programs, and books that encourage children to explore the diverse lives people lead. Offer snacks and other food experiences that represent cultural variety. Plan activities in which children create artifacts that depict their own characteristics that may be similar to or different from their classmates, such as lists of activities that boys as well as girls in the class like to do or self-portraits that depict skin color. Invite family members and community people from many backgrounds to visit and talk with children about their heritage and experiences. Carry out field trips that introduce children to the diversity of their community.

10. *Respond openly and honestly to children's observations and questions about diversity.*

- Invite children to explain their thinking aloud ("What makes you think only men can drive trucks?").
- Provide accurate information ("Some truck drivers are men. Some are women.").
- Point out examples that gently challenge children's mistaken ideas ("Here is a picture of a woman truck driver.").
- Use props that contradict stereotypes (Display photographs of women exhibiting physical strength and men performing home tasks such as caring for children).
- Challenge children's thinking by providing opportunities for them to experiment and investigate ("Donna thinks the brown color on my hands will wash off. Let's go to the sink and see if that happens.").

11. *Give children chances to practice democratic skills.* Plan activities in which children identify, generate solutions for, and carry out solutions addressing group problems. For instance:

- "How will we decide on a name for the guinea pig?"
- "Some children want to use the grassy space to run, and other children want to use the grassy space for playing with the balls. What should we do?"
- "The girls said, 'No boys in the block house?' Is that fair? What should we do?"

After a solution has been enacted, encourage children to evaluate it and adjust their strategies if necessary ("You decided to use the grassy area for running in the morning and for balls in the afternoon. How is that working?"). Introduce vocabulary associated with democratic principles: *fair, more, less,* and *majority rule.*

Materials for the Social Domain

Most materials can be adopted for social learning-related activities. However, some items are especially well-suited to this domain. A few examples are listed in Figure 15.9.

FIGURE 15.9 **Materials that support social learning**

✔ Simple table games children can use to practice working together and following simple rules.

✔ Pretend-play materials children can use to enact family living—expand traditional materials with items that represent various cultures, dolls of both genders and different skin colors, and so on.

✔ Chart paper and markers children can use to post signs describing child-made agreements.

✔ Containers in which supplies such as scissors, crayons, or tabletop building materials can be placed centrally in an area or on a table, prompting children to share the materials versus each child having a separate set for himself or herself.

✔ Large, hollow blocks and a big enough supply of unit blocks to prompt children to build together.

✔ Jump ropes, balls, hoops, parachute (materials that invite children to play in pairs or larger groups).

✔ Assorted picture books (fiction and nonfiction) depicting characters behaving prosocially, stories

involving rules and agreements, and stories illustrating different family customs and traditions. Here are examples:

- Beaumont, K. (2002). *Being friends.* New York: Dial Books for Young Readers.
- Bunnett, R. (2003). *Friends at work and play.* Bellingham, WA: Our Kids Press.
- Wagner, R. (2011). *A friend for Einstein, the smallest stallion.* New York: Hyperion Books.
- Meiners, C. J. (2004). *Join in and play.* Minneapolis: Free Spirit Publishing.
- Aliki. (1990). *Manners.* Hong Kong: South China Printing Company.
- Dooley, N. (1991). *Everybody cooks rice.* Minneapolis, MN: Lerner Publishing Group.
- Holman, S. L. (2002). *We all have a heritage.* Davis, CA: Culture CO-OP.

Planned Activities in the Social Domain

Besides using teaching strategies typically associated with the social domain, you can develop small-group and large-group activities to enhance children's social competence. Here are six activity ideas that illustrate social lessons. The goal numbers referred to in each activity correspond to the numbered goals listed earlier in this chapter.

Exploratory Play Activity: Playing House

Ages 3–6

Goal 13: For children to explore their own and others' human attributes and cultural practices.

Content: People in families often care for each other, eat, sleep, work, learn, and play together.

Families sometimes do things the way other families do; sometimes they do similar things their own way.

Materials: Provide variations on "traditional" housekeeping props in pretend play:

Eating and Cooking: rice bowls, chopsticks, wok, clay baker, hot pot, stew pot, tortilla warmer, tortilla press (tortillero), cast-iron plate or griddle (comal), mortar and pestle (molcajete), rattan trays, wooden bowls, Swedish pancake pan (plattar), wooden spoons, straight wooden rolling pin (no handles, very thin), food packages representing different ethnic traditions, cookbooks and pictures of foods from different ethnic traditions, cushions on the floor, and low tables for eating

Sleeping: mat, feather bed, futon, and hammock

Clothing: modern scarves, hats, footwear, jackets, cloth, and jewelry representing different cultures

Shopping: cloth or string bags, baskets to carry or wear, and squares of cloth to wrap around packages

Procedure: Select a few items to interject in the housekeeping area. Invite children to play. Observe children as they interact with the materials. Encourage children to try out or experiment with the materials. Avoid telling them what to do or how to use specific items unless safety is a concern or children ask you directly. Verbally acknowledge children's play using behavior reflections and paraphrase reflections. Invite children to communicate their thinking through actions and words.

To Simplify: Add only one or two new items at a time.

To Extend: Show children some items you intend to put into the pretend center; talk about their origin prior to children playing with them.

Guided Discovery Activity: Beautiful Skin

Ages 3-6

Goal 13: For children to explore their own and others' human attributes and cultural practices.

Content: Your skin is part of you when you are born.
The color of people's skin differs from person to person.
There are many different shades of skin tones.

Materials: Washable tempera paints in at least five different skin tones
Cotton swabs
One small paper plate per child
Smocks
Newspapers
A plastic dish pan with soapy water
A plastic dish pan with clear water for rinsing
Easel pad with large marker for recording results

Procedure:

1. Begin with a demonstration at group time or in a small group activity in the art area. Show children the different colors of paint in the bottles. Tell them you will try to find a paint that matches your own skin color. Dab a bit of paint on a Q-tip and put it on your hand. Ask the children to tell you if it is a match. If not, try another color, or mix a little of another shade with the one you originally chose on your hand or on a paper plate. Continue until the children declare that you have a match. Name the colors you blended to make your skin shade (peach, mahogany, terra cotta). Ask another adult to record your name and your paint combination on the easel pad.

2. Compare your skin shade to the skin of a child in the group. Invite the children to talk about what they notice.

3. Encourage the child to find a paint shade that is a good match. Repeat the mixing and comparing process until the child and the group are satisfied that a match has been achieved. Record the shades used.

4. Continue this process until everyone has recreated a personal skin color.

5. Use behavior and paraphrase reflections as well as open-ended questions to promote children's self-discovery of the activity content.

6. Answer children's questions nonjudgmentally and with accurate information.

To Simplify: Works with pairs of children.

To Extend: Encourage each child to create a paint sample to match the skin tone of another child in the group. Or invite children to compare their skin tones to see what color combinations they have in common or what ways their skin tone combinations differ.

Problem-Solving Activity: Democracy at the Play Dough Table

Ages 3-6

Goal 16: Carry out democratic principles and practices.

Content: One way people solve a group problem is to discuss what the problem is and how they might solve it.
The best solutions take into account everyone's needs.
There is more than one way to solve a problem.

Materials: A large grapefruit-sized ball of modeling dough

A child-sized table with three chairs for children and one chair for an adult

A plastic knife (safe for children to handle)

A pair of child-sized scissors

Procedure:

1. Invite three children to play with you at the play dough table.

2. *Observation*: Place the ball of dough in the center of the table and draw the children's attention to it. Keeping a hand on the dough, say, "I have one big ball of dough here and there are three children who want to play with it. Tell me how everyone can have a chance."

3. *Information Gathering*: Listen to the children's ideas; elicit suggestions from all. Paraphrase each child's suggestion. "Sarah thinks she could have it first and then you all could take turns one at a time." Follow up with, "What do the rest of you think of that idea?" Paraphrase their answers. Remain impartial throughout this discussion. Do not show agreement or disagreement with any idea, regardless of how logical or outlandish it may seem. Remind children that before anyone can play with the dough, the group must decide how that will happen. If the conversation stalls, make an observation such as, "Sometimes when people are trying to figure out how to share, they decide that each person can have a little or take turns." After several solutions have been posed, children generally gravitate toward one (this may involve compromise or combining suggestions). Acknowledge children's hard work and good ideas as they proceed. Remind them periodically that the goal is to make sure everyone gets a chance to play with the dough.

4. *Experimentation*: Summarize the children's solution and help them carry it out.

5. *Drawing Conclusions*: After the children have been playing with the dough for a while, ask them to describe and evaluate their initial solution. Invite them to make modifications if needed.

To Simplify: Limit this activity to two children.

To Extend: Invite children to develop alternate solutions and to try those solutions in a future activity with different materials but the same central problem.

Discussion Activity: Look or Touch: Making a Rule for Show-and-Tell

Ages 3-6

Goal 5: For children to conform to reasonable limits on behavior

Content: Rules are guides for behavior.

People make rules to keep living things safe, to protect people's rights, and to protect property.

In a discussion, people talk one at a time and listen carefully to whoever is talking.

Materials: An object the child brings from home or that the child has selected from a collection provided by the teacher

Procedure:

1. Each day, invite one child to show an object for other children to see or touch. During small-group or whole-group time, have the child display the object on a small table and tell something about it (What it looks like, what it is, where it came from, etc.). If the child is not interested in "telling," invite other children to describe what they see ("It's red." "It's made of cloth").

2. Next, ask the child to make a rule—is the object a *looking-thing*, meaning the other children may only look to find out more about it, or is it a *touching-thing*, meaning the other children may handle it carefully?

3. Help the rule-maker and the children carry out the rule as they examine the object.

To Simplify: Keep the object on a tray or a small table to make it easier for children to follow the rule if it is a looking-thing only.

To Extend: Follow up on the child's decision by asking him or her to give a reason for the rule (focusing on safety, property, or rights). If the child cannot articulate a reason, ask other children what reasons might apply.

Demonstration Activity: Beanbag Name Game

Goal 1: For children to develop social skills.

Content: Friends know each other's names.

Friends like to do some of the same things.

People feel friendly toward people who take turns and share.

Materials: Small beanbags (such as might be used in a beanbag toss)

Procedure:

1. Play this game with small groups of children or at group time with the whole class. Invite the children to sit in a circle. Demonstrate passing a beanbag to the person on your right as you say your own name. Ask the next child to say his or her name while passing the beanbag on. Continue this process, coaching children as necessary, until the beanbag has made it around the whole circle. Go around the circle a few times so everyone has multiple chances to say his or her name aloud to the group. Differ the speed of the game and the volume of the names to add variety.

2. Next, ask children to say the child's name along with him or her.

3. After children are fairly successful remembering everyone's name, tell them you will try naming everyone. Their job is to look and listen and help you get the names right. Name each child. Pause once in a while and let the children assist you by saying the child's name. Make an obvious and humorous mistake or two and let the children correct you.

4. Invite each child to try all the names with help from one another but without you leading the effort.

To Simplify: Play in small groups.

Repeat the procedure over multiple days.

To Extend: Ask the child with the beanbag to say the first and last name of the person to his or her right before passing it on.

Direct Instruction Activity: Playful Elephants

Goal 10: For children to demonstrate skills associated with cooperation (working with others toward a common goal).

Content: People cooperate by playing together.

One way to cooperate is to share physical space.

Another way to cooperate is to wait and take turns.

Materials: Circle-time area inside or outdoors

Procedure:

1. Teach children the following song, sung to the tune of "Twinkle, Twinkle, Little Star"

   • *One little elephant went out to play,*

   sat on a spider's web one day.

   • *She (he) had such enormous fun,*

   she (he) called other elephants to come.

2. Next, give directions for playing the game. Incorporate the cooperation content in the description. For instance, "You are cooperating when you go into the circle when a friend calls your name." Or, "You are cooperating when you sing along while people go into the circle."

   • Children form a circle.

   • One child goes in the center and pretends to be an elephant having fun on a spider web (pantomime motions).

   • Encourage all other children to sing.

   • At the words, "She called other elephants to come," the elephant in the middle picks another child to be a second elephant. That child joins the first and the group sings "Two little elephants. . . ." As the last line is sung, the second child chooses a third child, and so on.

   • Continue until all the children are on the spider web.

To Simplify: Limit the number of elephants on the web to four or five at a time. When the web becomes "full," send the elephants back to the circle and start with a new set of elephants.

To Extend: Invite children to come into the circle in pairs. The child in the center picks the first child and then that child picks a friend to enter the web with him or her.

Meeting the Needs of Diverse Learners

The physical environment either communicates that individual children are valued members of the classroom learning community or that they are lesser members of the group. Figure 15.10 provides a checklist to help you monitor the messages you convey and to make it more likely that all learners will feel at home in your program.

FIGURE 15.10 Diversity checklist

IMAGES When children look around the program, they see images that:	Clearly Evident	This Needs Improvement
1. Show males and females of differing ages, cultures, ethnicities, abilities, and body types		
2. Show diverse people engaged in everyday activities wearing modern clothing (not historic costumes)		
3. Depict a variety of family compositions, economic circumstances, and environments (work, play, home, community, urban, suburban, and rural)		
4. Include print in children's home language		
5. Are free of stereotypes (no exaggerated human features, no images depicting all people within the same group as looking exactly alike or people across groups having identical features with different-colored skin, no pictures showing only male firefighters or female teachers)		
6. Counter stereotypes (for example, women engaged in manual labor outdoors, men engaged in caregiving, modern photographs of a Mexican doctor or a Native American child using a computer, depictions of both males and females as firefighters, teachers, or health professionals)		
ACTIVITIES AND MATERIALS Children have access to:		
7. Books that include and represent the diverse children, adults, and families in the program		
8. Books that include illustrations and stories about diverse people engaged in a variety of activities and settings		
9. Books in which characters with diverse attributes are represented as wise, powerful, and good		
10. Music experiences (tunes, dancing, songs, and finger plays) and music-making objects that reflect different cultures, languages, and musical traditions		
11. Cooking and other food experiences that make a connection between culture and preparing, cooking, and eating food		
12. Puzzles, games, and other manipulatives that reflect diverse attributes and that are structured to accommodate children of diverse abilities		
13. Sensory experiences that address diversity, such as including cultural items in water/sand play (Chinese spoons and cups, African ladles, East European designs on objects)		
14. Art experiences that promote exploration of diversity (paper and paint in a range of skin tones; brushes and tools from a variety of cultures for painting, printing, and stamping; fabric, beads, and other decorations that reflect varied cultural traditions; art reproductions depicting many cultures and styles)		
15. Dress-up clothes for boys and girls, dolls, figures, and other props from various culture groups		

Source: Based on Anti-Defamation League (2012), Rhomberg (2004), Derman-Sparks & Edwards (2010).

COUNTERING STEREOTYPES

Think about attributes that characterize you: your gender, language, race, ethnic background, physical appearance, and so forth. Choose three. Identify at least one potential stereotype that someone might have regarding each attribute (e.g., girls are not good at math). Imagine you have a child in your class with the same attributes who is also susceptible to these stereotypes. How could you use the physical environment to counteract stereotyping?

Personal Attributes	Potential Stereotypes	Strategies
1.		
2.		
3.		

Communicating with Families About the Social Domain

Parents often name "sharing" as one of the first and most important social skills they want children to learn (Borba, 2005). Yet, sharing does not come easily in early childhood. Children's immature thinking makes it hard for them to consider the needs of others. They also lack the experience and words necessary to trade objects, take turns, or cooperate with peers. As a result, whenever young children come together to play, squabbles over toys are bound to happen. When these disruptions occur, typical adult reactions are to tell children to "Play nice," or "Share." Neither script is very effective. These words do not give children clear enough direction on how to meet their needs while also addressing the needs of others. Thus, children as well as adults benefit from learning the language of sharing. See Figure 15.11 for an example you might use to address this issue.

NEWSLETTER/WEB READY COMMUNICATION

FIGURE 15.11 • The Language of Sharing

"Share your toys." These are words children hear a lot at school and probably at home, too. As soon as children start playing together, they are reminded to share. Yet sharing does not come naturally to preschoolers. It takes several years to master. One way we help children learn to share is by giving them lots of practice taking turns, using toys together, and trading objects back and forth. Another is by teaching children the language of sharing. Most young children lack the words to express their needs or wants adequately. Here are some words we have been offering children to make sharing easier.

For the child who wants something:

- "I get it next."
- "When will you be done?"
- "How will we know when your turn is over?"

For the child who has something another child wants:

- "I'm not done yet."
- "You can have it next."
- "You can have it after I . . . ."

For the child who is waiting to say to himself or herself:

- "It's almost my turn."
- "I can wait."

Next is a powerful word. Most children can wait for a turn if they know for sure they are next or if they understand when the turn will be over, not only in time (e.g., 2 minutes) but also in terms of action (e.g., when this painting is done, when she has gone around the track three times, when the bucket is full). Finally, children need to know their special toys and comfort items (blanket from home, stuffed toy) do not have to be shared. Those are things other children can look at, but not touch or use themselves.

15 Applying What You've Learned

1. **Elements of the Social Domain.** With a peer, identify and describe the four elements of the social domain. Give an example for each.

2. **Key Concepts and Skills in the Social Domain.** Arrange to observe two young children at play. Identify two social skills each child displays and provide examples to illustrate these skills.

3. **Strategies for Teaching in the Social Domain.** Arrange to visit an early childhood classroom. Observe the children and teachers interacting. Look for at least two examples of a teacher using modeling, coaching, or elaborating to promote children's social competence.

4. **Planning Activities in the Social Domain.** Choose two of the activity plans presented in this chapter to turn into long-form lesson plans. Add objectives and evaluation questions to expand each into a fully developed plan.

5. **Meeting the Needs of Diverse Learners.** Tour the classroom in which you are working or volunteering now. Using the checklist provided in Figure 15.10, look at images on the walls and objects on the shelves. What messages about diversity do you see? What would you add or take away to make those messages more effective?

6. **Countering Stereotypes at Home.** Visit the toy section of a store. Check out the games and other toys on display. What stereotypes do you detect? How might a family counter these at home? Find at least two toys that would help families promote positive feelings about diversity.

References

Anti Defamation League. (2011). *Talking to our children about race and diversity.* Leadership Conference on Civil and Human Rights. Washington, D.C.: Author.

Anti-Defamation League. (2012). *ADL checklist for creating an anti-bias learning environment.* Retrieved from www.adl.org/education/anti-bias.pdf

Borba, M. (2005). *Nobody likes me, everybody hates me: The top 25 friendship problems and how to solve them.* San Francisco, CA: Jossey-Bass Publishers.

Derman-Sparks, L. (2011). Addressing children's questions about differences. *Early Childhood Today.* Retrieved from www.scholastic.com/browse/subarticle.jsp?id=4459

Derman-Sparks, L., & Edwards, J. O. (2010). *Anti-bias curriculum: Tools for empowering young children and ourselves.* Washington, D.C.: National Association for the Education of Young Children.

Dombro, A. L., Jablon, J., & Stetson, C. (2011). *Powerful interactions: How to connect with children to extend their learning.* Washington, D.C.: National Association for the Education of Young Children.

Epstein, A. S. (2009). *Me, you, us: Social-emotional learning in preschool.* Ypsilanti, MI: HighScope Press.

Gartrell, D. (2006). Guidance matters. *Young Children, 61*(2), 88–89.

Gonzalez-Mena, J. (2010). *Foundations of early childhood education: Teaching children in a diverse society.* New York: McGraw-Hill.

Hyson, M. (2004). *The emotional development of young children: Building an emotion-centered curriculum.* New York: Teachers College Press.

Hyson, M. (2008). Enthusiastic and engaged learners: Approaches to learning in the early childhood classroom. New York: Washington, D.C.: NAEYC and Teachers College Press.

Ladd, G. W. (2008). Social competence and peer relations: Significance for young children and their service providers. *Early Childhood Services 2*(3), 129–148.

National Council for the Social Studies. (2012). *Expectations of excellence: Curriculum standards for social studies–Executive Summary.* Retrieved from www.socialstudies.org/standards/execsummary

Rhomberg, V. (2004). *Diversity, anti-bias conductive checklist.* Toronto, Ontario: Mothercraft Institute for Early Development.

Seefeldt, C., Castle, S. D., & Falconer, R. (2010). *Social studies for the preschool/primary child.* Upper Saddle River, NJ: Pearson.

Shrestha, L. B., & Heisler, E. J. (2011). *The changing demographic profile of the United States.* Washington, D.C.: U.S. Congressional Research Service. RL32701.

Smith, P. K., & Pellegrini, A. (2008). Learning through play. In R. E. Tremblay, R. G. Barr, R. D. Peters, & M. Boivin (Eds.), *Encyclopedia on early childhood development* [online]. Montreal, Quebec: Centre of Excellence for Early Childhood Development; 2008:1-6. Available at: www.child-encyclopedia.com/documents/Smith-PellegriniANGxp.pdf

Wheeler, E. J. (2004). *Conflict resolution in early childhood.* Upper Saddle River, NJ: Pearson.

Willis, C. (2009). *Creating inclusive learning environments for young children.* Thousand Oaks, CA: Corwin Press.

16 Putting It All Together: Organizing Children's Learning Over Time

TO DO:

✔ Get apples for the apple sorting activity on Monday and the applesauce cooking activity on Tuesday

✔ Borrow three copies of *The Seasons of Arnold's Apple Tree* book for small groups on Wednesday

✔ Check with Sam's dad to make sure he is still coming to talk about insects on Thursday or Friday

✔ Reserve magnifying glasses prior to "Insect" visit

✔ Drop the apple collage activity, continue to make wet clay available in the art area, add more smocks

Grace Robbins reviewed her child observations for the past several days and then went over her plans for the coming week. Next, she began a to-do list of things she needed to accomplish before Monday.

Grace's to-do list reveals important things about planning activities for an entire classroom of young children over multiple days. She had to plan ahead, consider more than one activity at a time, obtain materials, and decide what changes to make in her plans based on child observations. These are all critical elements in putting together an effective educational program for children every day, all year long.

There are many things you must do to create a developmentally appropriate program. These include fostering caring relationships with children; guiding children's behavior; preparing safe, stimulating physical environments; assessing what and how children are learning; and creating individual activities for each of the six curriculum domains that make up whole-child learning. Now it is time to combine all of these skills to develop whole-day and multi-day plans.

Let's start with what it takes to plan a complete day from children's arrival to their departure.

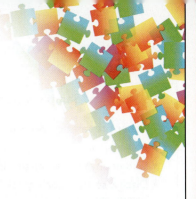

Daily Planning

It is not unusual to hear children ask:

What are we having for snack?
Can I ring the bell at cleanup?
Will we have paints at choice time?
Is it almost time to go outside?

All of these questions demonstrate children's awareness of the activities that make up their day at the center. Early childhood teachers are responsible for arranging such activities into a day-by-day schedule that breaks each day into manageable chunks for children to navigate. This schedule provides the framework through which early childhood programs are delivered and determines how children and teachers spend their time. The daily schedule also influences classroom climate. The way it is put together can make participants feel secure or uncertain, absorbed in their work, or at loose ends. A well-designed schedule can make it easier for children to be successful and behave appropriately. A poorly designed one can provoke misbehavior. Creating an effective daily schedule is so important to children's learning that it is one of the specified criteria for what constitutes developmentally appropriate practice (NAEYC, 2009).

PARTS OF THE SCHEDULE

Some events that are part of every daily schedule include whole-group times, small-group times, learning-center times, and outdoor play. Arrival, departure, dressing, eating, resting, and toileting are additional routines you must incorporate into each day's agenda (Gordon & Browne, 2011). See Figure 16.1 for a sample full-day schedule that includes all these parts. Figure 16.2 provides an example of a schedule for children in a half-day program.

Schedules such as the ones in Figures 16.1 and 16.2 can be adapted in many ways. One teacher's choice time may include centers designated as blocks, pretend play, art, manipulatives, math and science, books, sand table, and open snack. Another teacher may opt for a combination of learning centers mostly focused on language and literacy in the morning and varied across other domains in the afternoon. A third might flip the schedule by starting outdoors and ending with a free choice time from which children make their departure home. Another teacher might greet children at the door and then have them flow into a free choice time, followed by teacher-directed small groups and then a snack time in which everyone eats simultaneously. Teachers base their schedules on children's needs, staff availability, access to common spaces, and transportation factors. In each case, the ultimate focus is to support children's learning.

LEARNING OUTCOMES

After you read this chapter, you will be able to:

- Construct a daily routine that supports a good day for children.
- Plan smooth transitions.
- Create a weekly overview of activities that address whole-child learning.
- Use projects to build on children's interests and enhance their learning.
- Explain ways to address the needs of diverse learners in your overall planning.
- Communicate with families about children's cumulative learning.

These teachers are coordinating their daily schedules to share space on the playground effectively.

FIGURE 16.1 Sample schedule for a full day for teachers and children

Teacher preparation prior to children's arrival

- Review plans
- Gather any needed materials
- Discuss specific goals for children (individuals and group goals) with other staff members
- Prepare physical environment as necessary

Children and families arrive

Doors open at 7:30 AM, intermittent arrivals, not all children come early or all at once, most children are on site by 9:00 AM

- Greet children and families
- Breakfast and quiet self-selected activities for early arrivals
- Group meeting and introduction to day
- Choice time (includes learning centers, open snack, toileting, and 15 minutes of assigned small-group work with a teacher)
- Outdoors

- Circle time
- Lunch
- Story and rest
- Outdoors
- Choice time (includes some of the same centers as in the morning and some new ones, open snack, and toileting)
- Cleanup
- Circle time and group meeting at end of day
- Prepare to go home, farewells, and family interactions—intermittent departures until 6:00 PM

Teacher closure following children's departure

- Review observations/highlights of the day
- File child observations
- Restore room as necessary
- Revise next day's plans as needed
- Pull out key materials for following day

FIGURE 16.2 Sample half-day schedule for children

8:55 to 9:10	Arrival
	Greet children (children arrive on bus at same time), children read stories from the book basket or talk with an adult on the circle-time rug
9:10 to 9:30	Group time
9:30 to 9:35	Transition to choice time
9:35 to 10:40	Choice time (includes open snack)
10:40 to 10:50	Clean-up
10:50 to 11:10	Small groups
11:10 to 11:20	Dressing to go outdoors
11:20 to 12:10	Outdoor time and closing group time
12:15	Departure from playground (some children go home, some children go to lunch and then go home)

CONSTRUCTING A SCHEDULE THAT PROMOTES LEARNING

Each part of the day represents learning opportunities for children. By now you know how small-group and whole-group activities can serve as vehicles for addressing curriculum goals. In Figure 16.3 we provide some examples of how typical classroom routines can also fulfill this function.

Sometimes addressing goals through classroom routines comes about naturally as a result of children's actions and interests. However, teachers also intentionally plan

FIGURE 16.3 Sample goals associated with typical classroom routines

Routine	Domain	Goal	Example
Arrival	Affective	Self-awareness	Find own cubby and nametag
	Language	Speaking	Greet teacher, talk about yesterday, talk about upcoming day
		Reading	Read the daily message
	Social	Social responsibility	Put belongings in cubby, find job on job chart
Departure	Aesthetics	Self as artist	Show teacher/parent art work to take home
	Cognitive	Mathematics	Count steps to cubby from circle-time rug, count belongings going into backpack
	Physical	Gross motor	Hop, skip, or jump to cubby from circle-time rug
Dressing	Cognitive	Mathematics	Describe first, second, third step in putting on outdoor clothing
	Physical	Fine motor	Snap, zip, tie
	Social	Social responsibility	Ask for help or offer help to others—learn scripts for seeking and offering help
Eating	Affective	Self-efficacy	Set own place at table from start to finish, serve self, express preferences, make choices, clean up
	Cognitive	Mathematics	One-to-one correspondence—napkins to cups to children, count crackers/grapes at snack
		Science	Explore properties of food—colors, textures, smells, hot versus cold; observe changes in food through cooking, chilling, freezing
	Physical	Fine motor	Use utensils, handle finger foods, pour and serve foods; help to prepare food—tear, chop, mix
Resting	Aesthetics	Musical awareness	Listen to quiet music during rest time; listen to music representing different cultures
	Affective	Emotional competence	Practice relaxation techniques
	Social	Socialization	Practice impulse control and self-regulation, calm self
Toileting	Affective	Self-awareness	Awareness of body functions, gender differences, caring for own body, comfort with own body
		Self-efficacy	Follow pictograph for washing hands and toileting routine, self-care skills
	Language	Speaking	Body part names
	Social	Socialization	Manners related to personal hygiene—flushing, rinsing out sink when finished brushing teeth, throwing away paper towel

ways to make sure routines target the curriculum. How they structure the environment, the materials they provide, and what they say to children all make it likely that certain program elements will be stressed. For example, consider how the teacher in the Dragon Fly Room planned for children's learning during snack time using the strategies presented in Figure 16.4.

This teacher's plans are simple but intentional. They add substance to the snack routine and make it more likely that a variety of domains and goals are covered (Epstein, 2007). Of course, there are times when children take a planned lesson

FIGURE 16.4 Intentional planning for snack time

| Monday | Tuesday | Wednesday | Thursday | Friday |
Affective Domain	Social Domain	Cognitive Domain	Language Domain	Physical Domain
Children set their own snack place following a three-step pictograph	Each child invites one other child to snack	Children create combinations of snack items that total six, choosing from celery sticks, carrot sticks, and crackers (e.g., one carrot, two celery, three crackers)	The teacher invites children to describe their snack using adjectives such as crunchy, slippery, yellow, and so on; she writes their ideas on chart paper	Children peal chunks of banana for their own snack

This child is working on self-help skills before going outside to play.

in another direction, as happened on Thursday when the children quickly gravitated from describing their snack to talking about a problem that had just happened in the block area. In this case, the teacher followed the children's lead and supported their problem-solving discussion. She kept her "adjective idea" for another day when it might be more relevant to the children. As it happened, she still had opportunities to support language learning, albeit in a way that was different from what she had initially intended.

BEST PRACTICES

There is no one best schedule for every child, teacher, or school. However, there are principles of best practice that set good schedules apart from poor ones. The key to creating an appropriate schedule is to pay attention to five criteria:

- Consistency
- Pacing
- Time management
- Balancing variety and familiarity
- Whole-child learning

CONSISTENCY

From the time they are born, children benefit from consistent routines. Knowing what is going to happen next gives children a sense of security and helps them to more successfully predict what to expect and how to behave (Hemmeter, Ostrosky, Artman, & Kinder, 2008). Alternately, young children find it disconcerting if each day's events are totally unpredictable. The best daily schedules follow a similar *pattern* day after day. In other words, if Monday begins with greeting time, it helps if the same is true most of the time. Similarly, children benefit when the *sequence* of events remains approximately the same each day—for instance, greeting time, followed by free choice, followed by music, followed by outdoor time, followed by lunch and rest. This kind of consistency gives children a sense of order and provides continuity from one day to another.

PACING

Pacing refers to how children experience the speed of the day. Just like Goldilocks, children need a schedule that is paced "just right"—not too fast and not too slow. Schedules that require children and teachers to rush pell-mell from one activity to the next are exhausting. A day with a pace that is too slow can lead to boredom. Schedules designed to keep children on track within strict time limits ignore children's individual needs. Yet schedules that have no time limits lose their predictability and sense of purpose. None of these circumstances supports optimal learning and all of them contribute to potential behavior problems.

The best-paced schedules help children avoid becoming overly tired, accommodate children's individual needs, and allow enough time for children to become absorbed in activities, make choices and decisions, and solve child-sized problems within the context of the day's events (Hohman, Weikart, & Epstein, 2008). To achieve this ideal, teachers use the following strategies to influence the pace of the schedules they design.

- Alternate quiet and noisy activity times
- Alternate short times of having children sit and listen with much longer times of active engagement
- Alternate short times of adult-initiated or adult-directed activities with much longer times of child-initiated and child-directed activities
- Alternate short whole-group times with much longer times for individual and small-group interactions
- Alternate required routines (e.g., greeting time or lunch) with routines that emphasize child choice (e.g., choice time, outdoor time)

Young children benefit from periods of vigorous, self-directed physical activity throughout the day.

TIME MANAGEMENT

When formulating a schedule, it is important to remember that all parts of the schedule require an allocation of time, even if it is only a few minutes. A typical beginner's mistake is to account for the time needed to carry out the big chunks of the day, such as group time or free choice, but to forget to include time for children to make the transition from indoors to outside or to allow enough time for cleanup. Since everything children experience during the school day is meant to enhance learning, it is important to incorporate enough time for children to take advantage of that learning. The following strategies contribute to good time management in constructing a developmentally appropriate schedule.

- Include time for all routines and transitions (greeting time, cleanup, dressing to go outdoors, gathering to come indoors, mealtime, rest time, departing each day)
- Take into account seasonal shifts in the schedule (more time for dressing to go outside in winter weather, less time for this routine in the spring)
- Plan a long session of free-choice activities in the morning and another in the afternoon for full-day programs (60 minutes per session is recommended in many state standards)
- Plan each portion of the day with enough flexibility to accommodate variations in children's level of involvement (e.g., the children need a little more time to finish cleaning up, the children become restless at group time and the teacher decides to shorten the singing and let them go outdoors a few minutes early)

Jen and Tonia are absorbed in making chalk pictures. Although it is time to go inside, the teacher waits a few more minutes so the girls can finish their drawings.

BALANCING VARIETY AND FAMILIARITY

The old saying "variety is the spice of life" holds true when putting together a daily schedule that children will find interesting and teachers will find manageable. At the same time, children and adults gain a sense of security and competence with repetition and by building on what they already know and can do. Consequently, the best schedules balance variety with familiarity (NAEYC, 2009). As teachers strive to achieve an effective combination of each, they take into account the variables depicted in Figure 16.5.

WHOLE-CHILD LEARNING

The hallmark of developmentally appropriate practice is paying attention to all areas of child development and learning. Effective teachers look at every part of the daily schedule to make sure they have planned engaging learning experiences in every

FIGURE 16.5 Guidelines for balancing diversity with familiarity

Variables	Guidelines
Active play versus quiet play	• Intersperse active experiences (e.g., dancing with scarves) with quiet activities (e.g., small-group snack) • Physically separate noisy activities (e.g., acting out the "Three Bears") from quiet activities (e.g., lap reading)
Familiar activities versus new ones	• Offer a greater number of familiar activities than new ones • Introduce new activities throughout the day or week, not all at once • Refresh familiar activities with new props (e.g., animals in the blocks a few days; people figures added later in the week) • Repeat the same activity using new materials (e.g., children sort shells one day; sort rocks another day)
Child-initiated versus adult-guided experiences	• Offer more child-guided experiences than adult-guided ones
Individual, small-group, and large-group activities	• Approximately 1/3 of the day should be free choice, 1/3 small group, 1/3 whole group (the younger or more inexperienced the children, the shorter the time allocated to whole-group activities)
Simple versus complex activities	Complex activities are ones with multiple steps to complete, more safety features to consider, and involved setup or cleanup, as well as ones that require greater self-control from children and more adult support • Limit the number of complex activities going on simultaneously • Spread complex activities out over the day and week
Messy activities versus less-messy activities	• Avoid having two messy activities going on at once unless you have enough protective gear, cleanup supplies, and adults to supervise
Activities that are independent in contrast to activities that require close adult supervision	• Create a majority of activities that children can manage with minimal adult supervision • Introduce or demonstrate activities prior to asking children to do them on their own • Rotate into activities frequently enough to provide continuing support to all children in the room • Provide visual cues (pictographs) or auditory cues (recorded directions) to support children's learning and use of materials
Indoor times and outdoor times	• Make sure children go outside to play each day • Design portions of the day during which children can flow between outside to inside without a formal whole-group transition • Address each domain outdoors as well as inside

domain daily (Jacobs & Crowley, 2010). Use the following guidelines to help make whole-child learning an integral part of your daily plans.

- Address each domain every day
- Address each domain within different learning centers and routines throughout the week
- Address each domain indoors and outdoors
- Vary the learning activity types you use within and across domains (exploratory play, guided discovery, problem solving, discussions, demonstrations, and direct instruction)

One more thing to consider in the schedule is the times that lead from one experience to the next—these are called **transitions**. Transitions are critical routines that must be planned as carefully as all other parts of the day.

transitions The in-between times that happen as children shift from one segment of the daily schedule to the next or from one environment to another.

TRANSITIONS

Transitions are the in-between times that happen as children shift from one segment of the daily schedule to the next (e.g., from indoor time to outdoor time, from lunch to rest). Children also make transitions from one environment to another (e.g., from school to home, from the breakfast program to the preschool or kindergarten classroom). These are all critical intervals that have the power to help everyone move seamlessly and happily through the day or to throw a classroom into chaos (Ostrosky, Jung, & Hemmeter, 2012). Which result occurs is directly related to planning and implementation. All transitions need to be thought out in advance and all need to take into account how children learn, the availability of adults, and the physical environment. Most important, transitions need to be treated as part of the curriculum, not as afterthoughts. Just as all other portions of the schedule contribute to children's educational experiences, transitions must do the same.

PLANNING SMOOTH TRANSITIONS

It is estimated that within early childhood programs, children may spend up to a third of their time in transitions (Essa, 2011). This time can simply be wasted or it can be used to help children anticipate, figure out, work through, and successfully manage change (Gordon & Browne, 2011).

To achieve the most productive outcomes, early childhood teachers employ many of the strategies presented in Figure 16.6.

The strategies outlined in Figure 16.6 make transitions easier for everyone and keep the focus on learning versus simply moving from one thing to another. However, even well-planned transitions can be challenging for children if they happen too often during the day. Preschoolers and kindergartners become frustrated over frequent interruptions and the accelerated pace that accompanies having to constantly shift their attention, thinking, and actions away from what they are doing toward something else (Gallick & Lee, 2010). The most effective way to reduce such stress is to minimize the number of transitions children experience.

Martin is deeply involved in rolling the cars down the track. To help anticipate cleanup, the teacher walks over to him and says, "Five more minutes until cleanup. That means you have time to roll the car down the track five more times and then it will be time to put the cars and ramp away."

MINIMIZING TRANSITIONS

Having no transitions at all is neither desirable nor realistic. Transitions provide a bridge between one part of the day and another and enable teachers to vary the pace and activity level of the classroom in concert with children's needs. It is possible, however, to

FIGURE 16.6 Tips for creating successful transition times

Transition Tip	Examples
Teach children what is expected during transitions	Post a picture schedule outlining the events of the day, including the transitions.
	Demonstrate some transitions in advance.
	Model what you expect and draw the children's attention to your actions ("I'm finding all the crayons to put back in the bin." Or, "I'm turning off the water in this sink. You turn off the water in yours.").
	Point out peer models ("See how Jennifer turned on the water. You try it.").
	Physically and verbally walk children through each transition.
	Invite children to describe their potential actions during an upcoming transition ("What will you need to remember?" Or, "Tell me what we will do first as we get ready to go outside.").
Move children toward the next activity	Say, "You can hop over to your locker to get your coat," versus "You can leave group now."
	Give children information about what to do when they arrive at the next activity ("Go to the rug and pick out a book," Or, "When you go to the art table, put on your smock.").
	At the end of greeting time, ask each child individually what he or she would like to do first during choice time—paraphrase what they tell you and dismiss them a few at a time, reminding them of their "plan."
	As cleanup time approaches, invite a child to tell you what he or she is going to clean up and then help the child get started.
	Be at the circle-time rug before the first child arrives so you can greet children and get them engaged right away.
Keep waiting to a minimum	Give children who are waiting something to do—sing a song, act out a finger play, or play "I Spy."
	Divide the large group into small groups to reduce wait times (less time waiting to take a turn at a game, talking in the group, having a chance to tell about the day, having a chance to hear the teacher read "their" story).
	Rotate children through routines that typically require waiting (toileting, washing hands) in easy-to-manage numbers. Begin with a small group of two or three children, and send them to the bathroom while others are still playing. Other children can follow when the first group returns.
Warn children about transitions in advance	Teacher gives a 5-minute warning in advance of any transition.
	Child walks around room with a sign that says, "5 more minutes," or rings a bell that children have been told is the 5-minute warning.
Provide cues to help children move through transitions more easily	Child walks around the room at cleanup time, holding a sign and announcing that it is time to clean up.
	Provide pictographs that show the steps involved in a transition such as setting the table or putting on winter clothing while also talking children through the steps.
Make transitions fun	Sing a song at cleanup, jump on two feet to move from circle time to the cubbies to put on coats, walk on tiptoes coming in from outside, or slither like a snake from snack to group time.
Give children enough time to make each transition comfortably	The teacher says, "You have time to finish that painting and then it will be time to clean up." Or, "One more time around the trike track and then it will be time to put the trikes away."
	Allow extra time for children to wipe up the tables, put away the paints, or gather the trikes to put them in the shed. Adults could do such jobs faster themselves. However, rushing children or doing the tasks for them deprives children of valuable practice and opportunities to learn new skills.

(continued)

FIGURE 16.6 Tips for creating successful transition times (*continued*)

Transition Tip	Examples
Provide extra support for children who need it	Involve some children early in carrying out the transition.
	Ask the child to work with a peer to carry out the transition.
	Give an earlier warning prior to the overall warning to alert the child that the transition is coming.
	Carry out the transition along with the child.
	Invite the child to tell you in advance how he or she will carry out the transition.
	Break the transition into smaller steps.
	Give the child an individual choice card.
Provide positive feedback to children in the midst of and following transitions	Use behavior reflections and statements of information to draw children's attention to their appropriate actions during the transition ("You're putting all the crayons away." Or, "You remembered to wipe out the sink.").
	Use effective praise to reinforce positive behavior and to give children specific information about its impact ("You found your coat right away. Now we can go outside!").

FIGURE 16.7 Ways to eliminate transitions

Original Schedule	Revised Schedule
8:15–8:25 Arrival/hand washing **8:15–8:45 Free play** **8:45–9:15 Calendar, weather, and lesson** **9:15–10:00 Centers/small groups** – *Children rotate every 15 minutes between three small group activities or play in a designated center.* **10:00–10:15 Hand washing/snack** **10:15–10:30 Music** **10:30–10:40 Book time** – *Everyone is dismissed from circle at the same time to put on coats.* **11:00 Dismissal** – *Children wait for families or bus to pick them up.*	**8:15–8:45 Arrival/hand washing/table toys** – *Children have a choice of table activities, such as play dough, cutting scraps, or manipulatives, allowing easy entry after finishing arrival routine.* **8:45–9:00 Large group** – *A few routine activities, plus review of the day's schedule and center time plans.* **9:00–10:20 Center time/hand washing/snack** • *Teachers support play and teach skills in small groups or with individual children.* • *Snack is a center choice, allowing varied lengths of time to eat.* **10:20–10:40 Book time and music** • *Children finish cleaning up, then choose a book to read.* • *A few children at a time are dismissed to get coats while the other children continue singing.* **10:40–11:00 Outdoor time** **11:00 Dismissal** – *Class sings good-bye song and plays waiting games until arrival of families or bus.*

Source: Based on Hemmeter, M. L., Ostrosky, M. M., Artman, K. M., & Kinder, K. A. (2008). Planning Transitions to Prevent Challenging Behavior. *Beyond the Journal: Young Children on the Web,* Washington DC: NAEYC. May 1–7. Used with permission.

reduce the number of transitions that take place. The key to fewer transitions is to avoid making a separate time slot for every routine and to make very few routines ones that all the children have to do at the same time. Instead, certain routines (such as snack, toileting, or dressing) can be embedded into extended periods of free-flowing, child-directed time (such as free choice or outdoor time), allowing children to proceed at their own pace and with smaller numbers of peers at a time. How a schedule might be revised to decrease the number of transitions using these strategies is illustrated in Figure 16.7.

The revised schedule outlined in Figure 16.7 has several advantages over the original one (Hemmeter, Ostrosky, Artman & Kinder, 2008). These include:

- Fewer whole-group transitions in which all the children have to move together
- Smaller amounts of time in which children are having whole-group instruction and more time for children to interact in smaller groups
- Extended center time so adults have more time to interact with individual children or only a few children at a time
- Inclusion of snack as part of the center time (referred to as *open snack*) so children can eat when they are hungry and stay at the table for as long as they wish.

TRY IT YOURSELF

Think about your day today. From the moment you woke up to right now, what are three main activities (e.g., getting ready in the morning, riding the bus to class, your first class, etc.) that made up your schedule? Identify these in the following chart. Next, think about the transitions associated with those parts of your day. Were the transitions easy or difficult to manage? How did they affect how you felt or what you did? What does this tell you about transitions in your own life?

	Activities in My Day	Assessment of Transitions: Easy (E) or Difficult (D)	Impact
Activity 1			
Activity 2			
Activity 3			

PITFALLS TO AVOID IN DAILY PLANNING

In addition to the do's you have learned about daily planning, there are some don'ts to consider as well. Take a moment to reflect on these planning pitfalls and how to avoid them.

star activities Complex activities that involve a great deal of setup, cleanup, or close adult supervision.

1. *Implementing too many "star" activities in one day.* Star activities are complex activities that involve a great deal of setup, cleanup, or close adult supervision. Examples might be: marble painting, cooking with a hot plate, or bringing an animal guest to class. All of these activities have good education potential. Yet they could be difficult to manage (messy, dangerous, or emotionally provocative) and need particularly thoughtful adult preparation and support for children. The best way to address this pitfall is to avoid planning too many such activities in a given day—only one per day is usually best.

2. *Too little change in activities and materials.* If materials remain on the shelves week after week with no variation, children lose interest and become bored. This detracts from children's learning and contributes to potential behavior problems. To avoid this pitfall, refresh core activity areas (e.g., blocks, pretend play, puzzles) by rotating some items and by adding or taking away props based on children's interests and growing skills. Do this on succeeding days, not all at once, so that children discover something new each day while also having access to old favorites. Introduce new materials

Today the teacher makes watercolors available in the art area. This is a change from the markers that were featured yesterday and attract several children to the art table to try out the new materials.

at whole-group or small-group times and then incorporate those materials into your learning centers and outdoor activities. Go outside with materials that are traditionally used indoors and bring outside materials inside to add interest and variety to each day.

3. *Failing to provide enough activity spaces for children at choice time.* It is important to plan at least one-and-a-half to two activity spaces for each child in the class during free choice. Thus, for a class of 18 children, you must plan at least 27 to 36 activity spaces. When teachers fail to provide enough spaces, children wander the room in search of something to do or get into conflicts over too few materials or spots in a desired activity. Prevent this pitfall by reviewing your plans and figuring out how many children each activity can comfortably include. Make a tally of the number of spaces available and adjust activities to make sure you have enough.

4. *Neglecting to factor in availability of resources.* Problems arise when teachers forget to consider classroom management issues such as availability of materials and number of adults available to help in their plans. For instance, if you have scheduled easel painting and tie-dyeing for the same time of the day but have only four smocks, you might not have enough to go around. In addition, both these activities might require a great deal of adult support. If help is limited, the demands of these two activities going on at once will make supervising the rest of the room difficult. To avoid soiled clothes and other supervisory challenges, switch one of these "smock-related" activities to another time or another day. Reviewing each day's plans with classroom resources in mind is the best means for steering clear of such dilemmas.

Assembling a Daily Plan

Putting together a good day for children involves more than simply filling in the blanks on a planning sheet. It is not a one-size-fits-all activity, either. Plans that fit last year's class or that you find on the Internet may not fit your current group of children. The place to start is always by thinking about the individual children in your group and what interests them. Note the things that have captured children's attention (e.g., several children are excited about everything to do with art; Ralph and Tonia are working their way through the most challenging puzzles; Michael, Robert, Jessie, and Mindy spend much of their time in free choice creating block bridges and roads; etc.). Think about how you might use these things to extend children's learning. Then, consider ways to use the children's interests as a foundation for addressing concept and skill development described in relevant program goals or state standards. Create activities that address these aims and begin to distribute them on the page. As you prepare a written overview of the day, ask yourself the following questions:

- What are my goals for children's learning?
- What materials do I need?
- Where will the adults be stationed during various times of the day?
- Do I have enough activity spaces planned in each portion of the day?
- How will each transition take place?
- Have I addressed each developmental domain?
- Does this overview include a variety of activity types?
- Have I addressed a variety of goals or do I repeat the same few and neglect others?
- How well have I addressed the unique needs and interests of individual children?

Plan in pencil (either literally or figuratively) so you can edit and move things around to create a plan that avoids the pitfalls you just read about and that takes into account the five criteria of good planning (consistency, pacing, time management, balancing variety and familiarity, as well as whole-child learning). Look at Figure 16.8 for an

FIGURE 16.8 A portion of Cherry Gonzalez's daily plan

Time	Area and Number of Spaces	Goals and Domains	Activities	Cherry's* Thinking
1:00–1:15 Greeting Time	Group-time rug 18 children	Affective: Self-awareness and self-efficacy	Hello Song and greetings Job chart Demonstrate still life pictures and materials available in art area	I lead group time Jeremy* stays at door until last child arrives Flo* provides support at group time
1:15–2:15 Free Choice				I float and manage room Jeremy moves back and forth between art and math/science Flo reads books and checks on snack periodically
	Art area 6 children	Physical: Fine motor Aesthetic: Recognize and respond to basic elements of art	Tearing and cutting paper Objects children can use to create their own still life models Easels and paint: red, green, yellow, and brown	Mix paint in advance Will need four smocks for easel Make sure drying rack is up Encourage children to move from here to pretend-play to connect activities and build on their interest in art
	Block area 4 children	Cognitive: Mathematics	Children create structures using at least four different block shapes Children draw pictures of their structures	Create "challenge" sign for this area Make pencils and manila paper available for block depictions Plan to hang these up around room
	Library 3 children Listening center 34 children	Language: Alphabet knowledge Rhyming words Aesthetic: Exploration of color Oral language and print	Include alphabet books and books about art New book: *The Artist Who Painted a Blue Horse* by Eric Carle Read-along stories	Use *Blue Horse* book for group time on Tuesday Make available *Blue Horse* flannel board on Wednesday and Thursday Include *Blue Horse* tape plus train story for Talia Added listening center to expand activity spaces available
	Math and science area 6 children	Cognition: Mathematics Cognition: Science	Seriating and sorting brushes artists use Estimating jar Color paddles that illustrate color combinations Measuring length of potato vine, enter findings on chart	Make sure to have a collection of brushes of different lengths, widths, colors, and shapes Would like to do liquid color mixing—may be too much on the day we are doing easel paintings of still life arrangements (today's star activity)—introduce color mixing later in the week

(continued)

FIGURE 16.8 A portion of Cherry Gonzalez's daily plan (*continued*)

Time	Area and Number of Spaces	Goals and Domains	Activities	Cherry's* Thinking
	Open snack 4 children	Language: Following "written" directions	Making cracker sandwiches following pictograph directions Crackers, two kinds of cheese, juice	Children enjoyed this last time; since they are familiar with the activity this will be less challenging to supervise Use pictograph with 3-step directions (pictures and words) Flo should check in periodically to keep conversation going and to support following directions
	Pretend play 5 children	Social: Cooperation	Housekeeping Begin creating an art gallery of children's work next to pretend play	This will be a good follow-up to the children's visit to the 5th-grade art gallery last week Encourage children to move from here to art area to connect activities and build on their interest in art
2:10—Warning for cleanup 2:15–2:25 Cleanup		Social: Social responsibility	Child rings cleanup bell Sing the cleanup song Pairs of children choose an area to clean up	Art will have a lot to clean up Flo will get children in art area to start cleaning up soon after warning When Jeremy's areas are clean, he will send his kids to the art area to help
2:25–2:45 Small Groups	3 Round tables	Alphabet knowledge	Focus on literacy skills	Tues. Oral language Wed. Phonics Thurs. Print awareness Fri. Concept development One adult at each table—works with same small group each day, makes written observations of each child
2:55–3:45 Outdoor Time	Preschool playground	Aesthetic: Explore materials Cognitive: Science Physical: Gross motor Physical: Fine motor	Sand sculptures, chalk on the walk Making mud clay, creating different consistencies Trikes Weaving rag strips in chain link fence	Jeremy will float and manage outdoor time I will supervise mud clay. Make sure outside water is working and hose is connected for mud play cleanup Flo will keep eye on trikes and other gross/fine motor areas

*Cherry: head teacher; Jeremy: assistant; Flo: aide

example of how head teacher Cherry Gonzalez considered all these things in the plan she made for the 18 preschoolers in her mixed-aged class. Although this is just a portion of a complete day's schedule, it will give you an idea of the thinking that goes into creating an effective daily overview.

Planning for Multiple Days

As you can see, there are many things to keep in mind when preparing for a day of teaching. The same guidelines hold true when planning multiple days. Typically, early childhood programs ask teachers to plan at least one week at a time. In creating weekly plans, teachers think about each day from beginning to end and also how one day's activities relate to the next. For example, on Monday the teacher plans for the children to build a "box town" out of cardboard containers. She intends for the activity to last several days and plans to introduce new materials a few at a time to keep children engaged (carpet tape on Tuesday, small vehicles on Wednesday and Thursday, miniature people on Friday). In addition, teachers plan for the same activity areas to address different curricular domains throughout the week—puzzle plans are socially focused on Monday and Tuesday, cognitively oriented on Wednesday, then designed around affective goals Thursday and Friday. In any weekly plan, some activities last the whole week; others appear for only a few days and are then replaced by something else (there is water in the water table Monday through Wednesday; the teacher switches to sand on Thursday). These variations give children access to materials long enough to explore them thoroughly but also provide diversity to keep the weekly agenda interesting.

Another way teachers extend their plans is to make sure the same curricular goals are addressed using different activity types throughout the week. For instance, children are exposed to the social goal of helping as they participate in exploratory play, guided discovery, problem-solving activities, discussions, demonstrations, and direct instruction. Some of these variations occur on the same day; some happen on different days. The cumulative effect is that children have multiple chances to enhance their learning and teachers can accommodate the diverse learning needs of individuals. Keeping all this in mind, teachers engaged in whole-week planning look over their plans to make sure they have a selection of activities that:

- Lead from one day to the next
- Vary in the number of days they are offered
- Address each curricular domain several times
- Make use of different activity types throughout the week

Making Use of Themes

Of course it is possible to plan an excellent week of activities using all the strategies you have learned so far. However, some teachers add another tool to their teaching repertoire, that of planning activities around a central concept or theme. In other words, they plan several activities during the week around a topic of particular relevance to the children, such as leaves, vehicles, or storytelling.

Theme teaching is popular in preschool and kindergarten classrooms because if done well, themes offer the possibility of meaningful connectivity among activities. Children take what they have learned in one activity and apply it to their experiences in another (e.g., children explore the shapes and textures of real leaves in a sorting activity, examine leaves outside, and read about different kinds of leaves at story time). These connections have the potential to deepen and scaffold children's learning. However, if they are done poorly, themes can become trite—based mostly on props that are cute or entertaining (e.g., pockets, marshmallows) but not educational. The difference between educational themes and less educational ones lies in the source of the theme and how well it is supported by factual knowledge.

themes Multi-day plans that involve several activities around a topic of particular relevance to the children.

WHAT IS A GOOD THEME?

The best themes are based on what interests children, combined with a focus on program goals and curriculum standards (Kostelnik, Soderman, & Whiren, 2011). Good choices also allow for plenty of first-hand experiences with the content. For instance, several children in Kelly Maher's class showed a real interest in the vehicles they saw, heard, smelled, and otherwise experienced at home and on the road. Children pretended to drive vehicles on the playground and in the classroom. They made vehicle sounds and enjoyed singing about the wheels on the bus and the tractor on Old McDonald's farm.

They often pointed out different kinds of vehicles in the parking lot or on the road that passed in front of their classroom. Kelly decided to capitalize on the children's vehicle interests by incorporating some planned activities about vehicles in her weekly overview. Before committing anything to paper, however, she thought about what children might learn about vehicles. She looked up the term *vehicles* and was surprised to discover that not every machine that moves people or goods around is a vehicle. Instead, vehicles are defined as "devices having wheels or runners that travel on land." Airplanes and boats are categorized as vessels, not vehicles. This reminded Kelly that she could not teach children off the top of her head. She needed to look things up so she would be sure to have accurate information on which to base her plans. Following some more fact finding, Kelly created a planning web to help her identify interrelated concepts about vehicles she might refer to in her teaching (Petersen, 2002). Figure 16.9 is an example of Kelly's web.

Based on what she had learned about vehicles and her initial observations of the children's play, Kelly decided to introduce the topic by focusing on different kinds of

Brent shows Molly how he is using the steam shovel to fill his bucket. Both children are among several in Ms. Maher's class who are fascinated by vehicles and machines.

planning web A visual diagram of the interrelated concepts associated with a particular topic.

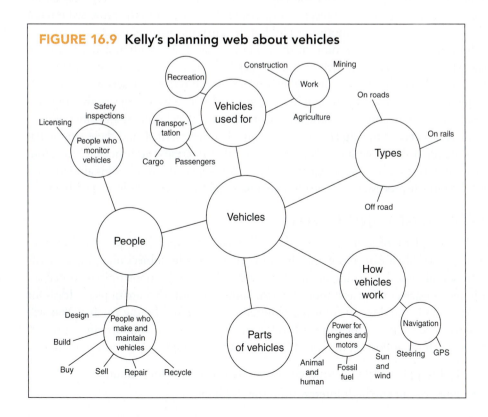

FIGURE 16.9 Kelly's planning web about vehicles

vehicles and the jobs they do. The content that supported her lessons included these terms and facts:

- A vehicle is a piece of equipment with wheels or runners that is used to transport people and things.
- Examples of vehicles are wagons, scooters, tricycles, bicycles, motorcycles, cars, trucks, buses, tractors, trains, snowmobiles, and sleds.
- Vehicles come in a variety of sizes, shapes, and colors.
- Vehicles have certain parts that make them suitable for certain jobs.

As Kelly developed the week's overview, she kept this factual information in mind and planned to address it through several hands-on activities. Not every activity she planned for the week related to the theme, but many did. Vehicle-related experiences were distributed across activity areas, across domains, from Monday through Friday. Some activities focused primarily on vehicle-related content (e.g., the kinds of vehicles), others used miniature vehicles or pictures of vehicles to address more general goals (e.g., counting and sorting). As Kelly interacted with children in the classroom, she did not recite the content verbatim, but she did refer to it as children participated in activities. Throughout this process Kelly noticed what the children talked about, the questions they asked, and how they transformed activities to suit their purposes. In this way, she obtained important information about what the children were learning and how she might use her observations to plan subsequent lessons. She could also determine whether children had enough of the theme and were ready to move on to something else or whether some facet of the theme had captured the children's attention enough to warrant their carrying out an in-depth project on the subject.

What Is a Project?

project An in-depth exploration of a topic that unfolds in three phases and that is driven by the children's interests.

Projects often evolve out of themes. However, they may also occur based simply on children's strong curiosity about something in their environment. A **project** is an in-depth exploration of a topic, object, or experience that stems from the expressed interest of children. This interest motivates children to carry out various hands-on activities to form a deeper understanding of the subject at hand. As children actively investigate whatever has captured their attention, they learn new concepts and skills. Whereas themes tend to be broad and initiated by teachers (based on child observation), projects are more strongly driven by the children's agenda. Additionally, in projects, the emphasis is on child investigation and problem solving (Helm, Beneke, & Steinheimer, 2007). Activities are chosen to help children represent what they studied, and these representations are often shared with family members or other interested audiences. Throughout the project, teachers document what children have done and learned. This all transpires in a three-phase process: getting ready, investigating the project, and sharing with others.

PHASE 1: GETTING READY

In the first phase of a project, possible topics emerge. Successful projects build on the things children care about and that intrigue them. The subject of a project needs to be a topic worth learning about. It should provide rich opportunities to deepen children's understanding and support curriculum standards that are in place. Ideas for projects can come directly from the children or be sparked by the teacher. You will need to decide whether the topic is feasible and has the potential to become a project. Ask yourself the following questions to see whether the topic has project potential:

- Is this topic worthy of children's time? Is it worth learning about?
- Does it generate high interest from the children?

- Does it support program and curricular goals that are already in place?
- Is there potential to include the topic in all areas of the curriculum?
- Are there practical opportunities for hands-on experiences to help children learn about the topic?
- Are resources available to extend children's learning?

If your answers to the previous questions are all *yes*, the topic is appropriate for further exploration by the children. Children require some knowledge of the subject before they can enter into a project. You will need to determine what children already know and what prior experiences they have had related to the subject. As noted earlier, including some introductory activities to expose children to the topic in your weekly teaching plan will provide a set of common experiences for children to refer to as they enter into the project. As their interest in the topic builds, you will help children formulate questions about the topic and ideas about how they might get answers to their questions. You will find that when children determine the questions, they are motivated to find the answers. Even figuring out how to get the information to answer their questions becomes an exercise in problem solving! During this initial phase, think about what resources are available to help the children learn more about the subject. This is an excellent time to invite parents with expertise on the topic to participate in some way.

PHASE 2: INVESTIGATING THE TOPIC

During the second phase of the project you will plan opportunities for the children to do fieldwork and to speak to experts. Fieldwork provides children with the chance to engage in hands-on, in-depth investigations to answer their questions and learn more. For example, you might arrange for children to visit a grocery store to learn about how the store operates, the different jobs at the store, or where the store gets its merchandise. Field-site visits provide opportunities for children to examine relevant equipment or materials and to interview experts who know about the topic. Figure 16.10 lists things to consider when choosing a field site.

In addition to field-site visits, real objects, books, and other materials are included in the classroom as resources to help children investigate the topic. Children's family members are often happy to lend artifacts or resources to the classroom to support children's learning. Adding project-related materials to different learning centers throughout the classroom stimulates children's interest in the project and provides opportunities to extend their learning and for them to represent what they know. As children carry out projects, teachers utilize a variety of teaching strategies such as reflections, scaffolding, questions, and challenges. Children also need opportunities to represent their knowledge. This might happen through drawing, telling stories, or building with blocks. These work samples can be displayed for further reflection by

fieldwork Visits to real settings during which children engage in hands-on, in-depth investigations. Such visits may be repeated more than once during a project.

FIGURE 16.10 Evaluating possible field sites

- Is the site safe for young children to visit and easy to monitor?
- What is available at the site for children to investigate (instead of just hear about)?
- Are there things available for children to handle, manipulate, move, touch, and so on, to spark their curiosity and help them learn more about the topic?
- Will there be an expert available for children to interview?

Source: Based on Helm & Katz, 2011.

the children and to communicate to classroom visitors what children are learning. Work samples also give you a means for assessing what children have accomplished through the project.

PHASE 3: SHARING WITH OTHERS

Once the project seems to be nearing its end, you need to think about ways for the children to communicate what they have learned. Children may share the highlights of the project with their families, classmates who were not a part of the project, or another class. You will help the children review what they have done by carefully examining work samples, reviewing photographs, and talking with their peers. Children can demonstrate what they have learned through art, sculpture, drama, and stories. You and the children will work together to create a display of photographs, artifacts, or other items collected through the project.

Next, let's see how Jenny Miller carried out a project in her preschool classroom.

JENNY MILLER'S TRACTOR PROJECT

The project began when several children became interested in the small lawn tractor that was used to cut the grass on the playground. The children watched carefully and then continued to show interest as they built "mowing machines" in the block area, pretended to drive tractors during outdoor play, and drew pictures of different types of mowers they imagined. Janson told the children that his grandfather used a "really big" tractor to cut down all the hay in his field. This idea captured the imagination of many of the children, and it was obvious the children wanted to know more.

PHASE 1: GETTING READY

Mrs. Miller began by helping the children create a list of what they already knew about tractors, what they wanted to learn, and ideas about how they might find the answers to their questions. Figure 16.11 lists some of the ideas children shared during this initial discussion with Mrs. Miller.

Mrs. Miller used the ideas from the children to create a preliminary planning web. She identified the concepts she thought could be addressed through an investigation of tractors and brainstormed activities that could be used to support children in gaining these concepts. She then reviewed the *Nebraska Early Learning Guidelines* (Nebraska Department of Education, 2005) to add to her planning web. She matched

---

FIGURE 16.11 Ideas from Mrs. Miller's class about tractors

What We Know About Tractors	Questions We Have About Tractors	How We Might Be Able to Find the Answer
There are big tractors and not so big tractors.	"Why are there different kinds of tractors?"	Look in a tractor book.
Some tractors pull things.	"How come some tractors pull things?"	Ask Mr. Cahill (the school groundskeeper).
Tractors can cut grass and some tractors cut hay.	"Can all tractors pull things?"	Ask Janson's grandfather.
Tractors are green.	"How do you learn to drive a tractor?"	Go to a tractor store and look at real tractors.
Somebody needs to drive the tractor.	"What are the parts of a tractor?"	

FIGURE 16.12 **Activities to support Nebraska early learning guidelines**

Approaches to Learning

- *Uses communication to ask questions and seek answers*
  - Help children create a list of questions and possible sources to answer questions.
- *Uses active exploration and trial and error to solve problems*
  - Have children create tractor sculptures using clay. Encourage problem solving as they add details to the sculpture (how can you attach the steering wheel to the body of the tractor?).
- *Reflects on experiences and information and draws conclusions from information*
  - Have children write thank you cards to the tractor museum telling what they learned from the visit.

Language

- *Uses new vocabulary that has been introduced*
  - Introduce a word wall with tractor terms.

- *Shows interest in early writing—uses writing to represent thoughts and ideas*
  - Have children bring clipboards to the tractor museum to sketch what they see.
  - Add "tractor words" to the writing area for children to copy.
  - Encourage children to make tractor books.

Mathematics

- *Develops knowledge of geometric principles—learns about shapes*
  - Create tractor pictures from simple geometric shapes. Provide photographs of tractors for children to use as references.
- *Recognizes different types of measurement can be made (height, length, width)*
  - Bring tape measures to the museum. Assign specific children to record measurements.
  - Use measurements to draw a scale tractor in the parking lot.

Source: Nebraska Department of Education. (2005). *Nebraska Early Learning Guidelines 3- to 5-year-olds.* Lincoln, NE: Author.

the *Guidelines* that were likely to occur through the project to those concepts and planned activities listed on her web. See Figure 16.12 for examples of *Early Learning Guidelines* Mrs. Miller planned to address.

PHASE 2: INVESTIGATING THE PROJECT

Mrs. Miller planned a visit to a tractor museum located on the campus of the local university. Since she had been to the museum several times in the past, she knew that there were many things the children could investigate up close and that the museum staff were more than willing to listen to the children's questions and provide thoughtful answers. Because the museum was close to the school, it was possible to make several visits, allowing the children to focus on one or two things during each visit. She prepared the children for each visit by helping them think about what they wanted to know as a result of the trip. Children identified the questions they would be responsible for investigating during the visit and how they would share what they learned with others when they returned to the classroom. Some children decided to tally the different types of tractors at the museum, others wanted to measure the tractors, and several decided to do an observational sketch of certain parts of the tractor. Over the course of the tractor project, children worked on various tasks including creating books about tractors, dictating stories in which tractors were featured, and representing different tractors using various building and art materials. The project really took shape when the children decided that they wanted to create a large tractor using cardboard boxes and recyclable material. They paid great attention to the details of their tractor, referencing photographs and their sketches when they disagreed about how to complete certain aspects of the tractor. Additional visits to the museum provided opportunities for children to concentrate on aspects of the tractors they had previously overlooked. Throughout the process, Mrs. Miller documented what the children were doing and noted what they had learned, displaying different work samples and photographs for the children to view in the classroom.

observational sketch Detailed drawing of an object or area based on focused observation. The focus of this type of drawing is to look carefully, draw details, and compare the real object to the drawing.

PHASE 3: SHARING WITH OTHERS

As a concluding event, the children invited their families to see the work they had done. The highlight of the occasion was showing the large tractor they had built to their family members. The children were particularly proud of the fact that the wheels on the tractor actually turned, and invited staff from the tractor museum to attend the party as special guests. Each child had a role in sharing a part of the project and what they had learned.

An Observational Sketch of Tractors

Logan carefully examines the tractor and draws what he observes.

As a part of our project on tractors we visited the Tractor Museum on the university campus. Logan was very interested in the wheels of the tractors. He made sketches of the tractors as a way to record what he observed. This type of observational sketching encourages children to observe carefully and record details to help them later recall what they have seen.

He then compares his drawing to the tractor. *"These are big wheels, there are lots of spokes! I have to put that in my picture."*

Logan shows Clark his sketch. Clark asks, *"Why did you put this here?"* (pointing to the drawing).

Logan explains, *"See, this is where the steering wheel is. You need that to drive the tractor."* Logan then shows Clark the steering wheel in his drawing and points to the steering wheel on the actual tractor.

Logan's sketch of a Row Crop tractor.

Look carefully at this documentation board. What do you notice that Logan has learned about tractors?

As you can see, doing project work with young children provides rich opportunities for learning. However, it is unlikely that projects will offer all of the learning experiences that should be included in the curriculum (Helm & Katz, 2011). Not all children will participate in any given project, and some children will be involved in a given project more than others. You will also find that some children may participate in one aspect of a project but show little interest in another. For these reasons it is important to include non-project-related activities into each day and learning center. Projects are well matched to many curricular approaches. Teachers who are comfortable with project work often incorporate aspects such as observational drawing and documentation into other types of learning experiences (Helm & Katz, 2011). The key is designing a variety of activities and experiences that actively engage children and support their growing understanding of a concept.

Meeting the Needs of Diverse Learners

Using projects provides opportunities for including all children. Teachers encourage children to develop their interests and utilize their individual strengths through project work. Each child's contributions are valued. The very nature of project work means a variety of activities and experiences take place. Not all children are required to participate in each one. Individual differences and interests are taken into consideration. Children are able to work at different paces and contribute in a variety of ways to the project. Children at all different levels of development can find some way to contribute to the work on the project. A large amount of project work is done in small groups of children, making it easier for the teacher to make adaptations or accommodations to include children with special needs.

Communicating with Families

Helping families and others in the community understand the value of project-based instruction depends on our ability to communicate what children are doing and learning. Many people fail to recognize the rich learning taking place through a project. You will find that family members want to understand what their child is learning and will look to you for explanations. Providing ongoing communication to families about classroom happenings, including project work, helps families feel they are a part of the classroom community and to better appreciate the meaningful learning taking place in the group. See Figure 16.13 for an example of information you can provide to families on the importance of projects.

TECH TIP

Documenting Children's Projects

Keep your cell phone, tablet, or other mobile device with you while children participate in project work. Use it to record children's work. Focus on the process rather than the product, emphasizing children's ideas and words. Later, add your own reflections about the project.

NEWSLETTER/WEB READY COMMUNICATION

FIGURE 16.13 • The Potential of Projects

Children are interested in the world around them. It's common to hear children ask many questions about something that captures their attention. When children find something that matters to them, they want to learn all about it. Helping children think carefully about what they want to know and identify ways to get answers to their questions helps children see themselves as capable learners. Having opportunities to find answers for themselves also helps children in developing the disposition of a learner. Children tell themselves, "I know how to find answers to my questions." One way children may discover new knowledge is to participate in an in-depth study of a particular topic in order to learn more about it. This investigation may last several days or even weeks or months, depending on the children's interest. This type of learning is called *project work*.

Through project work children learn to:

- Ask questions to learn about things they are interested in
- Predict the answers to their questions
- Use experts and other resources to gather information
- Find answers to their own questions and compare these answers to their earlier predictions
- Exchange ideas and opinions
- Test their ideas
- Learn to work with others toward a common goal

The topic of the project is not as important as the skills children develop by working on the project. Once children become absorbed in and challenged by a project on one subject, they realize they can learn about all sorts of things. And most important, children are able to experience the satisfaction that comes from solving problems and overcoming obstacles. These are exactly the skills they need to have as lifelong learners.

16 Applying What You've Learned

Based on what you now know about organizing children's learning over time, carry out these activities to increase your knowledge and skills.

1. **Constructing a Daily Routine.** Plan a sample daily schedule for a full-day classroom. Carefully review your schedule to make sure it includes all the best practices discussed earlier in the chapter.

2. **Planning Smooth Transitions.** Look over the schedule you outlined above, identifying several places where transitions would be needed to help the children move from one segment of the schedule to the next. Now, think about transition strategies you could use to support children during these times.

3. **Creating a Weekly Overview of Activities that Address Whole-Child Learning.** Observe a group of young children over the course of several days. Identify a topic you believe the children are interested in learning about. Outline a week's worth of activities connected by this topic. Think about the following questions as you put together your weekly plan:

   • How do I know children are interested in this topic? How will I stimulate continued interest in the topic over the week?

   • How will I provide the opportunity for children to pursue activities over time?

   • Are all the developmental domains included?

   • Is there a variety of activity types included each day and throughout the week?

4. **Using Projects.** Thinking about the topic you identified for your weekly plan, consider what opportunities may be available in your area for a field-site visit. Identify several potential possibilities and visit the sites. Using Figure 16.10, evaluate the feasibility of the sites you identified.

5. **Diverse Learners.** Explain to a peer how you could use project work to support the language development of an English language learner in your classroom.

6. **Communicating with Families.** Create a card for the block area of a classroom with the following information:

   In the block area children are (*list several things the children do in that area*).

   Through this type of play, they are learning to (*describe what children learn through the activities you listed*).

   Now develop a series of cards that could be placed throughout the classroom that explain what children are doing and learning in various activity areas.

References

Epstein, A. S. (2007). *The intentional teacher: Choosing the best strategies for young children's learning.* Washington, D.C.: NAEYC.

Essa, E. (2011). *Introduction to early childhood education* (6th ed.). Clifton Park, NY: Thomson Delmar Learning.

Gallick, B., & Lee, L. (2010). Eliminating transitions. *Exchange.* July/August. 48–51.

Gordon, A. M., & Browne, K. W. (2011). *Beginning essentials in early childhood education.* Clifton Park, NY: Thomson Delmar Learning.

Helm, J. H., Beneke, S., & Steinheimer, K. (2007). *Windows on planning: Documenting young children's work* (2nd ed.). New York: Teachers College Press.

Helm, J. H., & Katz, L. (2011). *Young investigators: The project approach in the early years.* New York: Teachers College Press.

Hemmeter, M. L., Ostrosky, M. M., Artman, K. M., & Kinder, K. A. (2008). Planning transitions to prevent challenging behavior. *Beyond the journal: Young children on the Web.* Washington, D.C.: NAEYC. May, 1–7.

Hohman, M., Weikart, D. P., & Epstein, A. S. (2008). *Educating young children: Active learning for preschool and child care programs* (3rd ed.). Ypsilanti, MI: HighScope Foundation.

Jacobs, G. M., & Crowley, K. E. (2010). *Reaching standards and beyond in kindergarten.* Thousand Oaks, CA: Corwin.

Kostelnik, M. J., Soderman, A. K., & Whiren, A. P. (2011). *Developmentally appropriate curriculum: Best practices in early childhood education.* Upper Saddle River, NJ: Pearson.

National Association for the Education of Young Children (NAEYC). (2009). *Developmentally appropriate practice in early childhood programs serving children from birth through age 8.* Position statement. Washington, D.C.: Author.

Nebraska Department of Education. (2005). *Nebraska early learning guidelines 3- to 5-year-olds.* Lincoln, NE: Author.

Ostrosky, M. M., Jung, E. Y., & Hemmeter, M. L. (2012). Helping children make transitions between activities. *What works briefs #4.* Champaign, IL: Center for the Social and Emotional Foundations for Early Learning. Retrieved from csefel.vanderbilt.edu/briefs/wwb4.html

Petersen, E. A. (2002). *A practical guide to early childhood methods planning and materials.* Upper Saddle River, NJ: Pearson.

Appendix

Lesson Plans

Exploratory Play

Children are very interested in exploring materials. In this plan, they can explore water (with and without soap), wax, the process of evaporation, the sponges, and waxing cloth. They are also exploring the idea of what they are likely to perceive as real work or contribution to the group. This should be unhurried with the focus on the process of doing. This activity is set up for two or more sessions.

Domain	Affective
Activity Name	Cleaning the Blocks
Goal	Children complete a task they have begun
Objectives	Given guidance and the materials, children will:
	1. Exhibit an interest in the materials.
	2. Examine the materials.
	3. Experiment with the materials.
	4. Ask questions or describe their observations.
	5. Communicate their thinking through actions, words, or the things they make.
Content	Wash: to clean with water.
	Wax: to rub with wax.
	Washing objects removes visible soiling and disinfects the objects.
	Real work is satisfying.
Materials	2 tubs with warm water
	Small amount of Spic and Span® (or any other cleaner that does not require rinsing); put some in one tub only
	2 or more scrubbing sponges
	Absorbent rug (under the tubs of water)
	Towels to wipe off excess moisture and clean up spills
	Plastic aprons
	Adult mop
	Clean rug where blocks can dry
	Later, or the next day:
	Floor paste wax and clean soft cloth (shop cloths work well)
	Unit blocks (regular maintenance is to clean and wax once a year)
	Tray padded with towels
	Digital camera
	Note: Blocks should not be left to soak in the water. Therefore, guide children to wash one at a time.

Procedure

Segment 1

1. Children will exhibit an interest in the materials.

Do	Say
Prepare the washing station in advance, bringing several blocks to it. Wash and rinse a block, placing it on the tray to drip. Move it to the drying rug. Invite children to participate.	*Our blocks need to be washed. You can do it.* *Later, when the blocks are dry, you may wax them.*

2. Children will examine the materials.

Do	Say
Move aside. Observe. Use behavior reflections and open-ended questions.	*You noticed a black mark on that one. Which side of the sponge do you think will work better?* Or *You are interested cleaning the blocks.*

3. Children will experiment with the materials.

Do	Say
Observe. Use paraphrase and behavior reflections based on what you see and hear intermittently. Take notes of what they say and do.	Examples of possible comments: *The water with the soap feels different from the clear water.* *You noticed that wet blocks look different than dry ones.*

4. Children will ask questions or describe their observations.

Do	Say
Make a few comments that do not require a response but are an opening if children wish to engage. Respond to questions. Observe. Mostly remain silent.	*You have really scrubbed a lot of blocks.* *You wonder what made that mark on the block.* *Tell me your idea about that.*

5. Children will communicate their thinking through actions, words, or the things they make.

Do	Say
Photograph children in action. Take notes on their comments during the activity. Ask quiet children about what they did. Clean up and prepare for transition.	*Cassandra, see this picture of you. Tell me what you were doing.* *Thank you for working, Mimi. When you have put away the sponge, what do you plan to do next?* *Caleb and George, you should be proud of all the blocks you washed. What activity will you do next? Please hang the wet towels on the line.*

Segment 2 (after the blocks are dry)

1. Children will exhibit an interest in the materials.

Do	Say
In advance, prepare the soft cloths by rubbing them into the paste wax so that they are waxy but the wax is not in chunks. Repeat as needed. Demonstrate wiping each block carefully and putting it on the shelf (if needed).	*Now you may complete cleaning and waxing the blocks.* *Each cloth has a little wax on it.*

2. Children will examine the materials.

Do	Say
Move away and observe. Use behavior reflections.	*You noticed that some wax has stuck to your fingers* [etc.].

3. Children will experiment with the materials.

Do	Say
Observe how children apply the wax to the blocks and play with the blocks. Comment periodically on what you see or ask leading questions. Take photographs.	*You noticed that the block feels different once the wax is on it.* *How do you get the wax from the cloth on the block?*

4. Children will ask questions or describe their observations.

Do	Say
Listen and take notes on children's comments. Use paraphrase statements to clarify questions.	*You are wondering why we rub wax on the blocks. The wax helps the blocks remain smooth and clean.*

5. Children will communicate their thinking through actions, words, or the things they make.

Do	Say
Prepare a photographic record with the children's comments from objectives. Review it with them. Use affective reflections as children reflect on their work.	*Thank you for showing me the really big pile of blocks that you waxed. You worked at this a long time.* *You are very pleased with the work you have done yesterday and today.* *It really feels good to get a big job done.*
Facilitate individual transitions.	*The art table is open and so is the puzzle table. Which one do you want to go to?* Or *Tell me what you plan to do next.*

Simplification   Children may just swish water and squeeze sponges and towels.

Extension   Allow children to dip into the paste wax, rub it into the cloths, and do more independently. (You may need extra wax.)

Most likely, block building will occur as a natural extension.

Evaluation (child)   Document what the children did and how they did it by using their comments and photographs.

What did the children learn from exploring the materials?

Were they successful in exploring materials while engaging in a task?

What would come next in meeting the goal for these children?

Which children had difficulty completing both parts of the task?

What appeared to be the difficulty for them?

What comes next for helping them to complete a task they have begun?

Evaluation (self)   1. Was I able to stand back and let the children lead in this activity?

2. What could I have done differently in setting up the activity or in closing it?

3. Did I focus my behavior reflections on the efforts children were making in meeting the objectives?

Guided Discovery

This plan can be used over months (or years) as children discover the properties of wet and dry sand indoors or outdoors. The standard measures are used so that children may observe weight differences in wet and dry sand. Focus on the process of observing closely. If you have not played in wet and dry sand recently, do so before implementing the activity: listen to the sound of dry and wet sand as you use it; smell them both; examine each carefully visually, noting tactile differences. Younger children will focus on the first few objectives. The oldest, most experienced children could engage in all of them.

Domain	Cognition
Activity Name	Wet and Dry Sand
Goal	Children examine natural objects by using their multisensory abilities
Objectives	Given instruction and the materials, children will:

1. Examine the material.

2. Experiment with objects.

3. Ask related questions.

4. Make relevant observations (describe what they are doing, tell someone to do something, explain something).

5. Make representational records of objects and events for future reference.

Content

1. People learn about nature by examining things carefully.

2. People can examine something by looking at it, smelling it, touching it, and listening to it.

3. Recording observations is one way to help you remember.

4. Sand and water take the shape of their containers; they can be poured.

5. Water changes the texture and weight of dry sand.

Materials

Sand (outdoors, if possible)

Water in buckets or faucet

Measuring scoops or measuring cups

Plastic containers that hold up to 1 gallon but are of various shapes; some that hold, 4, 8, or 16 ounces.

Funnels

Sifters

Table knife or straight-edge spatula

Spoons

Magnifying glass

3 × 5 or 5 × 7 cards

Felt-tip pens

Clipboard

Procedure

1. Children will examine the materials.

Do	Say
Invite children to participate.	*Come and dig in the sand. There are lots of containers for you to fill. Try moving the sand with your hands. Hold some and look at it carefully.*
Use behavior reflections.	*You are allowing the dry sand to flow through your fingers.*

2. Children will experiment with the material (or objects).

Do	Say
Make sure that all children have access to tools. Observe what children do and use behavioral reflections. Pose if/then questions.	*You are filling containers.* *What do you think will happen if [sand dries, gets wet, won't come out of the container, etc.]?*

3. Children will ask related questions.

Do	Say
Restate children's questions before answering them and wait for their comments.	*You wonder why the darker sand does not flow through the funnel like the brighter sand does. Do you have an idea about that?*

4. Children will make relevant observations (describe what they are doing, tell someone to do something or explain something).

Do	Say
Encourage children to share ideas.	*Louis, tell Theodore what you noticed about the light and dark sand. How did you get the light, warm sand darker and cooler?*
Ask children open-ended questions.	*How did you discover . . . ?* *What else did you try?*
Pose problems that children can act on with the materials to facilitate their thinking and observation.	*Nao, please explain what happened when you [turned a container over, added water, used a measuring cup].*

5. Children will describe results or conclusions.

Do	Say
As children clean up their area or are about to leave the activity, ask them to describe what they have done. Continually ask children how they found out something, what they saw, felt, or heard. Use some sample probes.	*Tell me what you did.* *What did you see?* *What happened when . . . ?* *How do you know that . . . ?*

6. Children will communicate results.

Do	Say
Encourage children to communicate the results of their experimentation.	*Tell Paul what happened when you . . . .*
Children may use words, pictures, or symbols that have meaning to them.	*Would you like to draw something to help you remember what you found out?*

Simplification   Children may engage in sensory experience related to Objective 1.

Extension
1. Point out the relationship of the measuring tools to the containers if a child does not point it out. Suggest that they count the number of cups needed to fill a larger container.
2. Look at specific grains of sand under a magnifying glass.

Evaluation (child)
1. Use a participation chart that allows you to record children's activity over a long period of time. Eventually, after several opportunities to play, develop a plan for discussing the properties of wet and dry sand.
2. What were the various strategies that children used to investigate the sand and water?
3. How did the children tend to communicate their findings?

Evaluation (self)
1. How would I revise this activity?
2. Were the materials adequate to explore the sand in different states?

Problem Solving

The processes defined in the objectives train children to think logically and to test their ideas. Scientific discovery is a process of elimination of possible answers to a problem, so predicting an incorrect answer and then testing it is desirable. Children do not need to get the right answer to think effectively. They can learn the properties of materials and make observations. The process can be used for all kinds of knowledge where outcomes can be observed.

Domain	Cognitive
Activity Name	Effects of Adding Materials to Tempera
Goal	Children explore first hand a variety of cause-and-effect relationships
Objectives	1. Children will explore the materials.
	2. Children will observe a physical or social phenomenon.
	3. Children will gather information or make a prediction.
	4. Children will experiment/test out their ideas.
	5. Children will describe the results or conclusions.
	6. Children will communicate their results.
Content	Same: identical, alike
	Different: unalike, dissimilar, not the same
	More: greater quantity
	Visual properties of tempera might or might not change by adding materials to it.
Materials	Liquid tempera or prepared dry tempera (red, yellow, blue, white, black)
	Brushes and paper for each child
	Container and water for rinsing brushes
	Pitcher of water
	Stirring sticks
	Several small containers and teaspoons (used to add materials)
	Sand
	Salt
	Liquid detergent (clear, uncolored)
	Powdered detergent (white)
	Paper and marker
Procedure	1. Children will explore the materials.

Do	Say
Encourage children to smell, touch, or examine all materials. Have a little in small containers. Name materials.	*We are exploring some materials today. Some you know, some you may not know.* *This is liquid detergent and this one is dry detergent . . . .*

2. Children will observe a physical or social phenomenon.

Do	Say
Give each child a brush and white construction paper. Put red tempera in a small container for children to dip brushes into.	*Paint a mark down the page. Look closely at the paint and tell me what you see.*
Use probes.	*Is the paint sticky, wet, smooth, rough [etc.]?*

3. Children will gather information or make a prediction.

Do	Say
Ask for a prediction.	*What do you think will happen if you add liquid detergent?*
	Or
	Guess what the paint will be like if we add sand.
As children say what they think will happen for each addition, record it on a large paper and repeat it.	*Miranda predicted that the liquid starch would not change the paint. Let's try it out and see.*

4. Children will experiment/test their ideas.

Do	Say
Try out the predictions.	*I poured liquid detergent into the red paint. Paint another mark on your paper.*

5. Children will describe results or conclusions.

Encourage the children to compare the marks.	*How is it the same or different from the first mark?*
	What does it look like? Feel like? How does it smell?
Ask child to compare her prediction to her observation. Was it accurate? Avoid the word *wrong*.	*Miranda, earlier you thought that the liquid starch would not change the paint. What do you think now?*

6. Children will communicate results.

Label each paint mark. Hang the paper where others can see it after it dries.	*Your record of what you did will help you remember. Hang it to dry. Later we can post it on the board.*
After it dries, ask child to recall the process.	*Miranda, tell me what you did to make each of these marks.*
Facilitate individual transitions.	*David, tell what you are going to do next, then hang up your apron and wash your hands.*

Simplification   1. Focus on Objectives 1 and 2.

2. If necessary, paint the marks yourself.

Extension   1. Repeat procedure starting at #3 for each material used in the same session. Otherwise begin with #1. Explore the effects of adding more of the material (lots of detergent) or combining materials such as sand and detergent.

Add each material to fresh paint; stir. Use a clean container for each combination.

Paint + sand; Paint + salt, etc.

2. Repeat as written, using a different color.

3. Repeat, adding one hue to another without altering texture, then with altered texture.

Evaluation (child)   Use a dated objective checklist with children's names on it to record whether children met each objective with a column for comments.

Note where children had difficulty with the process.

Evaluation (self)   1. To what extent were my comments focused on cause and effect or the observations children made?

2. How useful was my plan for evaluation for multiple experiences with the same process and material?

3. How should I alter my implementation to be more effective?

Discussion

The problems for discussion A through D are set up to demonstrate how you introduce an issue. By altering the wording slightly the strategies can be used for many different issues. Select the problem that is presented by the activities in your group. Do not use all of them at once, even with older children. Avoid discussing issues if you have made decisions already. This plan may be completed over a 2- to 3-year period and repeated as new variations emerge.

Domain	Social
Name	Establishing Shared Expectations for Rough and Tumble Play
Goal	Children show awareness of and concern for the rights and well-being of others
Objectives	1. Children will sit with other children during a discussion.
	2. Children will listen to one another without interrupting.
	3. Children will contribute at least one idea to a discussion.
	4. Children will ask questions related to the topic.
	5. Children will come to some agreements on how to play.
Content	All children enjoy movement and action.
	Some children enjoy playing roughly with other children part of the time.
	Hitting hard with a fist, biting, kicking, and other hurtful, angry acts constitute fighting not play.
	Fair: all people have an equal chance
Materials	Easel
	Markers
	Lots of large paper
	To save time, add headings for each problem on separate sheets of paper.
Procedure	1. Children will sit with other children during a discussion.

Do	Say
Call children together during a regular group time.	*Today we are going to talk about how we can play safely and be fair to everyone. All of you will get a chance to listen and to talk.*

2. Children will listen to one another without interrupting.

Do	Say
Paraphrase or repeat each contribution. Write a word or two on the paper.	*Remember to listen when one of your friends is talking. Then they will listen to you. I will write down your ideas so we do not forget them.*
A. If the children are very inexperienced, use a statement or questions to establish the purpose of the discussion.	*Being safe means no one gets hurt badly. Or What does it mean to be safe?*
	Being fair means that everyone gets to enjoy active play without someone hurting or scaring them. Or What does it mean to be fair when we play actively with others?
B. Set up the problem of "who is playing" using two acceptable but very different alternatives. Write down every suggestion, including the completely unacceptable ones.	*Some children like to play chase and tag, other children just like to run or play at other things. How will you know who wants to play tag with you and who doesn't?*
C. Set up the problem of where children play rough and tumble by establishing criteria first and asking children what spaces meet it.	*We use tumbling mats so people won't get hurt when they fall. You don't run in the classroom so that you won't bump into others or the furniture. You walk quietly in the hall so you don't disturb other groups. Where can you play noisily or actively without getting hurt or disturbing others?*
D. Set the problem of where to tag a person or where to hold them when wrestling. Use examples from older children that they might have seen. Note: You are asking children to evaluate using criteria established in the beginning.	*I have noticed that when the older children are playing tag, they touch the shoulder or back of the person they are tagging. It is someplace between the waist and the neck or on the arms. Do you think that this is safe and fair? Why? or Why not?*
E. Set the problem of how to stop playing vigorously.	*How should somebody let you know that they do not want to play anymore? and/or What do you think of having a 'safe zone' where someone can stop playing for a while? Where should that be on our playground?*

3. Children will contribute at least one idea to a discussion.

Do	Say
Keep track of who has commented and who has not. If necessary, ask a specific question or request a point of view from children who have not spoken.	*Philip, tell me how you would like others to let you know that they are not playing chase any more.* *Nick, do you agree with Phillip or do you have a different idea?*

4. Children will ask questions related to the topic.

Do	Say
Paraphrase any question asked so that everyone can hear it. If other children are able to answer, encourage them to do so.	*Jordan, maybe you can answer Kevin's question.*

5. Children will come to some agreements on how to play.

Do	Say
Review all suggestions as to possible answers as children appear to be finished providing them as each problem is addressed. Bring closure to the discussion (of each question) with a plan to try one. If you get agreement, verify it and write it out on a new piece of paper. If not, you may either choose one to try or vote on it. Transition	*You have shared your ideas, now it is time to decide. It seems most of you like XXXX. If you agree we will try that. I will write it out.* **Say** *You have been thinking very hard and everyone has a better idea of how we will play chase. It is time for lunch now, so children who sit at the red table can go wash their hands. The rest of us will sing…*

Simplification

1. Shorten the plan to address only Objectives 1 and 2. Accept participation by listening and answering general questions yourself.

Extension

1. Continue this discussion into a voting sequence if children generate more than one good alternative to solve a problem. Point out that once everyone has voted, then that is the strategy everyone will use.

2. Continue the discussion with additional problem statements. Generally these will be generated by your observations of your children. Some examples are:
   - "If you are bigger and faster than other children, they don't have a chance to tag you. What can you do to give others a fair chance?" (Establishing a handicap)
   - "If someone tags you hard and is laughing, what does that mean?" "If someone tags you hard and looks mad, does it mean the same thing?" (Using nonverbal cues to determine fight or play)
   - "If someone falls and gets hurt after you tagged him, what should you do?" (Avoiding aggressive escalation)

Evaluation (child)

Record summaries of comments made by children on an antidotal record related to the goal (see sample chart). Children may have participated in the discussion, but not demonstrated competence related to the goal. That is, he or she may know what safety means but demonstrate no particular interest in others.

Show awareness of and concern for the rights and well-being of others.

Child name	Child name
Notes:	Notes:

Evaluation (self)

1. How effective was I in setting the problem(s) so that children felt comfortable and safe?

2. Which strategies were most useful in involving the more timid children? The more dominating children?

3. How well did I respond to issues children brought up that I had not anticipated?

Demonstration

Use a demonstration when teaching a skill. Children learn best when they observe it, hear it described while observing again, and then try it themselves. This plan is for the beginner, regardless of age. Coach children using the same language that you use in instruction when they are practicing. Emphasize the actions of your hands when demonstrating in this plan.

Domain Aesthetics

Activity Name Pasting

Goal Children use a variety of materials, tools, techniques, and processes in the arts (visual art, music, dance, and drama)

Objectives
1. Children will observe/listen to a demonstration.
2. Children will describe what they observe.
3. Children will imitate a desired action.
4. Children will practice a desired action.
5. Children will carry out the desired action in a situation in which it is relevant.

Content
Paste is a sticky substance.
Paste goes between layers to stick them together.
There are various types of adhesives.

Materials
Paste (glue, mixture of glue and paste, flour and water paste, glue sticks)
9 × 12 construction paper
Recycled paper scraps (various types of paper or small items such cotton balls, wood chips, or bottle caps that can be adhered to paper)
Small dishes to hold paste
Newspapers to cover the table

Procedure
1. Children will observe/listen to a demonstration.

Do	Say
Place newspapers on the table. Lay out construction paper, assorted paper scraps, and small dishes of paste. Invite a small group of children to engage in the activity. Print the child's name on the 9 × 12 paper. Pick up a paper scrap and put it on the newspaper beside the construction paper. Put a small amount of paste on it. Turn it over and place it carefully on a piece of construction paper. Smooth it down without getting paste on the top.	*Today I will show you how to use the paste. (Pointing) This is the paste. These are papers that you may paste to the colored paper that you choose. Now watch my hands carefully.*

2. Children will describe what they observe.

Do	Say
Use the children's language to reinforce the sequence of events and then repeat the sequence orally as you carry it out again. Pause as needed to prompt them to supply the next step orally. A possible example is provided. You may ask, "What do I do next?" as needed.	*Now tell me what you saw first.* *First select a piece of paper to paste on. Then put a small amount of paste on it and smooth it all the way to the edges. Then pick it up and put it carefully just where you want it with the sticky side down. Push it down gently all over.*

3. Children will imitate a desired action.

Do	Say
Observe children carefully. Some additional coaching statements are included. You may repeat statements from #2 as needed.	*Now it is your turn. You do it.* *Smooth the paste to the edges.* *The paste goes between the papers, not on top.* *Think about where you want to put your paper before you lay it on.*

4. Children will practice a desired action.

Do	Say
Observe children as they make a simple collage. Use behavior reflections that reinforce the skills.	*Miranda, you have selected some bright colored papers to paste on your sheet.* *Nico, I notice that you have smoothed out all the lumps and the paper is sticking nicely.*

5. Children will carry out the desired action in a situation in which it is relevant.

	Do	Say
	Remind children about the process of pasting things together periodically as they do other projects.	*Recall that when you paste things together, they are more likely to stick if you have covered most of the surface smoothly.*
Transition	Remind children to place their collages to dry and to wash their hands before they leave for another activity.	*When you are finished, put your paper on the shelf to dry, then wash your hands.*

Simplification   Assist children physically by guiding their hands in smoothing out the paste and turning the piece over. Avoid doing it for a child. You may need to lift up a corner of a paste-covered scrap so the child may place it.

Extension   Use other adhesives listed above. Point out that the mixture of glue and paste is better for pasting heavier objects. Also point out that small drops of glue are sufficient.

Evaluation (child)   Use a general competence checklist that includes several basic techniques such as cutting, pasting, and using the easel with brushes. Repeat the demonstration as needed for individual children until they are proficient.

Evaluation (self)   1. How did I encourage the children to watch my hands?

2. Was I able to incorporate the children's oral descriptions into my oral statements and directions?

3. Were the materials for the specific activity appropriate?

Direct Instruction

This plan is for the child who does not seem to learn from a demonstration alone. A large ball is easier to catch than a small ball. A small ball is easier to throw. This plan can be carried out many times, implementing objectives based on your previous assessment of the skills the child has. Note that you may implement Objectives 1 and 2 many times before going on. You may also begin a particular episode with Objective 3 if you have done 1 and 2 on other occasions.

Domain   Physical

Activity Name   Catching a ball

Goal   Demonstrate appropriate form in the control of objects: throwing, catching, kicking, and striking

Objectives   1. Children will attend (watch/listen) to the instruction.

2. Children will carry out an action as requested (do something or say something).

3. Children will point out examples of the instruction.

4. Children will point out non-examples of the instruction.

5. Children will apply what they learn.

Content   1. A ball is a round toy.

2. Catching a ball by grasping it with the hands and arms and chest is easier than with the hands alone.

3. Watching the ball carefully is necessary for catching it.

4. Sometimes people move their position in space, their arms and hands in order to catch a ball.

Materials   6" to 8" ball(s) 3" to 6" Nerf® balls

Procedures   1. Children will attend (watch/listen) to the instruction.

Do	Say
Throw the ball to an adult or skilled child and verbalize what you see. (Or observe two children successfully playing catch.)	*Notice how Mimi is ready to catch the ball. She holds her hands up in front of her and watches where the ball is going.* *She had to scoot to the side and stretch her arms up to get the ball.*

2. Children will carry out an action as requested (do something or say something).

Do	Say
Stand fairly close to the child and with each successful throw, move backward to increase the distance. Match your comments to the child's ability.	*Get ready. Put your hands up and about 6 inches (demonstrate) apart.* *Watch the ball all the way into your hands.* *Move (forward, to the side, or backwards) so that the ball will land in your hands.* *Pull the ball into your chest.* *You caught that one!*

3. Children will point out examples of the instruction.

Do	Say
Observe other players and structure your verbal comments and questions to focus the child's attention on specific skills. Repeat objectives one and two as needed, with more practice.	*What did David do with his feet that helped him catch the ball?* *Tell me what you see Omir doing. How did he do it?* *Let's try again.*

4. Children will point out non-examples of the instruction.

Do	Say
Option A. Ask someone to throw you the ball. Deliberately gaze around, put up your hands late, and fail to move your feet. Incorporate some of the skills that the child does well as well as the errors. Exaggerate and engage in physical humor.	*Now I will catch the ball. Tell me if I am doing it right or if I am making mistakes. What should I do differently?*
Option B. Point out other children who are in the learning process. Ask the child to tell you what is going wrong and then follow up by helping another child by calling out coaching tips or encouragement.	*You can see that Chase is having a hard time catching the ball. What could you tell her to help her?*

5. Children will apply what they learn.

Do	Say
Set up conditions so that the child is playing with someone who has similar skills. Encourage them to coach each other.	*Practice playing catch with Chase and helping each other. Remember to watch the ball. When it is your turn to throw the ball, throw it gently directly to her.*

Simplification   From a standing position, roll the ball. Encourage the child to move to catch it and bend in time to grasp it. Then throw a ball in the air, with a short distance between you and the child.

Extension	Use smaller balls and increase the distance between thrower and catcher.
	Encourage child to use hands to grasp the ball without pulling it into the chest.
Evaluation (child)	Develop a checklist based on content.
	a. Catches ball with arms and body.
	b. Watches ball all the way to hands.
	c. Moves body to connect with ball
	forward
	sideways
	backward
	d. Catches ball with hands (without pulling it to the chest).
Evaluation (self)	1. Was I encouraging as the child approximated a catch?
	2. Did I maintain a low-key approach?
	3. Were the simplification and extension effective in providing each child with success and challenge?

Glossary

adherence Relying on external controls such as physical intervention or tangible rewards in order to behave.

adult-guided Adults determine the content, approach, and direction of an activity.

aesthetics A person's ability to perceive, be sensitive to, and appreciate beauty in nature and creations in the arts.

affective Having to do with self-understanding, emotions, and emotional expression.

alphabetic awareness Understanding that there are 26 letters in the English alphabet and that individual letters and letter combinations have names and match specific sounds in oral language.

amoral The inability to make judgments about whether something is right or wrong.

arts The creative work and the process of producing the creative work.

authentic assessment Carrying out useful strategies in the regular classroom to see whether children are making progress.

authoritarian style Demanding unquestioning obedience in lieu of all else.

authoritative style Having warm relationships and high expectations of children and enforcing rules in constructive ways.

autonomy A sense of oneself as a separate, self-governing individual.

body of group The main purpose of the whole-group instruction time.

child-guided Children mostly control the content and direction an activity takes.

classroom community A sense of common purpose and values that is shared by the teachers and children within a classroom, which leads to a sense of belonging by classroom members.

closing of group When the teacher summarizes the activity and guides children to the next portion of the day.

communication The amount and type of information and instruction adults offer children about how to behave.

concepts about print Understanding how print works (e.g., leaving spaces between words, capitalization, punctuation, reading from top to bottom and left to right).

content standards Level of quality or excellence related to educational content as identified by and agreed upon by experts in the field.

content The terms (vocabulary) and facts relevant to the lesson.

control The amount and type of ways adults enforce children's compliance with their expectations.

cycle of learning The 5-phase process (i.e., awareness, exploration, acquisition, practice, and generalization) of learning something new whereby gaining new knowledge and skills.

demonstrations Activities in which children learn how to do something through purposeful modeling by someone else.

direct-instruction activities Experiences in which adults primarily determine the goals, content, and process of the activity in order to teach children facts or routines.

discussions Activities designed to promote children's conversational skills and to contribute to children's sense of community within the classroom.

domains The six curricular areas related to child development and learning: aesthetics, affective, cognitive, language, physical, and social.

ecomap A graphic representation of the significant people in a child's everyday world and a timeline of critical events that have occurred since birth.

emotional competence Recognizing your emotions and using constructive means for expressing and managing emotions in daily interactions.

evaluation Including or adding meaning or value to an assessment.

evaluation (in activity plans) Ways to assess children's learning and the teaching methods used.

exercise Planned, structured, repetitive movement.

expectations The standards adults set for children's behavior.

exploratory play Activities in which children carry out firsthand investigations of people, places, objects, roles, and events. Through these open-ended experiences, children determine what to explore, how to explore, and the pace of exploration.

extensions Ideas for making an activity more challenging as children demonstrate the desire and ability to expand their knowledge and skills.

facts Something known to exist or to have happened.

fieldwork Visits to real settings during which children engage in hands-on, in-depth investigations. Such visits may be repeated more than once during a project.

fine motor skills Use of the hands to move objects precisely.

fluency Functional literacy, ability to read smoothly, expressively, and with greater automaticity (automatic recognition of words).

fundamental motor skills The basic movement from which more complex movements are made in sports, dance, and games (e.g., throwing, running).

genres Types of literature (e.g., poetry, narrative, fiction, short story).

goal Desirable behaviors relevant to children's development and learning within a domain.

graphemes The written letter symbols in an alphabet.

graphic organizers Visual representation used to organize information, thoughts, and ideas.

guided-discovery activities Activities in which children pursue answers, information, and strategies for "finding out," guided by a supportive teacher. Teachers determine the general direction of learning; children determine specific details.

guilt Feelings of shame resulting from rejection.

hazard Something that can cause injury and thus must be avoided.

identification The child relying on imitating someone he or she admires as the primary rationale for behaving in a certain way.

inclusive programs Programs emphasizing the acceptance and full participation of all students regardless of the student's ability. Children are included in all program activities as members who belong, with the supports and services they need to participate.

indirect guidance Altering the physical environment to clarify expectations you have for children.

individualized education plan (IEP) A program that determines what services children with special needs will receive, how services will be provided, and the outcomes a child might reasonably be expected to accomplish in a year. Every IEP includes these elements: a description of the child's strengths, needs, goals; short-term objectives; special education services and program modifications; and the frequency, duration, and location of the services to be provided.

initiative Sense of ambition and responsibility.

inquiry approach Teachers guide children in examining objects and events, posing questions, investigating, solving problems, drawing conclusions, and communicating findings.

internalization The child relying on his or her own values and conscience to guide actions and behavior.

learning center Well-defined interest area where children engage in hands-on learning.

literary arts Creative writing such as writing stories, poems, plays, jokes, or skits.

locomotor movement Moving from one place to another (e.g., rolling, jumping, galloping).

logical consequences Consequences for mistaken behavior that teach children alternate behaviors.

loose parts Anything that is small and can be manipulated by children; often what adults call junk (e.g., stones, seeds, sticks or other natural materials, or small tools or recycled material such as Styrofoam peanuts).

manipulative movement Controlled moving of an object with hands or feet (e.g., throwing or kicking a ball or threading a bead).

mastery Demonstrated control of a skill or concept.

materials All necessary props or equipment needed for an activity.

mistaken behaviors Undesirable things children do because they don't know any better or because they lack the skills to behave appropriately on their own.

mistrust Sense of hopelessness and suspicion.

nonlocomotor movement Staying in place while moving the body core or extremities (e.g., twisting, bending).

numeracy The ability to understand and apply basic numerical concepts of addition, subtraction, multiplication, and division.

nurturance The amount and type of care and concern adults express toward children.

objectives Specific statements of desired child behaviors leading to individual goals and tailored to meet the needs of the children involved.

observational sketch Detailed drawing of an object or area based on focused observation. The focus of this type of drawing is to look carefully, draw details, and compare the real object to the drawing.

opening of group Strategies used to signal the beginning of group time and capture children's attention.

oral language development Includes receptive vocabulary (words we understand) and expressive vocabulary (words we use to express our thoughts and needs).

perception The integration of sensory input, cognitive processing, and muscular response, if it is called for. All perception is both sensory and cognitive, never just one or the other.

perceptual motor skills Movements that lead to academic or cognitive outcomes (eye-hand coordination, figure-ground discrimination).

performing arts Art carried out through the artist's face, body, or presence, such as singing, dancing, or puppetry.

permissive style Having loving relationships with children, but setting few limits on their behavior.

personal messages Messages from adults that acknowledge children's positive behaviors or redirect mistaken behavior in three parts: Acknowledgement of the child's perspective, statement of adult emotion, reasons for reaction.

phonemic awareness Understanding that the speech stream consists of a sequence of distinct sounds—or phonemes—in a language.

phonological awareness The ability to hear differences and similarities in the sounds of words or parts of words, the ability to separate and blend sounds in words, the ability to manipulate sounds to make new words.

pictogram or rebus chart Chart with pictures or symbols to provide a simple guide through a process.

planning web A visual diagram of the interrelated concepts associated with a particular topic.

position statement A statement examining a specific issue pertinent to an organization and a declaration of the organization's stance on the issue.

primary sources First-hand sources of information such as real-life objects, field sites, or topic experts.

problem-solving activities Activities specifically designed to enhance children's observing, analyzing, experimenting, and reporting abilities.

procedures A step-by-step description of how to implement an activity. Procedures may include multiple teaching strategies.

productive aesthetic experiences Experiences that involve the creation of an artistic expression such as painting a picture, performing a dance, or singing a song, among others.

project An in-depth exploration of a topic that unfolds in three phases and that is driven by the children's interests.

prosocial Positive behaviors that are the opposite of aggression—acts of kindness such as helping, cooperating, encouraging, and comforting.

rational counting Matching each numeral name to an object in a group.

rehearsal Having children approximate or practice a desirable behavior in place of some mistaken behavior.

resilience The ability to rise above adversity and stressful circumstances.

responsive aesthetic experiences Experiences that involve learning appreciation for the arts, recognizing beauty in art and nature, and forming judgments about art.

restitution Having children make amends to rectify mistaken behavior.

risk Something that has the potential for causing harm but can be managed by supervision or planning.

rough-and-tumble play Movement play where children run, hop, fall, chase, wrestle, or kick while laughing or showing pleasant expression. May include play fighting.

scaffold To organize into incrementally more difficult steps while providing cues for success.

science content Factual body of knowledge developed by the scientific community.

scientific process Also known as scientific inquiry, the process used by scientists to gather information and answer questions.

secondary sources Indirect sources of information such as books, models, or photographs.

self-efficacy A person's belief that he or she can accomplish what he or she has set out to do.

self-esteem The positive or negative judgments a person makes about his or her self-identity.

self-identity The set of characteristics, abilities, attitudes, and values that a child believes defines who he or she is.

self-regulation Making judgments about behaviors being right or wrong and then voluntarily acting in ways that match those beliefs.

shame and doubt Feelings of helplessness and lack of control.

simplifications Ideas for reducing the complexity or abstractness of an activity. Ways to adapt an activity for children with less experience or with special needs.

social competence The ability to recognize, interpret, and behave effectively and appropriately in social situations.

social responsibility Caring for one another and for the world in which we live.

social skills Interacting with others appropriately.

social studies Developing the ability to contribute to the public good in a diverse and democratic society.

socialization Adopting the values, beliefs, customs, and rules of society.

socialization The process through which adults communicate the norms, values, behaviors, and social skills they think children need to function as successful adults.

standard Something that has been established by experts as a measure of quality. A criterion or yardstick.

star activities Complex activities that involve a great deal of setup, cleanup, or close adult supervision.

stress The body's reaction to change that requires a physical, mental, or emotional adjustment or response.

subitize To recognize how many objects are in a small group without having to count each object in the group again.

syntax Grammatical structure of a sentence.

targeting Putting one object in another or precisely on another (e.g., to hit a target).

task analysis Thinking in advance about necessary steps to achieve a specified outcome.

temperament The distinctive personal characteristics that children are born with and that remain constant over each child's lifetime.

temporary spelling Approximations of spelling of words that children use in the emergent stage of literacy.

terms The vocabulary that is used for activity-related objects and events.

themes Multi-day plans that involve several activities around a topic of particular relevance to the children.

transitions The in-between times that happen as children shift from one segment of an activity to the next, one segment of the daily schedule to the next or from one environment to another.

trust The belief that another can be counted on or is reliable. Trust in oneself, trust in one's caregivers, trust in the world.

uninvolved style Taking little notice of children and putting minimal effort into relating to them or teaching them how to behave.

usable arts Creation of art that is functional or practical in some way, such as weaving, ceramics, or quilting.

Venn diagram A diagram using circles to represent sets, with the position and overlap of the circles indicating the relationships between the sets.

visual arts The creation of art that is primarily visual in nature, such as painting, drawing, or sculpture.

whole-group time Those portions of the day in which all or most of the children in a class gather in one place to share the same learning experience simultaneously.

Name Index

Subject Index

Note: Bold page numbers refer to figures and tables.

STANDARDS AND KEY ELEMENTS	CHAPTER AND CONTENT
4. Using Developmentally Effective Approaches to Connect with Children and Families 4a. Understanding positive relationships and supportive interactions as the foundation of their work with children 4b. Knowing and understanding effective strategies and tools for early education 4c. Using a broad repertoire of developmentally appropriate teaching/learning approaches 4d. Reflecting on their own practice to promote positive outcomes for each child	Ch 2 Early childhood educators need to know about effective teaching strategies, p. 28 Ch 3 What adults need to know and do to support self-regulation, p. 43 Ch 3 Differing approaches to child guidance, p. 45 Ch 3 Authoritative guidance strategies, p. 49 Ch 3 Meeting the needs of diverse learners through authoritative guidance, p. 55 Ch 5 The role of planning, p. 79 Ch 7 Materials that support learning, p. 119 Ch 7 Meeting the needs of diverse learners by creating and maintaining learning centers, p. 135 Ch 8 Whole-group times in early childhood programs, p. 138 Ch 8 Planning effective group times, p. 139 Ch 8 Different group times for different purposes, p. 142 Ch 8 Planning group times, p. 147 Ch 8 Teaching strategies for whole-group time, p. 150 Ch 8 Addressing the needs of diverse learners in group time, p. 151 Ch 8 Pitfalls to avoid in whole-group activities, p. 151 Ch 9 Addressing the needs of diverse learners through aesthetic experiences, p. 161 Ch 9 Teaching strategies for the aesthetic domain, p. 166 Ch 10 Teaching strategies for the affective domain, p. 190 Ch 10 Meeting the needs of diverse learners in the affective domain, p. 194 Ch 10 Materials for the affective domain, p. 200 Ch 11 Materials that support science and discovery, p. 216 Ch 11 Meeting the needs of diverse learners in science, p. 220 Ch 12 Instructional strategies for mathematics, p. 232 Ch 12 Meeting the diverse needs of learners in mathematics, p. 234 Ch 13 Teaching strategies for the language domain, p. 249 Ch 13 Meeting the needs of diverse learners in the physical domain, p. 257 Ch 14 Teaching strategies for the physical domain, p. 270 Ch 14 Meeting the needs of diverse learners in the physical domain, p. 275 Ch 14 Typical materials to support learning in the physical domain, p. 276 Ch 15 Teaching strategies for the social domain, p. 300 Ch 15 Materials for the social domain, p. 302 Ch 15 Meeting the needs of diverse learners in the social domain, p. 307 Ch 16 Daily planning, p. 311 Ch 16 Assembling a daily plan, p. 321 Ch 16 Planning for multiple days, p. 324 Ch 16 Making use of themes, p. 324 Ch 16 Projects, p. 326 Ch 16 Meeting the needs of diverse learners through projects, p. 331
5. Using Content Knowledge to Build Meaningful Curriculum 5a. Understanding content knowledge and resources in academic disciplines 5b. Knowing and using the central concepts, inquiry tools, and structures of content areas or academic disciplines	Ch 2 Early childhood educators need to know about content, p. 27 Ch 5 Parts of the plan, p. 82 Ch 5 Putting all parts of the lesson plan together, p. 93 Ch 6 Learning activities in early childhood education, p. 100 Ch 6 The relationship between learning activities and materials, p. 110 Ch 6 How early learning activities relate to one another, p. 113

(Continued)